Paola Vettorel
English as a Lingua Franca in Wider Networking

Developments in English as a Lingua Franca 7

Editors

Jennifer Jenkins
Will Baker

De Gruyter Mouton

English as a Lingua Franca in Wider Networking

Blogging Practices

By

Paola Vettorel

De Gruyter Mouton

ISBN 978-3-11-032285-9
e-ISBN 978-3-11-033600-9
ISSN 2192-8177

Library of Congress Cataloging-in-Publication Data

A CIP catalog record for this book has been applied for at the Library of Congress.

Bibliographic information published by the Deutsche Nationalbibliothek

The Deutsche Nationalbibliothek lists this publication in the Deutsche Nationalbibliografie; detailed bibliographic data are available on the Internet at http://dnb.dnb.de.

Printing and binding: CPI books GmbH, Leck
♾ Printed on acid-free paper

Printed in Germany

www.degruyter.com

To Alessandro, may the wind be always at your back
and blow gently in your heart and mind

Acknowledgements

I became interested in ELF and ELF research in the mid–2000s, when I started working as a lecturer at the University of Verona after many years of teaching English to students of different ages. This prolonged educational intercourse in the classroom with children first, and then adults and teenagers allowed me to observe what English may mean to younger generations – for many of them, it is increasingly much more than just a school subject. English is the language of their favourite songs, the language through which they make international friends, the code they often see in their linguistic environment and they wear on their T-shirts. As I read through the works of ELF scholars – Henry Widdowson, Barbara Seidlhofer, Jennifer Jenkins and Anna Mauranen first, and then many others – those young people I have been so fortunate to teach kept coming back to my mind, with their wish to connect English as a school subject with the English they see around them, and with the English they use as a means to open up their communicative horizons. And, of course, this well resounded with the ELF research paradigm and empirical findings I was reading about, and then started researching. ELF readings, research(ers) and people, and the rich intellectual community I met at ELF conferences, together with this professional background, were the inspiration that brought to the development of this volume.

There are many people I would like to express my gratitude to. First of all I would like to thank Cesare Gagliardi and Roberta Facchinetti, Professors at the Department of Foreign Languages and Literature, University of Verona for their support in developing this volume. I would also like to thank my university for granting me a sabbatical year, during which I worked at the manuscript of this book, as well as my colleagues Roberto Cagliero, Marta Degani, Maria Ivana Lorenzetti and Anna Zanfei for their support in making the sabbatical leave possible.

I am also particularly grateful to Valeria Franceschi, Paola Caleffi and Maria Luisa D'Andrea for their continuous support and feedback on earlier drafts of this manuscript, to Francesco Padovani, and to the anonymous reviewer for her extremely helpful and insightful comments.

I would like to thank the series editors, Jennifer Jenkins and Will Baker, for their patient and generous encouragement all throughout the ideational process, and the De Gruyter Mouton team, particularly Julie Miess and Birgit Sievert for their precious support.

Last but not least, thank you “blogging ELFers”, and particularly the bloggers who granted permission for their words to be scrutinized with an ELF eye, and then included in this study.

Every effort has been thoroughly made to receive permissions to reproduce copyright material in this work, although in some cases it has not been possible to contact copyright holders.

The following Figures and Tables are reproduced under Creative Commons license (https://creativecommons.org/licenses/by–nc/3.0/):

p. 15 Fig. 1. “Post by language”. Source: Technorati *State of the Blogosphere* 2006, October 2006, as reported in D. Sifry, State of the Blogosphere blog post, November 6, 2006; http://www.sifry.com/alerts/archives/000443.html

p. 51 Fig. 5. “Bloggers worldwide”. Source: Technorati *State of the Blogosphere* 2010, Sobel J., Introduction; http://technorati.com/blogging/article/state-of-the-blogosphere-2010-introduction/

p. 53 Fig. 6. “Bloggers Worldwide”. Source: Technorati Media *State of the Blogosphere* 2011, Part 1; http://technorati.com/blogging/article/state-of-the-blogosphere-2011-part1/

p. 65 Fig. 7. “Community management”. Source: Technorati Media *State of the Blogosphere* 2011, Part 3; http://technorati.com/social-media/article/state-of-the-blogosphere-2011-part3/

p. 97 Fig. 8. “Which blogging platform is your main provider?”. Source: Technorati Media *State of the Blogosphere* 2011, Part 3; http://technorati.com/social-media/article/state-of-the-blogosphere-2011-part3/

I would like to express my gratitude to those who have replied and given their permission to reproduce the following materials:

pagina xixVII extract from *The 21st Century Flux* by Rowan Sawday Aka Dizraeli, 2010, lyric reproduced by kind permission of the author.

p. 11 Table 2. “Reported usage of national/official language on internet”, from H. Kelly-Holmes, Table 5, International Journal on Multicultural Societies (IJMS), 6/1, 2004, p.75, © UNESCO 2004, reproduced by kind permission of UNESCO.

p. 42 Table 3. “More blog to share experiences than to earn money”; source: Lenhart A. and S. Fox 2006; *Bloggers. A portrait of the internet's new storytellers*, p.8. Pew Internet & American Project, Pew Research Center. Washington, D.C., 19 July 2006. http://www.pewinternet.org/~/media//Files/Reports/2006/PIP%20Bloggers%20Report%20July%2019%202006.pdf.pdf; p. 46 Fig. 3. “The growth of the blogosphere 2002–2004; Source: Rainie L., Data Memo, The state of blogging, January 2005: 3; http://www.pewinternet.org/files/old-media//Files/Reports/2005/PIP_blogging_data.pdf.pdf; p. 47 Table 4. “Teen content creators and Internet users”; source:

Lenhart, A. & M. Madden, 2005. *Teen content creators and consumers*: iv. Pew Internet & American Project, Pew Research Center, Washington, D.C., 2 November 2005. http://www.pewinternet.org/~/media//Files/Reports/2005/PIP_Teens_Content_Creation.pdf.pdf; p. 48 Table 5. "Bloggers; Summary of findings at a glance". Source: Lenhart A. & S. Fox. 2006. *Bloggers. A portrait of the internet's new storytellers:* v. Pew Internet & American Project, Pew Research Center, Washington, D.C., 19 July 2006. http://www.pewinternet.org/~/media//Files/Reports/2006/PIP%20Bloggers%20Report%20July%2019%202006.pdf.pdf; p. 51 Fig. 4. "Americans online by age", Source: Jones S. and S. Fox. Generations Online in 2009, Pew Internet Project Data Memo: 2, Pew Research Center, Washington, D.C. (28 January 2009). http://www.pewinternet.org/files/old-media//Files/Reports/2009/PIP_Generations_2009.pdf; all reproduced by kind permission of the Pew Research Center – Internet & American Life Project.
p. 53 Table 6. "Bloggers by location in 2010", Source: http://www.sysomos.com/reports/bloggers/, reproduced by kind permission of Marketwire L.P.
p. 102 Fig. 10. "Languages on LJ", Source: Herring et al. 2007, reproduced by kind permission of IEEE.

Table of contents

List of illustrations

List of tables

Welcome to the twenty–first century flux
For now, English is the language of choice
And when it dies, as every tongue eventually must
Let it be said you added your voice
[…]
I said "Prof.! Language is the people that live it."
Get loose, give it some vision and foresight
And juice; we can fling the dictionary door wide.
I live in a city where it seems like
Every single idiom is intermingling stream–like,
Like streams, that know no barriers
No matter what dams and channels are established –
they are irrelevant. What matters is the message that is put across,
and the passion that's invested in it. Nothing's lost
it merely mutates, and lets the people speaking it
tweak it in new ways.
[…]
And if the English language is the lingua franca of this planet
Never say that it should be a closed system.

Rowan Sawday Aka Dizraeli. 2010. *The 21st Century Flux*
(Lyric reprinted by kind permission of Rowan Sawday Aka Dizraeli)

Introduction

One of the effects of the globalization of English has been the broadening in the range of cross–cultural contexts and functions in which the language is used as a lingua franca of communication, involving speakers of different linguacultures, for whom English is an additional language and is used as a medium for wider communication. As a result of globalization, communication routes and sites have developed into significantly diversified and variegated settings, and encounters in virtual spaces have become as real and meaningful as face-to-face ones. In a constantly interconnected world, where networks are continuously created and re-created for personal, professional or other purposes, in many cases via electronic media, English is most often employed as a commonly shared lingua franca of communication. In these globalized transnational spaces of interaction English can serve both more pragmatic, utilitarian communicative purposes, and/or be appropriated and localized to express identities and meanings that are peculiar to the participants and to the interactional contexts. Globalizing and localizing forces can thus be seen to be simultaneously at work in English as a lingua franca, and particularly so in electronically–based communication, where networks operate beyond territorial (and linguistic) boundaries by definition, be it at a local, national, international, intracultural or intercultural level. Indeed, despite the increasing presence of other (major) languages on the web, English constitutes the main code through which Internet users establish and maintain contact: "wider networking needs a lingua franca" (Seidlhofer 2011: 86), particularly when addressing a translocally located audience. English has found itself in a pivotal position to take on this role; it is not any longer a monolithic English, but one that has been and is continuously being appropriated and adapted by its users, most of whom are non–native, to serve their communicative and self–expressive practices and aims, often intermingling linguistic and other semiotic resources of different kinds. ELF is indeed a phenomenon of late modernity, which "qualifies well as an (almost prototypical?) instance of language in a postmodern world. It is fragmented, contingent, marginal, transitional, indeterminate, ambivalent and hybrid in various ways. Its users do not belong thereby to a well defined social group and their subjectivities are indeed diverse" (James [2005] 2008: 141).

Research in the field of ELF has developed particularly in the last decade, with the overall aim of investigating linguistic processes in successful communication, by recording tendencies in actual instances of language use by ELF speakers (Hülmbauer, Böhringer and Seidlhofer 2008; Jenkins, Cogo and Dewey 2011). The principal purpose of ELF research is to "describe how the language is manipulated in innovative ways to suit the communicative needs of speakers who interact in complex multilingual communities of practice, in settings where the language is sufficiently stable to act as a lingua franca, yet sufficiently variable to fit the infinite purposes it sets" (Dewey and Jenkins 2010: 89). ELF settings are by definition sites where the plurilingual and pluricultural resources of speakers interact. As Mauranen has convingingly argued, ELF settings and social groupings are characterized by non-locality, non-permanence, mobility and multilingualism (2012: 23). These properties all contribute to the shaping of the complexity of second-order language contact in linguistically hererogeneous ELF contexts:

> ELF takes shape in speaker interaction; interactants come together with their own hybrid variants, variants that resemble those of people who share their background (that is who speak their similect) but are different from those used by the people with whom they speak. ELF groups consist of speakers with hybrid repertoires where each individual may represent a different hybrid. Linguistic complexity in ELF communities and groupings is enhanced by the wider environments where ELF is spoken, which are usually multilingual (Mauranen 2012: 29)

Then, Mauranen continues, at a macrosocial level language change processes induced by language contact (e.g. simplification, levelling and reduction of marked linguistic features, 2012: 29–32) can be seen at work in ELF, together with "innovative hybridity [...] that meet the need of communication in circumstances of impredictability" (Mauranen 2012: 36). Indeed, in ELF "it seems that speakers use creative solutions to challenges arising in the heterogeneous and complex language environments that linguafranca entails" (Mauranen 2012: 47).

One of the main tenets of ELF is thus that innovations can be seen as part of language change processes that are inherent to any natural language, as it has been widely and long attested for English by sociolinguistic research in the inner and, more recently, outer circle varieties and World Englishes (WEs). Dewey and Jenkins (2010: 87) point out that the fact "[t]hat we are currently in an epoch of increased interconnection, in which communication takes place as much between communities as within them, means that these processes of shift are in many ways accelerated", as shown by findings in WEs as well as ELF research. And indeed, the expansion of internet-related connections over the last couple of decades can be said to have largely contributed to the "first generation of global ELF" (Mauranen 2012: 33).

The present study aims at providing and analysing findings based on an empirical research related to the use of English as a lingua franca in a corpus of internationally-oriented personal blogs, investigating how and to which functions English is employed in such blogging practices. So far ELF research has dealt mainly with spoken interaction; however, written modes may also constitute an interesting area of investigation[1], particularly so in electronic media (e.g. Mauranen and Metsä-Ketelä 2006; Mauranen 2012: 47). First of all in virtual spaces the traditional parameters of distinction between written and spoken language appear blurred. Secondly, they are increasingly used by bi– and multilingual users who employ English as the lingua franca of communication beyond traditional speech-community and territorial boundaries. Blogs, and cyberworlds in general, are not linked to geographically-related parameters, but act as across-boundaries communities where English is employed as the default lingua franca of "wider networking" (Seidlhofer 2007b: 315, 2011: 86). Internationally-oriented blogs can thus be considered an appropriate context to be investigated in ELF terms, as they represent naturalistic contexts of LF use, where (self-)expression and communication take place through English by deliberate choice.

Chapter 1 deals with Internet practices and characteristics of Internet users, with particular reference to the presence of English and other languages on the web, blogs included, and with the role that English plays as a lingua franca of communication in these wider networking spaces. The growth of the Internet in the last ten–fifteen years, due to the advent of advanced information technology and to the development of Web 2.0 interactive tools, has allowed on the one hand increased availability and dissemination of data, and on the other hand greater opportunities for interaction and communication at a global level. The penetration of the Internet in Europe, and to a lesser though increasing extent in Italy, too, involves in particular younger users between 16 and 25 years of age, who take advantage of the various communicative opportunities offered by the web, participatory practices in the first place.

The Internet and web-related modes provide myriads of occasions for 'wider networking', of which blogs are one but significant example, where (young) people adopt (and adapt) English as their international means of communication. Despite recent trends showing an increase in the presence of

---

[1] Cf. Horner 2011 as to pedagogic settings.

other major, as well as of minority, languages, English remains nonetheless the main lingua franca in web communication, and it appears it will continue to be so in the near future. The communicatively interactive opportunities provided by the Internet seem thus to constitute proper ELF contexts, where English represents the chosen language of communication across territorial boundaries. This chapter, after briefly outlining Internet practices in the EU and in Italy, will examine the presence of English and of other languages on the web and in blogs. The role of English as a lingua franca in virtual networking practices will then be looked at, with the consequent problematisation of traditional sociolinguistics concepts such as languages, and varieties, as discrete entities, which are realized by speakers within stable speech communities – all constructs the latter conceived of within a monolingual conceptual framework. Indeed, the use of English by non-native speakers in web-related practices is increasing, with communication shaped both by the specificities of the medium and by the communicative aims of the participants, who interact in communities that are no longer shaped by territorial, national (linguistic) boundaries. In these translocal spaces of communication, which have become a substantial part of our everyday habits, English represents a commonly shared code that is at the same time part of transcultural, transnational and translinguistic flows, and is bent and (re)localized to different practices. This is done by drawing on the multifaceted linguistic, cultural and semiotic repertoires of its users. In online communicative spaces English in its lingua franca function is thus appropriated and adapted to suit the users' communicative aims, which, while being globally oriented, are at the same time locally situated in terms of community-shared interests. Internationally oriented blogs can be said to represent instantiations of "*constellations* of interconnected practices" (Wenger 1998: 127–133) where linguistic resources are locally enacted and negotiated within specific groupings (Seidlhofer 2011) through shared practices and repertoires.

Chapter 2 outlines the characteristics of blogs, first introducing Web 2.0 participatory practices, then looking at blog-related specific features. Bloggers' traits and motivations for blogging are also dealt with, as well as the developments in the rapid spread of this Internet mode. Then, after briefly illustrating different typologies of blogs, personal journals are illustrated more in detail. Finally, interactivity affordances and practices in blogs, as well as their community-oriented features, are discussed. Web 2.0 practices with their participatory characteristics have contributed to broaden the possibilities of interaction at a global level, and blogs constitute one among such digital spaces. The popularity and spread of blogs have been continuous and consistent since their birth, alongside the recent growth in popularity of other social media. Teenagers and young adults appear to be major blog users, for whom this genre constitutes a privileged and open space for self-expression, interaction and sharing of common interests and experiences.

Despite the difficulty in defining clear-cut boundaries in blog typologies, due to the hybrid and highly flexible characteristic of this Computer Mediated Communication (CMC) mode, personal journals appear to be the most common type, usually dealing with personal musings, reflection, and sharing of experiences with a smaller audience. They are generally frequently updated, and most often created by young adults, for whom they represent a channel for personal relations. Despite communication in blogs being intrinsically asymmetrical, potential interactivity via hyperlinks and, above all, through comments is indeed a focal characteristic, especially in personal journals, where narratives about the self often combine with creative writing and multimodal sharing practices. Interactivity, commonly shared interests and participatory sharing practices are central elements to a sense of community in blogs, whether with smaller and more intimate audiences, or in larger and more open ones, which at times intersect. The boundaries – if any – that define these communities are not territorial in a geographical sense, but rather revolve around common interests on the one hand, and old or newly-made relationships on the other. English in its lingua franca role is the main linguistic means that allows communication, together with an elastic widening of such boundaries in internationally-set blogging practices.

Chapter 3 looks into language in Computer Mediated Communication. It has been argued that Internet language cannot be equated with written or spoken forms, but rather shares features of both along a continuum, also depending on the electronic discourse mode employed (e.g. Crystal [2001] 2006: Ch. 2; Baron 2000: 20–23, Ch.9). Despite variation across modes, several features seem to characterize language on the web; in virtual spaces, cross-linguistic language creativity, processes of code-mixing and code-switching, as well as appropriation and adaptation of the code to suit its users' communicative and expressive needs, appear to be common traits. Innovative linguistic features in CMC, which can be related to the dimensions of orality, compensation and economy (Androutsopoulos 2011a: 150), characterize the *e-grammar* of English (Herring 2011) and of other languages, particularly at the lexical level. For instance, characteristic typographic conventions are mostly used to express elements of orality or to make up for the lack of face-to-face paralinguistic elements; abbreviations and new morphological formations are frequently found, as well as syntactic brevity and colloquial grammar and vocabulary. Together with paralinguistic elements, they contribute to characterize CMC modes as 'conversational' as they respond to the need "to make written language suitable for social interaction" (Androutsopoulos 2011a:155). Recent approaches to Computer Mediated Discourse (CMD) have integrated the linguistic level of analysis within the situated practices of new media users, taking into consideration how the technological, situational and linguistic variables combine in CMD (cf. e.g. Herring 2007; Puschmann 2009; Androutsopoulos 2010, 2011a). Innovative language practices on the Internet are thus increasingly investigated in their (social) communicative functions, rather than in terms of language variation *per se*, looking at how users exploit the language as an expressive and interactional resource.

Blogs, and particularly personal journals, display characteristics of informal language and include many elements that make them socially interactive and conversational in genre. In general, language in blogs shares many features of CMC e-grammar, with some peculiarities typical to the genre: particularly in personal blogs, we find a widespread use of emoticons and 'deviances' from Standard English norms, the style is often colloquial and highly personal – all elements which are employed to reduce emotive distance and for interactive functions. Blog discourse, above all in personal journals, appears to be characterized by immediacy of writing which, together with the interaction-oriented affordances, makes it conversational in genre despite its asynchronicity. In personal journals monologic and dialogic modes tend to mix, through an intermingling of linguistic and visual codes, according to the bloggers' and to the participants' communicative purposes. When orienting at an international audience, English in its lingua franca role constitutes one among such codes – the one that allows verbal communication in these "wider networking" (Seidlhofer 2011: 86) practices. Self-expression and interaction thus intertwine, creating at times small interactive communities where all (linguistic) resources are employed to effectively interact and communicate.

In Chapter 4 the corpus of blogs from which the data object of the empirical study is drawn is introduced and described, together with the bloggers' characteristics; the ELF theoretical background, which constitutes my main backdrop in approaching the data, is also outlined, and the methodology and research questions illustrated. LiveJournal[2] has been selected among other blog-hosting services to our research aims given its international scope,

[2] http://www.livejournal.com/ (last accessed 15 November 2013)

the age range of its users, who are mainly in their twenties/early thirties[3], and its social networking characteristics; these elements are illustrated in the first part of the chapter together with the main features of LJ personal journals, users and languages employed in this blog-hosting service. Despite the possibility to create blogs in 32 languages, and the variegated locations of LJ users, in this cosmopolitan virtual space English indeed appears to be the main choice for LJ bloggers, many of whom non-native, "young, multilingual, geographically mobile" participants (Herring et al. 2007: n.p.).

The corpus of investigation is constituted by fifteen personal journals produced by Italian young adults communicating internationally on LiveJournal. Despite its relatively small size, the corpus data includes several instances of ELF-related phenomena as attested in literature, out of which some have been selected for this study, as Chapters 5 and 6 show. Findings from the questionnaire the bloggers were asked to complete, aimed above all to investigate their linguistic background and their main reasons for writing a blog in English, are also illustrated.

Salient points related to the ELF paradigm of research are then outlined, together with the methodological approach to data analysis, that is investigating to what extent, how and to what functions English is employed as the lingua franca of communication on these LJ internationally-oriented personal journals by the bloggers and their interactants. Approach to data analysis has been qualitative, within the ELF research framework. Findings have thus been analysed not in terms of correctness/incorrectness – i.e. as deviation from standard NS norms – but rather investigating which linguistic processes and communicative mechanisms constitute 'marked' examples of effective communication; the focus has therefore been on variation rather than on 'variety' (Hülmbauer 2007: 14; Seidlhofer 2011: 77–81); indeed, "English as a lingua franca research observes language, not a language and not a variety of language" (Baird 2012: 5).

Findings have been organized according to tendencies as identified in ELF research: Chapter 5 deals with processes of regularization, economy of expression and redundancy reduction, increased explicitness and lexical creativity, while in Chapter 6 we examine findings as to the exploitation of plurilingual resources and code-switching/mixing by the participants.

As we will discuss in Chapter 5, findings from my data show that in their role of ELF users participants in the international blogosphere appropriate the code and adapt it to their purposes of expression and interaction. They

---

[3] Source: http://www.livejournal.com/stats.bml, statistics continuously updated.

stretch their language expertise to this aim, not least in terms of language creativity, exploiting the 'language potential(s)' of the code – i.e. the possibilities of the 'virtual language' not yet codified but yet inherent in the language (Widdowson 2003; Seidlhofer 2011). Findings show that this exploitation takes place at different linguistic levels via processes that range from regularization and redundancy reduction, to appropriation and adaptation of the code to the participants' self-expressive and communicative needs, which are at times specific to the constellations in which they are set. The chapter illustrates and discusses findings of my empirical research as to regularization (e.g. economy of expression and redundancy reduction, increased explicitness and lexical creativity), which, despite the corpus small size, appear widely present in findings. More specifically, the following aspects are taken into examination:

- processes of regularization, economy of expression and redundancy reduction (pluralization of uncountable nouns; regularization by analogy; non-marking of –s plurals in nouns; *This/there is* + plural; interchangeable use of who/which; zero third person singular marking in present tense verbs (3sg Ø); questions tags; zero derivation; extension in use of general verbs);
- several strategies at work in the shift in use of definite and indefinite articles;
- increased explicitness, e.g. by adding redundant nouns and prepositions.

As to processes of lexical creativity, innovations in findings are explored in terms of exploitation of the 'virtual language', that is looking at how regular word-formation processes are employed in the creation of not-yet-attested lexical items through prefixation, suffixation, as well as blending, reanalysis and addition and reduction strategies.

Chapter 6 focuses on how the participants pragmatically exploit the plurilingual resources in their repertoire. The concept of multicompetence in ELF is explored before analysing the data both in terms of borrowings (e.g. Hülmbauer 2007, 2009; Pitzl et al. 2008) and of adaptation of idiomatic and fixed expressions (Pitzl 2009, 2012a); effective use of code-switching and code-mixing by participants is also examined to its different functions as hypothesized in ELF (Klimpfinger 2007, 2009; Cogo 2009, 2010, 2011), that is, appealing for assistance, specifying an addressee, introducing another idea and signalling cultural affiliations both in terms of primary linguacultures and in indexing belonging to in-group shared interests and 'constellations of interconnected practices', set against the specific CMC setting of the data as to blogging practices. The way in which idiomatic/fixed expressions are 're-shaped' by these ELF users in the light of their multilingual and multicultural repertoires is also looked into.

Chapter 7 deals with the implications of findings in pedagogical terms. The pervasive presence of English in young people's lives in Europe makes it increasingly difficult to draw a clear distinction between the roles of *learner* and *user*. Indeed, English represents a consistent part in younger generations' lives both in 'top-down' processes in education and in 'bottom-up' contacts, especially in pop culture and the media: music and computers, increased mobility and personal networks, which are created and maintained also via the Internet, constitute for them prominent opportunities of contact with this language. ELF is often the only commonly shared code employed to communicate across linguacultural backgrounds, frequently de-linked from its 'native territorial' implications. My findings also show how English represents a consistent part in the participants' worlds, and is employed in virtual spaces to connect and establish relationships in beyond-boundaries spaces.

However, the ability by these multicompetent ELF users to effectively exploit their (cross)linguistic skills often clashes with their negative self-perception with regard to their proficiency in English, which is at times overtly connected to the native speaker model. Despite their 'declarations of linguistic incompetence', the participants in my corpus appear to effectively make use of linguistic resources to meaning making, to establish relationships and self-expression as well as to effectively interact in their blogs, as exemplified and discussed in Chapters 5 and 6. Their non-nativeness is often exploited as a common, binding and shared resource "for sense-making" (Firth and Wagner 1997: 290), creating a sense of commonality in "accomplishing transcendent interpersonal meaning" (Firth 2009: 156). Furthermore, these multicompetent L2 participants display a high level of language awareness in their linguistic practices, which is instantiated in flagging practices, as well as variety awareness, translation and language play.

ELF is increasingly employed as the lingua franca of communication in wider networking – face-to-face as well as digital – international, multilingual and multicultural contexts. ELF users, such as the participants in this study, seem to effectively interact across territorial boundaries and beyond nativeness paradigms through a linguistic common denominator – ELF – which, together with other semiotic resources, allows them to carry out their genuine networking wishes and aims. This consistent contact with English and active use of ELF by young people is however not always acknowledged in educational settings. Looking at how the language that is (being) learnt in the classroom is effectively used in the 'real world', at what learners "make of their language" and how they have learnt "how to mean in English" (Widdowson 2012: 24) can provide indications as to reconceptualizing notions of communicative competence, native-speaker models, proficiency and competence. Furthermore, the ease with which these ELF participants draw on their plurilingual repertoire of multicompetent L2 users ought to be taken into account as a constituent part of the mobile resources (Blommaert 2010: 41–47) needed to effectively and appropriately communicate in globalized and localized settings. Fostering awareness of such issues in ELT, of how ELF *learners-users* (D'Andrea 2012: 82–83) effectively exploit all resources to languaging practices (Seidlhofer 2011: 189–190), could consistently contribute to take their communicative needs into account, and thus shift from a native-bound primacy to the development of the capability (Widdowson 2003: 171–173, 175–178; Seidlhofer 2011: 197–198) to appropriate and appropriately (in a Hymesian sense) use the language, and hence to a more positive sense of ownership for ELF users.

Chapter 1
Internet worlds, languages, users

> There are very different Englishes at play, at very different scale-levels, and with very different effects and functions (Blommaert 2010: 195).

It is undeniable that English, as the language which has 'accompanied' globalization processes, has now come to represent the main common contact language and lingua franca in an interconnected globalized world. The spread of English at a global level, its use an international means of communication by users who belong to different linguacultures and communities and employ it across territorial and linguistic boundaries, are both unprecedented and unparalleled.

It is certainly also undeniable that globalization has had homogenizing and detrimental 'corporatization' effects (Pennycook 2007: 24), both in economic and cultural terms, leading on the one hand to McDonaldization processes, and to great inequalities on the other (cf. e.g. Blommaert 2010 Block 2004). At the same time, however, the extensive opportunities for mobility, both physical and virtual, offered by technological means "are enabling immense and complex flows of people, signs, sounds, images across multiple borders and in multiple directions" (Pennycook 2007: 25) and have opened up possibilities for local(ized) diversity realized as "part of complex networks of communication and cultural flows" (Pennycook 2007: 31). In opposition to a hyperglobalist, homogenizing view to globalization, or to a sceptic one (Held et al. 1999), a transformationalist perspective, while acknowledging the outward projection of globalization "away from local communities towards the global arena" (Dewey 2007a: 336), highlights at the same time the importance of looking at how globalizing processes are realized in localization practices in that "[g]lobal transmissions are locally consumed, and in their consumption are remodelled, reconstituted, transformed" (Dewey 2007a: 337). That is, the fact that "English is currently the dominant language on a global scale, but is constantly being refashioned by interaction between people and institutions on various scales in response to globalization wherein the core-periphery structures of colonial globalization no longer exist" (Saxena and Omoniyi 2010: 213; cf. also Mufwene

2001, 2008). Such a perspective appears particularly relevant when thinking about the flow of information and interconnectedness which has been made possible by new technologies, the Internet in the first place: individuals can communicate over distances that are vast only in geographical terms and become irrelevant since participants gather and interact successfully in virtual spaces, using English as a common lingua franca, appropriating and adapting it to their (local) communicative aims. Thus, "ELF international settings" are viewed "as sites where distinctions such as these [between internal and external affairs, between the international and domestic and thus the local and the global] are indeed blurred, and where there is considerable linguacultural intermixture"; in ELF settings speakers "borrow from multifarious linguistic resources in the way they make use of English to achieve communicative goals", developing hybridized realizations that are locally enacted (Dewey and Jenkins 2010: 79).

This chapter, after briefly outlining Internet uses in the EU and in Italy, will examine the presence of English and of other languages in web-related practices and in blogs. The role of English as a lingua franca as employed in virtual networking will then be looked at, with the consequent problematization of traditional sociolinguistics concepts such as languages, and varieties, as discrete entities, realized within stable speech communities, by speakers conceived of within a monolingual conceptual framework. In online communicative spaces English in its lingua franca function appears appropriated and adapted to suit the users' communicative aims, which, while being globally oriented, are at the same time locally situated in terms of identity and community-shared interests.

1.1. Internet users

One of the most visible effects of globalization has been the massive diffusion of the Internet; from over a billion users at the end of 2005 (Internet Wold Stats[4]; Danet and Herring 2007a: 3), since 2011 the Internet connects more that two billion users (Internet Wold Stats[5]). Crystal ([1997] 2003) identifies in increased mobility, both physical and electronic, one of the main reasons for the spread of English as a global language, and reports that from 1990 to 1993 the number of Internet users had grown from a million to 20 million, and to 40 million in 1995; this rise continued exponentially "at a rate

[4] http://www.internetworldstats.com/emarketing.htm (accessed 15 November 2013).
[5] http://www.internetworldstats.com/emarketing.htm (accessed 15 November 2013).

of about 10 per cent a month in 1996", reaching 544 million users across 201 countries in 2002 (Crystal 2003: 119). One implication of this expansion is that users from different territories and linguacultural backgrounds access the web; as Crystal notes, "already in 1999 predictions were being made that in the early 2000s non-English users would exceed English users" (Crystal 2003: 119.). This forecast appeared to be true and realistic, and Internet usage reflects "the world's linguistic demographics, with English users hovering around 30 per cent" (Crystal 2003: 119.). Although globalization practices related to the media and Internet use have affected "elites far more than other groups, and having access to the technology divides the world into the haves and have-nots", trends show that even "in parts of the world where there has been low participation (e.g. Africa and South America), Internet access is increasing at a rate of about 20% a year (NUA 2002), which suggests that disparities may narrow if not close" (Wright 2004: 158–159). Looking at recent 2012 data reported by Internet World Stats[6], in the distribution of Internet Users in the world Asia adds up to 44.8%, with 10.4% for Latin America/ Caribbean countries, 7% for Africa and 3.7% the Middle East, while Europe and North America respectively amount to 21.5% and 11.4%.

As to the old continent, according to Graddol (1997: 50), in 1997 out of 50 million Internet users, 20% were based in Europe, mainly in Germany, the UK, the Netherlands and Sweden; apart from the UK, where English is a native language, in the above-mentioned other countries the competence in English is reckoned to be high (Nunberg 2000, quoted in Graddol 2006: 45), in some cases nearing the role of a second rather than a foreign language (e.g. Berns 1995: 43–44).

The 2004 *Mediappro* research (Rivoltella 2006) involving young people aged 12–18 across several countries mainly set in Europe[7], showed that the Internet had fully become part of 90% European young people's personal and social life. Together with other communication devices – mobiles in the first place, owned by 95% respondents – the web represented for younger generations an opportunity to keep in touch with their friends, bearing thus a social function. Blogging practices appeared particularly widespread in Belgium, where 38% respondents said they have a personal blog which, together with MSN and e-mails, was for them a way to socially interact with peers (Rivoltella 2006: 72).

[6] http://www.internetworldstats.com/stats.htm (accessed 15 November 2013).

[7] Belgium, Denmark, Estonia, France, Greece, Poland, Portugal, the UK, Italy and Quebec.

According to the European Interactive Advertising Association (EIAA) Mediascope 2008 data[8], in the same year 178 million Europeans were online every week, 55% of whom each day, particularly in the age range 25-34. The top reason indicated by 73% Europeans who used the web was to keep in touch with friends and relatives; 11% Europeans (7% for Italy) shared self-created content (text, images, photos, videos or music) on websites. The *Eurostat ICT* survey 2010[9] reports that 65% Europeans used the Internet at least once a week, a figure which reached 90% for the age range 16–24. Almost 50% Europeans post messages in blogs, chat and social networking sites, reaching 80% for the 16–24 age range; this appeared confirmed in the *Pillar 1 Digital Agenda Scoreboard*[10] data**:** Internet usage in the 27 EU countries in 2010 was higher for younger, as well as medium and well-educated middle-aged people.

Recent data from the 2011 and 2012 Internet World Stats[11] show that the penetration of the Internet in Europe amounts to 63.2% (58% in 2011) and, when compared to the world average (34.3% in 2012 and 30.2% in 2011), figures are almost doubled, with 68% for Russia (59.7% in 2011), Germany 67.5% (65.1 in 2011) and the UK (52.7% in 2012 and 51.4% in 2011) ranking top[12], and Italy placed sixth (35.8% in 2012 and 30.0% in 2011).

The 2011 European Commission *User Language Preferences Online* Flash Eurobarometer reports that about 80% Europeans use the web on a daily basis; younger people are confirmed to be 'heavier' Internet users, with a 65 per cent daily presence on the web for the15–24 age range (2011: 8). Younger respondents still in the educational system appear more willing to visit websites in English, with 65% in the 15–24 age range agreeing or strongly agreeing.

---

[8] http://newmediagr.files.wordpress.com/2009/07/eu081126mediascope.pdf (accessed 15 November 2013).

[9] http://epp.eurostat.ec.europa.eu/cache/ITY_OFFPUB/KS-QA-10-050/EN/KS-QA-10-050-EN.PDF (accessed 15 November 2013).

[10] Within the European Commission Information Society "101 Digital Agenda" actions , http://ec.europa.eu/information_society/digital-agenda/scoreboard/pillars/index_en.htm (accessed 4 November 2012).

[11] Internet Penetration in Europe, March 2011, Internet World Stats http://www.internetworldstats.com/stats4.htm (accessed 4 November 2012).

[12] Top Ten Internet Countries in Europe, March 2011 and June 30th 2012. Source: Internet World Stats, http://www.internetworldstats.com/stats4.htm (accessed 4 November 2012 and 15 November 2013).

When looking at Italy, in 2003 the majority of Internet users were under 35, particularly in the 25–34 age range, with a significant presence of teenagers (Rivoltella 2006: 85). The latter however, apart from instant messaging, seemed to rely more on mobile phones than on the Internet for social communicative practices, differently from their European peers (ivi: 99ff.). Half of the respondents in the 2004 *Mediappro* research conceptualized the web mentioning its social dimension (Rivoltella 2006: 134) as a space for meeting and friendship.

Even more recently (Internet WorldStats 2011) the penetration of the Internet in Italy continues to be lower than in other European countries; the *Digital Agenda Scoreboard 2011* illustrates[13] how, despite the percentage of frequent Internet users being close to the European average, that of regular users (48%) is one of the lowest in the EU, and, similarly, that of people who never used the Internet is one of the highest, reaching 41%. Nevertheless, in line with European trends, younger generations are heavy Internet users: according to national statistics (ISTAT 2009, cited in Ferri 2011: 34–37) 86% young people in the 11–24 age range regularly use the Internet and use Web 2.0 tools, a figure that appears similar to the findings of the Pew surveys for the U.S.

According to the Numedia Bios survey[14], 98.4% Italian university students regularly use a personal computer, and 68.7% an Internet connection for more than 5 hours a day. 42% have a personal blog, and 78% read other blogs. Three Internet users typologies appear to emerge from this survey: 30.1% are defined as "*internet@ttivati*" [internet@ctivated], i.e. spending a lot of their time on the web; 22.4% as "*neo-analogici*" [neo-analogical], i.e. still in a way new to the web, and 47% as "*digital mass*", holding a critical stance to the interactive qualities of the web (Ferri et al. 2010a, 2010b).

As to online activities, only 2.26% young Internet users write e-mails every day, while 57% employ instant messaging daily, and 63% have created a profile on a social networking website: the latter is thus becoming, particularly in European contexts, the main tool for distance communication, in line with findings of the latest Pew surveys: social networking sites are for a large proportion of teens and young people the preferred means to keep in touch with friends.

Web interactive and participatory practices appear thus to hold a prominent role: according to the above mentioned Numedia survey data, "prosum-

[13] http://ec.europa.eu/information_society/digital-agenda/scoreboard/countries/it/index_en.htm (accessed 4 November 2012).

[14] Osservatorio sui Nuovi Media, Università di Milano Bicocca, http://numediabios.eu (accessed 15 November 2013).

ers" (or "produsers" in Bruns and Jacobs' terms, 2006) actively participate in the web with content creation and sharing. Despite a decrease in blogging practices by American young people from 55% in 2006 to 28% in 2010 (Ferri 2011: 32), in the *Numedia Bios* study 42% Italian university students have a blog, and 78% read blogs by other people; the "blogito ergo sum" expression well sums up the self-expression and connection role of this online practice: in the words of a student-informant, "nel momento stesso in cui creo il mio blog, il mio profilo, è proprio perchè sto cercando di connettermi agli altri. Di creare un noi" [in the very moment I create my blog, my profile, it is exactly because I am trying to connect with other people. To create an 'us'", my translation] (Ferri et al. 2010b[15]).

The 2011 European Commission *User Language Preferences Online* Flash Eurobarometer[16] shows how the most popular Internet activities in Italy are in line with the EU, i.e. looking up information about education, training or courses; in 2010 only uploading of self-created content and retrieval of information about training and educational opportunities appear for Italy to be above the UE average in terms of Internet users[17], with a significant increase in the first from 2007[18], following the EU trend.

The overall picture emerging from these data is that of a widespread and increased/ing penetration of the Internet in the European, as well as in the Italian scenery. Regular web practices are particularly prominent for younger generations, who use the Internet to keep in touch with friends; a significant proportion reads or maintains a blog, and social networks are on the increase in their social communicative purposes. The wider networking spaces allowed by new technologies provide thus significant room for internationally oriented, translocal practices, where English in its lingua franca role allows connections with other users of different native languages, in practices that are at the same time global and local in that they are realized

[15] http://www.numediabios.eu/giovani-e-media-digitali/snack-culture-2010/ slide 56 (accessed 15 november 2013).

[16] Cf. Internet users in Italy by percentage of internet users, http://ec.europa.eu/public_opinion/flash/fl_313_en.pdf (accessed 15 November 2013).

[17] Although not in overall population terms, where all fields appear lower that the UE average, cf. http://scoreboard.lod2.eu/index.php?scenario=4&indicator-group%5B%5D=Internet%2Busage&year=2010&countries%5B%5D=IT#chart (accessed 15 November 2013).

[18] Cf. http://scoreboard.lod2.eu/index.php?scenario=2&indicators%5B%5D=i_iuse+IND_TOTAL+%25_ind&countries%5B%5D=EU27&countries%5B%5D=IT#chart (accessed 15 November 2013).

in virtual communities of different types, as we will see in the last section of this chapter.

1.2. English and the multilingual Internet

> On the Net, all languages are as equal as their users wish to make them, and English emerges as an alternative rather than a threat
> (Crystal ([1997] 2003: 120)

The web has been, at least initially, regarded "as the flagship of global English" due to two main factors: firstly, most Internet hosts were based since the beginning in the U.S. or in English-speaking countries. Secondly, software technology did not initially support the reproduction of alphabets and characters for many non-western languages such as Arabic, Chinese and Japanese, thus limiting multilingual browsing (Graddol 1997: 50, 61; cf. also Warschauer and De Florio-Hansen 2003: 5; Danet and Herring 2007a: 8–11, 2007b; Crystal [1997] 2003: 115–116). As Yates explains, "[t]echnological standards such as ASCII, which are based on the English language, have helped tie the new communication media to the English language, making it harder for non-English speakers to exploit the opportunities provided by new media" (1996: 118). Moreover, Internet usage has for long been based in the USA (Yates 1996: 117); even though more recently there is on the web a wider representation of users located in different parts of the world, a large proportion of Internet resources are still located in North America and Europe, a situation which is likely to continue, thus favouring the predominant status of English on the web (Paolillo 2007: 424–426; Crystal ([1997] 2003: 15–120). When compared to other big languages, as for example Chinese, a further factor to be kept in mind is that, differently from English, the former are, at least so far, spoken mainly by a population of native speakers and generally do not function as an international, globally spread lingua franca of communication among native as well as non-native speakers. In the hierarchy of language choice on the Internet (as well as in other contexts, cf. Graddol 2006: 44–45; 2007: 250–252), English is generally at the top, followed in turn by regional and local languages (Graddol 1997: 61; Herring 2002b; 2010b; Danet and Herring 2007a: 22–23, 2007b).

Indeed, Graddol maintained since his 1997 publication that the web would have become increasingly multilingual, in global as in local communities. According to Global Reach data (quoted in Dor 2004: 98), in 1997 English speakers using the web amounted to 45 million, against 16 million non-English-speaking users; by 2003, however, the web had already become much more multilingual: about 230 million users were English-speaking, while non-English speakers had risen to 403 million, and in 2004 the first accounted for 280 million and the latter to at least 657 million (Dor 2004: 99). In 1996 English as the language of home pages was reported to amount to 84.3% (Graddol 1997: 51), while in 1999, this percentage had lowered to 72% (Paolillo 2005: 57).

According to the figures reported in Crystal ([2001] 2006: 232) in 2004 English was the first language of the Internet (35.2%), followed at a distance by Chinese (13.7%), Spanish (9%), Japanese (6.9%) and German (3.2); other languages were represented in much minor proportions. When compared to earlier data referring to the 1990s (Crystal [2001] 2006: 217), however, significant changes can be noticed: English was then reported to be in a totally dominating position with 82.3%, followed by a mere 4% for German, 1.6% for Japanese, 1.5% for French and 1.1 for Spanish, with other languages all well below 1%. Figures referred to 2010 (Crystal 2011: 79) rank English at 27.5% and Chinese at 22.6%; the latter has been growing in the last ten years at a pace which is 4 times quicker than English. These figures appear to be confirmed by Graddol: while in 2000 English accounted for 51.3%, it had decreased to 32% in 2005 (Global Reach 2005, quoted in Graddol 2006: 44; cf. also Paolillo 2005); Barton and Lee (2013: 43) report that according to 2010 Internet World Stats "about 73% of internet users in the world have a first language other than English and the proportion is continuing to grow". This picture shows that, despite English still remaining the first language of the Internet, other languages have gradually been gaining ground, such as Chinese, Japanese and German.

Thus, while at the beginning English was certainly *the* language of the web, in the last decade the presence of other major languages has become much more predominant: besides the exponential rise of Chinese when compared to less than a decade ago, we find among the ten top Internet languages Spanish (7.8%), Japanese (5.3%), Portuguese (4.3%), German (4.0%), Arabic (3.3%), French (3.2%), Russian (2.5%) and Korean (2.1%), plus a 17.4% for other languages (Crystal 2011: 79; cf. also Gardner 2007). In terms of globalizing forces, however, Block (2004: 35) points out that

> greater diversity does not necessarily mean that all languages are equal: bigger is still better in the pecking order of world languages as much of the

proportional weight wrested away from English has been in favour of a few major languages. Thus Japanese, German, Chinese, Spanish, Russian and other languages of the economically advantaged nations of the world, have managed to establish a strong presence on the Internet.

Internet World Stats report the following data (Table 1.) related to the top 10 languages on the web, significantly highlighting that "tallying the number of speakers of the world's languages is an increasingly complex task, particularly with the push in many countries to teach English in their public schools" (http://www.internetworldstats.com/stats7.htm, last accessed 15 November 2013).

Table 1. Top 10 languages used in the web as of 31 May 2011. Source: http://www.internetworldstats.com/stats7.htm (accessed 15 November 2013)

Top Ten Languages in the Internet	*Internet users by Language*	*Internet penetration by Language*	*Growth in Internet (2000 - 2011)*	*Internet users (% of Total)*	*World population for this Language (2011 Estimate)*
English	565,004,126	43.4%	301.4%	26.8%	1,302,275,670
Chinese	509,965,013	37.2%	1,478.7%	24.2%	1,372,226,042
Spanish	164,968,742	39.0%	807.4%	7.8%	423,085,806
Japanese	99,182,000	78.4%	110.7%	4.7%	126,475,664
Portuguese	82,586,600	32.5%	990.1%	3.9%	253,947,594
German	75,422,674	79.5%	174.1%	3.6%	94,842,656
Arabic	65,365,400	18.8%	2,501.2%	3.3%	347,002,991
French	59,779,525	17.2%	398.2%	3.0%	347,932,305
Russian	59,700,000	42.8%	1,825.8%	3.0%	139,390,205
Korean	39,440,000	55.2%	107.1%	2.0%	71,393,343
TOP 10 Languages	**1,615,957,333**	**36.4%**	**421.2%**	**82.2%**	**4,442,056,069**
Rest of the Languages	350,557,483	14.6%	588.5%	17.8%	2,403,553,891
World Total	**2,099,926,965**	**30.3%**	**481.7%**	**100.0%**	**6,930,055,154**

According to these figures, only 2.6 percentage points separate Chinese from English (cf. column 5 in Table 1.), and the overwhelming majority of users employ a language other than English on the web; to be noticed also that Arabic, Russian and Chinese have grown immensely from 2001.

When looking at Europe, according to Mollin (2006: 77–80), English is most frequently used on the Internet for international and intra-European communication: Europeans tend to employ English as a lingua franca with speakers of different L1s also online, and this appears confirmed in Durham's study (2007), where English was the most employed language in a Swiss medical students' mailing list by all language groups (Italians, French and German-speaking students); in this case one of the factors influencing language choice towards English may have been the lingua franca role it plays for all participants, not least in intranational communication in multilingual Switzerland (Durham 2007: 332). As Danet and Herring (2007a: 18) well summarize, despite the variety of languages spoken in the European Union and the EU's commitment to multilingualism, "local languages often cede to English and regional lingua francas when speakers of different languages backgrounds seek to communicate". Wodak and Wright's investigation about language choice in an online discussion forum hosted by the EU *Europa* website shows that "even in a public space where discussion can take place across a range of languages – and it is evident that a range of languages are spoken by users – English nevertheless became the lingua franca of communication" (2007: 396), and it is most likely bound to be "ELF with the linguistic features accounted for by Seidlhofer" (Wodak and Wright 2007: 399).

Within a research commissioned by UNESCO[19], Kelly-Holmes' 2004 study about language repertories and choices of high-school students across eight countries, most of which in the EU (Ukraine, Poland, Macedonia, Italy, France) and some in other geographical contexts (Tanzania, Oman and Indonesia), highlights that perceived self-competence in English ranges from 50% (Oman) to 100% (Indonesia), with 70% for Italy (2004: 72). Reported Internet sessions in the national languages and in English appear variegated, with higher percentages for smaller national languages such as Macedonian, as illustrated in Table 2. below. In the case of major languages, "there is less need for these students to be more flexible linguistically, since there are Internet resources available for them in their own languages" (Kelly-Holmes 2004: 74).

[19] http://portal.unesco.org/ci/en/ev.php-URL_ID=14697&URL_DO=DO_TOPIC&URL_SECTION=201.html (accessed 15 November 2013).

Table 2. Reported Usage of National Languages on the Internet. Source: Kelly-Holmes 2004: 72

Country	Percentage of Reported Sessions in National Language	Percentage of Reported Sessions in English
France	86% (French)	29%
Italy	91% (Italian)	17%
Macedonia	13% (Macedonia)	84%
Oman	100% (Arabic)	25%
Poland	84% (Polish)	49%
Tanzania	82% (Kiswahili)	90%
Indonesia	19% (Indonesian)	84%

These results appear to be confirmed also in Wright's comparative study involving several countries (2004): findings show that when Internet resources are available in the users' first language, the use of English decreases. Together with English as the lingua franca of communication at the international or global level, there seems thus to be a tendency to increasingly use one's L1 in local settings: "[t]oday, while internet users around the world still must use English for global communication, they increasingly turn to their own language to reach web sites or join discussions in their own country or region" (Warschauer and De Florio Hansen 2003: 160). English and native languages, in this perspective, retain thus a very different role, with complementary and overlapping rather than competing functions, confirming trends in face-to-face contexts (e.g. Hülmbauer, Böhringer and Seidlhofer 2008: 29).

Concerning Italy, in Kelly-Holmes' study 72% Italian respondents stated that they knew English well enough to use it on the web, and 75% maintained they employed English as well as Italian on the Internet (Kelly-Holmes 2004: 56). The recorded sessions were mainly aimed at academic work (47%), while only 10% accessed the web to get news and information and 5% for leisure activities (Kelly-Holmes 2004: 69). On the whole, only 4% sessions were reported to be monolingual in English, and Italian was used in 91% cases, with 15% sessions reported as bilingual, in which the combination of English/Italian resulted the highest (55 out of 75). Noteworthy that for all respondents "English was the most frequently reported second language used on the internet" in 71% bilingual or trilingual sessions (Kelly-Holmes 2004: 69). However, in the case of the Italian sample, the self-perceived competence in English (70%) does not seem to correlate with its frequency of use on the web, which amounts to only 17%.

With some exceptions (Tanzania, Macedonia, Indonesia[20]), findings in Kelly-Holmes' study show that national languages are more frequently used than English to surf the web. It would have been interesting to see whether these findings are confirmed also in more interactional web activities, as respondents said they mainly use the Internet to gather information and for academic work. As Kelly-Holmes points out, "the inference is that where English language use increases, the user tends to employ the language both for passive understanding and for active communication", and "the flexibility and competences of bilinguals in these settings seem to contribute to this shift" towards English (Kelly-Holmes 2004: 74–5).

When looking at more recent data as reported in the 2011 European Commission *User Language Preferences Online* Flash Eurobarometer, 55% respondents state they use "at least one language rather than their own" to read/watch content and to write on the web (European Commission 2011: 5). This language is most often English, in 48% cases to read or watch content, and in 29% in writing practices; significantly, 62% respondents state they employ a language different from their L1 to communicate with friends and acquaintances online; although blogs are not specifically mentioned in the survey, they are presumably used together with other social interactive online activities and among other web genres to this purpose. Frequent Internet users are more likely to employ a language other than their own mother tongue in their Internet browsing or writing activities, and particularly so for 15–39 year old full-time male students living in urban areas (European Commission 2011: 10). The majority of respondents (48%) state they use English occasionally to read and watch content (13% always, 26% frequently), mostly well-educated or full-time students, young (49% 15–24 year old), male (46%) and living in urban areas (European Commission 2011: 14). As to online writing activities, 29% overall respondents say they use English in 56 per cent cases, with demographic percentage shares similar to the ones for reading and watching content. When communicating with friends and acquaintances, 6% and 15% respondents respectively state they always or frequently use a language other than their own, 41% occasionally and 38% never, with higher

[20] Other non-European countries investigated in the study commissioned by UNESCO (Wright 2004) were the United Arab Emirates, Oman, Japan and Ukraine. As Leppänen and Peuronen summarize, "the survey's findings indicated that there is a digital and linguistic divide between Internet users in richer and poorer countries", whereby in the latter Internet users tend to rely more on English-medium sources given the scarcity of "resources available to provide services in local languages (2012: 387).

figures for 'heavy' Internet users. The 2012 Special Eurobarometer survey *Europeans and their Languages* also highlights that 34% Europeans use foreign languages on the Internet (European Commission 2012: 7), and English is mentioned as the most useful language by 70% people using the Internet on a daily basis (European Commission 2012: 81).

According to the data in the 2011 *User Language Preferences Online* Flash Eurobarometer, on the whole, younger users aged 15–24 seem to surf the web in a language other than their mother tongue more frequently, either to get information, to read/watch content, for entertainment, to learn about educational or job opportunities, or to communicate with friends and acquaintances (76% for the latter) (European Commission 2011: 28; cf. also Special Eurobarometer *Europeans and their Languages* 2012: 52–53). Opinions related to the availability of websites in different languages show that the majority (68%) of respondents would rather visit a website in their own language when available, an option which is also highly advocated; despite significant country variations, overall 32% respondents strongly agree they would accept to use English when their L1 is not available (21% rather agree, 17% rather disagree, 27% strongly disagree, European Commission 2011: 29); opinions appear thus quite evenly distributed between acceptance and refusal attitudes.

When looking at Italy, the 2011 *User Language Preferences Online* Flash Eurobarometer reports that in this country daily Internet use amounts to 73%, close to the 80% average of the other EU member states; 35 per cent Italian respondents state they use English besides their own mother tongue to read/watch content on the web, and 22% for writing online activities. As to communicating with friends and acquaintances, Italian respondents rank among the lowest figures, with only 3% always using another language, 12% frequently, 33% occasionally and more than half – 52% – never, with an overall percentage of 54% (European Commission 2011: 27). 61% Italian respondents strongly or rather strongly disagree they would accept to use English when their L1 is not available, an attitude they share with the Latvian and Romanian respondents; they also state that interesting information would be missed when visiting websites in languages they do not understand.

These figures appear to show that English is largely employed in online activities to internationally-oriented purposes, either to retrieve information if, and when, it is not available in local languages, or to communicate with a wider audience via a shared lingua franca. The mother tongue and English are often used in combination, and the latter is chosen to connect online with internationally-set people, particularly by younger and frequent Internet users. Together with the increasingly multilingual nature of the web, English in its lingua franca role among speakers of different linguacultures, whether native or non-native, appears to be the most frequent choice in these wider virtual networks. Nevertheless, a preference for using the L1 (in particular for Italian respondents) appears common in several studies both in online reading and writing activities. In the next section we will take into examination the presence of English, as well as of other languages, in blog practices which, as we will see, present a somewhat different picture.

1.3. Languages in blogs

> Language choice does not tell where you are, it tells whom you want to read your text (Myers 2010: 53).

English seems to represent the main language of the blogosphere, too. Herring et al. (2007: n.p.) report that in 2004 the NITLE Weblog Census[21] estimated 61.9% of the 2.1 million weblogs in their sample to be written in English, a figure that in 2005 had risen to 68.7% of the 2.9 million weblogs taken into account. Other languages appear nevertheless to be well represented: Catalan was reported in 2005 to be second to English, followed by French, Spanish, and Portuguese. In Herring et al.'s study, in 2002 Brazilians seemed to be the second-largest group in Blogger[22], comprising 13% of its total 750,000 users. By 2004, the Portuguese speaking population of the social-networking and blog-hosting website Orkut was estimated at 41.2%, while English-speakers made up only 23.5%; in 2006, their number had reached 65%, with an U.S. 13.5% share. Other languages in the blogosphere included a relevant presence of Iranian, South Korean, Polish and German users.

According to the 2006 Technorati estimates, posts in English counted for 39%, followed by Japanese (33%), Chinese (10%), Spanish (3%) and Italian (2%) (cf. Fig. 1. below). As Sifry (2006[23]) points out, the blogosphere was emerging as increasingly multilingual and deeply international. English, while being the language of the majority of early bloggers, appeared to be decreasing in presence, and blogs in Japanese and Chinese had grown

[21] National Institute for Technology & Liberal Education (NITLE), http://www.nitle.org/ (accessed 15 November 2013); updates to the Weblog Census are no longer available.
[22] http://www.blogger.com (accessed 15 November 2013).
[23] http://www.sifry.com/alerts/archives/2006_11.html (accessed 15 November 2013).

significantly. Japanese, Chinese, English, Spanish, Italian, Russian, French, Portuguese, Dutch, and German were the languages with the greatest number of posts tracked by Technorati in 2006. When looking ad distribution in time, posts in Japanese and Chinese had "a daily pattern that indicate heavily localized posting", while those in English and Spanish displayed more globalized patterns (Sifry 2006[24]).

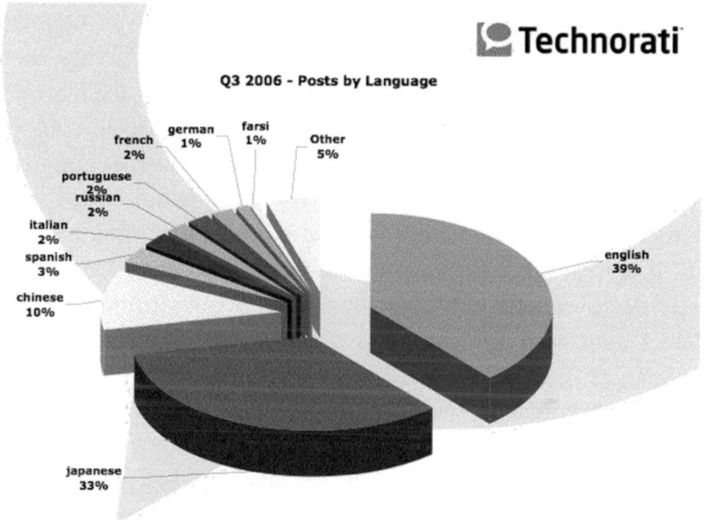

Figure 1. Posts by Language, Source: Technorati *State of the Blogosphere* 2006, October 2006, as reported in D. Sifry, State of the Blogosphere blog post, November 6, 2006 http://www.sifry.com/alerts/archives/2006_11.html (accessed 15 November 2013).

In 2007 the four top languages reported by Technorati were English with 36% (in 2006 it amounted to 39%), closely following Japanese (37%, from 33% in the previous year report), Chinese (8%) and Italian 3%, the latter overtaking Spanish (Sifry 2007). It is worth of note that in the Technorati report, while Asian languages generally appeared geographically correlated, for English this correlation was relatively lacking, possibly testifying to the different global locations from which bloggers posted.

In June 2008 blogs in 81 languages were tracked in the Technorati survey with respondents from 86 countries (Winn 2009[25]), who said they published

[24] http://www.sifry.com/alerts/archives/2006_11.html (accessed 15 November 2013).
[25] http://technorati.com/social-media/article/state-of-the-blogosphere-introduction/

blogs in 20 different languages; significantly, 72% declared to write their blog in English (White 2009[26]).

In Efimova and de Moor's analysis (2005) multiple language usage (English and German in particular) was identified in entries and comments in a community blog, a fact which could be attributed to the international nature of the examined weblog community, whose members were located both in Europe and the U.S. The same findings apply to Herring et al.'s 2007 study on language networks on LiveJournal: although English was the predominant language, it also played the role of a lingua franca in the international blogosphere, and bloggers often employed different linguistic codes in what the authors define as "bridging" journals (cf. § 4.1.4), displaying awareness of the cross-cultural, cosmopolitan nature of their audience. Language mix is a frequent feature in Myers' sample of blogs in English, too; language choice often marks some kind of affiliation, and code-switching may also be used to signal that a blogger is "comfortably cosmopolitan" (Myers 2010: 54) and easily switches between languages. Myers also exemplifies how posts are at times translated into English or French, and comments are posted in either language. This data shows that language choice in blogs appears to be most likely determined by the scope of the audience the blogger intends to address: when it is perceived as international, i.e. made up by participants of different languages and linguacultures, the language is typically English, that is often mixed with the bloggers' L1s, and/or other languages, which often assume localizing functions, too.

In her study related to Slovenian blogs Šabec highlights how in net-communities "the kind of English that is an integral part of this communication is not any specific variety of English such as British, American or perhaps Australian variety (though the American influence prevails), but rather a kind of international, global English" (n.d.: 9). According to Šabec, English is used not only as a communication tool, but also as a social marker to indicate "the users' belonging to a particular online community" (Šabec n.d.: 9), as well as identification with a particular culture, where English is perceived as a prestige language. "Thus some bloggers express their most intimate thoughts and feelings in English rather than in Slovene. It is not unusual for some to choose English slogans and quotations to represent their blog" or "to use English nicknames, blog titles and blog entries" (Šabec n.d.: 10–11).

(accessed 15 November 2013).

[26] http://technorati.com/social-media/article/day-1-who-are-the-bloggers/ (accessed 15 November 2013).

In their wish to reach a global audience, "for some bloggers their global identity seems to take precedence over their local one" (Šabec n.d.: 10–11). The same stance is taken up by Brala who, in her investigation of Croatian blogs, concludes that in an increasingly multilingual and cross-lingual society, in across-geographic and territorial boundaries contexts as the web, language contact brings about new varieties which are then spread. In Brala's view, "[i]n the case of the Internet, the universal language is without any doubt English […], or perhaps more correctly, it is a clumsy, misspelled English, a sort of 'lingua franca' international(ized) English" (Brala 2008: 90), albeit recognising that "the phenomena of languages and cultures in contact, or rather, the features resulting from that contact, can also be seen as a development of *both* the guest (usually English) and the host national language", where (quoting Crystal 2006) the language is adapted to the new communicative situation (Brala 2008: 91).

Despite recognizing the role of common language for international communication that English plays in blogging practices, in these latter studies the language is clearly looked at in its 'divergence' and 'deviating features of "clumsy and misspelled lingua franca" and, albeit not openly, measured against native (standard) models. As the next chapters will illustrate, in my data English appears to be the chosen lingua franca of communication in blogs when addressing an international audience, and it is adopted and at the same time adapted for this aim working as a lingua franca beyond territorial and national (language) boundaries. Despite its global function of a common language that allows communication in wider networks, language choice and language practices in blogs can be regarded as adaptively employed by the participants to suit the local and/or wider networks according to the participants' communicative and interactional aims within their online communities and interactants.

To sum up, we can say that the blogosphere appears to be an increasingly multilingual setting, where language choice is mostly related to the audience bloggers aim at addressing. On the one hand English constitutes the lingua franca that allows communication in these, as in other, beyond-territorial boundaries settings; on the other hand, code mixing, code-switching and local languages often serve 'more localized' functions. As Herring and colleagues (2007) suggest, "trends towards English use and other language use co-exist on the Internet, along with the tendency for bridging individuals to blur the boundaries between language groups". In the wish to communicate in international networks, ELF enables Internet users in socially-based networks to "connect based on common interests and concerns across languages and communities" (Seidlhofer, Breiteneder and Pitzl 2006: 5; cf. also Mauranen 2012: 18–23), at the same time incorporating in their discourse elements of their L1s, and of other languages, according to their self-expressive and communicative needs, to their purposes and to the communities in which they participate. As Leppänen and Peuronen highlight, on the Internet as a "translocal affinity space", participants with different languages in their repertoire "can come together with other like-minded people to share their interests, concerns or causes" (2012: 389). In these gatherings, "the translocal Internet has also become a linguistic contact zone in which multilingual resources and repertoires can turn out to be crucial capital for successful communication, action and interaction" (Leppänen and Peuronen 2012: 389).

1.4. Wider networking and ELF

As we have outlined in the previous sections, it is undeniable that web practices made possible by the developments in technology and connected to globalization have accelerated the spread of English as a common language of communication across territorial boundaries. As we have seen, despite the increasing presence of several languages, in the hierarchy of language choice on the web English appears generally at the top, followed in turn by other national, regional and local languages (Graddol 1997: 61; papers in Danet and Herring 2007b). English on the Internet is frequently employed in its role of lingua franca, rather than as a native language, across linguacultural backgrounds, by and for people who wish to communicate with an internationally-oriented audience.

English, in its already prominent position of global language in the media and in political, cultural and business communication, has indeed found itself in a privileged position to become the lingua franca across language groups and in cross-linguistic contact on the web, too (Warschauer, Blood and Chou 2010: 490). At the same time, as Warschauer and De Florio Hansen (2003: 159) point out, "by bringing together users in many countries, the Internet has furthered the need for people to communicate in an international lingua franca and strengthened the position of English in that role" (cf. also Crystal [1997] 2003: 115–120). The use of English as the lingua franca in wider Internet networking appears thus to have been a natural consequence of the role it plays globally in many fields and discourse communities, extending "its domain of use to become the main lingua franca for the many new kinds of users who have come on line in the 1990s" (Graddol 1997: 50). To a decline in the overall presence of Internet users for whom English is the mother tongue corresponds indeed an increase of non-native English speakers communicating over the web (Graddol 2006: 44); as CyberAtlas data show, already in 2003 about two thirds of Internet users were non-native speakers of English, and "hundreds of millions of people are already participating online today in languages other than English, in some form of nonnative English, or in a mixture of languages, and this trend is projected to continue in the years to come" (Danet and Herring 2007a: 2); communication and interactions among people in the world, "a number of whom employ English as a language of wider communication", is of course also linked to its spread via technology in other areas, such as visual media and (popular) music (Danet and Herring 2007a: 22) The increased use of English by non-native speakers on the web is also highlighted by Herring, even in communicative contexts that would normally favour the use of the user's native language; as Herring underlines, "[w]hile the numerical domination of English-language users has decreased considerably over the past decade, the use of English as a lingua franca appears to be growing as speakers of different languages come into contact with the Internet and use English as a common language" (Herring 2008a: 2643).

The spread of web-related practices, and the role played by English in these online communities, have therefore unsurprisingly become major issues of research in the last decades. The changes brought about by online practices in communication, together with the role and function of English, have been addressed in several, non specifically ELF-oriented studies related to language(s) use on the web. As early as 1996, when technological affordances allowing the participation on the web of non-western language scripts had not yet fully evolved, and ELF research had just started to develop, Yates (1996: 130) noticed that

> today, when we think of English as a language we may not think of England, the country where it first developed. We may be from the USA or from Singapore and speak an English whose features are part of our nationality. There are also many speakers of English as a foreign language for whom the language does not play an important role in their sense of national identity. When we attempt to define nationality, we obviously cannot use language as a definition; one is not English because one speaks English.

Yates then, pointing to English in its international role of lingua franca, concludes saying that the new media "could play the role of removing the 'imagined community' of nationalism, in favour of other communities based either upon global economic ideologies or patterns of personal interests and opinion" (1996: 133), thus further stressing how in its lingua franca role English cannot be any longer equated with notions of nativeness, nor to Anglo-centred 'ownership' of a language that has become global (cf. also Mauranen 2012: 17–23).

The same notion, albeit from a different stance, is highlighted by Posteguillo (2002), who argues that the "Internet is constructed on a set of overlapping speech and discourse communities or communities of practice. First of all we find two major speech communities: native English speakers and non-native speakers of English, and then a variety of purposes around which net users of both speech communities get together" (2002: 32). Posteguillo sets forward the notion of "netcommunities" to define "a networked community of practice made up of Internet Users who share the use of one – or a few – cybergenres for a certain set of common purposes. Net users in a netcommunity may belong to different speech communities of either native or non-native speakers of English", and share also the use of English as a lingua franca of communication[27] (Posteguillo 2002: 32).

Thus, the global use of English on the web, as in other contexts, calls into question a number of conceptual issues, in the first place that of "ownership of English" (Widdowson 1994; 2003: Chapter 4), related to "who controls English and sets its standards" (Warschauer, Blood and Chou 2010: 490), as well as to the variety(ies) employed on the web. As pointed out by Baron (2003: 8–9), first of all, "since the majority of English speakers in the world already are non-native users of the language (Crystal [1997] 2003), content writers for the Internet cannot assume that even the majority of readers will understand complex grammatical constructions, idioms, or less common vocabulary"; secondly, given this scenario, Baron also questions which "dialect'" of English should be selected in online communication even among native speakers of English, as well as issues related to intercultural communication.

Moreover, given the diversified users and uses of English in online contexts, 'the language on the web' cannot any longer be defined as a unique and undifferentiated variety (a point to which we will return in Chapter 3): "[w]hen the internet first emerged, there were simplistic notions of a single online English, which contrasted with both spoken and written English. In fact,

[27] To be pointed out that Posteguillo talks about "Englishisation" referring to the use of English as a lingua franca on the web, and refers to code-switching practices as a "lack of proficiency in English" (2002: 32).

there are many varieties and genres of online English, just as such diversity exists in the spoken and written realms" (Warschauer, Black and Chou 2010: 500). As the authors point out, one important commonality in this diversity is the trend which "involves the challenge to traditional gatekeepers of English language use", as exemplified by Wikipedia and blogs "challenging the mainstream media, or tens of millions of youth challenging notions of correct English" (Warschauer, Black and Chou 2010: 500). Furthermore, the web, besides being (or precisely because it is) a "language contact situation of unprecedented scale" (Paolillo 2007: 424), significantly represents "a place where languages and scripts can be mixed in new ways, and where this mixing plays an important role in indexing identity" (Seargeant and Tagg 2011: 503). Notions of ownership, standardness, national-language boundaries and speech communities as traditionally conceived of are thus significantly challenged by and in these spaces, where communicative practices are created in ways that are afforded by the peculiarities of the medium, as well as shaped by the aims of its participants.

1.5. Linguistic resources and English: global and local practices

Globalization processes have obviously had a tremendous impact on language practices, as the available and easy-to-use possibilities of connection between and among people have opened up new ways of communication and of language use. In this scenario of increased virtual mobility and interconnectedness, due to an intermingled and complex set of socio-cultural, historical and economic reasons (e.g. Crystal [1997] 2003), English has certainly represented the language through which globalization practices have taken place. At the same time, however, they have also on the one hand substantially contributed to a further pluralization of English*es*, since English is employed in a variety of contexts and to different local meanings (Blommaert 2010; Pennycook 2007, 2010); on the other hand, these extended transnational communicative contexts have brought about an intermingling of different linguistic (as well as non-strictly linguistic) resources, which may be locally employed to interactive practices. As Warschauer and De Florio-Hansen maintain, while "[g]lobalization heightens the role of English as an international lingua franca [...] re-localization creates space for other national and local languages to reassert themselves; the broad mix of international, regional and local discussion channels on the Internet first accelerated the spread of global English and now provides opportunities for those who challenge English-language hegemony" (2003: 177).

The different contexts of use and usage brought about by the global spread of English are extremely fluid, and cannot any longer be measured against traditional notions of stability, whereby languages are conceived of as ideological and institutional constructs. Rather, they ought to be contextualized in terms of mobility and language resources in use, as "language-in-motion, with various spatiotemporal frames interacting with one another" (Blommaert 2010: 5): language resources are mobile, they cut across the constructs of national languages, varieties and speech communities, and can thus have significant repercussions at several levels in how language/s, speakers and their practices are to be conceptualized. Indeed, mobile resources are framed in terms of trans-contextual networks, flows and movements" (Blommaert 2010: 9). As Mauranen and Metsä-Ketelä remark (2006: 2; cf. also Seidlhofer 2011: 73, Chapter 4; James [2005] 2008: 141):

> English as a lingua franca is a child of the postmodern world: it observes no national boundaries, and it has no definite centres. In many ways, it is part of a transcultural flow, with its speakers using it in their own ways, constructing their own identities and forming their own groupings. It is also, importantly, used by a plethora of in-groups and special domains all over the world, but not only in a general or standard way. It takes many shapes, as we might expect of a language which is used in an age of accelerated mobility and new contacts.

Indeed, it has been pointed out that the World Englishes paradigm of research, although it has substantially problematized traditional notions of a unitary English, and is inherently set within a plurality perspective (Pennycook 2007, 2010), has not questioned matters of 'ideological' terminology'; in Pennycook's words, the WEs model, "while attempting to achieve sociolinguistic equality for its varieties, is not epistemologically different from this model of core, variation and exclusion: for a World English to be such, it must adhere to the underlying grammar of central English, demonstrate enough variety to make it different, but not diverge to the extent that it undermines the myth of English" (2007: 23; cf. also Saraceni 2010: Chapter 4). Furthermore, the WEs approach is still 'variety' based, as recognizable for instance in the labeling of distinct local varieties such as Indian English, Singaporean English (cf. Pennycook 2007: 20–21); even the three circles Kachruvian model reproduces the nation state/ language construct, thus not fully capturing the global, across-circles use of

ELF (e.g. Seidlhofer 2011). In understanding the spread and use of English today, both pluralization (its global spread) and localization practices need to be taken into account: "[g]lobal Englishes are now what they are not because English has spread and been adapted, but because local practices have been relocalized in English" (Pennycook 2010: 74). These relocalizations are each time different since they emerge from the use of English as employed to locally-meaningful practices, which may thus take on variable linguistic instantiations (e.g. cultural references) which are highly complex and often relocated "from transnational to a national set of indexicalities" (Blommaert 2010: 189). Localization of the global can for instance take place by combining several repertoires "constructed out of bits and pieces of conventionally defined languages" (Blommaert 2010: 43) in diversified ways and at different linguistic levels, from accent (Blommaert 2010; Pennycook 2007), to lexicogrammar and syntax (Pennycook 2007, 2010): "[s]ociolinguistically, globalization is a strongly local and localizing phenomenon, in which strong features of local sociolinguistics regimes operate on the bits of globalized language that enter the local environment" (Blommaert 2010: 101; cf. also Cogo and Dewey 2012: 18–24). This applies even more in the case of ELF due to the fluid nature of its speakers' constellations and to the consequent flexibility with which the language is used, combining emerging traits that are "distinctive to ELF communication" with more localized usages (Dewey and Jenkins 2010: 85).

Linguistic practices in global settings involve the deployment of differentiated resources, where languages and language varieties cannot any longer be considered as discrete entities, a paradigm the latter which is closely connected to the nation state, one language-one nation construct (cf. e.g. Wright 2004; Anderson 1983), and still remains deeply embedded in popular thinking, as well as in linguistic categorization also at an institutional level (Pennycook 2010, Blommaert 2010). As shown by Blommaert in the case of Joseph, whose asylum application in the UK was rejected by the Home office on the basis of his 'unusual' linguistic history, "[a] monoglot ideology makes time and space static, it suggests a transcendent phenomenology for things that define the nation state, and presents them as natural, neutral, a-contextual and non-dynamic" (2010: 165).

In a constantly interconnected world where "distances are continuously being compressed through communication technology, traditional boundaries become more fluid, and are more often transgressed" (Dewey 2009: 77). In these globalized scenes, which have become part of our everyday practices (at least in the Western world), "the local […] often becomes defamiliarized and the global familiarized, blurring the boundaries between what is local and global" (Dewey 2007a: 337). The increasing presence of English in language-mixed practices in different (local) contexts and domains challenges the 'neat' division of languages into discrete, nation-based entities. Thus, traditional categories like a/the language(s), varieties, dialects, as well as code-switching and mixing, borrowing, and hybridity, are increasingly perceived as inadequate to investigate and describe such a fluid inter/multilingual deployment of resources (Blommaert 2010; Pennycook 2010; Canagarajah 2007; Heller 2007a, 2007b). Most often, the use of differentiated linguistic resources we witness in the use of English as a translocal language of communication (but also of other languages, Jørgensen 2008) cannot be connected to languages seen as separate and countable entities; rather, they appear as "translingual practices" taking place "across communities other than those defined along national criteria" (Pennycook 2010: 84). Such cross-linguistic practices are increasingly present also in de-territorialized settings such as electronic communication (e.g. Seargeant and Tagg 2011; Androutsopoulos 2010), and have been otherwise defined as "polylingual languaging" (Jørgensen 2008: 170), whereby language users draw on whatever (inter)lingual resources at their disposal in the realization of communicative acts, "with all their skills and knowledge" (Jørgensen 2008: 169).

Recent views of multilingualism have similarly problematized these issues. Plurilingual repertoires "should not be seen as a collection of 'languages' that a speaker controls, but rather as a complex of specific *semiotic* resources, some of which belong to a conventionally defined 'language', while others belong to another 'language'" (Blommaert 2010: 102). These resources consist of "concrete accents, language varieties, registers, genres, modalities such as writing – ways of using language in particular communicative settings and spheres of life, including the ideas people have about such ways of using, their language ideologies"; they are instantiated and recognizable in actual practices of language use (Blommaert 2010: 102; cf. also Heller 2007a: 11–12, 2007b) as enacted by multicompetent L2/Ln/ELF users by drawing on all the interconnected resources they have at their disposal (cf. e.g. Cook 2002a, 2007, 2010b; Seidlhofer 2011: Chapters 5 and 6).

Hence, when looking at language in a globalized society, ideal and idealized categories may no longer be adequate to account for the increasing complexity, variability and mixed-characteristics of language usage (Pennycook 2007). In this perspective, "[t]raditional notions related to multilingualism, such as code-switching, then become moments of voice in which people draw resources from a repertoire that contains materials conventionally associated with 'languages'", which would however be better seen as "heteroglossic practices in which different voices are blended" (Blommaert 2010: 181; cf. also Androutsopoulos 2010: 212–214).

The new contexts in which English is employed cutting across territorial boundaries have significant repercussions also on the conceptualization of the distinction between native/non-native speakers: what appears to be central in the use of English in these communicative spaces is "not so much whether or not one is born in a particular kind of community but rather what one does with the language" (Pennycook 2007: 35). The polylingual, translingual (as well as multi/transmodal) practices consistently enacted by language(s) users in transcultural and transnational communicative spaces can show how people employ their communicative resources "interacting across different linguistic and communicative codes, borrowing, bending and blending languages into new modes of expression" (Pennycook 2007: 47). Thus, as Pennycook points out elsewhere, "rather than trying to sort out the local from the derived – the constant comparison between peripheral and metropolitan forms of English – we need to consider what language users do with English, how they understand its relationship to their own condition, and what new meanings are generated by its use" (Pennycook 2010: 74). And in terms of English as employed in its lingua franca function, looking into how hybridized English(es) are developed in the construction of ELF localized discourses (Dewey and Jenkins 2010). Cogo directly relates the high variability of ELF "in terms of the constellation of users, the sociocultural background of speakers, their sociolinguistic repertoires, and their migration patterns" (Cogo 2012b: 289) to the concept of super-diversity (Vertovec 2007). Besides the above characteristics, a super-diversity approach in ELF is particularly valuable on two grounds: a) the use of plurilingual resources is seen as a natural element of communicative practices since these resources are part of language users' sociolinguistic repertoires (Cogo 2012b: 289–291); b) the focus is "on the user rather that the code of language. It is the user that shapes, moulds, and constructs their repertorie in the social collaborative activities, carried out within the multilingual ELF community" (Cogo 2012b: 291), or, as we will see, within each communitiy and 'constellation of interconnected pratice', given their highly changeable and variable nature within ELF.

The adaptation of communicative practices to localized, and glocalized, users' aims can be well observed in new communicative genres such as the ones on the web, which are characterized by mostly informal and hybrid language use in form and in language choice (Seargeant and Tagg 2011: 500; Barton and Lee 2013). Furthermore, glocal youth cultures and subcultures often constitute essential elements in online communication practices, where "bilingualism 'from below'" can act to "eventually reinforce a *dissociation* of language and nation, as counter-normative uses of non-native English construct imagined alliances with global cultural movements and may well be used to challenge the hegemony of English-speaking countries" (Androutsopoulos 2007: 225, emphasis in original). Internet users may thus choose to employ Standard English in certain modes, and code-switching/alternation in others: this can also result in an "an act of cultural resistance against monolingual America and Europe as well" (Warschauer, Black and Chou 2010: 500), since language use is adapted and bent in creative and locally-meaningful ways.

1.6. Virtual communities, communities of practice, networks of ELF users

A similar shift in perspective, leading to the need for a post-variety approach, has been called upon in ELF research: in its global spread English cannot be seen with reference to a community of speakers as traditionally and territorially conceived, and languages and varieties as separate bounded entities: "[t]he use of English in ELF interactions occurs not as the deployment of a particular set of language norms, but rather as a constantly renewed, co-operatively modified, somewhat HYBRIDISED linguistic resources, leading us to similarly call into question our conventional frames of reference and descriptive/analytical practices in applied linguistics" (Jenkins, Cogo and Dewey 2011: 15, emphasis in original).

The unprecedented changes in communication (Crystal [1997] 2003), mainly due to technology developments that have taken place in the last decades, together with the spread of English as the global lingua franca, have also called for a transformation in the concept of 'community' in sociolinguistic terms. The multiple connection affordances brought about by the Internet entail that communication patterns cannot be any longer defined only in terms of face-to-face communication. As Seidlhofer (2011: 86, emphasis in original) significantly highlights, these new modes have deeply modified both communication patterns and the function English plays:

> with the current proliferation of possibilities created by electronic means and easy global mobility, changes in *communication* have accelerated and forced changes in the nature of *communication*: the *media* now available have

> *changed* the *modes* of use. And in all this English is in a pivotal position: already established as a widespread language, it is particularly well placed to play a crucial role in these changed conditions, where communities can no longer be defined mainly in terms of face-to-face contact, and certainly not by a common language. [...] Wider networking needs a lingua franca.

Indeed, we may have more frequent, and intense, contacts with friends, either professional or personal acquaintances, through the Internet than in face-to-face contexts, whether via e-mail, social networking, Instant messaging, Skype, videoconferencing or blogs: "[c]ountless interaction networks are independent of physical proximity and are instantiated through interaction over vast distances, often without the participants ever meeting 'in the flesh'" (Seidlhofer 2011: 85, cf. also Dewey 2009: 75).

Traditional speech communities, conceptualized in a physical, local sense, are connected to primary socialization and related to "assumptions of stability and separation" (Hülmbauer, Böhringer and Seidlhofer 2008: 28; cf. also Seidlhofer 2007b). The recent socio-economic and cultural transformations, and the emergence of global networks due to diaspora dispersals and to other globalization processes, mean that communication may no longer be based solely, or primarily, on local, face-to-face interaction. In such settings, where English is often employed as the (only) commonly shared lingua franca, traditional definitions based on speech communities are thus to be re-examined (Seidlhofer 2011: 83–85): Indeed, in online worlds "geographical boundaries do not coincide neatly with linguistic ones", as "individuals may belong to more than one speech community" (Danet and Herring 2007a: 7), which, as we have seen, may or may not intersect in online communication, depending on the linguistic choices operated by the participants, as well as on the setting and on the participants' communicative aims.

Moreover, online communities, "unlike those based in 'real life', are mobile in that they are not restricted by geography. Moving to the other part of the world does not hinder your ability to participate in a LiveJournal community. Anyone can use a LiveJournal from any location, provided, of course, that they have an internet access" (Raynes-Goldie 2004: 7). The same may be said to apply to other web-based communication contexts.

As a consequence, in global patterns communication takes most often place beyond territorial boundaries as traditionally conceived, where communities are less and less related to geographical proximity and cohesion. In these highly fluid and mobile realms, English is most likely to serve as a commonly shared means of communication, a lingua franca that cuts across primary socialization speech communities and settings, to serve secondary socialization communicative aims (Seidlhofer 2007b: 314–315). When communicating internationally, most often "ELF speakers do not live in immediate physical proximity with each other and do not constitute a speech community in this sense" (Seidlhofer 2011: 83). In such contexts, Seidlhofer continues, ELF represents the main tool "for conducting transactions and interactions outside people's primary social spaces and speech communities, for enabling 'transcultural flows' (Pennycook 2007)" (2011: 84). And these "virtual worlds [...] are beginning to have a substantial impact on the way we communicate, relate to each other, and especially in the way in which we see ourselves as belonging to a community" (Dewey 2009: 77). As we have seen earlier in the chapter, the web has relatively quickly become, for younger generations especially though not only, a substantial location for interpersonal relations and a major way to connect with people who may equally be geographically nearer or far away.

Indeed, as Seidlhofer points out, "[a]t a time when many of us, and particularly those who are regular users of ELF, tend to spend more time communicating with people via email and Skype than in direct conversation with participants in the same physical space, the old notion of community based purely on frequent local, non-mediated contact among people living in close proximity to each other cannot be upheld any more" (Seidlhofer 2011: 87). Rather, these communities, in which communication can be seen as a primary aim, may be better conceptualized as virtual communities, or, as more recently suggested, 'communities of practice' (CofP, Wenger 1998), operating at the same time at a local and global level.

The concept of CofP is particularly relevant to ELF research, and has been applied to several studies and settings, since in ELF the 'shared repertoire' of linguistic resources is locally enacted and negotiated within specific settings and domains of use, such as in the case of professionals, in academic research communities, as well as chatrooms in online environments (Seidlhofer 2011: 86). Communities of practice were initially defined along three main dimensions: mutual engagement of participants in shared practices; jointly negotiated enterprise; and a shared repertoire of communal resources (routines, sensibilities, artifacts, vocabulary, styles, etc.) that members develop over time (Wenger 1998: 72–85). In a later definition CofP were seen as "groups of people who share a concern, a set of problems, or a passion about a topic, and who deepen their knowledge and expertise in this area by interacting on an ongoing basis" (Wenger et al. 2002: 4).

In the case of ELF, the concept of CofP could on the one hand be intended in a broader and more fluid sense than its original formulation, given the "protean nature of ELF communities" (Dewey 2009: 77); on the other hand, the different, and frequently ad-hoc formed grouping of ELF users may, or may not, meet the three main criteria outlined above to constitute communities of practice.

When looking at the use of English to communicate with larger audiences in wider networks, and therefore in its role of lingua franca across different linguacultures, ELF can be regarded in principle as part of a commonly shared repertoire in that it is locally appropriated and adapted to suit the communicative needs of the participants and in each communicative act. Ehrenreich however argues that, since in many ELF settings English is employed to the main purpose of serving pragmatic communicative functions, in some ELF groupings "English does not form part of the joint enterprises, but is used as one resource together with other resources as their 'shared repertoire'" (Ehrenreich 2009: 135). Furthermore, given the inherent variability in ELF settings and participants, practices, groupings and even evaluation of appropriateness may vary substantially, the notion of CofP may then be better conceptualized as "*constellations* of interconnected practices" (Ehrenreich 2009: 134; Wenger 1998: 127), a concept which can account for broader configurations, whether at a global or at a local level, than that of CofP (Wenger 1998: 126–133.).

Whether ELF settings are regarded, according to their specific and unique characteristics, as CofP or as constellations of interconnected practices, a salient point remains that English is employed as the lingua franca in a growing number of different settings, where communities and grouping cannot any longer be characterized in terms of local (speech) communities, but by looking at how the language is adopted and adapted in these translocal practices. Thus, while English as a lingua franca is a globalized phenomenon, its realisations are local and localized, pertaining to each situation, each constellation of speakers, and realized in ad-hoc groupings, where ELF users treat "the language as a shared communicative resource within which they have the freedom to accommodate to each other, code-switch, and create innovative forms that differ from the norms of native English and do not require sanctioning by native English speakers" (Jenkins 2011a: 931). ELF can thus be seen to operate between the global, the local and often the individual level(s), and is realized in hybrid and fluid ways which are peculiar to the participants' constellations (e.g. Baker 2009: 585–586; Canagarajah 2007). As Wright (2004: 159) insightfully notices,

> technologies have redrawn the imagined communities that we construct. Anderson's (1983) idea that we perceive ourselves as part of the national group

> as we read the daily national newspaper or the latest fiction in the national language may no longer hold to the same extent as in the recent past. We may be just as disposed to construct our identities in relation to the transnational networks we belong to as we cross former boundaries for our information, contacts and exchanges. The satellite television channels we watch, the websites we access, the email groups we belong to may well be as influential in the construction of group identity as our national media.

Indeed, as Mauranen perceptively points out, a parallel can be drawn between global communities and imagined communities for patterns of interaction, which differ substantially from traditionally conceived ones: "members of imagined communities do not directly interact with all other members of the community, even in principle. […] Imagined communities are based on people's mental images of their affinity. Such images are fostered through communication, which in turn requires a common language that is able to maintain a sufficient level of mutual comprehensibility" (2012: 18). ELF, as a common means of communication in these transnational contexts, may be defined as an "archetypal setting in which communication transcends conventional linguacultural boundaries, with the result that cultural practices and language resources become interactionally transformed as they are performed" (Jenkins, Cogo and Dewey 2011: 16).

In taking on a transformationalist view on globalization processes, and further pointing out how the use of English transcends traditionally-conceptualized (speech) communities as it takes place "*between* rather than within communities" Dewey (2007a: 347, emphasis in original) draws attention to the fact that in ELF contexts speakers "locally 'transform' linguistic resources and mutually construct a fairly broad set of common lexicogrammatical resources" to effectively communicate – resources which do not necessarily need to be conformed to (Standard) ENL norms, but are rather hybridized in their local realization and communicative goals (cf. also Dewey and Jenkins 2010: 87–88; Baird 2012: 6, 10). The same point is made by Hülmbauer, who maintains that ELF users become part of locally created *situational speech communities* bringing about their resources which become part of a *situational resource pool* and are employed to the local processes of meaning construction (2009: 325, emphasis in original). In order to serve interconnected communicative functions, the language gets thus untied "from any geographical centre" (Dewey 2007a: 349), and adapted to suit the participants' communicative needs and aims in each ELF setting, cutting across traditional categorizations such as native / non-native / ESL / EFL users, too (cf. e.g. Baker 2009: 570, 586).

As we have outlined, new contexts of use need consequent adjustments, both in the notion of community in sociolinguistic terms, and in that of linguistic variety: "[a]longside local speech communities sharing a dialect, we are witnessing the increased emergence of global discourse communities, or communities of practice, or other groupings sharing their particular modes of communication, with English being the most widely used code" (Seidlhofer 2011: 88). Online spaces of interaction often constitute, as in the case of blogs, gatherings of, and meeting points for such groupings, for whom English represents the chosen language of communication when aiming at wider networking. Weaker or stronger ties may be created among the participants, depending on the purposes, frequency and regularity of their online networking practices. In any case, interactions in these wider social networking spaces take place through a lingua franca (Mauranen 2012: 21), which is in most cases English.

As we will see in the following chapters, Web 2.0 participatory spaces, blogs included, allow for heteroglossic practices in which a number of linguistic and semiotic, multimodal resources are deployed as self-expressive and communicative practices (e.g. Androutsopoulos 2010: 214). English in its lingua franca, connecting function represents one of such resources, where the language is not necessarily conforming and conformed to native standard norms, but rather appropriated 'from below' and globalized or localized according to the aims of the participants, who may be "simultaneous, developing global norms and local norms as they come to use English for both intercultural and intracultural purposes" (Sharifian 2010: 138). Such instantiations of language use often include, together with the hybridity and non standardness of e-grammar, innovative language forms, which are created drawing on the ELF users' plurilingual repertoires, as well as by exploiting the potentials of the 'virtual language' (Widdowson 2003: 48-49, 173; Seidlhofer 2011: 109-120). As Wright (2004: 175) points out:

> the role of English in globalisation derives from more than the usual reasons for adopting a lingua franca. It is not only being learnt because it gives access to the power and prestige of a centre, but because it enables the flows, networks and structures of an increasingly postnational system. It is the medium that allows individuals to transcend their group membership, and this is what people appear to want to do.

In this sense ELF is characteristic to the ever developing communication affordances of our contemporary world, which have made fast communication beyond any kind of border a daily reality (Dewey and Jenkins 2010: 79–80) – of which, as we will see in Chapter 2, blogs constitute relevant spaces.

Chapter 2
Blogging worlds

As we have seen in Chapter 1, English as a lingua franca constitutes the most common linguistic means of communication across territorial, as well as virtual, boundaries. Web 2.0 practices with their participatory characteristics have contributed to widen the possibilities of interaction at a global level, and blogs constitute one of such digital media spaces. In this chapter we will outline the characteristics of blogs, first introducing Web 2.0 as to participatory practices, then looking at blog-related specific features. Motivations for blogging will also be illustrated, as well as the developments in their rapid spread since their birth, also in terms of bloggers' characteristics. Then, after briefly outlining different typologies of blogs, we will look at personal journals in more detail. Finally, interactivity affordances and practices in blogs, as well as their community-oriented features will be dealt with.

2.1. Web 2.0-based practices

A major development in interactive practices on the web has been brought about by the advent of the so-called Web 2.0. While the Web 1.0 can be said to have been characterized predominantly by information retrieval and thus a "unidirectional, information-oriented medium" (Androutsopoulos 2010: 207), in Web 2.0 (O' Reilly 2005) environments active participation and sharing practices have become a regular feature. The publication of user-generated textual and multimedia content, and participation in web spaces such as social networks, media-sharing websites, wikis and blogs, have expanded the possibilities that were technologically provided by the Web 1.0, so that Web 2.0 may be defined as "an attitude, not a technology" (O' Reilly 2005). Wesch (2007[28]) has highlighted how the Web 2.0, when compared to the Web 1.0, is characterized by the "linking of people", rather than by the "linking of information", with a shifted focus on interactive rather than receptive-only processes[29]. As Herring points out, Web 2.0

[28] Retrievable at http://www.youtube.com/watch?v=NLlGopyXT_g (accessed 15 November 2013).

[29] Although the Web 2.0 as a new concept has been criticized, cf. e.g. Metitieri 2009: Chapter 2; Berners-Lee 2006; Herring 2012b.

today, taking into account to Wikipedia and other online resources, refers to "*changing trends, and new uses of*, web technology and design, especially involving participatory information sharing; user-generated content; an ethic of collaboration; and use of the web as a social platform. The term may also refer to the *types of sites* that manifest such uses, e.g., blogs, wikis, social network sites, and media-sharing sites" (2012b: 2, emphasis in original).

Androutsopoulos identifies in the notions of 'convergence' and 'participation' the distinguishing traits between Web 1.0 and Web 2.0: the first is "related to the accessibility of localized, bottom-up productions and distribution of on line content", while the second "refers to the fusion of formerly distinct technologies and modes of communication into integrated digital environments" (2011b: 4-5). Multimodal file-sharing and collaborative content authoring can thus be said to be main and characterising features of Web 2.0 environments, through which heteroglossic practices are realized, and codes, semiotic signs as well as languages are employed as indexes of different voices and identities (cf. Androutsopoulos 2011b).

Besides the availability of blog-hosting platforms with easy-to-use blog software, since the early 2000s services allowing easy creation of web content by individuals were launched and soon became extremely popular: some were focused on a specific content type (e.g. Flickr for photos, YouTube for videos, del.icio.us for bookmarks), and some provided a complete social-networking type platform with the possibility to create blogs, groups, profiles, to upload photos and other multimedia content, such as MySpace and LiveJournal (cf. Herring 2013: 3-4). Web 2.0-based software tools have thus allowed several functions, such as photo and video sharing, private and public messaging, self-presentation in the form of personal profiles. They have also made the creation of blogs highly feasible also for people who are not familiar with HTML (see below). Together with blogs, participatory culture is characteristic to "social websites like Facebook, MySpace, Xanga and Bebo; collaborative writing sites like the Wikipedia, OhMyNews and Slashdot; social bookmarking sites like del.icio.us, Digg and Furl; media sharing sites like Flickr, YouTube and Freesound; micromedia sites like Twitter and 43 things; and other sites that organize all these threads of publication like Technorati" (Walker Rettberg 2008b: 3). Through Web 2.0 tools users can become active content creators at different levels: by editing and uploading texts, either in their original form or modifying creations of other users, by commenting on them, and/or by linking different kinds of texts (Androutsopoulos 2010: 207). Web 2.0-based CMC interactive spaces, of which blogs are one exemplification, thus allow 'produsers' (Bruns and Jacobs 2006: 6-7) to be at the same time users and producers of content, information and knowledge; participatory media constitute frameworks which make contribution possible in broader terms, and blogs have "provided the first genre and technology to make self-publication and genuine participatory media really accessible to ordinary citizens" (Walker Rettberg 2008: 3; cf. also Herring 2013: 4).

In Web 2.0, as Androutsopoulos remarks, "contemporary forms of online talk largely share with their predecessors in web forums and newsgroups a relative lack of institutional regulations and a proliferation of the features that have come to characterize informal written language online: spoken-like and vernacular features, traces of spontaneous production, innovative spelling choices, emoticons [...] and the like" (2010: 209). Yet, in Web 2.0-based practices "new patterns of discourse organization emerge as well, for instance comments on published content, which were popularized by blogs, and are now ubiquitous on content-sharing sites" (Androutsopoulos 2010: 209; cf. also Barton and Lee 2013). Indeed, sharing of multimedia material has become a common feature, which is often treated as a prompt for "short exchanges among 'friends' on social networking sites" (Androutsopoulos 2010: 209) – an element the latter which can also be detected in conversation-like interactive exchanges in blogs, as it will be illustrated in the next sections.

2.2. Blogs

> By personalizing content, blogs go beyond a purely informative role, and provide a platform for debate, deliberation, and the expression of personal identity in relation to the rest of the (blogging) world (Bruns and Jacobs 2006: 5).

Academic interest in blogs and blogging practices developed steadily since the emergence of this Internet genre in the late 1990s, and in parallel to the diversification and proliferation of blogging practices. Researchers have examined blogs from differentiated disciplinary perspectives, and scholarly definitions of blogs vary accordingly. From the point of view of communication, sociology and ethnographic studies, blogs have been examined as "*practice and process*" (Puschmann 2013: 78), focusing on bloggers' motivations, activity, interaction (e.g. Efimova and de Moor 2005; Ali-Hasan and Adamic 2007) and relationship management (Stefanone and Jang 2007). Blogs have also been investigated from a linguistic points of view (e.g. Herring, Kouper et al. 2005; Puschmann 2010b, 2013; Myers 2010; for an overview of different approaches see Puschmann 2013, 2010a). From a more technical and content perspective, research has concentrated predominantly on "*user-produced data*", i.e. posts and linking practices (Puschmann 2013: 78).

The birth of weblogs is reported to date back to 1998[30], when a few self-created websites similar to the format we know today were listed by Cameron Barrett on his weblog. These blog forerunners developed out of personal home pages, and contained "a mixture in unique proportions of links, commentary, and personal thoughts and essays" (Blood 2002: 2). Knowledge of website design was needed to create and maintain blogs, as they were generated in HTML and then manually uploaded to a web server; indeed, early bloggers generally worked in the technology industry, and used blogs to share information (Miller and Shepherd 2009: 266-267).

The term weblog was abbreviated into 'blog' in 1999, after blogger and web designer Peter Merholz[31] interpreted and de-constructed the term as 'we-blog'. A milestone to the increasing popularity of the genre was the launch in 1999 of free and easy-to-manage blogging tools, hosted by websites such as Pitas.com (then followed by diaryland.com) and Blogger.com (the latter by Pyra Labs), Livejournal.com, Xanga and later Typepad[32] (Blood 2000, 2002: 3-5; Miller and Shepherd 2009: 267). The launch of these software tools has since allowed the creation of blogs even with minimal HTML skills, and has been one of the main factors contributing to their exponential rise and popularity, particularly of the personal journal type, which by 2004 had become the majority (Herring, Scheidt et al. 2005; McNeill 2009: 147; boyd 2006a: n.p.). Blog users became "younger and less technically adept", and "a new emphasis on personal commentary rather than links, self-disclosure rather than information sharing" was developed (Miller and Shepherd 2009: 267). In Walker Rettberg's words "to judge by the success of blogging in the last few years, it seems that the 'push-button publishing' Blogger.com offered in October 2000 was exactly what people wanted" (2008: 3).

The variety of dedicated blog-hosting services and the development of blog software packages, most of them open source and free of charge, which have become widely available since the 2000s, has substantially contributed

[30] While the term itself first appeared in 1997, when used by John Barger to refer to a list of shared interesting websites (Blood 2002; Baron 2008).
[31] http://www.peterme. com (accessed 15 November 2013).
[32] Typepad was launched in October 2003.

to the spread of blogs. Examples are Blogger, LiveJournal, GreatestJournal, Twoday.net[33], plus some specifically focused on diary writing like OpenDiary and Diaryland. These blog-hosting services allow users to choose from a variety of formats according to personal tastes and technological features. Some, like Wordpress or MovableType, offer blog script packages which can be installed and managed on the user's web server, and require a higher degree of technical expertise when compared to the management of the software provided by blog-hosting services (Schmidt 2007: 1417). To be noticed that some websites, such as LiveJournal and Diaryland, differ in structure from blog-hosting services like for instance Blogger, and were at the beginning not thought of as blogging tools, so that "their users do not always conceptualize their practice as blogging" (boyd 2006a: n.p.).

2.2.1. Characteristic blog features

Definitions of what constitutes a blog abound in literature, and vary according to the approach taken to their study. Moreover, technological developments in time have affected blogging practices, too: technical affordances have made it possible to develop content into increasingly multimodal rather than text-only posts; the number and typologies of bloggers, both single and group, has significantly become more and more diversified. Undoubtedly, it can be argued that "blogging is rapidly progressing from a novel, even subversive practice to something quite mainstream" (Puschmann 2010a: 13).

From a technical point of view, the basic characteristics generally referred to when defining a blog are the fact that it is a frequently updated website, with most recent posts appearing at the top of the page, and previous entries listed in a reverse chronological order (Herring, Scheidt et al. 2005; Nardi et al. 2004a, 2004b; Myers 2010: 21 among others). The majority of blogs are created by one individual, and multiple author blogs are less frequent than single-author blogs (Herring et al 2004; Hearst and Dumais 2009).

Distinctive characteristics of blogs are their easy-to-use format, and the possibility to allow comments by readers. Furthermore, links to other websites or blogs are usually present, and can be located in the blogroll,

[33] A quite comprehensive list of websites offering free blog-hosting services can be found at http://www.masternewmedia.org/create-a-blog-best-free-hosted-blog-publishing-services-mini-guide/ (accessed 15 November 2013).

or within a post. Links represent one of the typically networking tools available to bloggers, since they generally mirror the blogger's interests as for what pages are worth reading; in Myers' words, "[l]inking is the currency to the blogosphere" (2010: 30). Links are employed to perform different functions: to provide additional information, evidence or to add something different to the text, to give credit or ask to perform an action (Myers 2010: 37-44.). Though a characteristic feature of blogs, linking practices appear less widespread in blogs than comments (Herring, Scheidt et al. 2005; Miller and Shepherd 2004); links often constitute a characteristic of blogs aiming at public visibility (cf. Granieri [2005] 2007: 40-44; Metitieri 2009: 41-49).

As mentioned, posts are displayed in reversed chronological order, with the most recent appearing at the top of the page; this reverse chronological organization gives blogs a sense of immediacy and authenticity (Blood 2000). Earlier posts are archived in chronological or thematic sequences, and can be accessed at a click of the mouse in the archive, which is usually positioned on a sidebar located on the blog home page, and permit retrieval of earlier posts and, if allowed and present, comments.

Although blog-hosting websites provide bloggers with differentiated formats to personalize and customize their pages, a set of basic features appears consistent throughout blogs (Miller and Shepherd 2004). Unlike personal home pages, blogs are frequently updated, generally have an identifying title and contain individual time-stamped entries named posts. A post typically includes a title, the date of publication, a main text body and, usually, the author's name. Tags, which are textual labels assigned to posts to facilitate organization and navigation of the blog's content by topic, are frequently added too, and generally appear both at the end of a blog post and as a navigational tool in the sidebar; the URL/location of the item on the web is also present in posts. Author and time of publication are generally automatically assigned by the blogging software, thus constituting extra-textual information, and making deictic language possible (Winer 2001; Puschmann 2009, 2012). Blogs still tend to be text-predominant: however, the inclusion of multimodal elements, such as pictures, sounds and video, is technically afforded by the medium and is becoming more and more common (Herring et al. 2005: 161; Herring et al. 2006: 6; Baron 2008: 110).

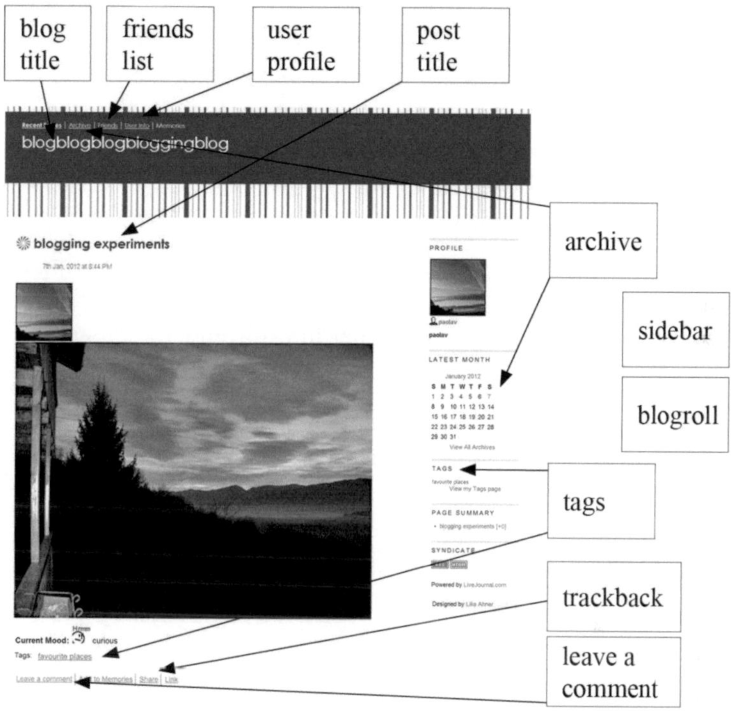

Figure 2. A personal LJ journal home page with main features

Figure 2. above illustrates the main features of a blog page on a LJ journal, which can be summarized as follows:

Sidebar: contains the links to other blogs or to websites considered worthy of quotation by the blogger, or can be used "to create a personal snapshot" to list the blogger's "current reading, music rotation, recent films, videos and the like" (Blood 2002: 48).

Blogroll: usually located in the sidebar, it contains the list of the blogger's favourite blogs, which are either regularly followed, or considered particularly interesting; it thus constitutes both a mark of the interests of the blogger, and of the networks he/she has with other blogs; it often includes citations of the blogger's affiliations in the blogosphere (Schmidt 2007: 1415). Though not always featured, it is quite commonly included; community-oriented blog platforms like LiveJournal and Xanga automatically incorporate a blogroll with the blogger's friends list into the user's profile page.

Permalinks: usually placed at the end of a single post, they provide a permanent link to that entry, even when posts get moved to the archive. Permalinks thus constitute a useful tool in navigating a blog, as well as an important element in terms of 'conversational' characteristics, since references in comments or in other blogs can be made to a specific entry (microcontent), rather than to the blog as a whole.

Archive: as new entries are added, older posts are generally automatically archived by the management tool. Archives are often visually organized as calendars, and can thus be accessed by date. They serve as a reference to previous entries, for the blogger her/himself and for other bloggers (Blood 2002: 45).

Trackback: usually placed at the end of a post, this protocol allows notification to blog followers that a new post has been published containing references to his/her post/blog. The referenced post will usually include a short excerpt from the original blog and link back to it. This feature makes links reciprocal and contributes to establishing group relations.

Comments: nowadays comments are generally afforded by all weblog management software, though the blogger may decide not to activate this function. Through the commenting system other users can leave a comment, express agreement or disagreement, provide feedback about the post or additional information; the blogger may leave a comment, too, usually to respond to his/her readers/commenters. Comments are displayed in chronological order after the post itself, with the latest comment appearing last. In some platforms, as for instance LiveJournal, they are grouped into threads, thus resembling online discussion boards. The possibility to leave a comment is characteristic of blogs (and more recently of other Web 2.0 environments like YouTube or Flicker, cf. Barton and Lee 2013), and it represents one of the main affordances in creating a sense of community (Miller and Shepherd 2004) and potential interaction, both with the blogger him/herself and with other readers/commenters, who can be either 'regulars' or part of a larger audience.

In blogs, as in other Web 2.0 based CMC modes, the possibility to include a special "profile" page about the blogger is frequently provided; it contains information such as age, gender, geographic location, profession, interests and hobbies. The level of details included in the profile page varies individually and in relation to the different blog-hosting services; some blogging platforms (e.g. LiveJournal) also allow the inclusion in the profile page of metainformation about the blog such as statistics about visitors, posting, comments and links to other blogs by the author. According to Herring et al. (2006) the usage of profile pages and non-anonymous information is increasing, thus allowing readers to catch a glimpse of the blogger's world, interests and personality right from this page.

Together with permalinks, two are the main features that can potentially contribute to interactivity in blogs. On the one hand we have trackbacks, which notify other bloggers about new posts via a link to the original post, and are frequently displayed alongside comments (Puschmann 2010a: 55). On the other hand, we have comments that allow readers to react and provide feedback to blog entries, thus constituting potential conversational opportunities, either with people the blogger already knows, or with new visitors (Ali-Hasan and Adamic 2007). Bloggers are generally attentive to their readers and respond to comments, creating what Nardi et al. have defined as a "studied minuet between blogger and audience" (2004b: 225), a point to which I will come back later.

To summarize, the macrostructure of a blog consists of individual posts, which constitute a blog's microstructure; they are automatically marked with metainformation about author and time, and displayed diachronically in reverse chronological order. Most recent information is thus presented first, but older posts can still be accessed in the archive. Despite significant variation both in terms of topic (personal experiences/narration, external events, multimodal material) and style even within a single blog, the above-illustrated genre-specific features are always included and constitute the characterising marks of this CMC mode.

2.2.2. Motivations for blogging

> Part of the allure of blogs is the easy way they move between the personal and the profound (Nardi et al. 2004a: 44).

Blood (2002: 60 ff.) identifies three main reasons for which bloggers create and update a blog: as a means of self-expression, to keep in touch with family and friends, or to share information, either on general or on specific topics; furthermore, particularly in the case of professionals or corporate blogs, they may serve to build a reputation in specific areas of expertise. These motivations appear to have held true over the years: Nardi et al.'s (2004a, 2004b) informants (all well-educated, middle-class Americans) stated they blogged to document their life, to update family and friends with activities and whereabouts, to express opinions and points of view; for them blogging represented a form of democratic or "catharthic" self-expression and an "outlet for thoughts and feelings" (2004a; 44), or was used to "think by writing" (Nardi et al. 2004b: 227; cf. also Blood 2002: 60-62; Viégas 2005) and to participate in community forums in diversified settings (e.g. poets, class blogs).

In the 2006 *Pew Internet and American Life Project* (Lenhart and Fox 2006) the most popular blogging type was the personal journal, and the motivations given for blogging were to cover "life and activities" (37%), to express oneself creatively (52%), to document personal experiences or share them with others (50% of all respondents and 76% among younger users); the latter was chosen as the primary blog topic by 37% of bloggers[34] – although more than half bloggers stated that they wrote for themselves. Staying in touch with family and friends was also popular for 60% of respondents, more so for younger 18-29-aged women, while sharing practical knowledge or skills appeared more frequent among older users aged 50-64. (cf. Table 3. below).

Table 3. Reasons for personal blogging (source: Lenhart and Fox 2006: 8, Pew Research Centre, Washington, D.C. http://www.pewinternet.org/~/media/Files/Reports/2006/PIP%20Bloggers%20Report%20July%2019%202006.pdf.pdf) (accessed 15 November 2013)

More Blog to Share Experiences Than to Earn Money

Please tell me if this is a reason you personally blog, or not:	Major reason	Minor reason	Not a reason
To express yourself creatively	52%	25%	23%
To document your personal experiences or share them with others	50	26	24
To stay in touch with friends and family	37	22	40
To share practical knowledge or skills with others	34	30	35
To motivate other people to action	29	32	38
To entertain people	28	33	39
To store resources or information that is important to you	28	21	52
To influence the way other people think	27	24	49
To network or to meet new people	16	34	50
To make money	7	8	85

Source: Pew Internet & American Life Project Blogger Callback Survey, July 2005-February 2006. N=233. Margin of erroris ±7%

[34] Followed by politics (11%), entertainment-related topics (7%), sports (6%), general news and current events and business (5%), technology (4%), religion, spirituality or faith (2%).

According to the 2008 Technorati *State of the Blogosphere* (White 2009), self-expression, meeting and connecting with like-minded people and sharing expertise ranked respectively first, third and second among the main reasons for blogging (cf. also Hollenbaugh 2010b). Although bloggers wrote about multiple topics, and personal and professional subjects were equally popular, personal lifestyle predominated (54%), with technology ranking second (46%); 69% of bloggers had personal blogs dealing with topics of personal interest. Bloggers defined their style as "sincere, conversational, humorous" (White 2009, Report Day 2). As for interactional features, 67% said that they had made friends via blogging, with whom they communicated online but had never met in person; 85% allowed comments on their blog.

In the 2009 Technorati *State of the Blogosphere* report (Sussmann 2009) self-expression and sharing expertise are still primary motivations, and 45% of all respondents say they blog about personal musings, a figure reaching 53% for hobbyists. These findings appear confirmed in the 2010 Technorati *State of the Blogosphere* (Sobel 2010), where self-expression, that is, "to meet and connect with like-minded people" and "to speak my mind on areas of interest" are the most cited reasons, with sharing expertise ranking third. 62% of bloggers say that they have made friends through their blog and have interacted online (cf. also Lenhart et al. 2010).

The 2011 Technorati *State of the Blogosphere*[35] highlights that 70% of all bloggers use their blog primarily to share their expertise and experience with others; for hobbyists, expressing themselves on areas of interest, becoming more involved with their passion areas and meeting and connecting with like-minded people rank from second to fourth. 54% of respondents agree that they have made friends through their blog, and as many state that they have become more involved with their passion areas as a result of blogging. As to topics, personal musings rank first for hobbyists, followed by technology and news, the latter also with reference to reading other people's blogs (but not as to writing). 79% of all respondents describe their blogging style as "sincere," and 67% define their style as "conversational".

When looking at social media, 82% of bloggers say they use Twitter to promote their blog (77%), to follow friends (60%), and to highlight interesting links (59%); 89% use Facebook, and 50% of all bloggers have separate Facebook pages for their blog and for their personal account, with

[35] http://technorati.com/social-media/article/state-of-the-blogosphere-2011-part2/ (accessed 15 November 2013).

an increase of 34% from the previous year. Among Google+ users, the most common reasons for using this social network is to mention interesting links (43%) and to promote their blog (33%) (cf. also Smith 2011). Personal and creative self-expression, together with the wish to document personal experiences and to connect to like-minded people, appear thus to be steady and predominant reasons for blogging, particularly in personal journals (Baron 2008: 112), as an opportunity "to tell stories in a mediated forum to a potentially large, though distant and invisible, audience" (Miller and Shepherd 2004; cf. also Blood 2000). In terms of personal narrative, "[o]verall, bloggers appear more concerned with themselves than with others, and with writing to write more than with writing to be read" (Puschmann 2010a: 43); personal self-expression rather than topics related to the 'external world' figures as a constant motivation for blogging over the years. Keeping in touch with family and friends, and meeting (new) people are also predominant aspects, which, as we will see below, are fostered by the dynamic and interactive affordances of this medium, too.

2.2.3. Spread of blogs

> In 2004, when Technorati started, the typical reaction to the word 'blog' was 'huh – can you repeat yourself?'. Today [2008] blogs are everywhere – even presidential candidates have blogs (B. Feld, quoted in Winn 2009, Technorati *State of the Blogosphere 2008*).

Establishing exact numbers for blogs is not always a straightforward matter, and estimates are at times contradictory. Moreover, statistics do not always differentiate between active blogs, i.e. frequently and regularly updated ones, and blogs that are just created, or created and quickly abandoned (cf. Caslon analytics http://www.caslon.com.au/weblogprofile1.htm[36]). We will here refer mainly to data reported in the Perseus Development Corporation, Pew Internet & American Life Project and Technorati *State of the Blogosphere* reports, since they represent three among the main surveys which have regularly investigated blogs demographics over the years.

Earlier days certainly saw a significant and quick blog spread: according

[36] Last accessed 15 November 2013.

to the 2003 Perseus Development Corporation survey on eight major blog hosting services, the number of new blogs "increased by more than 600% between 2000 and 2001", for a total of more than 4 million blogs at the time (Miller and Shepherd 2009: 267; cf. also Herring et al. 2006: 4). The Technorati *State of the Blogosphere* found that the number of blogs was doubling every six months from March 2003 to June 2006, and the growth of blogs happened in parallel with social-networking services: Facebook, Friendster and MySpace were all launched between 2002 and 2004 (Miller and Shepherd 2009: 267).

According to Perseus data, in 2003 the majority of blogs were created by teenagers: 51.5% in the age range 13-19, and 39.6% by young people aged 20-29 – making up for a total of 92.4% under-30 bloggers; the typical blog appeared to be written by "a teenage girl who uses it twice a month to update her friends and classmates on happenings in her life", in a very informal style, with slang spellings and abbreviations (Perseus Press Release 2003[37]).

In 2004, the *Pew Internet and American Life Project* reported that 2-7% adult Internet users had created a blog, and the 2005 survey showed a growth at a rate of 58% in the use of blogs in the USA, with 8 million people having a blog, and 12% Internet users posting comments or materials on blogs; Technorati and blo.gs reported that in the same year the number of blogs was between 1.5 and 2 million (cf. also Herring et al. 2006). In the age range 18-29, about 25% posted on other people's blogs. 15,000 new blogs were created every day, and 10,800 updated every hour; 7% of 120 million adult Americans had a blog or a web-based diary (Bruns and Jacobs 2006: 2). Blog creators appeared quite well off and well educated, 48% were under the age of 30 and 57% male (Rainie, Data Memo, *The State of Blogging*, January 2005[38], cf. Fig. 3. below).

---

[37] http://www.perseusuk.co.uk/survey/news/releases/release_blogs.html (accessed 15 November 2013).).

[38] http://www.pewinternet.org/Reports/2005/The-State-of-Blogging/Data-Memo-Findings.aspx (accessed 15 November 2013).

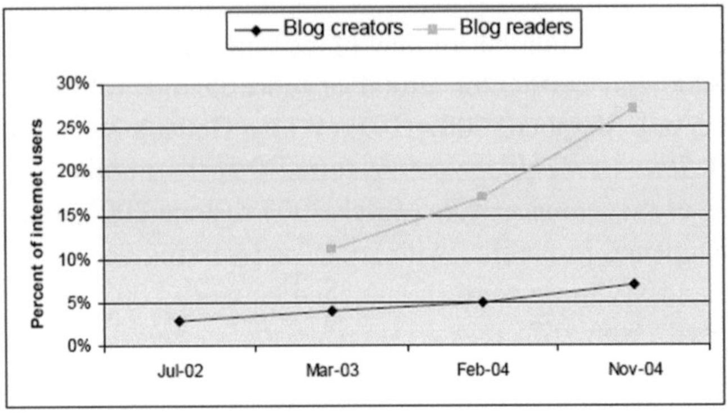

Figure 3. The growth of the blogosphere 2002–2004 (Source: Rainie L., Data Memo, The state of blogging, January 2005: 3, Pew Research Centre, Washington, D.C.; http://www.pewinternet.org/files/old-media//Files/Reports/2005/PIP_blogging_data.pdf.pdf) (accessed 15 November 2013)

In 2004 57% of online teenagers (aged 12-17) were content creators on the Internet: 19% had created a blog and 22% a personal webpage; 32% had developed or worked on a webpage for school, a friend, or an organization; 33% had shared original content such as artwork, photos, stories, or videos online, or remixed online content into a new personal(ized) work (Lenhart and Madden 2005: 8-9). Teens were much more likely than adults both to blog and to read blogs: 25% of girls 15-17 blogged (against 15% boys), 53% girls and 34% boys said they read blogs of people they knew, and blogged for an audience of family or friends (Lenhart and Madden 2005: 8). In comparison, only 7% of adult Internet users said they had created their own blog and 27% to read blogs[39]. For many teens blogging was about the "maintenance and extension of personal relationships" in the form of a personal journal, to communicate with friends, post ideas and share personal experiences (cf. Tab. 4. below); in fact, the Internet appeared to be employed by the majority of users as a tool to communicate with friends and family (Boase et al. 2006, quoted in Stefanone and Jang 2007: n.p.).

[39] Although Herring et al. (2006: 10) found that in their sample adult bloggers either predominated (March-April 2003 and April 2004) or equalled teens (September 2003), while young adults aged 10-25 increased across the samples.

Table 4. Teen content creators and Internet users (Source: Lenhart and Madden 2005: iv, Pew Research Centre, Washington, D.C.; http://pewinternet.org/~/media/Files/Reports/2005/PIP_Teens_Content_Creation.pdf.pdf) (accessed 15 November 2013)

Teen Content Creators and Consumers: Summary of Findings at a Glance
More than half of online teens are Content Creators.
19% of online teens keep a blog and 38% read them.
Older girls lead the blogging activity among teens.
Teen bloggers are tech-savvy and heavy internet users.
Half of online teens say they currently download music files and close to one-third say they download video.
Most teen downloaders think that getting free music is easy and it's unrealistic to expect people not to do it.
Teens are as likely now to have paid for music online as they are to have tried peer-to-peer services.
Source: Lenhart, A. and Madden, M. *Teen Content Creators and Consumers.* Washington, DC: Pew Internet & American Life Project, November 2, 2005.

Fifty million blogs were tracked in the Technorati *State of the Blogosphere* 2006 (Sifry 2006, November[40]), and the blogosphere was over 100 times bigger than in 2003 with about 175,000 new blogs created every day. From 2004 to 2006, the number of blogs doubled every six months (Sifry 2007[41]). The 2006 Pew report figures indicate that 54% bloggers in the USA were under the age of thirty, and evenly distributed between men and women, mostly but not only white (Lenhart and Fox 2006: ii). As in the previous year, a large proportion of bloggers (77%) also shared materials (photo, art work, stories, videos) and 44% remixed them (e.g. songs, texts or images) into their own artistic creations or artwork; nevertheless, blogs still appeared largely text-based (80%). 90% bloggers read other people's blogs, usually on a regular basis, and a predominant 77% allowed comments on their blog; 41% also had a blogroll/friend list on their blog.

Bloggers were also heavily engaged in other forms of digital communication: 78% sent or received instant messages, and 55% text messages via a cell phone. For a vast majority of respondents blogging was a hobby, and only 13% updated their blog daily. 62% did not have a personal website before creating their blog, or published their material anywhere else. 52% bloggers stated they posted mainly for themselves, 32% for their audience, whom they believed was composed mostly by people they knew, and 35% for people they had never met (cf. Table 5. hereunder).

[40] http://www.sifry.com/alerts/archives/2006_11.html (accessed 15 November 2013).
[41] http://www.sifry.com/alerts/archives/000493.html (accessed 15 November 2013).

Table 5. Main findings for bloggers and blogging in 2006 (Source: Lenhart and Fox 2006: v, http://www.pewinternet.org/~/media/Files/Reports/2006/PIP%20Bloggers%20 Report%20July%2019%202006.pdf.pdf) (last accessed 15 November 2013)

Bloggers: Summary of Findings at a Glance
Blogging is bringing new voices to the online world.
Telephone surveys capture the most accurate snapshot possible of a small and moving target.
Contrary to the impression created by the press attention on political blogging, just 11% of bloggers say they focus mainly on government or politics.
The blogging population is young, evenly split between women and men, and racially diverse.
Relatively small groups of bloggers view blogging as a public endeavor.
The main reasons for keeping a blog are creative expression and sharing personal experiences.
Only one-third of bloggers see blogging as a form of journalism. Yet many check facts and cite original sources.
Bloggers are avid consumers and creators of online content. They are also heavy users of the internet in general.
Bloggers are major consumers of political news and about half prefer sources without a particular political viewpoint.
Bloggers often utilize community and readership-enhancing features available on their blogs.
Source: Lenhart, Amanda and Susannah Fox. *Bloggers.* Washington, DC: Pew Internet & American Life Project, July 19, 2006.

As to data for Europe, in 2006 2% Internet users based in the UK wrote blogs, and 13% among them had read a personal blog in the preceding week (compared to 40% in the USA), 25% in France, and 12% in Denmark (Baron 2008: 109). However, it was noted that in 2006 "Médiamétrie, dismissing claims that 10% of French population 'have blogs', claimed that there were just over three million active French blogs. UK market researcher Synovate claimed in June 2007 that only 10% of British 18 to 24-year-olds have ever blogged" (Caslon Analytics[42]).

In the 2007 Pew survey *Teens and Social Media* (Lenhart et al. 2007: 2) the use of the Internet as a space for social interaction by teenagers emerged as central: 93% teens used the web, and 55% of online teens had created a profile on a social networking website such as Facebook or MySpace. Instant Messaging (IM) and social networking were privileged over e-mails to keep in touch with friends, thus confirming that blogging was used in combination with other digital communication tools.

Blogging activities had almost doubled: 28% respondents had created their own online journal or blog, in comparison to the 19% figures of 2004 (8% for adult bloggers); 49% read blogs, compared to a 38% figure in 2004.

[42] http://www.caslon.com.au/weblogprofile1.htm#ephemerality (accessed 15 November 2013).

We still find a prevalence of girls in the blogosphere: 35% female against 20% male teens engaged in blogging activities, although in video-sharing websites boys uploaded more than girls (Lenhart et al. 2007: 8-10).

As to the youngest, 64% online teens aged 12-17 participated in one or more content-creating online activities, (compared to 57% in the 2004 survey): 39% shared their own artistic creations online, such as artwork, photos, stories, or videos (33% in 2004). Digital images (photos and videos) appeared to play a major role in the life of teenagers: 26% remixed online content into their own creations, 47% had uploaded photos and 14% videos, and such postings often gave way to commenting and conversation-like interactions. In general, 76% online teens posted comments to a friend's blog (Lenhart et al. 2007: i, 2-4).

33% respondents had created or worked on webpages or blogs for others, such as groups they belonged to, friends, or as part of school assignments, a figure basically unchanged from 2004 (32%); 27% maintained their own personal webpage, compared to 22% in 2004. Activity on social networks (SNS) also appeared highly correlated to blogging: 42% of those who used a social network site had also created a blog (as opposed to 11% of those who did not use SNS), and 70% reported reading the blogs of others (Lenhart et al. 2007: i, 7).

These figures show a particularly relevant increase in teenager blogging practices, which can on the one hand be associated to social-networking activities, and on the other to the spread of the mode, both in general and in educational contexts: "blogging has been embraced and encouraged by the educational and library community, and some schools are now incorporating blogging tools into their curriculum" (Lenhart et al. 2007: 8).

In 2007 the incessant growth pace in the blogosphere appeared to somewhat slow down; nevertheless, more that 70 million blogs were tracked, and about 120,000 new blogs were created every day. As for 2008, Technorati[43] (Winn 2009) reported how numbers for blogs varied according to different sources: out of the 184 million worldwide (Universal McCann, March 2008), figures for the U.S ranged from 22.6 (e-Marketer) to 26.4 million (Universal McCann); MySpace, on the other hand, claimed that the blogs hosted in their space in 2008 amounted to more than 150 million (Miller and Shepherd 2009: 267). The typology of blogs included personal (79%), professional (46%) and corporate (12%) ones. Respondents for Europe amounted to 27%,

[43] http://technorati.com/social-media/article/state-of-the-blogosphere-introduction/ (accessed 15 November 2013).

were mostly male (73%); 48% were 18-34 years old, 52% over 35 and half of them blogged for hobby and fun (Winn 2009).

In 2009 BlogPulse tracked 126 million blogs, and Puschmann (2010a: 6) reports that between 100 and 180 million were based in the USA. According to the Technorati 2009 *State of the Blogosphere*[44] (Sussman 2009), two thirds were male and 60% aged 18-44, with a relatively high income and educational qualifications. Hobbyists represented 72% of the respondents, and said they blogged for fun and personal satisfaction (76%) and to express their "personal musings" (45%), while 71% stated their main motivation for blogging was "to speak their minds", particularly so for hobbyists. Including photo (82%) and video (53%) material in posts was becoming increasingly popular: only 13% respondents said they posted text-only entries, and 73% stated they created the photos, video, or audio themselves. However, the diversity of the blogosphere, and the passion for sometimes very niche topics, was revealed by 30% respondents who said their primary subject in blogging was 'other', despite the fact that the 23 choices that were provided included most broad fields of inquiry.

As to teenagers, The Pew Project *Generations Online in 2009* reports that "teens and Generation Y (Internet users aged 18-32) were the most likely groups to use the web for entertainment and to communicate with friends and family" (cf. Fig. 4. below), and blogs were created to update friends about their life and experiences (Jones and Fox, Project data memo, January 28[45], 2009: 3). 49% teens, 43% Generation Y, 34% Generation X (aged 33-44) reported respectively to read blogs, and 28% teenagers, 20% Generation Y, 10% Generation X to have created a blog, confirming the trend that blogs constitute a privileged space for self-expression and interaction for younger generations (Jones and Fox, Project data memo, January 28[46], 2009: 5)

---

[44] http://technorati.com/social-media/article/day-1-who-are-the-bloggers/ (accessed 15 November 2013).

[45] http://www.pewinternet.org/~/media/Files/Reports/2009/PIP_Generations_2009.pdf (accessed 15 November 2013).

[46] http://www.pewinternet.org/~/media/Files/Reports/2009/PIP_Generations_2009.pdf (accessed 15 November 2013).

Chart: Percentage of Americans online by age (Teens, 12-17, Nov. 2007-Feb. 2008, margin of error = ±3%. Adults, December 2008, margins of error differ by subgroup. See methodology).

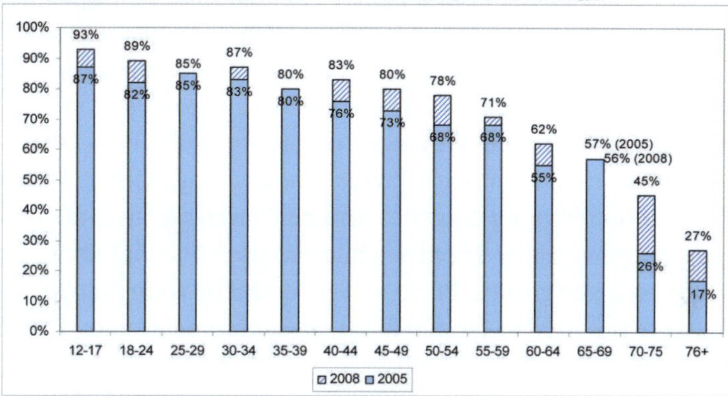

Figure 4. Americans online by age (Source: Jones and Fox. 2009. Generations Online in 2009, PEW INTERNET PROJECT DATA MEMO: 2, Pew Research Centre, Washington, D.C.; http://www.pewinternet.org/~/media/Files/Reports/2009/PIP_Generations_2009.pdf) (accessed 15 November 2013)

Coming to more recent data, the Technorati *State of the Blogosphere* 2010[47] (Sobel 2010) claims that, although almost half respondents are located in the U.S., European bloggers amount to 29% (Fig. 5. hereunder).

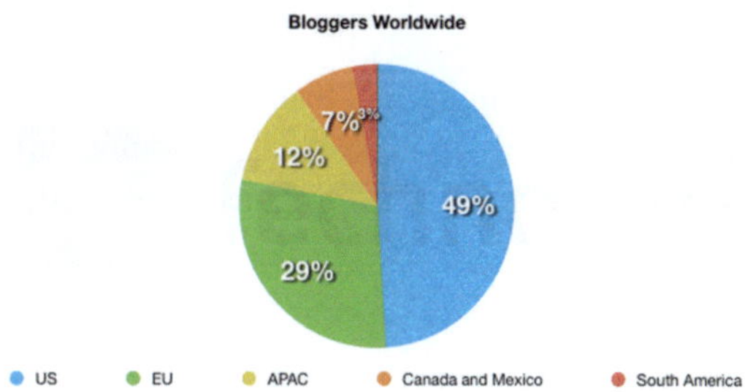

Figure 5. Distribution of bloggers worldwide (Source: Technorati *State of the Blogosphere* 2010, Sobel J., Introduction, http://technorati.com/blogging/article/state-of-the-blogosphere-2010-introduction/) (accessed 15 November 2013)

The use of social media by bloggers seems to be expanding, and the boundaries between blogs, micro-blogs and social networks are at times blurred: for instance, blog posts are increasingly shared via social networks. Nevertheless, blogging practices in general still appear on the increase: 47%

---

[47] http://technorati.com/blogging/article/state-of-the-blogosphere-2010-introduction/ (accessed 15 November 2013).

hobbyist bloggers have more than one blog, and their use has been modified by smartphones or tablets: 40% bloggers say that this "has changed the way they blog, encouraging shorter and more spontaneous posts" (Technorati *State of the Blogosphere* 2010 Report, Sobel 2010[48]). According to a substantial part of the respondents, their blogging habits will expand and include a wider range of topics in the future. However, according to the Pew 2010 report on the use of social media among teenagers and young adults (Lenhart et al. 2010), since 2006 blogging practices dropped among teens and young adults but increased among older people, while the use of social networking sites had risen for both age groups. From a 28% figure for young bloggers in 2006, only 14% were reported to blog in 2010; also, commenting on friends' blogs decreased from 76% to 52%. Creative content sharing and remixing practices seem instead to be in line with previous Pew surveys findings.

In the 2010 Technorati *State of the Blogosphere* report[49] (Sobel 2010) the majority (64%) are hobbyists, who blog for fun, 65% are aged 18-44, and two thirds are male; respondents were from 24 different countries, the majority (71%) was based in North America, and 19% in Europe.

As for hosting services, Wordpress, Blogger and Blogspot were the most popular, the latter two particularly with hobbyists, while LiveJournal ranked quite low.

A different picture is although provided by the Sysomos report[50], which states that in 2010 younger people were the most active accounting for 53.3% of total bloggers in the 21-35 age range, teens for 20.2%. 36-to-50 year-olds were 19.4%, while over 51-year-old bloggers amounted only to 7.1%. As to gender, bloggers appeared almost equally distributed, with 50.9 female and 49.1 male bloggers.

According to the same report, when looking at geographic location, as Table 6. below illustrates, most bloggers are set in the U.S., followed by the UK with 6.75%, Japan (4.9%), Brazil (4.2%), Canada (3.9%), Germany (3.3%), Italy (3.2%), Spain (3.1%), France (2.9%) and Russia (2.3%).

48 http://technorati.com/blogging/article/state-of-the-blogosphere-2010-introduction/ (accessed 15 November 2013).
49 http://technorati.com/blogging/article/state-of-the-blogosphere-2010-introduction/ (accessed 15 November 2013).
50 http://www.sysomos.com/reports/bloggers/ (accessed 15 November 2013).

Table 6. Bloggers by location in 2010 (Source: http://www.sysomos.com/reports/bloggers/) (last accessed 15 November 2013)

Country	Share percentage
USA	29.22%
UK	6.75%
Japan	4.88%
Brazil	4.19%
Canada	3.93%
Germany	3.34%
Italy	3.21%
Spain	3.14%
France	2.87%
Russia	2.31%
Australia	2.22%
India	2.14%
Sweden	2.05%
Malaysia	1.7%
Netherlands	1.69%

Source: sysomos.com sysomos

In the 2011 Technorati *State of the Blogosphere*[51], the average number of blogs per respondent increased slightly from 2010, from two to three. The bloggers who responded were located in 45 countries, nearly half in the United States, but with a significant presence in Europe, as Fig. 6. hereunder shows.

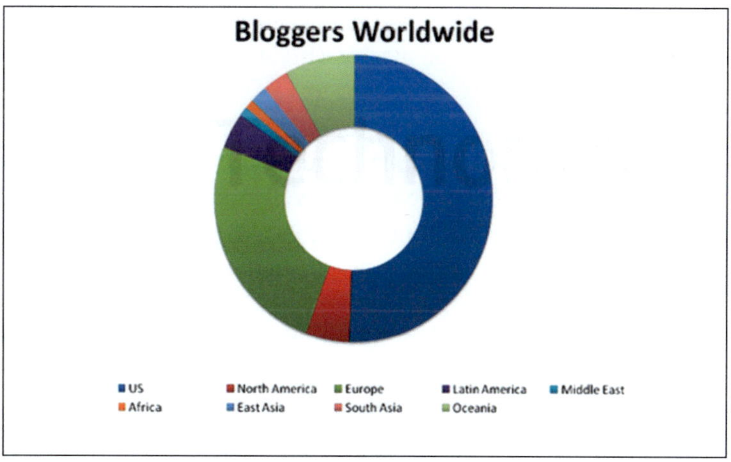

Figure 6. Bloggers Worldwide (Source: Technorati Media *State of the Blogosphere* 2011, http://technorati.com/blogging/article/state-of-the-blogosphere-2011-part1/) (accessed 15 November 2013)

[51] http://technorati.com/blogging/article/state-of-the-blogosphere-2011-part1/ (accessed 15 November 2013).

According to the same survey, overall, 14% of bloggers spend at least 21 hours per week visiting social media sites. About three fifths of bloggers, for all blog types, are male; the majority are in the 25-44 age range, with a third over 44. Hobbyist bloggers still represent the majority, with 60% of the respondents to the survey; 72% blog to speak their mind, and half of them primarily to express their personal musings; they also state they individually respond to comments from readers. The majority say their blog is a way to share expertise and experience with others, though for 31% hobbyists it is a way to speak their mind on an area of interest, and personal satisfaction is how they measure the success of their blog. Overall, blogging has a positive impact on the respondents' personal life; 54% say they have made friends through their blog and that they have become more involved with their passion areas as a result of blogging.

The growing relevance of social media is confirmed: 89% respondents use Facebook, mainly to promote their blog; 82% are on Twitter, and nearly half of them link their blogs to it[52].

As these figures show, in general the youth use online media to extend their range of friendships and interest, either through private communications (IM or mobile phones) or public practices in social-networking sites. Teenagers consider these virtual settings, such as social networks and online journals, as "friend and peer spaces" (Ito et al. 2009: 38). Interest-based communities of various kinds also represent relevant aggregating spaces; fan sites and specialized networks can be found within larger websites, a case in point being LiveJournal. An example in this sense is represented by Anime fans, which produce "a wide range of creative works", including fansubbing, as well as a range of fan-related online events (Ito et al. 2009: 62-3).

To sum up, despite at times contrasting estimates, it is undeniable that blogs have seen a rapid development since their beginning in the mid-1990s, especially in the first years. Blogging emerges as a favourite activity for younger people, who often use it concurrently to other forms of digital communication and social network media. Amongst the most prominent motivations for blogging, we find expressing personal musings and connecting with like-minded people, both belonging to their sphere of family and friends, or as new encounters. Creative content sharing practices are also increasingly widespread for regular and young bloggers. Although most statistics report

[52] The Pew Internet survey *Why Americans Use Social Media* (Smith 2011) shows that 66% Americans use social media platforms as Facebook, Twitter, MySpace or Linkedin mainly to stay in touch with new and old friends.

bloggers being mainly based in the USA, other geographical areas are increasingly represented, as Table 6. and Fig. 6. above show.

At an international level, "while cultural differences in blogging communities exist, overall the blogging community shares remarkable similarities with each other despite geographic distances" (Su, Wang and Mark 2005: 4), not least as blogging often revolves around common interests and communities. Although broad generalisations are not possible, nor feasible or appropriate since digital media include a vast range of individual and community variation, at the linguistic level, as we will see in Chapter 3, personal blogs in particular are generally characterized by a certain speech-like informality, a frequent use of abbreviations and emoticons, creative spelling and punctuation (e.g. Šabec n.d.; Brala 2008; Moraldo 2005; for an international perspective on blogging cf. also Schlobinski and Siever 2005; Russel and Echchaibi 2009).

2.2.4. Types of blogs

> What complicates the analysis of blogs is that they are both the product of blogging and the medium through which the bloggers produce their expressions. Blogs emerge because bloggers are blogging (boyd 2006a: n.p.).

Different categorizations of blogs have been developed alongside their spread. As we have seen in the previous section, since the early years, blogging practices have grown exponentially and developed into specific sub-genres (Bruns and Jacobs 2006: 3) or sub-types (Herring 2007), and today blogs increasingly display wide variation in structure and content (e.g. Nardi et al. 2004a: 42, 2004b: 222). As pointed out by Baron, "[t]he scope of blogs has expanded dramatically over the past decade, making blogging more of a multifaceted tool than a specific type of internet platform"; blogs have increasingly incorporated features of social media, such as profile pages or privacy settings, which are controlled by the blogger (Baron 2008: 109).

Miller and Shepherd (2009) suggest three main phases in the development of blogs: the first, prior to the changes in blog design tools in the late nineties, characterized by a selection of links and commentaries; the second marked by the creation of blog hosting sites and easy tools, which boosted the popularity of the genre, particularly in the self-expression opportunities associated to personal journals. The third phase, contemporary to the advent of social-networking services, has also been influenced by the technological developments of Web 2.0, which, as we have seen, has in the first place allowed sharing of user-generated content and a higher level of interactivity and participation.

Blogs can be classified differently depending on the point of view taken in looking at their development: for instance, according to whether they are private or corporate (the latter for business purposes), developed by a single or by a group of authors, devoted to personal experiences, to a community or to research aims, to what kind of media they incorporate[53]; definitions also vary: a video blog can be referred to as a 'vlog', a blog mainly containing links can be defined as a 'link log', a 'sketchlog' when containing an art portfolio, or a 'photoblog' when incorporating photos (cf. Miller and Shepherd 2004; Baron 2008: 110; Miles 2006 for video and audio blogging).

Typical categorizations are those made with reference to blog content, differentiating among weblogs that deal with 'external' events, usually public (like filter or topical weblogs, notebooks, K-logs, public-affairs blogs) and personal journals (Blood 2002: 6-9). Filter blogs are characterized by openness to the 'external' world: as the name underscores, they filter, comment and evaluate information, often deal with news and political issues, frequently include links, and are characterized by a topic-centric style (Puschmann 2013: 92; cf. also boyd 2006a; n.p.). Topic blogs generally focus on particular subjects or products; notebooks may deal either with 'external' or with personal matters; in knowledge blogs, expertise in a field is shared. More recently, we also find science and research blogs as a developing genre (Mauranen 2013).

Personal journals are most typically characterized by content related to the blogger's day-to-day activities, thoughts and feelings, as well as his/her wish to network with family and friends, and have an author-centric style approach (Puschmann 2013: 92). They may also be used to keep record of life events, thoughts and/or (research) projects (Brady 2005: 10-11). Mixed blogs incorporate characteristics of at least two of the above-mentioned types (Blood 2002: 8-9).

A categorization that combines form and function in blogs has been proposed by Krishnamurthy (2002), who has suggested classification along two vector scales, that is, "personal vs. topical" and "individual vs. community",

[53] Cf. e.g. http://www.blogossary.com/ for a comprehensive glossary (accessed 15 November 2013).

which can help in capturing the distinction between personal/individual and group/community blogs (cf. also Treem and Thomas 2010: 347).

A dichotomic categorization that distinguishes internal and external focus is put forward by Puschmann (2009: 3; 2010a: 41-2; 2012: 94): the first are defined as "ego-blogging", and the second as "topic blogging". The two are characterized by several contrasting aspects: the focus may be internal or external; the audience narrow, close and familiar, or wide, distant and unfamiliar; the aim may be to record thoughts, to reflect on one's life and to maintaining relationships, or to inform and influence others. Blogs may be anonymous or, as most generally, not anonymous, characterized by narration and a stream of consciousness flow or by exposition, by a more formal vs. less formal style; finally, they may contain either few or no hyperlinks, or some as well as frequent hyperlinks. According to this interpretative model, blog focus (ego vs. topic blogging) can be paired with audience scope (narrow vs. wide): "ego blogging correlates with a narrow scope (self, family, friends), while topic blogging correlates with a wide scope (all people interested in a certain issue or topic)" (Puschmann 2010a: 42). Personal journals, which, as we have seen, appear to be preponderant in the blogosphere, can in this perspective be defined as ego-blogging, and be associated to previous off-line diary practices, while topic blogging addresses a specialized, 'expert' audience and can be related to journalism and publishing practices. As Puschmann summarizes, "[t]he reasons for choosing ego blogging or topic blogging are varied and fundamentally depend on how users conceptualize their blogs and on what their communicative needs are" (Puschmann 2010a: 72), possibly also alternating or mixing the two modes along a continuum.

In applying her faceted classification scheme to blog analysis, Herring identifies the following as specific to blogs: asynchronicity, one-way message transmission, persistence of messages in archives linked to the sidebar of the blog, web-based delivery and tendency for text-only messages, entries in reverse chronological order, a comment option below each entry, a one-to-many participation, though imbalanced (2007: 24-25 *passim*; see also Chapter 3). Puschmann has expanded Herring's scheme, adding further elements in relation to blogs and to recent developments in technology. For instance, as to the dimension of synchronicity, Puschmann (2010a: 27) highlights that the spread of Internet connection packages and of mobile devices and their connectivity allows Internet users to be constantly connected and logged in, which may consequently modify the notion of synchronous and asynchronous modes. Moreover, microblogging formats such as Twitter allow potential synchronicity in mode to its users (cf. also Crystal 2011: 38).

In any case, whichever classification is taken into account, blogs represent the author(s)' point of view and can be seen as a medium for self-expression (Blood 2002: 60-61; Puschmann 2009: 2; Miller and Shepherd 2004): either in ego- or in topic blogging, "the reader gains an insight into what the blogger deems important enough to record or present. Whether a blogger tells a story or makes an argument in a post […], the reader can observe the process of expressive self-construction through time in the blog as a whole" (Puschmann 2010a: 123); "an 'ego component' is therefore virtually always present in blogs, whether topic or ego blogs" (Puschmann 2010a: 73). Blogs are indeed characterized by self-centredness in that a blogger's individual personality traits and personal narrative choices at different discourse levels are identifiable: in expression via explicit first person self-reference by the blogger; in temporality, i.e. tense information related to the entry's post date; in spatiality, i.e. "the origo of spatial adverbials is either the blogger's location at coding time, or the blog in the role of a virtual place on the (spatially conceptualized) Internet"; in topicality, i.e. "the blogger features in her own discourse" (Puschmann 2010a: 58-62). Together with formal features, frequency and brevity, personality thus appears "one of the driving factors in weblogs' popularity" (Turnbull 2002: 83, cited in Miller and Shepherd 2004 n.p.).

As McNeill (2009: 151) underlines, "the majority of blogs occupies a middle ground, with 'diaries' including links, and 'blogs' personal commentary as well as annotations, suggesting that, despite their apparent desirability, rigid generic distinctions will not hold". Rather than in straight and tight borderlines, personal journals, topical, filter and mixed blogs operate along a computer-mediated communication continuum: at one end we find static web pages or standard HTML documents such as personal pages, which are less frequently updated, and characterized by a unilateral one-to-many communication; at the other end stand various forms of asynchronous CMC, such as newsgroups, e-mail and blogs, which are regularly updated, and characterized by a more symmetrical typology of exchanges with reciprocal communication. As Herring, Scheidt et al. (2005: 160) argue, "blogs are in fact a hybrid of existing genres, rendered unique by the combination of the source features of the genres they adapt, and by the distinct technical affordances". It is often difficult to clearly categorize blogs according to their content since, despite some bloggers following a precise focus, 'external' and 'internal' elements are often mixed. This has been acknowledged in recent approaches to the study of blogs; Puschmann (2102: 75-76) highlights that in recent research "there appears to be a gradual move away from definitions that tie blogs exclusively to a specific style or content closely resembling antecedent practices, such as diary-writing and journalism, to definitions that are more open and recognize what boyd [2006a] refers to as 'the efficacy of the practice'".

Alongside other web modes, in several – above all earlier – studies blogs have been conceptualized and defined as a CMC genre (Herring, Scheidt et al. 2005; Miller and Shepherd 2004). Herring and Paolillo (2006: 442-443) define genre characteristics in blogs as including "common structural features such as dated entries displayed in reverse chronological sequence and sidebars containing links and calendars", a "culturally recognized name (Swales 1990), and the common purpose of sharing content with others through the web". However, as we have seen and as the authors point out, the rapid spread and differentiation in blogging practices and their consequent variation in topic, discourse and communicative purpose, has made their definition as a single, unified CMD genre, increasingly problematic. With Mauranen (2013: 11), "[i]nstead of one genre, it might be more reasonable to talk about several blog genres – maybe even an unlimited number, given that new kinds of blogs seem to crop up sooner that anyone can really hope to keep up with".

Boyd (2006a: n.p.), in fact, maintains that defining the blog "as a genre obscures its role in distributing and representing expression", arguing that blogs ought rather to be conceptualized as a medium through which communication occurs. Such a perspective would allow deeper understanding of their structure and content, as well as of the complex dynamics of orality/textuality, corporeality/spatiality and public/private that in blogs appear blurred. Furthermore, Miller and Shepherd (2009: 281-286) point out that blogs stand apart in Internet genres as they are native to the web, and are largely determined in format and content by the affordances, i.e. the technical capabilities of the medium, and consequently of the hosting websites in which they are created. "The affordances offered by blogs – interaction and connection, immediacy, instant access, low overheard" (Miller and Shepherd 2009: 283) have shaped their development, and blogs can therefore be defined as "a technology, a medium, a constellation of affordances" (Miller and Shepherd 2009: 283) rather than a genre in the narrower sense of the term.

A more adherent definition of blogging practices today may thus be that of a medium where content is created and shaped according to the way in which "a blogger has chosen to work within the set of constraints and affordances offered by blogging software" (Walker Rettberg 2008a: 20, cited in Lövheim 2011: 13), moulding them to the expressive and communicative needs of bloggers. With Puschmann, it seems thus "sensible to argue that users of different genders and age group pick styles appropriate to their envisioned target audience (ranging from the self to a broad public), and their communicative goals (ranging from self-expression to the accumulation of social capital) and they write accordingly" (2012: 95), exploiting the flexibility of the medium to their self-expressive and communicative purposes.

2.2.5. Personal journals

Despite the variability and interconnectedness of blog typologies, personal journals, also defined as lifelogs or online journals, appear to have a prominent role in blogging practices and have emerged as the most frequent type in several studies; as Schiano et al. note, "the majority of blogs are written by ordinary people for much smaller audiences [than 'heavy-hitting' blogs], and on largely personal themes" (2004: 1). In Herring et al.'s study (2005: 151) personal blogs account for 70.4% of the sample, which is noteworthy also given that sites specifically devoted to online journal writing, such as LiveJournal.com or Diaryland.com, were not included in their data. As Puschmann summarizes, "the prototypical use of blogs as a medium for personal publishing by private non-professionals still dominates over other scenarios" (2009: 1; cf. also Granieri [2005] 2007: 72-73; Metitieri 2009: 48 concerning Italy).

Research on personal blogs as online journals has focused on their specific characteristics, particularly on the higher frequency with which they are updated, the limited number of links to other websites (Herring, Scheidt et al. 2005: 158), and the fact that they appear to be addressed to a smaller audience than other web genres, one mainly made up of family and close friends (Huffaker 2006).

Depending on the affordances provided by the software in the different blog-hosting services, individual bloggers can adapt the mode to suit it to their communicative needs in creating and updating their blog, in addressing their posts to the perceived or imagined audience in the blogosphere, as well as in responding to the comments and feedback of their readership. "The content they [bloggers] choose to share varies as widely as communication, ranging from reflections to to-do lists, philosophies to references to found digital objects" (boyd 2006a: n.p.)

In terms of self-disclosure, personal blogs are usually characterized by making personal information openly available (Viégas 2005; Huffaker and Calvert 2005), and more so in the case of younger bloggers (Hollenbaugh

2010a). The fact that personal blogs are often used as a communicative channel for interpersonal relations may also be a prominent factor in self-disclosure (Jang and Stefanone 2009: 324).

In gender terms, personal journals tend to be read and produced more by (young) women (Herring, Scheidt et al. 2004, Herring, Scheidt et al. 2005; Lenhart and Madden 2005: 4-6; Herring and Paolillo 2006; Hollenbaugh 2010a: 1666), who write about their personal experiences (Lenhart and Fox 2006: 7-8) and use these virtual spaces also to "communicate with friends, manage relationships, and build communities" (Lövheim 2011: 4, citing Bell 2007: 103).

When looking at age, teenagers appear to engage more in personal blogs than adults and blogs are perceived by teens as a realistic space for self-expression (Herring, Scheidt et al. 2004; Huffaker and Calvert 2005; Huffaker 2006). However, as Puschmann (2102: 84) maintains, "[t]here appears to be a broad consensus that in blogs there is a dynamic relationship between style, genre, age and gender of the blogger, and behaviours such as linking and quoting, but clear and unambiguous causal relations between these dimensions have not been established". These variations may be certainly attributed to the flexibility of the medium, which allows choice in format and content that can be freely decided upon by the individual blogger according to her/his motivations in maintaining a blog. Personal blogs appear characterized by an informal and often personal style, which can be described as "hybrid in that blends, mixes and switches between narrative and non-narrative modes, but in which a total absence of narration is rare". The choice of mode and style, however, depend on the blogger's communicative goals, "which may change from one post to another and even within a single post" (Puschmann 2010a: 52).

Although according to Blood (2002: 9) blogs are "native to the web", personal journals in particular have been compared to previously existing genres, particularly to diaries[54] and to other web-based genres, such as pre-1988 online journals, personal home pages and community blogs (e.g. Hodkinson 2006). However, an important difference from the diary genre to be borne in mind is that personal weblogs as an Internet mode are on the one hand socially situated (Walker Rettberg 2008b; Miller and Shepherd 2004), and on the other can take advantage of the medium affordances which make them immediate since posts can be uploaded quickly and frequently, and foster

[54] For a discussion on the relationship between Internet diaries and blogs see McNeill 2003, 2009; Miller and Shepherd 2004, 2009; Van Dijk 2004; Puschmann 2010a; Adami 2008.

interactivity with readers through comments; as McNeill points out, "online participation in this genre allows writers to carry on diary conversations that will no longer be monologic, where the response will not just be imagined but actual" (2003: 29; 2005). Blogs, differently from diaries, provide as a medium potential interactivity between the blogger and his/her audience, as well as among readers, a characteristic that makes them substantially uniquely dialogic in the potential network of relationships that can thus be created, as the following sections will illustrate.

2.3. Blogs as communicatively interactive spaces

> For the blogger, the blog is corporeal, but for the reader, it is a space of conversation (boyd 2006a: n.p.).

> Blogging, with its viral spreading of messages, dense remixing of words, and sharp give and take both within and across sites, appears to be a perfect example of dialogic interaction (Warschauer and Grimes 2007: 16).

According to Kramsch (2009: 157), blogs can be seen as the "quintessential manifestation" of the connectionist model of language, which "places emphasis on the social use of texts in social interactions". The blog is "as unencumbered by standard uses of usage as the diary, as interactive as a conversation, and through the compression of time and space offered by the computer it enables users to shape and manipulate public opinion".

As Crystal notes, "blogging has introduced a new era of interactivity to websites" ([2001] 2006: 247), and it is precisely this element which makes them so attractive to users (Herring, Kouper et al. 2005). It is worth mentioning in this respect that since 2002 social networking sites like Facebook, Friendster or MySpace and Orkut, and microblogging services like Twitter[55], have provided further opportunities for Web 2.0-type interaction; significantly, some among these websites provide blog components, too (Huffaker 2006) and, as we have seen in § 2.2.2, blogging is often used in combination with other social media. Even the development of Twitter does not seem to have sensibly changed blogging practices so far, as blogging and microblogging are two different styles of expression, with different functions to them. Twitter posts are very brief, similar to the editable and more evanescent 'status updates' in

[55] Twitter started in 2006.

Facebook, conceived for faster production and consumption than blog posts. In Twitter, as in Facebook, "you live in an eternal now, and the past just gently vanishes from view" (Rosenberg 2010[56]), while in blogging, longer posts – which are also archived and easily retrievable – remain central: "there's a nearly infinite universe of things you might wish to express that simply can't fit into 140 characters" (Rosenberg 2010[57]).

Blogs "positively encourage many-to-many rather than one-to-many interactions" (Myers 2010: 84) or, in boyd's terms, blogging is "an *n-to-?* practice where some discrete number of bloggers share with an unknown number of readers" (2006a: n.p). Weblogs can thus be said to represent "communicational networks" (Mayfield 2003[58], quoted in Granieri [2005] 2007: 46), where relationships are created on the basis of the desire and choice to communicate, which is enacted on the blogger's side by posting entries and possibly by soliciting responses from readers, and on the audience's side by adding comments, which can in turn be answered by the blogger, creating at times a sort of asynchronous chat. Blogging practices thus potentially involve two/multi-party actors, the blogger and his/her reader(s), in communicative exchanges which are not one-way, monologic communicative acts, but dialogic and interactive. In Schmidt's words, "speaking in one's personal voice and being open for dialogue rather than engaging in one-way communication are core elements readers have come to expect from blog communication, be it in private online journals, corporate blogs, or political blogs" (2007: 1413). An audience is indeed always present by definition in blogs: even when bloggers write about their intimate thoughts, this 'external' presence, either conceptualized or actual, is always there, and can exert an influence also on topic, style and tone (Puschmann 2009: 4).

In blogs, the relationship between authors and their audience tends thus to be different when compared to other media, and bloggers are generally "acutely aware of their readers, even in confessional blogs, calibrating what they should and should not reveal" (Nardi et al. 2004a: 42-3; cf. also Warschauer and Grimes 2007; Viégas 2005). In blogs, the audience(s) can actually be shaped both by the width of its scope and by the social intimacy (or distance) between the blogger and his/her readers. This audience cannot be conceived of as a single, one-rounded concept, but should rather be conceptualized as multidimensional: it can be constituted by the specific

[56] http://www.sayeverything.com/postscript-four-cases-for-the-persistence-of-blogging/ (accessed 15November 2013); cf. also Rosenberg 2009.

[57] http://www.sayeverything.com/postscript-four-cases-for-the-persistence-of-blogging/ (accessed 15 November 2013).

[58] Cf. http://radio-weblogs.com/0114726/2003/03/30.html (accessed 15 November 2013).

(restricted) public a blogger has in mind when writing (conceptualized audience, CA); it can at the same time be seen as the actual readers of the blog (actual audience, AA), or the larger target audience constituted by all the potential readers a blogger is addressing (TA). Boundaries between the latter two – CA and TA – may be fuzzy, or they may coincide if a blogger presumes there are no 'lurkers' or overhearers among the readers (Puschmann 2013: 87; Puschmann 2009: 4). The range of audience can vary also according to the typology of blogs, from (potentially) none in ego-centred, diary-like blogs, to wider ones in topical or discussion blogs.

Interactivity in blogs is thus mainly afforded by the possibility of commenting to posts by readers and other bloggers (Blood 2002: 17), and particularly so in personal journals. Comments allow direct, personal and mostly unmoderated discussion and feedback to any post, to which readers and the blogger him/herself can participate if they wish so. Even "the relative lack of comments or links that is characteristics of many blogs means that no specific topical focus is forced onto the blogger – she is free to set her own agenda with every new post" (Puschmann 2009: 2). Since "interaction (via comments or trackbacks) is technically possible but not formally required" (Puschmann 2009: 4-5), it is the blogger's choice whether to allow his/her blog to become an interactive site. In other words, even though the relation is in principle asymmetrical as only the blogger can post entries and choose whether to allow comments, which are thus 'subservient' to the main post (Nardi et al. 2004b; cf. also Peterson 2011), the opportunity for interactivity is in any case granted by the medium itself. It is precisely this possibility for feedback that makes blogs a potentially interactive and dialogic virtual space. Furthermore, the fact that many commenters are bloggers themselves can be seen to contribute to a symmetrical interactional relationship (Puschmann 2010a: 35).

In Herring, Scheidt et al.'s study (2005), when compared to other blog genres (filter blogs and K-blogs), online journals involved a lower level of interaction and commenting activity (cf. also Herring et al. 2006; Nardi et al. 2004b; Baron 2008: 110). In other studies, however, this did not prove true: Hodkinson (2006), for instance, found that goth livejournal bloggers actively interacted in each other's blogs. In actual fact, most blogs include the possibility of leaving a comment: for instance, in the 2006 Pew report, 87% respondents said they allow readers to comment on their posts, and 82% they posted a comment on other blogs (Lenhart and Fox 2006: 20) and the Technorati 2011 *State of the Blogosphere*[59] reports that 87% respondents either moderate or respond individually to comments (cf. Fig. 7. below). As we will see in Chapter 4, all bloggers in my corpus have provided this possibility.

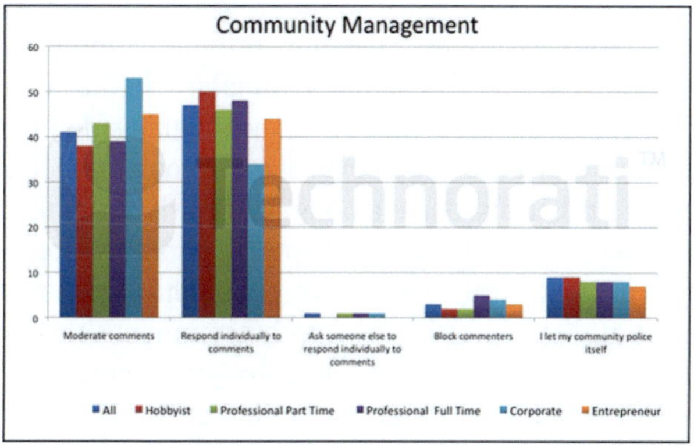

Figure 7. Comments in blogs (Source: Technorati Media *State of the Blogosphere* 2011, http://technorati.com/social-media/article/state-of-the-blogosphere-2011-part3/) (accessed 15 November 2013)

In their potential interactivity, blogs are also perceived to be less intruding than other Internet means of communication, e.g. e-mails or Instant Messaging, as they are more a 'pull' than a 'push' type in CMC communication modes: it is the reader's choice to decide whether to respond to a post through commenting, or rather not to take advantage of this potentially interactive tool (Baron 2008: 112; Nardi et al. 2004b; Gumbrecht 2004: 3; Puschmann 2013: 91). Blogs can in fact be considered midway between a 'push' and a 'pull' medium in that, while providing for new communication dynamics, it is the readers' choice whether to react to a post or to a comment (Puschmann 2009: 4-5). At times feedback may also come not directly in comments but through other media, since the social nature of blogs makes them part of a larger communicative "social arena" (Nardi et al. 2004b: 225; Schiano et al. 2004).

Indeed, bloggers frequently blog in order to receive feedback or advice from their audience, and often expect this feedback to come, thus capitalizing "on the interactive nature of the internet" (Stefanone and Jang 2007: n.p.; cf. also Schiano et al. 2004). As Granieri ([2005] 2007: 73) notes, in blogs – and particularly so in personal journals – dominant elements are human partici-

[59] http://technorati.com/social-media/article/state-of-the-blogosphere-2011-part3/ (accessed 15 November 2013).

pation, solidarity and empathy, where the desire to communicate interweaves with that of making personal (virtual) connections (cf. § 2.2.2). As we will see in the following chapters, these characteristics are also present in my corpus.

To sum up, blogs as a CMC medium provide communication means which are potentially dialogic in nature, particularly in the commenting system; when present, comments, indeed, do not stand aside but become part of the blog itself as they unfold, and the "diary becomes a meeting place and starting point for further discourse among previously disconnected readers" (McNeil 2003: 34). As we will see in Chapter 4, personal blogs on LiveJournal generally work as a truly interactive communication space: when the commenting activity to a post is present, the comments closely interweave both in respect to the original post and to other comments, thus creating dialogic spaces – which are at times very similar to conversational turns – between the blogger and her/his audience as well as among the members of the actively responding audience.

2.4. Blogs as constellations of interconnected practices

> "[I]t makes you feel good that people are reading it. You don't really want too many people reading it, but it's nice when somebody's reading it. Especially the people you want to, like your friends. So when you meet up again they don't have to say \what's new". . . I can't remember; I put it on the web!" (blogger, quoted in Gumbrecht 2004: 4).

As we have seen in § 2.2.2, primary motivations for blogging are meeting and communicating with like-minded people, as well as sharing experiences and expertise with others. These motivations combine with connecting to family and friends, as well as creating relationships with new friends. Social connections are thus one of the main motives in keeping a blog, together with the creation of content and information sharing, both in relation to group belonging and to the sense of a shared community, where participants cooperate (Hollenbaugh 2010b). Blogs are for the most part meant to be read, and many bloggers indeed live blogging as a way of creating and developing relationships (Miller and Shepherd 2004). Schmidt (2007) highlights how relations represent a structural aspect of blogging, both when they are hyypertextual, i.e. carried out through linking practices, or more socially constructed via friending (and commenting) practices. The first are made possible by the software technical affordances and instantiated in permalinks, trackbacks and comments; blogrolls and additional networking features which may be provided by the blog-hosting service (e.g. differentiated privacy settings for posts, can either be made visible to all or to a selected group of friends, as in Live Journal) also substantially contribute to relationship practices in blogs. It is through links and comments that bloggers "position themselves in the community of bloggers", indicating "the tribe they wish to belong to" (Blood 2000: n.p.): in the blogosphere, a sense of community is developed by individual bloggers through linking to other blogs, or by commenting on each other's posts, practices which become "forms of social control, signs of approval, acceptance, value" (Miller and Shepherd 2004: n.p.) and are salient to blogging practices.

The applicability of the notion of community to web interactions has been a debated issue (e.g. Androutsopoulos 2006a), and researchers tend to agree on the need for certain conditions for an online group to be defined as a community (Herring 2002a: 142). Virtual communities can be seen as a group of people regularly interacting online around a shared interest or purpose, with shared communicative history and norms (cf. Androutsopoulos 2006a: 421-423; Herring 2008b). Bloggers can be said to form communities that resemble Wenger's Communities of practice "in a more general sense: groups of people who share certain routines and expectations about the use of blogs as a tool of information, identity and relationship management"; the latter can be enacted in larger or smaller networks, "from users of larger platforms to rather small groups of bloggers sharing certain interests" (Schmidt 2007: 1419-20). Constellation, or a set of little sphericules as "multiple publics that pursue their own discussions" are thus locally created, within the small circles of a blogger and his/her readers, without necessarily referring to a larger national or global audience (Gitlin 1998, quoted in Myers 2010: 24).

As boyd (2006a: n.p.) points out, "practitioners often refer to the sociable aspects of blogging and blogs. They talk about the conversational qualities of blogging and the desire to share with others. They talk about community and how blogging helps them engage with a community of people". As we have seen, bloggers tend to build relationship with like-minded people who share the same interests, to mention each other in posts and to communicate through comments (Herring, Kouper et al. 2005), and "bloggers receiving many comments will comment on their own post in reply to others' comments" (Ali-Hasan and Adamic 2007: 2).

As outlined in the previous section, some blogs, particularly personal journals, are characterized by smaller audiences, which however in most cases form communities of individuals who most regularly read, comment and interact on a blog space. "While some bloggers aspire to a large audience, most are concerned with blogging to those they know as the potential of like-minded strangers who stumble upon their site" (boyd 2006a: n.p.). Even when bloggers and readers have become part of a shared community, partly constructed via sharing "private texts", they still expect to be able to continue reading "texts that are personal, even intimate" (McNeill 2003: 8) thus mutually contributing to a sense of close community. This appears to be confirmed in Stefanone and Jang's (2007) findings about communication in blogs being characterized by strong tie[60] networking contacts, also enhancing existing relationships. Online journals can in fact play "an important part in the development of strong, intimate relationships" (Hodkinson 2006: 192), at times leading also to other forms of interpersonal communication, either virtual or face-to-face. A sense of community is developed in blogs not only through membership, close intimacy and mutual support within and by the members of the group, but also in emotional terms, achieved particularly as personal stories are shared: indeed, "[f]ollowing well-organized stories, readers can feel familiar and intimate with the blogger, even more than in the face-to-face communication situation" (Shang, Chen and Chen 2007: 216; cf. also Baym: Chapter 4). This can be developed both at a more intimate, local level through interactive (commenting) practices that foster a sense of belonging to a 'regular' group of interactants in one or more blogs, or by reciprocally linking to each others' blogs. At the same time, it can be achieved at a wider level, too, feeling to be part of the bigger blogosphere (Kaye 2005: 90; Nardi et al. 2004b: 225), particularly for younger bloggers: "[t]hrough their LiveJournals or Xangas, teenagers not only express themselves, but create a communal sense of values and thoughts deemed worthy of being shared" (van Dijck 2004: n.p.). As we will see in the next chapters, examples of both can be found even within a same blog; posts may receive comments by frequent commenters, either in relation to more personal matters (such as diary-like reports, trips, personal musings, favourite songs/films, etc.), or on shared interests related to broader (web) communities, like icon-making, fanfiction, manga and anime. Concurrently, and particularly with posts con-

[60] Strong ties involve extensive familiarity, and can take place in a variety of domains, while weak ties are more superficial, "confined to a narrow shared interest and take place within a single domain" (Wellman and Gulia 1999, cited in Hodkinson 2006: 191).

nected to these less personal (although not less important) topics, we may find comments by a larger, more anonymous and open audience, which are prompted precisely by the shared interest(s) the topic of the post tackles. The participants in these 'gatherings' may change even from post to post, and often form quite long threads of 'microdialogues' between the blogger and the commenters. In this sense, they may be said to resemble 'constellations of interconnected pratices' (as we will see below), which are created and recreated according to the participants (and their interests) within a blog, but also in different posts and comments within the same blog.

As we have seen in Chapter 1, a community of practice can be defined along three main dimensions: mutual engagement of participants in shared practices; jointly negotiated enterprise; and a shared repertoire of communal resources (routines, sensibilities, artifacts, vocabulary, styles, etc.) that members develop over time (Wenger 1998: 72-85). In a later reading (Wenger et al. 2002: 4) CofP were defined as "groups of people who share a concern, a set of problems, or a passion about a topic, and who deepen their knowledge and expertise in this area by interacting on an ongoing basis".

The first defining criterion of CofP, mutual engagement, i.e. the members of a community meeting, cooperatively interacting and building relationships, can be said to characterize many online communities, and can apply to blogs, too. As outlined above, many personal journals operate interactionally and relationships are built among the participants, albeit not face to face but virtually in cyberspace. These relationships can take place within a smaller and 'more intimate' regularly interacting group of people, or at a wider level, with a higher number of participants who meet, possibly less frequently, around commonly shared interests (e.g. icon-making, manga/anime or fanfiction aficionados, cf. Baym 2010: 83). It is thus blog affordances, in the first place posting and commenting but also permalinks, trackbacks and blogrolls, that all contribute to the creation of online communities where relationships and meaningful interpersonal connections are built through interactional practices, both within and across 'constellations' of blogs.

The second criterion of a CofP, that of 'joint enterprise, refers to "some kind of goal or purpose which is defined explicitly or implicitly and shaped by the participants creating among them 'relations of mutual accountability'" (Ehrenreich 2009: 132). In personal blogs, self-expression on the one hand, and on the other hand sharing personal experiences (and/or expertise) with other participants in terms of both intended and actual audience, can be seen as commonly shared motivations. However, blogs cannot be said to constitute *per se* communities of practice as to joint enterprise, but can rather be seen as tools enabling personal voices to network within larger communities. As Wenger and Trayner point out, individual blogs can "give people a personal voice as contributors to a community[61]". Indeed, individual blogs may be part of larger communities spaces "for specific purposes, such as telling personal stories of practice" (Wenger and Trayner 2011), or individual blogs by community members may be included on the blog roll or through RSS feed services. This appears particularly relevant when considering web-hosting services like LiveJournal, which are community-oriented in nature and where individual blogs are often connected to larger interest-based communities, as we sill see in Chapter 4.

Despite personal blogs being more self-oriented than other digital media typologies, the kind of networks and ties that can be established among bloggers, as well as between bloggers and their readers/commenters, can be quite strong. As mentioned above for my corpus, they are created through differentiated communication-oriented practices which can "lead to the formation not only of hypertextual networks, but also of social networks of varying density", from "'communities of blogging practices' in a very general sense" to "smaller and more close-knit networks, which might range from users of particular blog platforms to rather small groups of bloggers sharing certain interests (e.g. knitting bloggers)" (Schmidt 2007: 1427) – or, as in our case, interests ranging from fanfiction writing to icon-making. Indeed, blogs can be seen as one of the virtual cyberspaces that are exploited to networking practices, and are often employed in a combination of tools, ranging from the possibility of personal contact via private message, email, Skype, to sharing images or artefacts and interaction in social networking websites. This variety of communication opportunities is frequent practice in blogs and serves as a potential to enlarge networking interactive practices among likely-minded people who share the same interests: "[i]nternet users increasingly apply a whole repertoire of applications for online-based networking, self-presentation, and information management. Teenagers are especially eager to create content online and to manage their social relations with peers through an array of tools for interpersonal communication, among them blogs, Instant Messaging, social networking sites, and mobile phones" (Schmidt 2007: 1427).

In general a weblog may thus be defined as a connecting tool, which can potentially provide the framework for a community, both within a blog in

[61] http://wenger-trayner.com/resources/how-do-communities-use-blogs/ (accessed 15 November 2013).

the collaborative conversation-like structure of posts-comments, as well as between and among blogs via other networking affordances. The relationships and ties are created among the participants as *people*, who can be part of CofP also as a network of bloggers, where ideas and expertise can be shared and discussed. Moreover, an action-based CofP may follow if a group of people interacting in blogs decide to meet around a commonly-shared enterprise to create a more formal structure, e.g. a collective blog. Therefore, although blogs cannot be said to possess *per se* the characteristics to meet the second criterion to qualify a CofP, in some cases, either by virtue of the strong ties which can be created around a common interest or passion, particularly in blogs characterized by a smaller but regular audience, or because of their association to larger communities, they can be considered as potentially meeting, at least in part, the CofP dimension of joint enterprise. This however depends much on how the blog is intended and construed by the blogger and by the audience.

The third parameter in evaluating CofP, that of a shared repertoire, refers to the set of resources – linguistic and of other kinds – used within the community to negotiate meaning, which can be "imported, adopted and adapted" to the community's purposes (Wenger 1998: 126). In personal blogs this dimension appears to be realized both via linguistic means (e.g. in-group jargon, also related to specific areas and domains of interest of the community of interactants), as well as by the use of different languages to different aims and of other multimodal resources, leading to heteroglossic practices (cf. Androutsopoulos 2010, 2011b). These shared communicative repertoires become an intrinsic part of commonly-shared practices among the participants.

As we have seen in Chapter 1, that of CofP is a relevant concept to ELF settings, too. ELF users' constellations can be characterized as communities where individuals build a shared repertoire of linguistic resources, which they deploy in communication, and where meaning is co-constructed also by drawing on the (diverse) linguacultural backgrounds of the participants. The way in which, in internationally-oriented journals, bloggers and their interactants make use of English as the main lingua franca of communication, together with other aforementioned resources, sets personal blogs within practices that are at the same time global and local. They can be considered global in that the use of English orients them towards a potentially international audience; furthermore, the interests, such as icon-making, manga, anime and fanfiction, which create ties between some of these blogs and their participants, are commonly shared by wider communities around the world. At the same time, both the posts and the interactive practices among bloggers and their readers/commenters that are enacted in these virtual spaces are often locally realized, within smaller communities that at times intersect with wider ones, each with their own communicative (shared) habits.

In such variable 'constellations of interconnected practices', as we have seen in Chapter 1, language(s) can be conceived of as a set of resources which are adapted and appropriated to differentiated communicative aims. They thus constitute a common but at the same time flexible means that allows self-expression, experiences to be shared, and interaction, where heteroglossic practices are enacted in different albeit interconnected ways: English may serve as the in-common lingua franca across the participants' L1s in a wider audience, while being at the same time appropriated in order to be suited to global and local meanings; other languages – the participants' L1s as well as other Lns – may either work as part of heteroglossic practices to express specific meaning in these wider contexts, be employed to express more local concepts and ideas, or used to address and interact with a smaller – though not necessarily local in terms of physical proximity – audience.

2.5. Conclusions

Despite the development and increased popularity of a whole set of Web 2.0 social networking interactive spaces, blogs still appear to constitute a preferred self-expression and communication mode, particularly for younger generations, who often use social networks and other digital media in combination to blogging. In this chapter we have looked into the characteristic features of blogs, an easy-to-use, flexible and hybrid web-related mode which has rapidly spread within participatory Web 2.0 practices. Potential interactivity via hyperlinks and, above all, through comments is indeed a focal characteristic in blogs, especially in personal journals, where narratives about the self often combine with creative writing and multimodal sharing practices. Among the main motivations for blogging we find self-expression and connecting with like-minded people, who can either be old or newly-made friends. Despite the difficulty in defining clear-cut boundaries in blog typologies, due to the hybrid and highly flexible characteristic of this CMC mode, personal journals appear to be the most common type, above all in relation to the aforementioned connecting practices.

Interactivity, commonly shared interests and participatory sharing practices are central elements to a sense of community in blogs, whether with a smaller and more intimate audience, or in larger and more open ones, which at times also intersect. The boundaries – if any – that define these communities are not territorial in a geographical sense, but rather revolve around common interests on the one hand, and friendship – or, better, 'friending' – on the other. English in its lingua franca role is the means that allows communication and an elastic widening of such boundaries in internationally-set blogging practices. The sense of community that is built in these 'constellations of interconnected practices' takes thus place through different and variable, albeit interwoven, resources: ELF and other languages, commonly shared interests, participatory sharing, all contributing to communication and interactive practices which can be locally and/or globally set, or both at the same time.

Chapter 3
Language and Computer-Mediated Communication

In the previous chapter we have examined the main characteristics of blogs, looking at how they constitute privileged interactive spaces in digital media communication. In this chapter we will first briefly outline how language is employed in Computer-Mediated Communication (CMC henceforth), as well as some among the main approaches to Computer mediated Discourse (CMD henceforth) analysis. Language in blogs will then be looked at, particularly in its specific interactive and socially-oriented functions.

3.1. Language and Computer-Mediated Communication (CMC)

The language of the Internet has attracted the attention of linguists since the late 1980s. The focus of early research was mainly set on characterising CMC linguistic features by measuring them against the traditionally categorized modalities of speech and writing. Issues revolved around whether CMD could be defined as: a) written language, due to its medium characteristics since it is typed on a keyboard and displayed on screen; b) "written speech" (Maynor 1994 quoted in Herring 2007: 2) given that it is characterized also by informal features of spoken discourse, or c) "interactive written discourse" (Ferrara et al. 1991; Werry 1996: 47-48) and "digital networked writing" (Androutsopoulos 2011a: 1) due to its interactive and dialogical nature (cf. also Herring 2010a: 2). Its characterization as an intermediate mode between spoken and written discourse, or even as a totally different and new variety – 'Netspeak' (Crystal 2001 [2006]: 17) – were also proposed, due to features such as abbreviations, emoticons and non-standard spelling. As Crystal notices, many *–speak* coinages "placed undue emphasis on the potential linguistic idiosyncrasy of the medium" suggesting that it "was more homogeneous than it actually is" (Crystal 2011: 2).

It soon became clear that language on the Internet cannot be measured against or equated with either spoken or written discourse, as it appears to include characteristics of both and be located on a continuum between 'typical' speech and 'typical writing'. With Baym (2010: 63), "it might be more fruitful to think of digital communication as a mixed modality that combines elements of communication practices embodied in conversation and in writing". Indeed, a simple, clear-cut and absolute dichotomy cannot be maintained between speech and writing, either: as Biber's 'textual dimensions approach (1988) has shown, communicative function and linguistic features are closely interrelated so that spoken and written texts frequently overlap along a continuum according to their function. CMC is thus often situated in-between, as a hybrid genre, where traditional parameters of spoken and written modes tend to blend according to the situation, mode, topic and setting, as well as participants and communicative purposes (e.g. Baron 2000; 21-22; 158-160; Kytölä 2012: 108; Herring 2011a: 4; Baym 2010: 63-65).

Crystal (2001 [2006]: 28-46) has looked at web genres taking into account several parameters of spoken and written discourse. When looking at the language on the Internet, what makes it different from speech is on the one hand the lack of simultaneous feedback, the slower rhythms of interaction determined by technology, the absence of non-verbal cues and a certain degree of contrivance (Crystal 2001 [2006]: 26-48; cf. also Crystal 2011: Chapter 2). At the same time, however, it appears to "display much of the urgency and the energetic force which is characteristic of face-to-face conversation" (Crystal [2001] 2006: 28), and it "selectively and adaptively displays properties of both" (Crystal [2001] 2006: 47). Language on the Internet appears to be of a hybrid nature in that it includes traits that can be ascribed both to speech and writing, in different measures depending on the CMC mode in which it is employed: for instance, while web-pages are more written-oriented, other genres such as e-mails, chats or virtual groups can display several speech-like features. These characteristics also vary across synchronous (e.g. chat) and asynchronous (e.g. e-mail) modes: in the first we find features that make it closer to speaking, since, similarly to unplanned speech, "synchronous modes of CMD impose temporal constraints on users that result in a reduction of linguistic complexity" (Herring 2001: 617), resulting on the whole in shorter, syntactically less complex messages. Asynchronous modes, on the other hand, are linguistically more similar to writing, although variation in levels of formality depends on social situational factors (c.f. e.g. Crystal 2001 [2006]: 44-48, 2011: 67-69; Herring 2001: 614-616, 621, 2010a; Danet and Herring 2007b). Rather than being strictly connected to the modality, in the same way as it happens across different written and spoken genres, CMC can range from highly formal and structured to unscripted and spontaneous communication. As Herring argues, "[t]here is much prima facie implicit evidence that text-based CMC is conversation-like" not least since participants themselves often refer to their exchanges in terms of "'talked', 'said', and 'heard'" (2010a: 1); also, they are often defined by scholars as 'speakers' who 'talk' in 'turns', and CMC is explicitly compared to conversation (Herring 2010a: 2, cf. above). Furthermore, the expansion of Web 2.0 communication includes "web-based modes such as blogs, wikis and social network sites", as well as "semi-synchronous modes such as instant messaging" (Herring 2008a: 3), which have been a contributing factor in making the distinction between synchronous and asynchronous web communication less clear-cut. Moreover, in CMC settings in particular, "'conversational'" should be "defined broadly to include not just orality, but the interactive and social dimensions associated with face-to-face communicative exchanges" (Herring 2010a: 3), as well as the medium-related traits that imitate – or make up for – spoken prosody and body language (Herring 2010: 4).

The expansion of the internet since its birth has brought to a proliferation of modes – or genres – each with common but at the same time different and peculiar characteristics. These new communicative environments are characterized by linguistic traits that reflect the social, cultural and interactive needs and purposes of its users at all levels. And, as argued by Herring, "CMC fulfils many of the same social functions as spoken conversation" (2010a: 4) since "people are already using CMC in place of spoken exchanges. Indeed, textual CMC has become a prime site for conversation, supplementing F2F and telephone for personal, professional and commercial interactions" (Herring 2010a: 5, cf. also Chapter 1).

As Giltrow and Stein (2009: 9) well highlight, the new spaces enabled by the internet reconfigure

> the conditions to which pragmatic features of language respond. The main components of this new communication setting are the vast and variable range, new pull and push mechanisms, new distance-synchronic forms of communication, new combinations of N-to-N – the number of people speaking and the number of people receiving the communication – and the high speed as well as the archiving of interaction, to name but a few.

While early research approached CMD as a uniform genre in terms of language features, its diversified forms and "socio-technical modes" (CMC subtypes as defined by technology) have increasingly been analysed in their own specificities (Herring 2007, 2002a). The speed of change in the different "outputs" – as these communicative digital spaces have been defined by Crystal – is very fast and continuously changeable, both across and within modes (Crystal 2011: 9-11). The proliferation of Internet technologies, genres and sub-genres, as well as its diversification in sociolinguistic terms, makes it difficult to draw clear-cut boundaries both at a macro and at a micro-linguistic level, since they are characterized by "volatility and chameleon-like properties" and by "greater fluidity and pragmatic openness" (Giltrow and Stein 2009: 9). Moreover, as Kytölä points out, "language users, social actors, *appropriate* any technological innovations or new communication formats to whatever usage they prefer" (2012: 108, emphasis in original). This appropriation can be applied to language – and languages – too: "even monolingual (e.g. English) online applications or interfaces have often been extensively appropriated and modified by different (ethno)linguistic communities for their particular communicative needs" (Kytölä 2012: 108; cf. also Androutsopoulos 2011a: 154-158; 2006a: 421). The myriad of internet outputs have thus provided people with new communicative spaces, where language, languages and other semiotic codes can be used and appropriated to suit the users' needs and communicative aims, tweaking the code(s) for self-expressive and interactional purposes, hence potentially strengthening their power as agents of language change.

3.1.1. "e-grammar"

Nevertheless, and despite variation across electronic discourse modes and even within a single genre (Herring 2002a: 139), several English CMC *e-grammar* traits (Herring 2012: 2) seem to commonly characterize language as used on the Internet across different outputs and at different linguistic levels, from spelling to morphology and syntax. As Androutsopoulos points out, three main dimensions can be identified in research related to innovation in CMC language: "conceptual orality", "semiotics of compensation" and "linguistic economy" (Androutsopoulos 2011a: 5). Orality "includes all aspects reminiscent of casual speech in written discourse" (Androutsopoulos 2011a: 5). As to compensation, in order to make up for the lack of extra-linguistic and paralinguistic elements of spoken face-to-face communication (intonation, stress, speed, rhythm, pause and tone of voice, Crystal 2001 [2006]: 34), genre-specific typographic conventions are frequently employed. Pauses may be graphically represented via punctuation in the form of periods; emphasis may be provided employing capital letters, italics/bolding or reduplication of letters, or by inserting asterisks on both sides of a word. Common typographic elements include thus either a minimalist or an expressive use of punctuation and capitalization, and substitution of part of words with numbers (e.g. Crystal 2001 [2006]: 36-38; 2011: 61-65; Baron 2003: 79-80; Thurlow 2001; Baym 2010: 60-61). As Baym summarizes, in socio-emotional terms "even text-based new media afford many ways to express emotion. We use emoticons to signal friendliness, we use punctuation and capitalization to insert feeling, we use informal language and talk-like phonetic spelling to create an air of conversationality" (2010: 103).

In order to compensate for lack of body language and other visual elements, or to add emotive hues, or even to playful effects (Baym 2010: 60), graphical icons in the form of smileys or emoticons are also used as kinesic cues across different Internet modes. Traditional emoticons are sequences of keyboard characters constructed by combining punctuation marks to be read sideways – the most commonly employed being the smiley *:-)* denoting a smiling face, or *:-(* indicating sadness. Asian-style emoticons of Japanese tradition (known as *kaomoji*) are to be read horizontally, e.g. ^_^ for a smiling face (Baron 2003: 116), and are often related to the world of manga (Katsuno and Yano 2007: 280-289); both types are widespread in English CMC (Herring 2012: 2).

At the orthographic level, we find unconventional spelling (particularly in teenager online language use, Crystal 2001 [2006]: 90; cf. also Androutsopoulos 2011a: 152), abbreviations (acronyms, clippings, vowel omission), onomatopoeic spelling, letter homophones, spelling that imitates informal or dialect pronunciation, or employed to reproduce prosody or other sounds. These orthographic innovations are rarely unintentional, but rather "deliberate adaptations of the technical and social contexts of interactions for social purposes" (Baym 2010: 64). They may 'save a keystroke', thus being related to the dimension of linguistic economy (Androutsopoulos 2011a: 150); they may be used to recreate features of spoken language (Herring 2012: 2; Al-Sa'Di and Hamdan 2005), or serve several other factors which can be conscious or unconscious (Crystal 2011: 62). Furthermore, abbreviations may also be employed to indicate group membership (Baron 2003: 21). As Androutsopoulos points out, the "indexical potential" of respelling "is broader than just linguistic economy. CMC respellings introduce new indexicalities by virtue of their continuity with spelling practices in other domains: popular culture, ICT, trade names, and specialised shorthand" (2011a: 8).

At the level of morphology, new formations are created via affixation (*e-, cyber-, hyper-),* blending, acronyms, conversion, or shift in meaning, and they may operate separately or simultaneously (Herring 2012: 4). A certain degree of lexical inventiveness through the aforementioned word-formation processes appears to be more frequent in blogging and microblogging, as well as in chat interactions (Al-Sa'Di and Hamdan 2005).

At the syntactic level, CMC is at times described as "'telegraphic and fragmented" (Herring 2012: 5) since elisions and incomplete grammar clauses are not uncommon; as Crystal notes, not being necessarily subject to processes of editing and proofreading, it is "a syntax that reflects the way writers think and speak" (2011: 68). It is also characterized by a certain level of informality and colloquial constructions, particularly in informal modes where the social dimension is prevalent, such as chatgroups, Instant Messaging (IM), microblogging and to a certain extent blogs. According to Crystal (2001 [2006]: 41), colloquial grammar and vocabulary in CMC are employed as a way to express warmth and reduce emotive distance, too.

Characteristic to CMC discourse are also emotes and predications; both are expressed in the 3rd person singular present tense, the first automatically produced by the system and denoting actions performed by the user (e.g. *Anna writes*), while predications are user-generated and employed to refer to states or actions, usually set between asterisks (e.g. **sighs**).

Many of the above linguistic and discourse features appear to characterize the *e-grammar* of English, as well as of other languages. Investigated e-features in languages other than English, such as French, Greek, Swedish and German, have shown that typographical and orthographical flouting are common elements (for an overview cf. Danet and Herring 2007a; 12-15). In German, for instance, graphical representation of standard and non-standard pronunciation, syntactic patterns typical of spoken language, elision and discourse markers seem common features (Androutsopoulos and Ziegler 2004). In Italian personal blogs (Moraldo 2005: 146, 159-161) the aforementioned typographical and orthographic devices appear frequently used, as well as features of orality such as formulaic patterns, taboo words, dialectal influxes. Croatian (Brala 2008) and Slovenian (Šabec n.d.) blogs also seem to include CMC linguistic features, albeit often 'anglicized' both in terms of terminology, abbreviations and acronyms specific to the web, and at the morphological and syntactic level.

Linguistic innovations appear to be mostly affecting lexis, while syntax, traditionally more resistant to language change, seems to be to a certain extent less influenced by innovative linguistic practices (Herring 2012; 2008a). Despite the fact that many lexical innovations have spread easily across the web, and that an increasing number has been included in dictionaries thus becoming part of the accepted lexicon, it is nevertheless difficult to determine whether these new Internet words will accelerate and lead to long-term language change (e.g. Crystal 2011: 57-58). Furthermore, at times it may even be questionable whether they originated on the web, as for instance in cases of semantic shift, such as 'lurker' or 'flame' (Androutsopoulos 2011a:

147; cf. also Crystal 2001 [2006]. 53-56). Nonetheless, they can be said to constitute characteristic traits of the language as used on the Internet, especially in informal-communication oriented modes.

3.2. Approaches to Computer-Mediated Discourse (CMD) Analysis

Computer-mediated discourse analysis takes into account both the verbal aspects of online communication as shaped by the medium, and the social practices which are enacted in CMD (Herring 2001, 2007, 2012b). In sociolinguistically oriented CMD analysis, three main variables can be identified: the technological (i.e. related to the medium), the situational (related to the participants, setting, purpose), and the linguistic/discourse one, which can be categorized onto four main levels of analysis (structure, meaning, interaction management and social phenomena), each related to different issues, phenomena and methods of investigation (Herring 20113: 4-5).

Herring's facets approach to CMD (2007) and to blogs in particular, is based on category conceptual parameters named "facets" and looks at the same time at the technological and the social dimensions. Since CMD "is subject to two basic types of influence: medium (technological) and situation (social)" (Herring 2007: 10), facets allow categorization of CMC data taking both dimensions into account. While technological features are determined by "messaging protocols, servers and clients", by the hardware and the software, the social factors are associated with "the situation or context of communication" (Herring 2007: 11). Factors related to the technological medium take into account whether communication is synchronous or asynchronous, "one-way" (message-by-message transmission, where receiver sees a message only once it is sent) or "two-way" (the sender and receiver can see the message while produced), the persistence of transcript (how long the message is stored), the number of characters allowed in a single message, the kind of channel (text-only or multimedia), the message format, as well as other technological affordances related to the possibility of anonymity, privacy, filtering and quoting. The situational factors in Herring's approach are based on Hymes' (1974) SPEAKING model, which have been intersected with CMD features: participation structure, participant characteristics, purpose, topic/theme, tonc, activity, norms and code (language).

Conceptualizations such as Herring's facets model, particularly in that it takes into account the social dimension as well the medium-determined technical affordances since both contribute to shape and characterize CMD communication (cf. also Puschmann 2009: 2), allow a rethinking of CMC modes as 'conversational'. Following Herring, conversation in CMD can be "defined broadly to include not just orality aspects, but the interactive and social dimension associated with face-to-face communicative exchanges", or "any exchange of messages between two or more participants, where the messages that follow bear at least minimal relevance to those that preceded or are otherwise intended as responses" (Herring 2010b: 3-4). Indeed, scholars have recently called for research practices that, beside being based on a discourse-ethnographic approach, rather than focus on language variation approaches *per se* investigate "the *situated* practices of new media users (i.e. communicators) and the intertextuality and *heteroglossia* inherent in new media convergence" (Thurlow and Mroczek 2011b: 224, emphasis in original; cf. also Androutsopoulos 2010, 2011b; Leppänen and Peuronen 2012; Barton and Lee 2013).

A further relevant factor to be taken into consideration are the modifications brought about by Web 2.0 based web modes, particularly – though not only – in the intermingling of language and multimodal practices characterising interaction in these new digital media discourses (Herring 2013: 5-7); Herring, indeed, suggests that following to such significant shifts in CMC, discourse ought to be reconceptualized as "Discourse 2.0" or "convergent media computer-mediated discourse (CMCMC)" (Herring 2013: 6), and an additional level – that of multimodal communication – ought to be taken into account in the CMDA paradigm of analysis (Herring 2013: 20-21).

As outlined above, numerous communicative and linguistic strategies which can be ascribed to orality are common both in synchronous and in asynchronous Internet modes, such as creative spellings, emoticons, "typographic patterns to imitate spoken prosody; discourse produced in chunks that resemble 'intonation units [...]; turn-taking" (Herring 2010b: 4), as well as code-switching and other heteroglossic practices. Moreover, as Androutsopoulos (2011a: 145) argues, "interactive written discourse" or "digital networked writing" is "interpersonal and relationship-focused" and "dialogical and interaction-oriented, carrying expectations of continuous exchange". Hence, language can be expected to be employed to suit the expressive and communicative needs of its users, and to serve their conversational and interactional purposes, being thus appropriated and moulded to the self-expressive and interactional needs of the participants, together with other semiotic resources characteristic of Web 2.0 practices.

Innovative linguistic features, which are realized at different linguistic levels within the dimensions of orality, compensation and linguistic economy, respond to the need "to make written language suitable for social interaction" (Androutsopoulos 2011a: 155). In CMD they may therefore be investigated not just as evidence of language innovations *per se*, but as expressions of the new communicative functions they come to express, both at the individual and at the group/network level. Digital media may thus be conceptualized "not as containers that determine the language they contain, but as resources for social practices, which do constrain, but do not determine the shapes and styles of network writing" (Androutsopoulos 2011a: 158). Furthermore, the use of language in digital media discourse is more often than not intentionally creative (and frequently playful, too), and "never simply about form" (Thurlow 2012: 180); creative uses of language are present at different linguistic levels: besides orthographic and word play, we find also interactional, identity, sound and topical play, and this "[c]reative practice is motivated by – and expressed in – the pragmatic, relational needs of participants as much as it is by their deliberate attempts to play with the norms of spelling, punctuation and grammar" (Thurlow 2012: 180). In other words, language use in CMD is shaped to respond to the communication needs of users, together with – and as part of – their online multimodal and heteroglossic practices. It can therefore be interpreted as an intentional exploitation of expressive and interactional resources among others, as a common new media practice for young people that "ought to be properly recognized for their creativity and cultural significance" (Thurlow 2012: 186, citing Willis 1998; cf. also Androutsopoulos 2011a). Several forces can thus be said to be at work in digital environments; first of all, the language is appropriated to its users' needs and aims, and "[w]ritten language norms are *pluralized* to the extent that different styles of writing can be deemed appropriate in different environments and genres and to different users groups" (Androutsopoulos 2011a: 156). Secondly, globalized/ing and localized/ing factors seem to entwine in virtual communication: they are at the same time globalized as "linked to global semiotic and cultural flows" and "*localised* in the more specific sense of being limited to particular online communities or networks" (Androutsopoulos 2011a: 156, emphasis in original; cf. also Barton and Lee 2013). Indeed, as we have discussed in Chapter 2, such entwining of global and local elements is particularly characteristic of personal blogs, where constellations are created and re-created according to the expressive and interactional aims of the participants. As we will see in the next section, the way in which language is employed in these virtual spaces constitutes a central element of self-expressive and connecting practices in blogs.

3.3. Language in blogs

> Some blogs are monologues, some have shared authorship, some are interactive (Crystal 2001 [2006]: 15).
>
> It is written language in its most naked form (Crystal 2001 [2006]: 245).

Research on blogs from a linguistic point of view has attracted the interest of numerous scholars. Even more than in other web genres, blog discourse appears to be characterized by hybridity: Herring, Scheidt et al. (2005: 161, 2004: 110, cf. § 2.2.4) in fact place blogs and the style in which they are written on a CMC continuum between personal web pages and newsgroups. Despite displaying characteristics of asynchronous web modes, particularly in personal journals, features of synchronicity are encouraged by the genre itself in terms of immediacy of writing, thus placing blogs in the middle of the spoken-written media continuum (Crystal [2001] 2006: 44). As discussed in Chapter 2, blogs are characterized by technical affordances that make them potentially highly interactive and dialogic, in the first place in the commenting function they allow.

Language in blogs is both space-bound (by the medium) and time-bound (dated entries, which are archived but still accessible via permalinks); both aspects are afforded and determined by the software (Puschmann 2010b: 168-169; cf. also Crystal [2001] 2006: 42-43). Features of immediacy, informality and non-standardness are frequent (Crystal 2001 [2006]: 244-5), and the fact that entries can be posted straight away after having written them means that bloggers may "have less opportunity to 'tamper' with their text, less time for hindsight to 'alter' the 'true' version of experiences" (McNeill 2003: 37). From a stylistic and linguistic point of view, variability in blogs appears high: "[d]epending on the blogger's conceptualization of the format, a blog entry can be speech-like or written-like, colloquial or formal, and can relate to private or public […] issues". Among different digital media, blogs thus represent a particularly flexible situational context for rhetorical and linguistic choices, which can be used differently according to the blogger's communicative aims (Puschmann 2013: 81-82). Indeed, as boyd argues, traditional distinctions of textuality and orality are blurred in blogs, where the "negotiation of communication" pattern is peculiar to the genre and yet at the same time "draws from both": it is the medium itself that "creates a dynamic that is synchronous and asynchronous, performative and voyeuristic" (boyd 2006a: n.p.).

Within the variability of the genre, personal journals in particular display "a variety of writing intended for public consumption which appears exactly as the author wrote it, which is not constrained by other genre conventions, and which privileges linguistic idiosyncrasy. I call it, on analogy with free verse, free prose" (Crystal [2001] 2006: 246). Following Puschmann (2012: 94), personal blogs in their author-centred characteristics (cf. Chapter 2) can be said to be marked by a less formal and spoken style, usually presented as spontaneous self-narrative, with frequent use of personal pronouns. We find an extremely frequent use of contracted forms and abbreviations, which are "used in all possible cases" (De Gerdes 2005: 110) and concentrated above all in private blogs. From a linguistic point of view, it is the "presence and availability of linguistic structures that users can associate with spoken discourse" (Puschmann 2009: 2) that highly contribute to the characterization of blogs as conversational in nature. Colloquial lexis, swear words included, are also frequent (De Gerdes 2005: 111-112), and at times dialectal forms are present, too. Coinages of new words, on the other hand, appear less common and mostly found in the form of compounds, or hyphenated chains of adjectives preceding a noun.

Blogs, above all when explicitly addressing the audience, seem to include specific language features such as:

- direct address to the reader and audience (Puschmann 2013: 93; 2010b: 171);
- pronouns, in particular *we – I/you,* appear common in personal blogs entries. They express a "first person voice" (Puschmann 2013: 93, 2010b, Myers 2010: 73-74), and can make the audience feel part of a group, either as an individual or collectively as a multiple audience; 3rd person pronouns, on the other hand, are more typical of filter blogs entries (Herring, Paolillo 2006: 453);
- questions, that can be used to elicit information or in a rhetorical function, or as directives (Myers 2010: 75-77);
- directives inviting the audience to take some sort of action (Myers 2010: 74-75);
- oral-style interactional discourse markers such as conversational particles/connectives (Myers 2010: 20; Puschmann 2013: 93), pause fillers, repairs, response cries, tags, interjections, as well as phatic exclamatives, which can all be said to be more typical of spoken rather that written language.

As to syntactical patterns, in personal blogs sentences generally appear less complex, with frequent elliptical expressions (e.g. the first person subject missing), in a way "similar to telegraphic writing" (De Gerdes 2005: 122).

When looking at paralinguistic features, generally those available in CMC such as smileys, emoticons, creative spelling and typography, abbreviations and acronyms are commonly found in blogs, too (Myers 2010: 20, 78). Emoticons in weblog online interactions are widely used to integrate verbal messages, a fact which may be only partly justified by their commonality in diverse CMC applications (Huffaker and Calvert 2005). Besides expressing emotional states, emoticons can also take up the role of enhancing friendliness, they may be used to prompt reaction from potential participants, to complement language as indicators of illocutionary force (Dresner and Herring 2010), or employed (at times playfully) in the function of discourse markers (De Gerdes 2005: 119-120) with an interactional emotive function. Additionally, as discussed in Chapter 1, multimodal material (photos, videos, art work) is more and more often included in posts, in combination with multilingual text entries, resulting in practices that are increasingly heteroglossic.

These linguistic and paralinguistic features can in general be seen as devices employed by bloggers to "manage interaction and keep it going" (Myers 2010: 102) and some, such as the use of first person pronouns either in the singular or in the plural form, can be directly ascribed to the interactive aspect of blog communication (Herring and Paolillo 2006: 453). Besides, pragmatic cooperative (or non-cooperative) linguistic attitudes towards the audience characterize blogs as a conversational and interactional mode (Puschmann 2009).

Therefore, although written by virtue of the medium affordances, blogs can conceptually be mapped onto conversation, which they situationally mirror "in that a) they are (at least potentially) interactive and b) four factors associated with interactivity (chronology of contributions, what was said, who said it and when it was said) are technologically reproduced in blogs (sequence of posts, post title and text, name of the blogger, timestamp)" (Puschmann 2010a: 63). These metainformative elements (author, time of posting, place) contribute to features of spoken language, too, independently from "whether or not actual dialog (via comments or trackbacks) takes place in a blog or not – the potential to create a persistent, retrievable record that can use the same linguistic constructions which are typical of spoken language is sufficient" (Puschmann 2010a: 123). Hence, besides providing the opportunity for interaction in comments, it is the very format that allows, albeit potentially, to address a multifaceted and plural audience. On the other hand, hyperlinks and other co-textual information in blogs partly combine "the situatedness of speech with the permanence and stability of writing" (Puschmann 2013: 86).

To recap, the hybrid nature of blogs derives from the coexistence of elements which are typical of speech with others that are peculiar to writing, in the first place the absence of "co-temporality and co-spatiality of speaker and hearer", with the consequent "implications for the structure of the discourse: pauses, fillers (cognitive load of on-line production), the need to cede the floor to others, issues of politeness and acceptable communicative conduct, etc." (Puschmann 2010a: 63).

In terms of interaction management, many CMC textual genres have been said to be "interactionally incoherent" (Herring 2001: 618), particularly in terms of turn-taking, on two levels: on the one hand the lack of simultaneous feedback, and on the other the "disrupted turn adjacency caused by the fact that the messages are posted in the order received by the system" (Herring 2001: 618). This can result in interactional fragmentation and overlapping messages both in synchronous and in asynchronous modes. It can be argued that in blogs, although the addresser (the blogger) and the time of speaking (publication time) can be identified, the lack in synchronicity due to the medium characteristics can nevertheless hamper the development of conversational turns in spoken discourse terms (Puschmann 2010b: 33). In asynchronous modes in particular, the adjacency of messages may be intensely disrupted also in extended sequences (Herring 1999; 2001: 618-820) given that everybody can hold the floor at any time, "all participants can produce messages independently and simultaneously" (Reyes and Tchounikine 2004: 296). Topics which are not linearly responded – or for which linearity cannot be immediately reconstructed – tend to be abandoned, leading to topic fragmentation (Herring 1999; 2001). Notwithstanding, as Herring points out, both synchronous and asynchronous computer-mediated communication are extremely popular, and "users regularly ascribe to both a conversational, interactive quality" (1999: 10). Turn-taking strategies in CMC may therefore just be differently perceived and organized (cf. also Garcia and Jacobs 1999; O' Neill and Martin 2003). In actual fact, Herring illustrates how CMC users adopt a differentiated set of compensatory strategic techniques to effective interaction, from (supportive) backchannels to turn-change signals and reference, such as quoting or linking, as well as topical organization; language play, greater intensity in hyper-personal interaction and conversational persistence (e.g. in blogs archives) are also widely present (Herring 1999:

11-14). O' Neill and Martin (2003) also demonstrate how in chats a (non) consecutive sequential organization of entries is more loosely interpreted by participants than in face-to-face conversation, and topic management is handled similarly to informal spoken contexts; rather than textual coherence in abstract, objective terms, it is more the "coherence for the participants" these interactions assume (O' Neill and Martin 2003: 7) that should be accounted for in conversational terms. Moreover, turn-taking in CMC can often be observed rather than within a single message, in "the whole of messages that each participant answers in each branch of conversation", i.e. in a group of messages (Reyes and Tchounikine 2004: 302).

Despite conversationality in blogs being a debated and controversial issue (cf. e.g. Peterson 2011; Herring 1999), the potentiality for allowing interaction of this genre is generally acknowledged. On the whole, CMC is being increasingly employed in conversational ways, adapting the constraints of CMC modes to make interactional communication possible (Herring 2010a: 1-5). As we have seen, blogs display conversational characteristics especially in the possibility of commenting, which can be "*employed* conversationally by users" (Herring 2010a: 4, emphasis added). From the single blogger's point of view, communication can thus be defined as a one-to-many/*n* (differently e.g. from unmoderated newsgroups, Puschmann 2010a: 35), since the –*n* audience members are potentially enabled to engage in interactional moves via commenting practices despite being the blogger who retains control of the discourse structure. Indeed, as Puschmann (2009: 2) highlights, in interactional terms blogs "are characterized by affording their users unlimited floor time in a quasi-speech situation that is potentially interactive but not encumbered by the constraints of synchronous communication".

Furthermore, mediated interpersonal conversation can be "conceptually mapped" onto the general frame of face-to-face conversation: "[t]he contextual information that the blogging frame provides – dated, attributed and archived entries, 'about' pages that describe the blogger, hyperlinks to other pages and the use of deictic expressions – make it possible to conceptualize a blog entry as a sort of uninterrupted, planned, organized and persistent conversation" (Puschmann 2010b: 3). This notion may well be applicable to comments, too, since simultaneity of speech is constrained by the medium itself. Blog deixis (Myers 2010: 36, 51; Puschmann 2013: 84-86), the potential possibility of feedback in the form of comments and trackbacks, and fact that blogs can be maintained by an individual, are all elements that contribute to the metaphor of conversation in the genre. Although blog communication is in principle asymmetric, i.e. a blogger can express his/her planned thoughts, feelings or opinions without having to cede the floor, all the aforementioned elements concur in making blog activity similar in many ways to spoken conversation (Puschmann 2010b: 3) where monologic and dialogic modes intermingle (Puschmann 2009; cf. also Efimova, de Moor 2005).

3.4. Conclusions

To sum up, the much diversified set of communicative functions performed by blogs, from self-expression to social interaction, allow the combination of monologic and dialogic modes, making them a hybrid mode that can flexibly be exploited to the users' needs.

While the focus of early research has been mainly on characterising CMC linguistic features by measuring them against the traditionally categorized modalities of speech and writing, later approaches have taken into account its diversified forms and "socio-technical modes" in their own specificities (Herring 2007) and dual characteristics – related to the medium as well as the situational factors.

Innovative linguistic features in CMD, which can be related to the dimensions of orality, compensation and economy (Androutsopoulos 2011a), characterize the *e-grammar* of English, as well as of other languages, particularly at the lexical level; such features, together with paralinguistic elements, contribute to characterize CMC modes as 'conversational' as they respond to the need "to make written language suitable for social interaction" (Androutsopoulos 2011a: 155).

Blog discourse, above all in personal journals, appears to be characterised by immediacy of writing which, together with the interaction-oriented affordances, makes it conversational in genre despite its asynchronicity. Indeed, personal journals, as we have outlined in Chapter 2, are most likely to be populated by participants aiming at reciprocal exchanges, dealing with topics which are in some way related to their life and interests. In these blogs monologic and dialogic modes tend to mix, by entwining linguistic and semiotic codes according to the bloggers' and to the participants' communicative purposes. Digital media can thus be regarded as spaces where "new resources and strategies for written language production and meaning making" (Androutsopoulos 2011a: 154) are appropriated and exploited by users, and can be conceptualized "not as containers that determine the language they contain, but as resources for social practices, which do constrain, but do not determine the shapes and styles of network writing", that are "materialized and performed by networked writers in late-modern, post-standardized societies" (Androutsopoulos 2011a: 158).

Such appropriation is carried out in ways that are often novel, in order to fulfil purposes of social interaction which cut across national (language) borders, speech communities as traditionally conceived of, as well as notions of linguistic standardization and languages as separate entities. The variability with which language resources are employed by internet users to their self-expressive and networking purposes can in this perspective be seen as part of late and post-modernity fluidity, bearing significant and interesting similarities with the ways in which ELF is employed and deployed to its users' needs and purposes (cf. § 1.5), combining global(ized) practices with local(ized) aims.

And, as we will see in the next chapter, when orienting to an international audience, English in its lingua franca role constitutes one among such resources, and that is frequently appropriated to communicate in "wider networking" (Seidlhofer 2011: 86) practices.

Chapter 4
Bloggers as ELF users

> English serves as a lingua franca for many LJers from different language backgrounds who choose to blog in English rather than their native language (Herring et al. 2007: n.p.).

As we have discussed in the previous chapters, weblogs represent a major digital area, which has significantly grown since free, easy-to-use blogging applications became available. Together with other digital spaces such as chats, instant messaging and more recently, social networks, blogs allow communication to take place in "wider networking", among people who share common interests and wish to communicate beyond territorial boundaries and across different linguacultures. This happens most often through English in its role of commonly shared lingua franca.

Weblogs are "naturalistic data in textual form" (Hookway 2011: 92), and as such they can constitute for researchers a meaningful space for investigation in linguistic terms, particularly from an ELF perspective: they represent 'real' contexts of ELF use, where bloggers and their audience give voice to their thoughts, ideas and opinions, (self-)expressing and communicating via English as a commonly shared code by deliberate choice.

In the following sections we will first examine the main features of LiveJournal, as to its users, blogs, and communities, to then look at the languages employed in this web-based service. The corpus of investigation will then be illustrated in terms of characteristics and methodology of selection; relevant data about the bloggers as emerging from the questionnaire survey will also be dealt with, particularly concerning their experience and use of English and of other languages, as well as their motivations to keep a blog in English. Finally, the ELF theoretical framework of reference will be outlined, the research questions and the methodological approach to the data illustrated.

4.1. LiveJournal.com

LiveJournal (LJ henceforth) can be defined as a web-based service that allows registered users to create online diaries and journals. These journals are parallel in structure to blogs, as they are frequently updated and entries are arranged in reverse chronological order. Through an open source blogging platform, even people with little technical expertise can create and maintain a journal on this (and similar) blog-hosting sites. LJ was one of the first social networks to be launched (boyd and Ellison 2007: n.p.); it was originally created in 1999 by Brad Fitzpatrick, who was nineteen at the time, "with a journaling practice in mind" (boyd 2006a: n.p.): the creator's main aim was then to keep in touch with his school friends[62]. It later became a blogging tool, and this term was overtly included in the 2004 description "... *a simple-to-use (but extremely powerful and customizable) personal publishing ("blogging") tool, built on open source software* (November 2004)" (quoted in boyd 2006a: n.p., emphasis in original).

In comparison with other blog services, LJ can be described as "a system of user – and socially – organized information that works as a system of knowledge creation. By combining personal journal keeping with bulletin board systems, LiveJournal facilitates the social production and sharing of knowledge" (Raynes-Goldie 2004: 3). Indeed, LJ describes itself by highlighting its mix of self-expression, community and social networking features:

> LiveJournal is a community publishing platform, willfully blurring the lines between blogging and social networking[63].
> LiveJournal encourages community and personal expression by offering users both a user-friendly interface and the ability to deeply customize their journal. The site allows users to set up their own virtual diary and communicate with their friends by posting and receiving comments on each other's entries. In many countries the site's most popular functionality is the community aspect which allows users to engage each other on issues of common interest[64].

These characteristics, as we will see in the next sections, make LJ a potentially highly interactive virtual space both in individual and in community-oriented terms.

4.1.1. LJ Journals

Several options are offered to LJ users, who can choose among paid, or free of charge (*basic* and *plus*) accounts; paid accounts allow a greater availabil-

[62] For a timeline see http://en.wikipedia.org/wiki/Timeline_of_LiveJournal (accessed 15 November 2013).
[63] http://www.livejournalinc.com/aboutus.php (accessed 15 November 2013).
[64] http://www.livejournalinc.com/press_releases/20081219.php (accessed 15 November 2013).

ity of software features, including the possibility of uploading multimodal content. LJ users can also customize their journal through differentiated pre-defined styles, and create their blog choosing from 32 languages. It is also possible to select from pre-defined or user-created personalized pictures and icons, which are graphics or avatars that can be displayed on journals to represent interests, moods, feelings, personality, according to the situation[65]. Icon making is indeed a common interest among LJ users, and many posts and sharing practices, even in community blogs, revolve around this common-based peer production practice: as Tarkowski notes, "[u]ser icons are a valuable symbolic good in the LiveJournal environment" (Tarkowski 2005: 10; cf. also Rebaza 2008). Icons also bear primary identity and symbolic meaning in LJ fan practices, as fans often "choose actors or scenes that comment on the show or fannish debates" (Helleckson and Busse 2006: 12). In icon-making practices, most often references from popular culture are (re)mixed with the life of the icon-creator and serve as a further means of communication and socialization, as well as to in-group practices, together with the frequent use of emoticons and acronyms (Helleckson and Busse 2006: 17).

Compared to other blog-hosting services, the LJ interface appears to be quite sophisticated, as users are provided with different options, such as showing links to 'friends' and including a 'mood' indicator, which are potentially afforded for each entry and can be accompanied by an icon, too; it is also possible to display the music the blogger is listening to, and to tag each entry. The number of comments to a post is automatically created by the software, and a 'search' feature is also available. Journals can be easily updated via the LJ web interface, or with the help of client programmes.

The user profile page, which is quite articulated and recalls in many ways the socially-oriented architecture of social networks (Marwick 2008: 1-4) has been a peculiar feature of LJ since the very beginning. A set of personal information data can be uploaded and updated on the profile page (User Info), such as biography, contact information, the schools the blogger has attended in the past and/or he/she is currently attending[66], as well as his/her interests and LJ communities. The user's friends list (abbreviated to *flist*), which is crucial to the community aspect of LJ (Raynes-Goldie 2004: 4), is defined by the blogger and generally includes people sharing similar interests, thus also serving to delimit visibility for a post (*friendslocking*) (Helleckson and

---

[65] While free accounts users are granted 3 pictures, paid ones can have from 15 to 100.

[66] Including fictional establishments such as Hogwarts – Harry Potter, Starfleet Academy – Star Trek.

Busse 2006: 12). Friends lists can include communities and provide RSS[67] feeds to individual users, too.

In general, blogging software allows three degrees of privacy: besides anonymity via the use of a pseudonym, a blog can be private in that it is password-protected and thus accessed only subsequent to the blogger's permission; it can be listed by the blog service, and thus be easily retrievable, or unlisted and therefore less likely to be found (Nardi et al. 2004b: 223). "Making the choice between public or private is a primary way bloggers manage their potential audience", as a public blog can in principle be retrieved and read by anyone (Hollenbaugh 2010a: 1659), even without having a LJ account and/or logging in as a LJ user. Indeed, in LJ the term 'friend' is closely connected to the privacy features at the bloggers' disposal. LJ journals may be publicly available to anyone, but they can also be designed to be readable to a restricted audience. When marked as "friends-only" – a feature which has long been a distinctive trait of this blog-hosting service[68] (Herring 2007: 25-26) and is now common on social networking websites, too – a blog can only be accessed by the blogger's (approved) friends. When marked as 'private, it can be read only by the writer him/herself; journals designed as 'custom' are open only to members of a specific filtered sphere of friends (Marwick 2008: 11). Furthermore, LJ also provides its users with an option to limit traceability of posts by search engines. In LJ a mid-option is that of setting privacy options as 'semi-friends only' whereby the blogger makes some content publicly available, while restricting chosen posts to his/her friends' audience. A further alternative is to mark single posts as 'private', thus making them accessible to a limited 'approved' audience. As in other blog-hosting services, comments can be allowed or disabled, or even screened so that they will be visible to readers (friends included) only subsequent to the blogger's approval. These multiple privacy options appear to be widely employed by LJ users: a LJ 2006 research showed that 95% of the 250 respondents marked their posts as 'friends-only', and 85% made use of filter options (Marwick 2008: 11).

[67] RSS stands for Really Simple Syndication. RSS feeds are automatically sent and received by those who have subscribed to those feeds.

[68] Now adopted also by Xanga and Myspace (cf. http://en.wikipedia.org/wiki/LiveJournal, accessed 15 November 2013).

4.1.2. Interactivity and community practices on LJ

Differently from other, more 'traditional' blog hosting services LJ can be employed at the same time in its social networking and blog-hosting features, "resulting in a hybrid user platform" (Stefanone and Jang 2001: 7; cf. also Marwick 2008: 9-10). The 'friending' option indeed gives LJ an additional socially-oriented aspect and in many ways makes it more similar to social-networking sites (such as MySpace and Friendster, cf. boyd 2006b) than to blogging ones (Marwick 2008: 5): for instance, two or more users can have no continuous relationship, or can list each other as friends, either with or without reciprocation; when reciprocated, they will appear on a 'mutual friends' list. As friends lists and their contents are generally visible to anyone[69], some users also include their friending and/or defriending policies in their profile pages (Cherny 2005: 1-2).

The above features can indeed foster the development of strong ties among 'friended' members, who often share common interests, and "encourage a long-term deep engagement between users that is comparable to real-life (usually abbreviated as 'RL' on LiveJournal) conversation" (Marwick 2008: 1). However, when compared to social networks, the fact that blogs allow longer entries can potentially enhance deeper connections as well as emotional involvement, as they are more liable to spark conversations and in-depth discussions than typically shorter comments on social networking websites such as Facebook. Furthermore, including someone in the friends list entails socially attentive commitment for many LJ users, for whom "identifying another user as a 'friend' does not only mean that you enjoy reading that person's journal, but also that you 'trust' or will 'vouch for' that person" (Marwick 2008: 5; cf. also Fono and Raynes-Goldie 2005).

In its double characteristic of blogging host-service and social community, LJ also hosts shared – or group – journals, which are defined as 'communities', a feature which may be strengthened even further in the future (Ungerleider 2012). Communities, or *comms* for short, can be moderated or non-moderated, and are in many ways similar to discussion forums, with all-to-all posts that can either be personal or records of interaction among users (Tarkowski 2005: 2). In community blogs knowledge is shared horizontally: users who have common interests and are "involved in communal dialogue and practice" jointly and discursively contribute to the community itself in a mutually supportive way (Raynes-Goldie 2004: 7). Petrochenko, a former

[69] Although friends lists can be hidden from public view, too.

LJ U.S. general manager, has recently defined LJ as "a trove of amazing community-driven, user-generated content", which "consists of not just blog entries and photos, but hundreds of thousands of comments posted by people who are passionate about the topic at hand" (quoted in Ungerleider 2012: n.p.). In line with the conceptualization of LJ as a community space, users can also voluntarily contribute to the service development in various ways, as well as support the site signing for a paid account (Gorny 2004: 5).

Besides textual and multimodal entries, popular on LJ are Memes, or quizzes and games[70], which spread from blog to blog in a process of "cross-pollination" that is emblematic of how community sharing works in LJ blogs (Cherny 2005: 3). Indeed, in terms of themes and contents LJ is quite heterogeneous (Tarkowski 2005: 2); fandom communities and fanwork were especially popular on LJ from 2002 to 2007, and common interests are music, technology, manga & anime, writing fiction, and fanfiction in particular, with the latter considered as a popular blogging niche community in the US and elsewhere (Ungerleider 2012).

As we have seen in Chapter 2 (cf. § 2.3), blog communication can in principle be defined as asymmetrical since it is mainly regulated by the blog author; nonetheless, interactivity represents a defining characteristic in blogs. LJ bloggers, indeed, generally enable comments to be posted to their blog entries, and most commenters also have their own blog "so everyone has a chance to both post and comment" (Herring 2007: 26). Comments in LJ are displayed on a thread, and may consist either of just a short feedback, or of more elaborated responses; further comments can also be posted in reply to previous ones, and sometimes a thread may become very long. Indeed, "vivid reaction and almost immediate commenting, in some cases maximally close to real time dialogues, is part of Live Journal etiquette" (Verschik 2010: 355). This frequent and at times almost synchronous commenting activity often gives threads on LJ dialogic-like characteristics, which display speech-like features also in turn-taking sequences.

4.1.3. LJ users

In terms of popularity, in Herring et al. (2006: 9) *Blogger* stood out as the preferred publishing site (about 70%), while LJ was used by a minority of bloggers (3.6% in September 2003, 3.5% in April 2004); on the other hand, according to Lenhart and Fox (2006: 14), LJ was in 2005/6 the most popular

[70] Popular also in other blogging websites such as Xanga.

blogging site chosen by 13% respondents, prominently young female bloggers, the latter representing 22% of the sample, against 7% male bloggers.

As to more recent data, the Technorati *State of the Blogosphere* 2011[71] reports Wordpress being the most popular blog hosting service with a 51% share, followed by Blogger and Blogspot (21% and 14% respectively), and LJ ranking quite low (cf. Fig. 8. below).

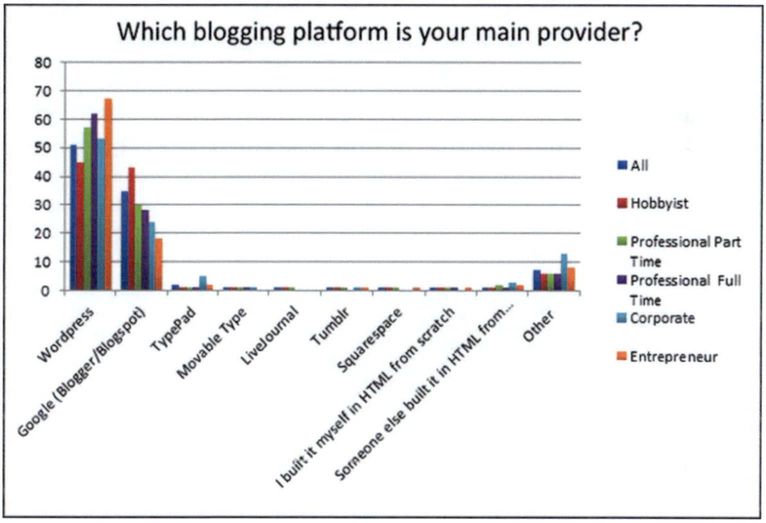

Figure 8. Blogging Platforms (Source: Technorati Media *State of the Blogosphere* 2011, http://tcchnorati.com/social-media/article/state-of-the-blogosphere-2011-part3/ (accessed 15 November 2013).

Despite sometimes contrasting figures, LJ has seen a rapid and dynamic development over the years: the million registered users in 2003 had doubled in 2004, and about half of them had an active account (Gorny 2004: 5). In September 2005 there were almost 8.2 million registered journals and 1.4 million active users, about "the size of a fair sized city that lives without a map or a telephone book" (Tarkowski 2005: 2), and in 2008 LJ had reached 1,9 million users (Marwick 2008: 1). In June 2011, 31,772,640 accounts existed on LiveJournal, with 1,959,750 listed as "active in some way[72]". The majority of LJ users were in the 17-25 age group, with a large

[71] Cf. http://technorati.com/blogging/article/state-of-the-blogosphere-2011-part3/ (accessed 15 November 2013).

[72] To be noticed that the number of dead or never updated journals constitutes in general a problematic issue in determining blog numbers.

presence of 31-year-old users. Of those who specified their gender, 62.7% were female and 37.3% male (cf. http://en.wikipedia.org/wiki/LiveJournal). As of 24.12.2011 LiveJournal statistics[73] reported that the total number of accounts was 34,852,708, of which 1,969,223 were "active in some way" and 18,750,645 ever updated; in mid-July 2012, the amount was of 37,975,882, of which 1,696,214 "active in some way" and 19,801,753 ever updated. Among users who specified their gender, 43.8% were male (40.1% in December 2011), and 56.2% female (59.9% in December 2011). As to age distribution (see Fig. 9. hereunder) the majority of users were between 21 and 34, partially confirming the peak as to 31-year-old users recorded in June 2011, which is now highly towards 32; this data can possibly be explained by LJ aficionados keeping with the blog service over the years.

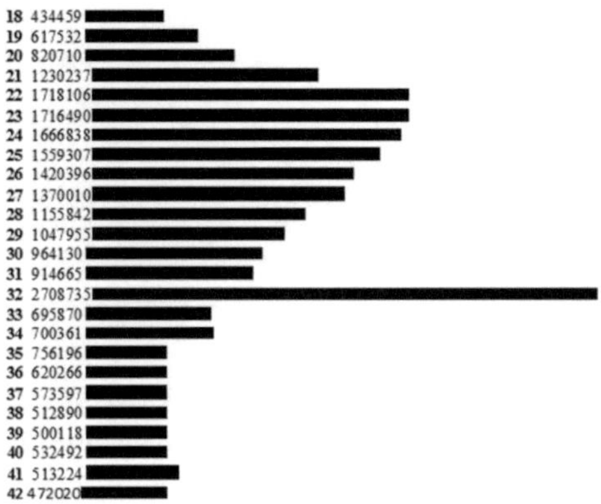

Figure 9. Age distribution on LJ (Source: http://www.livejournal.com/stats.bml; accessed 18 July 2012).

Together with Blogspot, LJ has been a popular hosting site with younger people (Herring and Paolillo 2006: 443). While other platforms, like Wordpress or Movable Type, appear to be designed to meet the needs of "more audience-driven practitioners", and Blogger to provide simple interfaces, LiveJournal and Xanga "focus on community-minded bloggers" (boyd 2006a: n..p.). LJ bloggers are usually savvy Internet users, who blog about their personal experiences (Herring 2007: 26) and take advantage of the LJ community-oriented characteristics illustrated above. As other similarly oriented blogging sites, LJ appears "heavily skewed towards younger users, provid-

[73] Source: http://www.livejournal.com/stats.bml , statistics are frequently updated.

ing a medium for active display of the intertwining of blogging, community and relationship-building among teens" (Lenhard and Madden 2005: 8). It is also worth noticing that, owing to its many lower-age users, mainly hobbyists, LJ has been at times considered "a lower member in the family of blogging tools" (Tarkowski 2005: 2; cf. also Gorny 2004: 8).

LJ appears to be associated especially with personal journals, a fact which is probably due also to the multiple chances of regular interaction with a selected group of friends provided through the "friends page", that "automatically collates new entries as they appear" (Hodkinson 2006: 188). Indeed, despite its social-software orientation, on LJ "the majority of interactions take place on the personal territory of one individual and are initiated, centred around and regulated by that individual" (Hodkinson 2007: 632).

4.1.4. Languages on LJ

When looking at LJ users in geographical terms, the following are the 15 most popular countries for LiveJournal users respectively as of May 2010 (Table 7.) and July 2012 (Table 8.):

Table 7. Top 15 countries, May 2010 (Source: http://en.wikipedia.org/w/index.php?title=LiveJournal&oldid=447359800) (accessed 15 November 2013[74])

Top 15 countries	**8,673,909**	**100%**
United States	4,895,360	56.43%
Russian Federation	1,593,894	18.38%
United Kingdom	451,142	5.20%
Canada	436,384	5.03%
Ukraine	256,373	2.96%
Singapore	209,879	2.41%
Australia	205,400	2.37%
Philippines	125,922	1.45%
Germany	96,105	1.11%
Brazil	83,867	0.97%
Japan	76,106	0.88%
India	72,559	0.84%
Belarus	61,746	0.71%
Finland	56,714	0.65%
France	52,458	0.60%

[74] Based on LJ statistics 22.05.2010, accessed 22.07.2010; edited by 98.144.64.15

Table 8. Most popular countries on LJ in July 2012[75] (Source: http://www.livejournal.com/stats.bml)

United States	4,478,099
Russian Federation	2,546,332
United Kingdom	445,707
Canada	394.903
Ukraine	383,801
Singapore	199,596
Australia	198,544
Philippines	154,174
India	139,064
Poland	130,855
Japan	105,708
Germany	105,252
Belarus	94,704
Korea (South)	90,058
China	71,943

LiveJournal appears to be most popular in English-speaking countries, with the United States ranking top (although recently acknowledging a decline in users, Ungerleider 2012), and consistently followed by Russia in second position: LJ was in fact sold to a Russian company in 2007, and has been since "focusing on growth in Russia and Singapore, where the blog service is incredibly popular"; LJ is the most appealing blogging platform in Russia (Ungerleider 2012; Gorny 2004: 6). Two Inner Circle countries (the UK and Canada) rank third and fourth, and two Outer Circle ones (Singapore and India) are significantly included in the top 10, together with several Expanding Circle countries; South Korea and China have also recently entered the top-15 countries. Although locations may not be indicative in terms of the language(s) spoken by users, they can nevertheless provide some reasonable hints about the array of codes present on

[75] Figures calculated on LJ users who have chosen to list their location; last accessed 15 September 2012.

LJ. Indeed, in language variety terms LJ was designed from the start as a multi-language environment, a fact which has contributed to its popularity also among non-English users (Gorny 2004: 7). When creating a LJ blog it is in fact possible to choose from 32 languages and language varieties[76].

As we have outlined in Chapter 1 (cf. § 1.3), despite other languages being increasingly represented, English still appears to be the main language of the blogosphere. Even more than other web modes, in blogs the choice of language seems to be related to the international range of potential readers and English is frequently consciously and intentionally chosen as the lingua franca of communication when aiming to reach an internationally-scoped audience.

In their investigation of languages in the blogosphere Herring et al. (2007) selected LJ as the site of enquiry in that it represents one of the largest web-hosting services in the world, and it is internationally oriented both in terms of users' location and languages employed: indeed, more than two-thirds of its 11 million users at the time of the study reported to live elsewhere than the United States. As we have seen, this picture appears on the whole to be confirmed in recent statistics, even though users located in the USA in 2011 still amount to more than 50%. Despite the fact that LiveJournal, as many Internet services and social networking sites, has for long been based in the U.S., its users have been quite geographically diversified. Herring and colleagues' study focused specifically on the demographics of language use in 1,000 randomly selected LJ journals: English emerged as the predominant language, with 84% LJ journals in this language; other less employed languages were Russian (11%), followed by Portuguese, Finnish, Spanish, and Dutch (all with 4%), and Japanese (3%); mixed language journals made up 2.3% (cf. Fig. 10. below).

[76] The LJ translation page (http://www.livejournal.com/translate/) includes the following: Afrikaans, Basque, Belarusian, Brazilian Portuguese, Chinese (Simplified), Chinese (Traditional), Danish, Dutch, English, English (LJ), English (UK), Esperanto, Estonian, Finnish, French, German, Greek, Hebrew, Hindi, Hungarian, Icelandic, Irish, Italian, Japanese, Latin, Latvian, Lithuanian, Malay, Norwegian Bokmål, Norwegian Nynorsk, Polish, Portuguese, Russian, Spanish, Swedish, Turkish, Ukrainian (accessed 15 November 2013).

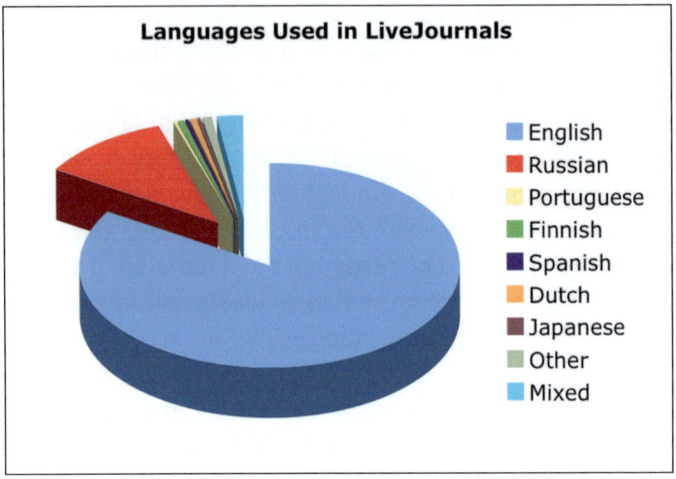

Figure 10. Languages on LJ (Source: Herring et al. 2007: n.p.)

According to Herring and colleagues the size in the presence of languages other than English in their sample data was correlated also to the number of journals on LiveJournal in that language, and to friending networks: "in general, the greater the presence of a language on LJ, the larger the universe of potential friends its speakers have to choose from, and the more friends they are likely to have" (Herring et al. 2007: n.p.).

As to English, it appeared significantly employed by many people who were not residing in the U.S., as well as by bloggers for whom English was not a native language. Some blogs were overtly multilingual, others contained links to journals in other languages. Those blogs written in more than one language were labelled by Herring and colleagues as "bridging journals", where three main patterns of users were identified:

1. students of a foreign language who wish to practice their skills in the language they are learning with speakers of that language on LJ, while employing their L1 to communicate with their friends;

2. expatriates blogging both in their native language and in the language of the place where they live, thus 'biculturally' including both their former and new social networks;

3. bloggers who make extensive use of non-verbal content: photographs, graphics and popular song lyrics were often included in bridging journals, in that they allow the (numerous) users and friends to interact even "with little or no understanding of the language of the journal" (Herring et al. 2007: n.p.); the latter may be run not necessarily by hobbyists only, but also by professional or semi-professional photographers, and by graphic or fashion designers.

The possibility of creating a blog in several languages, as well as the 'friending' and 'community journal' LJ characteristic features, provides the choice for users both for monolingual and cross-language interaction. Particularly in bridging journals, LJ bloggers "tend to be multilingual and multicultural, although some simply blog about content with international appeal" (Herring et al. 2007: n.p.).

In Herring and colleagues' investigation, English, and to a lesser extent other languages, was frequently used in limited/formulaic ways, for instance in templates, titles, photo captions, lyrics, poems, and quotations. Languages thus seemed to be employed also to a symbolic function, i.e. not necessarily in connection to the bloggers' level of language proficiency: "the frequency of this practice suggests that many LiveJournalers, even those who lack the linguistic or non-verbal means to interact directly with speakers of other languages, are aware that LJ is a cosmopolitan environment, and orient to that fact, albeit superficially" (Herring et al. 2007: n.p.). This can undoubtedly be seen as closely connected to the global presence of English, particularly in popular (visual) cultures: multimodal material is easily accessible on the web, and sharing practices are frequent, as we have seen, in digital environments, either in the original or in remixed forms. "Young, multilingual, geographically mobile bloggers link to, and are linked by, journals in different language groups, creating de facto bridges across cultures", as well as intersections between language networks, displaying awareness of "mutual other-language and other culture" (Herring et al. 2007: n.p.). As we will see in the next sections, the bloggers in my corpus too appear to display many among these characteristics, choosing English as the lingua franca that allows them to connect with friends of other linguacultures, sharing bits of their life experiences through heteroglossic posts and variegated comments, often overtly declaring their non-nativeness to a language that nonetheless allows them to interact in wider communicative arenas.

To sum up, the combination of the above illustrated features make of LJ not only a virtual space for self-expression via personal journals, but also a socially interactive area where individuals get in touch and communicate by means of their blog and/or within shared-interest communities, through friends lists or specific interest group journals. The high level of interconnectedness between users characterizes LJ as a peculiar space among blog-hosting services: the variegated communication tools available to LJ bloggers, such as friends lists and comment threads, which are made possible from a technical point of view since on LJ blogs are "kept on the same server in a single database", all contribute to the LJ characteristic "community-building architecture" (Gorny 2004: 8-9).

The cosmopolitan scope of LJ also implies that a commonly shared language is needed to communicate internationally, and in most cases this language is English. Thus, the "wider networking" practices enacted by LJ bloggers and their readers and interactants about commonly shared interests, personal musings and networking activities can take place also thanks to the lingua franca role they assign to English, either as native or as non-native users.

4.2. The Corpus - Methodology of selection

In order to select a corpus of blog interactions that could be suitable to research purposes as to how English is employed as a lingua franca in such practices, out of the several existing blog-hosting services[77], LiveJournal seemed particularly suitable given its aforementioned characteristics. My purpose has been to trace personal journals produced by young people communicating internationally online, in order to investigate their communicative practices in a virtual, internationally-oriented blogging environment. The main ground for focusing on Italian bloggers has been to investigate how English is actually employed by these 'ELFing bloggers' as a lingua franca to communicate in an internationally-oriented online setting. English is increasingly present in Europe both in formal instruction, and in the linguistic landscape at large; this is especially true for younger generations, who are also active web (prod)users, and Italy is no exception. My main focus of interest has thus been to investigate how these ELF users, who have Italian as their L1, exploit their bilingual, or plurilingual language expertise to communicate and interact with their potentially world-oriented audience.

As illustrated in the previous sections, the age group of LJ-users appears to be concentrated between 20 and 29, with a peak around 31-32[78]. Moreover, as we have seen, LJ has an international scope: although the main language on LJ is English, it is possible to create a blog in 32 languages, and the territories where LJ users are located are quite varied: as of today among the fifteen most popular locations for LJ bloggers, apart from Inner Circle

[77] Blog content management systems available, besides the popular Blogspot, include Blogger, Blogster, Xanga, GreatestJournal, Pitas, Diaryland, Opendiary, cf. Crystal 2001 [2006]: 239.

[78] Source: http://www.livejournal.com/stats.bml ; statistics are constantly updated.

ones (the USA, the UK, Australia and Canada), we find Outer Circle (India, the Philippines, Singapore) and several Expanding Circle ones (the Russian Federation, Poland, Germany and Brazil).

LJ thus appeared a particularly appropriate space to be investigated to my research aims. In order to make the retrieval of blogs produced by people located in different geographical areas possible, the website was searched using the search-by-school feature[79], which is organized by country. Indeed, as Myers (2010: 140) underlines, "blogs are hard to sample", both due to the incredible growth the blogosphere has experienced in the last decade, and to its consequent complexity, with an "endless criss-crossing hyper tracks and trails" (Hookway 2011: 98; cf. also Herring 2008b). And the blogs I came across on LJ during my selection process displayed a variety of typologies: many were created but never updated; quite a few included only a very small number of posts; many consisted mainly of pictures of different types (above all art work, photos, icons) with little or no textual posts; some were updated regularly and others once in a while, and many contained posts only in Italian – or exclusively in another language, frequently Russian. Finally, some were "friends only" and their content was set not to be freely and publicly accessed. These typologies had hence to be excluded from the corpus: as Table 9. illustrates, out of 766 blogs visited, only fifteen were finally included.

Since my main research aims were focused on investigating to what extent, how and to what functions English is employed as the lingua franca of communication by young Italian bloggers in the international LJ blog-hosting service, the main criterion of selection in the blogs visited has been the identification of those produced by bloggers aged 18-32[80] with Italian as their native language, containing a majority of posts in English, for a total of at least 1,000 words in each blog. In order to cover a more complete territorial sample, the search by school was carried out in different Italian regions, including areas in the north (Veneto, Lombardia, Liguria), centre (Abruzzo, Marche) and south/main islands (Sicilia[81], Sardegna). The results of the selection process are summarized in Table 9. below.

---

[79] Most web-hosting services include search features by demographic information (e.g. age or location), as well as interests and hobbies; LJ allows such search both by interest and by school.

[80] The mean age in the corpus being 25.2.

[81] Out of the 75 blogs visited, two were identified as suitable for Sicily; however, they have not been included as no answer was received from both bloggers to the request of consent to use the data in this study (see below).

Table 9. Total number of blogs visited per region and blogs selected

Area	N. blogs searched	N. blogs selected Corpus
Veneto	147	5
Lombardia	375	3
Liguria	46	2
Abruzzo	31	1
Marche	52	2
Sardegna	40	1
Total	766	15

4.2.1. Some methodological considerations

In principle, unless openly set up as 'private', most Internet content is freely accessible to anyone and thus public by default (Herring 1996). Nevertheless, one of the ethical dilemmas in academic research involving Internet data has been whether online publicly available material ought to be subject to request for consent from participants, and to be granted anonymity in order to protect the participants' identities so as not to be potentially harmful to them. Various strands of thought have emerged on this debated matter, from more open positions who argue that, as this material is publicly accessible to anyone, participant consent is not a requirement (e.g. Walther 2002), to others who maintain that privacy should in any case be safeguarded since online materials "though publicly accessible, are written with expectations of privacy and should be treated as such" (Hookway 2011: 105). A third position takes into account the fact that clear boundaries between public and private are blurred on the Internet (Eysenbach and Till 2001), and very often they depend on "how actors themselves construe their participation in an online environment" and thus in "how they are defined by users" (Hookway 2011: 105, citing Waskul and Douglas 1996; cf. also King 1996 as to 'perceived privacy'). Herring (1996) has argued that considering CMC data as inherently private would be in most cases problematic and would set serious limitations to the researcher, particularly within a (critical) linguistic approach. In fact, she points out that "the focus of linguistic investigation is the form rather than the content of the utterance", and that, while information about the participants ought to be preserved, in linguistic research "what is important are patterns across groups of speakers, rather than individual linguistic variation" (Herring 1996: 159).

A salient consideration to the issue is the fact that in CMC, e.g. in group discussions, social networks, as well as on YouTube and Flicker, technological affordances allow (prod)users to make data and content available to a more restricted set of people; relevantly, as we have seen, the same is true for blogs in LJ, where several privacy options are made available to bloggers, among which the 'friends-only' tool in order to make the content of a blog private rather than publicly available. Furthermore, it is worth mentioning that the LJ Privacy Policy informs LJ users about privacy settings, giving specifications about the public visibility both of usernames and content[82]. As Hookway points out, "[b]logging is a public act of writing for an implicit audience. The exception proves the rule: blogs that are interpreted by bloggers as 'private' are made 'friends only'. Thus, accessible blogs may be personal but they are not private" (Hookway 2011: 105; cf. also Herring 1996; Basset and O' Riordan 2002). And in our case, during the process of data gathering 'friends only' blogs, as well as private content in semi-friendly-only ones, were excluded from the potential corpus, in compliance with the bloggers' overtly expressed option for privacy.

Despite the data being openly accessible, not least given the need to include in the analysis extracts that could be exemplificative of English as a lingua franca use, it was deemed proper to ask bloggers for consent to use the data to the research aims[83], i.e. within 'fair use' (Herring 1996, 2002a; Hookway 2011). Permission was granted for the fifteen journals which have been included in the corpus. Request to complete the questionnaire aimed at investigating the bloggers' experience with English and the reasons why English was employed as the lingua franca of communication in their journal was subsequently sent to all the fifteen bloggers.

As to the observer's role, my stance can be identified as covert: in my role of researcher I remained a concealed observer, as I did not ask for LJ friendship to any of the bloggers involved in this study, nor did I intervene with any commenting or interactive activity in the selected blogs, in order to prevent any possible influence on the data observed. Regarding anonymity, all possible measures have been taken to preserve the participants' anonymity: usernames have been concealed by assigning participants a pseudonym, and all references to the blogs' title, or to data such as the time and date of the message, have been omitted (King 1996); to the same aim, visual representations of posts have not been included in the present study.

[82] http://www.livejournal.com/legal/privacy.bml (accessed 15 November 2013).

[83] Request for consent was sent via private message in LJ or e-mail, to the bloggers whose journals were identified as meeting the criteria of the corpus as outlined above.

4.2.2. The corpus: blogs characteristics

The blogs from which the data included in the corpus has been drawn were searched and a sample of posts and comments were selected from each journal. The blogs making up the corpus are differentiated both in the nature of posts and commenting activities and in length: some are updated regularly, and have been running for a considerable amount of time, thus presenting a 'rich' archive, while others are updated less regularly and contain a smaller number of posts. Word-counts for the data from each blog are thus differentiated, from 2,073 words for the smallest, to 42,790 in the largest, with a mean of ~20,650 words per blog. The rationale in including also the smaller blogs in the corpus resides in the fact that they contribute to the typological diversity of personal journals, which range from accounts of personal life and experiences, to sharing interests and hobbies such as icon-making, manga & anime and fanfiction, to posting quizzes, quotes and memes (cf. e.g. Hodkinson 2007). The corpus, though not aiming at being representative from a quantitative point of view given its relatively small size, can nevertheless be seen to constitute a reasonably varied sample in qualitative terms of common blogging practices on LJ as aimed at an international audience. The final corpus makes up for a total number of ~312.300[84] words, comprising both posts and comments; the latter indeed constitute an important feature in international blogs in English, where participants frequently code-mix and code-switch into their native, as well as other, language – a frequent characteristic for "[y]oung, multilingual, geographically mobile" bloggers who thus create connections among different languacultures (Herring et al. 2007: n.p.).

To sum up, the corpus of investigation is thus constituted by fifteen personal journals produced by Italian young adults communicating internationally on their LJ blog. As outlined above, this blog-hosting service has been selected among others given its international scope, with participants cutting across all three Kachruvian circles, as well as the relatively young age range of its users. All the blogs in the corpus belong to the personal journal genre (cf. Chapter 2), which "has been the fastest area of blog growth since 2001, and the one which has the most distinctive linguistic character" (Crystal [2001] 2006: 242). As we have seen in Chapters 2 and 3, although interaction in blogs – as in other CMC genres – may not have the same urgency of spoken interaction, with language mirroring their hybrid written-spoken nature, the structure of posts-comments often displays highly dialogic and

[84] Including text data available in the bloggers' profiles (~2,500 words).

conversational features (e.g. Herring 2004, 2008a). In many cases the commenting activity involves, beside the blogger, several other commenters, in interactive exchanges displaying traits that resemble short spoken interactions, "most reminiscent of everyday face-to-face conversations between friends than of discussion with any particular 'public'" (Hodkinson 2007: 636).

Taking into account the specificities of blogs as a CMC genre, the corpus can be regarded as spontaneously produced ELF data, which captures instances of self-expression and interaction taking place naturally, inasmuch as it is aimed at communicating via English at an international level, as findings from the questionnaire survey also testify. Indeed, a regular thread running through most blogs is the desire to communicate with other bloggers and, more in general, people who either share the same interests, or have sympathetic attitudes and are, so to say, on the same wavelength. The interest areas of the participants appear variegated, with icon making, manga, anime and fanfiction as frequent characteristics; the people who participate in the blogs via comments in many instances empathically take part in the community-like interactions which are created in and around the blog, or even at tomes within a single post. In actual fact, one of the characteristics of LJ is that accounts of personal life experiences in blog practices are often closely interwoven with participation in fan communities: with regard to fanfiction, Helleckson and Busse relevantly note that "[t]he constant intrusion of personal information between fannish discussions and fiction presents a different mode of interaction in which a writer's personal impression may influence the way we read her fiction and viceversa. One benefit is that the mix of fiction and other material allows fans who are not creative writers to interact more fully" (Helleckson and Busse 2006: 14). This also appears true for some of the blogs in my corpus, where fanfiction writers often include in posts direct links to their production; other fan practices, like icon-making, on the contrary usually constitute an integral part of the post. Both textual and multimodal materials represent opportunities for interactional practices which, particularly as to icon-making, are generally quite active[85] (cf. 4.1.1). Somewhat differently from Herring et al.'s (2007) bridging journals, in these blogs interaction frequently takes place in relation to multimodal material (pictures, art work), generally in more concise forms for comments to

[85] Fanfiction texts, as well as any other hyperlinked material, were not included in the corpus, as the choice was made to consider only posts and comments, due to their potentially dialogic traits.

icon-making entries (cf. also Rebeza 2008), often consisting of "little more (and often less) than a single sentence", somewhat like "bullet point conversations" (Hodkinson 2007: 638). Other times replies to posts are longer and more articulated, particularly in response to topics related to personal matters and musings, or in discussions about more general interests; as mentioned in § 2.4, a broader participation on more global themes frequently intermingles with local and personal topics.

The corpus is variegated in terms of the interests and thematic aspects that are dealt with. In some journals posts are mainly dedicated to personal musings and to everyday life and events, frequently in connection with the blogger's interests (e.g. cinema, music and music groups, reading) or experiences (university life and courses, trips etc.). Other journals' posts are more specifically focused on fandom and fanwork activities like fanfiction, manga and anime, or icon-making, which may also combine within the same blog.

Fanfiction refers to fans re-writing original stories, characters and / or settings, by developing new plots; fanfiction works can originate from literary works or favourite media, from TV series and films to manga and anime (cf. Black 2008; Jenkins H. 1992). LJ, as mentioned earlier, has always been a favourite site for fanfiction fandom, both in terms of individual blogs and of communities. In individual blogs, links to fanfics are frequently embedded in posts, leading to the platform / website where the texts have been uploaded; this is frequent practice in my corpus, too, and fanfics, when present, are mostly related to TV series or shows such as *Supernatural*, *So you think you can dance*, and *Stargate*.

Manga and anime fandom have become popular in many countries outside Japan, where they originated, and across Europe, too. Interest in manga and anime is quite widely represented in my corpus; posts often relate to well-known productions, such as *Naruto*, or to others like *Ai no Kusabi*, *Hetalia Axis Powers*, *Vampire Knight*, *Itazura na Kiss*, *Toshokan Sensou*, *Himitsu*, *Soul Eater*; we also find specifically anime-related references, for instance to *Code Geass* and the *Gundam* series, or productions connected to videogames like *Persona* and *Hakuouki Shinsengumi Kitan*. At times the participants' interest in anime and manga intersects with fanfiction writing, as well as with fanart icon making, since they are common practices in these specific fandoms. Because of the clear connection with Japanese culture, posts may include code-switches to Japanese, more frequently with reference to names and titles, which are however often provided in English, too. In some cases, and particularly for songs, texts are given both in Japanese script (*Kanji/hiragana*) and *Romaji* characters, and with their translation in English (only at times in Italian).

Icon-making is most often related to specific fandoms, and generally has to do with popular TV series (e.g. *NCIS*, *Gilmore Girls*, *Grey's Anatomy, Supernatural, Castle, White Collar*, *Smallville*), or even Japan-inspired videogames such as *Kingdom Hearts*, whereby icons 'as squee'[86], or series of icons, are created and shared; icon making is considered as part of fanart[87], particularly in the form of photo re-manipulation, and it is particularly popular on LJ also with dedicated communities. Icons (as well as banners and wallpapers) are generally posted by bloggers to be shared with the like-minded people visiting the blog, spawning in the great majority of cases a good deal of comments, mainly short ones to compliment and/or thank the author, and acknowledge credits for icons when taken to be re-used.

Although at times bloggers and commenters may know each other in real life, in the majority of cases communication seems to be mainly of a virtual nature. Multimodal material embedded in posts, as well as code-mixing and code-switching are regular features; in our case code-switches involve mainly English and Italian, but Japanese, Spanish and Latin are found, too, the latter often in the form of quotations. These common practices well exemplify the heteroglossic and plurilingual nature of these virtual environments. Varied are also the linguacultures of the people who interact in these blogs, as well as the nature and frequency of commenting practices: some blogs tend to be more closed communities, with regular posters interacting on a more frequent basis (fanfiction, personal diaries); others include a high number of comments from a variegated number of countries, albeit with a less regular activity. At times links are created among participants who take part in each other's blogs by regularly commenting to posts, giving way to conversation-like shared spaces of interaction (cf. e.g. Hodkinson 2007). In most blogs in my corpus comments are made by people from different linguacultures, while a few blogs present interactants who come mainly, though not exclusively, from an Italian background. The international blogosphere in the corpus data includes participants who are located in the UK/Ireland/Northern Ireland, the USA and, to a lesser extent, Australia, Canada and New Zealand, and who are presumably native speakers of English. A few countries are set in the Outer Circle: Malaysia, the Philippines, India, and many in the Expanding circle: Brazil, Paraguay, Japan, with a good representation of

[86] "A not-uncommon response to a fannishly happy-making episode of a fannish show, is a sudden set of 10, 20 or 30 icons, all from that single episode, made available to other watchers of the show", http://fanlore.org/wiki/Icon_%28image%29 (accessed 15 November 2013).

[87] Cf. http://fanlore.org/wiki/Fanart (accessed 15 November 2013).

Europe (Norway, Finland, Germany, Austria, Switzerland, France, Belgium, Greece, Spain, Portugal, Poland, Croatia, Bosnia, and Hungary). As Berns has pointed out (1995, cf. Chapter 7), Europe does not constitute a homogenous situation within the Expanding circle: in some countries, particularly in Northern Europe, English serves in several contexts the functions of a second language, whereas in others it mainly plays the role of a foreign language. The participants in our data corpus appear variegated in this respect, too. In some cases a visual record of the nationalities of the people visiting the blog has been added to the LJ blog sidebar, as Figures 11., 12. and 13. hereunder exemplify.

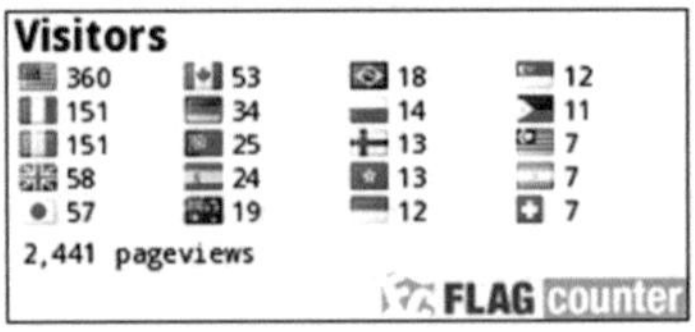

Figure 11. Flag counter for visitors

Figure 12. Flag counter for visitors

Figure 13. Flag counter for visitors

In Figure 11. we have a substantial number of representatives from the USA, Canada, the UK and Australia, as well as from Europe (Italy, France, Germany, Switzerland, Portugal, Spain, Finland, Poland) and other Expanding circle countries such as Morocco, Brazil, Argentina, Japan and Indonesia; Outer circle territories like Singapore, the Philippines and Malaysia are present, too. Figure 12. illustrates a similar network, albeit with a smaller proportion of countries and a higher number of visitors, with the USA figuring an overwhelming majority. The Flag counter in Figure 13., on the other hand, exemplifies a blog with smaller numbers of visitors located in Italy and in countries where English is spoken as a native language.

To recap, the corpus, despite its limited size, appears to represent a variegated sample of LJ personal journals from several points of view: firstly, interests are varied and range from icon-making to manga, anime and fanfiction; secondly, topics and aims go from self-expression to sharing life experiences and common interests. Thirdly, the range of friends and followers is quite varied, both in geographical terms and in frequency of interaction. The common thread is constituted by the wish to keep in touch with old and new friends and to communicate with people who, while often sharing the same areas of interest, may belong to different linguacultures and be geographically located in different parts of the world, across all Kachruvian circles. And English in its lingua franca role is the linguistic means that allows such wider networking of human relationships.

4.2.3. The questionnaire survey: bloggers' characteristics

In order to complement the corpus data and gain a more ethnographic perspective about the main participants (bloggers) and their experience and relationship with English and other languages, as well as their main reasons for keeping a blog in English, a questionnaire survey was deemed appropriate. The questionnaire was organized into 20 questions; after an introductory section related to personal, factual data (age, gender, level of education, L1, other languages in their linguistic repertoire), and aimed at gathering information related to the level and length of formal instruction in English, as well as the attested level of proficiency in English according to the CEFR; the final section dealt with the contexts in which the bloggers employ English, and whether its use is mainly related to oral, written or online Internet communication (cf. Appendix 1). Most questions were of the multiple choice type (e.g. Dörnyei 2007), and the possibility of leaving further comments was given in the last open question. Table 10. hereunder summarizes the main findings from the questionnaire survey:

Table 10. Main findings from the questionnaire survey

	Item	N.
Gender	M	1
	F	14
Education:	Secondary school	4
	Undergraduate	6
	Graduate	3
	PhD	2
Still a student	YES	9
	NO	6

L1	Italian	15
English – years formal instruction	5	2
	8	4
	10	2
	11	2
	12	2
	13	1
	14	2
International Certification for English – Level	NO	7
	B2	4
	C1	1
	C2	3
Lived in an Anglophone country	NO	10
	YES	5 (1-5 months: 4; 9 months: 1)
English-medium education	NO	8
	YES	7 (Secondary school: 4; University: 3)
Languages other than English	NO	4
	Spanish	1 C1/C2 (fluent) 1 A2 (3 years junior high school) Note: 3 bloggers: 2 additional languages; 2 bloggers: 3 additional languages
	Portuguese	1 A2
	French	5 (B2: 1; B1: 3; A1: 1)
	German	6 (B2: 1; B1: 1; A2: 2; A1: 2)
	Japanese	4 (B2: 2; A1:2)
Use English for… (more than 1 answer possible)	school/studies	12
	leisure activities (reading books, watching TV/ DVDs, travelling, etc)	15
	accessing information (news, articles, etc.)	15
	communication for personal/social purposes in international contexts	15
	communication for professional purposes in international contexts	4
	Other	1 writing, publishing original stories

Communication for personal/social purposes in international contexts (more than 1 answer possible)	Oral	3
	Written	9
	Oral and written	3
Online	e-mail	15
	Newsgroups	3
	Blog	15
	Chat	5
	Forum	11
	Gaming	3
	Other	1 social networks

The findings show that most respondents are female (14); indeed, according to LJ stats, women are in the majority among LJ users[88], and Herring et al. (2005: 152) report that teens and women tend to create more personal blogs than males and adults. The length of formal instruction in English of the bloggers in my corpus goes from five to fourteen years; most respondents (10) have never resided in an Anglophone country, eight have had English-medium instruction, and nine are still students. Eight bloggers have an international certification for English, ranging from B2 (4) to C2 (3) CEFR levels. Despite the length of formal education and the level of proficiency being varied, as most often the case in ELF settings (cf. e.g. Jenkins 2006a: 141; Mauranen 2011: 163), the bloggers' contact with the foreign language in formal instruction has been of at least five years, to a maximum of 14 years to date: given that nine of the respondents were still students, English has presumably continued to be part of their curricula. This area of enquiry in the questionnaire survey has been included in order to gain an overview of their 'relationship' with the English language, as well as with other languages, and has not in any way implied that they have been regarded in the context of this study in their role of learners, but as competent ELF users who communicate with other ELF users in the world-wide blogosphere. Particularly worth noticing that eleven bloggers can speak at least another foreign language besides English, in some cases at an A1 (for Japanese, Portuguese, French and German), but more commonly at an A2 or B1/B2 level; they are thus at least bilingual, and the majority plurilingual having at least three languages in their linguistic repertoire. As we will see in the next chapters, this is relevant both in terms of the differentiated communicative strategies that are enacted in the use of ELF by these multicompetent L2 users, and is

[88] LJ statistics report that LJ users are as follows: Male: 5,673,697 (41.8%); Female: 7,888,296 (58.2%); Unspecified: 4,357,350; source: http://www.livejournal.com/stats.bml (data accessed 7 April 2012, statistics continuously updated).

also very likely to have played a major role in the language-awareness they display.

All respondents said they use English in leisure activities, to access information and to communicate for personal / social purposes in international contexts; twelve indicated they use it also for their studies, and a minority of four to communicate for professional purposes in international contexts. As to online Internet contexts, all respondents include the use of English in e-mails and blogs, eleven in forum (with one specifically mentioning social networks), five in chat contexts and three in newsgroups and gaming. Three bloggers report using English only for oral communication, nine for written communication, and three for both; the written medium appears thus to be prevalent in their use of English, consistently with the answers related to the use of e-mails and blogs in Internet communication. Overall, English appears to be a constant and regular part of their personal, as well as educational, life.

When looking at the open question related to the reasons why they keep a blog in English, the answers plainly show that the main motive is to get in touch with people with L1s other than Italian, as the following extracts illustrate, respondents stated they use English "to be able to communicate with a lot of people" and "because in this way I can communicate with people from different countries". The use of English to this aim has in some answers been overtly connected to its global role of lingua franca, which allows networking with people of different linguacultures: "because English is a contact language the most of the people of the planet understand and so, using it, more people can have access to the material posted on my blog. Plus, I'm interested in broadening my horizons not talking only to Italian speakers". Using English for these bloggers thus emerges as a deliberate choice, in that it allows them to "to reach a wider audience", particularly on the web; as one respondent summarizes, "using English to communicate is certain way to be understood and to reach a bigger number of internet users that, like me, use English as lingua Franca".

In one single case a preference for communication with native speakers is mentioned: "I often write in English because all my readers and friends (except few ones) are British or American; I started writing in three languages: Italian, Spanish and English, but it was too complicated to keep translating everything". Even in this comment, the fact that English is in any case employed in its role of a shared lingua franca is somewhat detectable in the reference to the blogger's initial use of three languages in his/her posts, which then needed to be translated into English for the sake of his/her (wider) audience.

It is worth noticing that the role played by Anglophone cultures is often a palpable presence in the bloggers' interests, particularly in global products such as TV series, music or readings, as exemplified in the following remark: "besides, my interests (books, TV shows, etc.) derive from English-speaking countries – it's just easier to make my opinions known about them using English rather than Italian". This familiarity with English, which emerges as a 'natural' part of their lives when it comes to self-expression as well as in communication, is also revealed: as one blogger clarifies, "written English comes to me more naturally than my mother tongue when it comes to expressing my views and feelings". In two other comments this aspect is mingled with the international, wider audience granted when using English in blogging – as well as fanfiction – practices, as the following well highlights: "personally I prefer to write in English because I feel it's more direct than my mother language: also, my blog at livejournal was made for my international contacts/friends, since I was an active author on fanfiction.net (where I published my English-written stories) and writing in English allows me to reach and be understood by more people than with my mother tongue". Or' as another participant states, "I used English because I was talking about topics that didn't have a broad audience in my home country. By writing in English, I could get in touch with people from all over the world who were interested in the same topics".

Several other bloggers highlight how their networking and friending practices can be effective at an international level only by employing English as a common lingua franca to communicate with people "all over the world": "because the most part of my friends are from other countries, and I'm sure that if I write in English everyone understand what I'm saying"; "because it can easily reach everyone and most of my friends are not Italians nor they understand Italian, so it would be uneasy"; this appears particularly relevant in web-related activities, as the following comment highlights: "most of my on-line friends are an international bunch, using English to communicate felt like the most natural choice". In one case, a blogger overtly explains that many LJ communities are in English, adding that that is the main reason why he/she keeps a blog in this language: "my ljblog, which isn't my 'main' blog (I write in Italian in it), I use LiveJournal to watch and post in big communities […]. I made some posts on my personal page only because I thought it was a polite thing to do when I'm talking with other people. Also, some communities I only use English in don't accept you join request when you haven't written any posts". Indeed it is not unusual for bloggers to keep one journal in English and one in Italian, often hosted by two different services[89]; as a respondent in the Technorati *State of the Blogosphere* 2008 remarked, "I blog in Spanish and English for different reasons. In English I blog to communicate my ideas and views"[90]. At times an additional reason provided by my respondents for using English in blogs is "to meet people from foreign countries and to practice my English", which appears in line with one of the features characterizing bridging journals in Herring et al. (2007, cf. § 4.1.4).

To sum up, the results of the questionnaire survey show that these bloggers's contact with English in formal education ranges from five to fourteen years, and that many hold an international certification in English and can speak at least another foreign language besides English and their L1. They can therefore be considered multicompetent, at least bilingual, L2 users, who are aware of the role of lingua franca that English plays in the international blogosphere, and employ it to the precise aim of addressing an international audience via a commonly shared code.

4.3. English as a Lingua Franca: theoretical framework and paradigm of research

The field of ELF research has developed considerably over the last decade, focusing on different linguistic levels, from phonology (Jenkins 2000, 2002) to lexicogrammar (e.g. Seidlhofer 2001, 2004; Cogo and Dewey 2006, 2012; Björkman 2009; Mauranen 2010a, b) and pragmatics (e.g. Meierkord 2002; Cogo and Dewey 2006, 2012; Kaur 2009; Mauranen 2009; Klimpfinger 2009; Hülmbauer 2009; for a comprehensive overview cf. Jenkins, Cogo and Dewey 2011). ELF research is concerned with the investigation of linguistic and pragmatic features as connected to their functional significance in ELF communication, i.e. "*any use of English among speakers of different languages for whom English is the communicating medium of choice, and often the only option*" (Seidlhofer 2011: 7, emphasis in original). As emphasized by ELF scholars (e.g. Seidlhofer 2009b, 2011; Cogo 2008), and as will be discussed below, marked linguistic features are to be considered interesting in that they are revealing of processes and functions in communicative (and language variation and change) terms. As Seidlhofer (2009b: 49-50) puts it, "the main question is what variability tells us about the communicative

[89] blogspot.com and myspace.com being the most common ones.
[90] M. Varsavsky, quoted in Winn 2009, http://technorati.com/social-media/article/state-of-the-blogosphere-introduction/page-2/ (accessed 15 November 2013).

and interpersonal functions the observed forms are being used to express. The focus is on developing an understanding of how ELF users exploit the resources of the language to achieve their communicative outcomes". The primary interest of situated ELF studies, she continues, is "how ELF users, usually bi- or plurilingual, exploit the potential of the language in ways that result from the purpose of the talk and the interpersonal dynamics of the interaction".

Research into lexicogrammar has focused on the way ELF speakers manipulate and appropriate the language to their communicative and functional aims (Seidlhofer 2009b), investigating patterns of variation and innovation, which appear to be not random but regular. As Dewey points out, in ELF contexts these features can be seen as linguistic innovations, motivated by underlying processes as "*exploiting redundancy*, *enhancing prominence*, *increasing explicitness*, and *reinforcement of proposition*" (2007a: 339, emphasis in original), which are realized as "familiar processes of language variation in language use, but extended in non-canonical, creative ways" (Seidlhofer 2011: 108). These tendencies can be regarded as part of natural language change and language evolution processes, which are accelerated in ELF due to the mobile, multifaceted and complex contexts of use, where "speakers from a multitude of linguacultural backgrounds regularly make use of the language in infinitively varied contexts and for unlimited functions" (Dewey and Jenkins 2010: 88; cf. also Dewey 2007b; Jenkins et al. 2011: 7; Mauranen 2012. 27).

The ELF variants initially hypothesized by Seidlhofer (2001, 2004) have been researched and substantiated in a number of studies, both based on smaller-sized corpora (e.g. Cogo and Dewey 2006, 2012; Cogo 2009; Hülmbauer 2010) and on the VOICE[91] and the ELFA[92] corpora. Widely investigated lexicogrammar areas include processes of overgeneralisation/regularization of *–s* plural in nouns (e.g. Erling 2002; Björkman 2008a, 2008b, 2009; Erling and Bartlett 2006; Mauranen 2010a) and use of the demonstrative *this* both for singular and plural forms; the use of zero third person singular marking in present tense verbs (3sg Ø) (e.g. Breiteneder 2005, 2009; Seidlhofer et al.

[91] VOICE. 2011. *The Vienna-Oxford International Corpus of English* (version 1.1 online). Director: Barbara Seidlhofer; Researchers: Angelika Breiteneder, Theresa Klimpfinger, Stefan Majewski, Ruth Osimk, Marie-Luise Pitzl. http://voice.univie.ac.at (accessed 15 November 2013).

[92] ELF in academic domains, cf. ELFA 2008. The Corpus of English as a Lingua Franca in Academic Settings. Director: Anna Mauranen. http://www.helsinki.fi/elfa/elfacorpus (accessed 15 November 2013).

2006; Cogo and Dewey 2006, 2012); interchangeable use of *who* and *which* relative pronouns (e.g. Seidlhofer 2011; Cogo and Dewey 2012). Increased clarity and explicitness by adding redundant prepositions and nouns has also been looked into (e.g. Seidlhofer 2007a; Cogo and Dewey 2006) as well as preference for analytic/double comparative and superlative forms. Other researched areas include shift in the use of definite and indefinite articles, e.g. preference for zero article where L1 article use is idiomatic and preference for definite article to attach extra importance to a referent in a stretch of discourse (e.g. Cogo and Dewey 2006, 2012; Dewey 2007a, 2009); shift in patterns of preposition use (e.g. Cogo and Dewey 2006; Björkmann 2009), also in phraseological units (Mauranen 2005, 2006, 2010a, 2012); extension of the collocational field of words with high semantic generality (Cogo and Dewey 2006, 2012; Jenkins 2011b) and extended use and meaning of some 'general' verbs (e.g. *make*, *do*, *have*, *put*, *take*).

Studies based on the ELFA corpus have both confirmed the presence of most of the above-outlined features, and hypothesized additional morpho-syntactic elements in terms of ELF non-standardness[93] (Björkman 2008a, 2008b, 2009; Ranta 2006, 2009; Mauranen 2012) all at phrase levels.

While the above features have been found not to generally undermine effective communication, the areas of idiomaticity and phraseological units may indeed be problematic, particularly in what Seidlhofer has defined as "unilateral idiomaticity" (2001: 149) with reference to metaphorical language use, idioms, phrasal verbs and fixed ENL expressions (cf. also Seidlhofer 2004: 220; 2007a: 145; Seidlhofer and Widdowson 2007). ELF pragmatics has also been a widely investigated area, which has looked into the ways in which ELF speakers cooperatively co-construct meaning by means of several strategies, from repetition to code-switching and by drawing on their pluriligual repertoires (e,g. Meierkord 2002; Cogo 2009, 2010; Mauranen 2006; Hülmbauer 2009, 2010; Klimpfinger 2007, 2009).

Non-standard word formation is among the most noticeable innovations in ELF language use (Seidlhofer 2011: 101); non-standard morphological

[93] For instance, at the Noun phrase level, we find non-standard word formations, analytic/double comparative/superlative forms (e.g. *more easy, more safer, more bigger and bigger*, Björkman 2008b), non-marking *–s* for plural of nouns (Björkman 2008a, 2008b, 2009; Mauranen 2010a: 18), whereby speakers seem not to mark the plural (e.g. *respect for human right*), or to mark plural meaning merely by numerals, adverbs or determiners before the noun (e.g. *two different reactor*), as well as non-standard plural forms where uncountable nouns are regularised (e.g. *how many hydrogen,* Björkman 2009).

formations, as well as regularisation processes, appear conventional and creative at the same time, whereby novel functions are assigned to word formation processes (Mauranen 2010b) by creating new words, or collocating them differently. As Mauranen points out, 'morphological overproductivity' "seems to ensue from the nature of morphology, which is highly prolific and held back by convention rather than rule" (2010a: 18). Lexical creativity processes, which in ELF have been shown to follow well attested word-formation processes can be ascribed to language variation and serve functional motivations including those of increased clarity, economy of expression, regularization and filling gaps in the lexicon (Pitzl, Breiteneder and Klimpfinger 2008: 40-43). As Mauranen words it, "[t]here are always unused possibilities that are compatible with the word-formation rules of a language, but simply not taken up" (2012: 131). When this takes place in ELF settings, Mauranen continues, such morphological overproductivity "might not cause great disturbance under circumstances where participants make less precise predictions of form, that is, where they are ready to accept variability" (2012: 131).

Such processes may also involve influence from the participants' L1s: ELF settings comprise speakers from different linguacultures, who are at least bilingual by definition. In cross-linguistic creativity the non native status of the participants, who, as multicompetent users "stand between two languages" (Cook 2002a: 5), can be exploited as a "resource for sense making" (Firth and Wagner 1997: 290), coining 'true' friends, or emergent co-occurrence/collocations, which are often employed to supportive co-construction of meaning and effective communication (Hülmbauer 2009: 103; cf. also Cogo 2010: 303; Hülmbauer 2009: 337-341; Hülmbauer et al. 2008: 29). Cognates – or 'true friends' – can thus be seen in ELF contexts as manifestations of plurilingual competence, where translingual processes are applied, often also thanks to the commonalities in the different L1s of the speakers involved.

Similar underlying functional motivations can be seen in code-switching phenomena: L2 users "often code-switch from one language to another" (Cook 2002a: 4), and draw upon a range of linguistic competencies and repertoires, employing L1-2-3-N as additional tools to effective communication and co-constructed meaning (Cogo 2009: 266-269; 2012; Klimpfinger 2007: 51, 2009: 365-366; Hülmbauer 2007: 8, 2013). According to Pölzl (2003: 9-11), ELF users may choose to employ their L1 according to personal preference and to the context or the communicative goals, switching into their L1 aiming to display their cultural membership and to consciously show their loyalty to their own mother tongue.

It has also been highlighted that a good number among the non-standard features that have been researched in ELF are by no means confined to these contexts, but often occur also in many varieties of English, in situations of language contact, and/or are typical of spoken English grammar, a further point to support their interpretation as language change in progress, rather than learner errors. As Dewey (2007a: 339) points out, the processes that motivate innovation in ELF may not necessarily be conscious, but can instead be seen as a natural tendency in aiming at effective communication. Rather than typical errors or deficiencies produced by second/foreign language (permanent) learners, in ELF contexts these 'different' features can be seen as motivated by several functional underlying reasons as well as be part of natural language use, naturally complying with language change processes (Seidlhofer 2004: 222, 2008: 2).

Effective communication has in fact been one of the main tenets in ELF research, whereby the relationship between form and function is not measured against ENL (standard) norms, i.e. against notions of correctness/incorrectness, or deficiency and learner error (e.g. Cogo and Dewey 2012: 36; Hülmbauer 2007: 6-7; Seidlhofer 2008: 33-4). Rather, they are looked at as different manifestation of language use enacted to effective communication. In Hülmbauer's words, "comparison to ENL as a point of reference is not used to show what ELF lacks, but what is so typical of ELF" (2007: 14). ELF is thus analysed in its own right rather than as evidence of failed attempts to produce 'native-like' English and "in features that differ systematically and frequently from English as a Native Language (ENL) and are communicatively effective in ELF contexts" (Jenkins 2010: 103; cf. also Dewey and Jenkins 2010: 73).

It has indeed been argued by several ELF researchers (e.g. Dewey 2009: 62, 79-80; Seidlhofer et al. 2006: 9-10; Cogo and Dewey 2012: 36-38) that from a methodological point of view researching ELF entails taking into account how its unique traits, which derive both from the settings where it is enacted, and from its participants' characteristics, are strategically put into place in communication. In ELF settings, bi- or multilingual users employ ELF as a commonly shared means of communication, adopting it as the lingua franca and adapting it to their needs, which are communication- rather than accuracy-oriented and may thus not need to conform to ENL standardness. Also, ELF is locally realized in that the constellations of its users and settings are highly variable; as Dewey well summarizes, "ELF is best understood as a dynamic, locally realized enactment of a global resource, best conceptualized not as a uniform set of norms or practices, but as a highly variable, creative expression of linguistic resources which warrants a distinct analytical framework" (2009: 62). That is, researching ELF entails "an open engagement with similarity and difference" rather than a dichotomic stance between "'standard' vs. 'non-standard', 'ENL/normative' vs. 'ELF/expressive', or perhaps worse 'creative' vs. 'conforming'" (Baird 2012: 10). What ought rather to be investigated is the relationship between surface forms and "the contextual reasons, motivations, attitudes and social meaning associated with certain performances, forms and interactional choices" (Baird 2012: 10) within an emic perspective (Seidlhofer 2008; cf. also Seidlhofer 2011).

ELF users certainly share a common status of non-native bi-/multilingual speakers of English, and they have different linguistic, cultural and communicative resources available to them. These resources are variably enacted depending on several factors: "ELF speakers, with their individual backgrounds and resources contribute to a *situational resource pool* which changes as speaker constellation change" (Hülmbauer 2009: 325). Thus, while on the one hand ELF users display a shared and common non-nativeness, and appropriate and adapt the linguistic communicative resources in their repertoire to suit their contextual communicative needs, on the other hand this takes place in ways that are peculiar to each, variable and temporary contextual ELF setting. In this view, "*situational speaking communities*" of practice are created, undone, and (re)created anew "for each emerging interaction" (Hülmbauer 2009: 325), where and whereby ELF users from different language backgrounds, with different language(s) repertoires, and different levels of proficiency in the language aim to effectively communicate.

Rather than looking at forms in isolation, what appears mostly revealing in ELF is the investigation of how the underlying processes are employed to negotiate and produce co-constructed meaning, i.e. the "communicative potential" (Hülmbauer 2009: 332) forms hold despite – or because of – their non-standardness. Common patterns of exploitation of the virtual potential of the language (Widdowson 2003: 48-49, 173; Seidlhofer 2011: 109-120) have been by now widely attested in ELF research. Redundancy reduction, increased explicitness and enhanced prominence have been shown to be primary underlying motives in ELF language instantiations at different levels, from lexicogrammar to syntax. Pragmatic motivations have also been proved to be predominant in these processes, as well as influence from the L1/Ln in the repertories of ELF multilingual users. All these contribute, often simultaneously, to effective meaning making in ELF interactions, where "[v]irtuality interacts with plurilinguality. The theoretical possibilities of a language (in our case

English as a base of the lingua franca mode) are potentially reinforced, inhibited, or influenced in various other ways through the availability of linguistic resources from elsewhere" (Hülmbauer 2013: 56).

4.4. Research aims and methodology

Given the theoretical framework for ELF research outlined – though briefly – above, the following main research questions have been addressed in this empirical research study:

- RQ1: which ELF lexico-grammatical elements, as attested in relevant literature, are present in the corpus and at which linguistic levels?
- RQ2: in which self-expressive and interactional processes and to which function are they employed?
- RQ3: how are plurilingual repertoires exploited to meaning making, both in terms of exploitation of linguistic resources and as code-switching practices?
- RQ4 given the specificities of the research setting, not least in terms of 'constellations of interconnected practices', are the above characteristics employed to the same (or to different) functions as attested in ELF findings for oral data?

In order to investigate the presence of potential ELF-related elements and to answer the research questions, the corpus was searched with Wordsmith Tools 5 (Scott 1999), which has also served to look into regular patterns of language use. As to code-switching, the data has been manually scanned. As it will be illustrated more in detail in the next chapters, some features were selected for investigation, that is, those that responded to "underlying processes as '*exploiting redundancy*, *enhancing prominence*, *increasing explicitness*, and *reinforcement of proposition*'" (Dewey 2007a: 339, emphasis in original; cf. also Mauranen 2012 Ch.2), as well as those related to the exploitation of plurilingual resources. The data was checked for ELF features as identified in relevant literature, and all occurrences of morpho-syntactic non-standardness were extracted and noted down; whenever relevant, e.g. for processes of morphological creativity, occurrences were also checked with the VOICE corpus for similar instantiations.

Clearly, it was in some cases not easy to determine whether occurrences fully responded to non-standardness criteria and could thus be considered as language variations: firstly, "[t]here are differences of what is standard and therefore acceptable even within varieties of native Englishes" (Björkman 2009: 230-231). Secondly, and particularly so on the web, innovations in language use are far from uncommon (cf. Chapter 3). Thus, and specifically in relation to lexical non-standardness and idiomatic expressions, 'problematic' cases were also cross-checked with the BYU-BNC and the COCA corpora[94] and, when dubious, were not included.

Being Italian the L1 of all bloggers in the corpus data, a greater presence of linguistic elements potentially influenced by their linguaculture could easily be expected. However, given the aforementioned variegated nature of the bloggers' interactants locations, the data can still be considered in its linguacultural variety, of which we have tried to ensure representation of. Whenever relevant, the analysis has also included "selected passages analysed qualitatively" (Hülmbauer 2007: 13-14) in order to investigate not merely form *per se*, but the function to which a particular ELF feature has been employed, as well as its (interactive) context. Indeed, in ELF form and function have proved to be closely interrelated, where "form follows function" (Cogo 2008) since focus is primarily set on communication rather than on formal accuracy. Successful ELF communication does not necessarily rely on complying with ENL norms (cf. Hülmbauer 2007: 15-27, 2009: 331-342); rather, it can be considered as "any exchange that proves to be meaningful for the participants and that has reached the required purpose or purposes" (Cogo and Dewey 2012: 36).

One of my research aims has been to see whether some of the linguistic elements which are by now well attested in other ELF research findings were present in the data, and to interpret them in qualitative rather than quantitative terms. The findings could on the one hand constitute potentially interesting confirmation of ELF communication effective practices as for self-expression and interaction in blogs and online settings, and on the other hand uncover possible tendencies related to web environments which constitute relevant spaces for interaction in ELF terms. Indeed, despite its small-size, most hitherto ELF-investigated features do occur in the data, and often for similar communicative functions; their investigation could contribute to further substantiate attested patterns of change and variation in ELF language use. Generally, in ELF research the main criteria to include a feature as relevant are that it is systematically and frequently occurring in the corpus data, and

[94] The BYU- BNC, based on the British National Corpus from Oxford University Press (available online at http://corpus.byu.edu/bnc/), and COCA, The Corpus of Contemporary American English (available online at http://corpus.byu.edu/coca/).

has been produced by speakers of different linguacultures in multilingual settings (e.g. Björkman 2009: 229-230; Cogo and Dewey 2006: 64; 2012: 47). Its communicative effectiveness has increasingly been considered as a highly relevant criterion (e.g. Cogo and Dewey 2012: 36; Hülmbauer 2009: 328-332), on the ground that such instances can be seen as a potential sign in terms of language change and innovation, as well as a valid non-ENL based benchmark in evaluating their relevance to communicative and pragmatic functions. As Hülmbauer (2010: 59) points out, given that "ELF speakers often use rather unconventional methods to reach their communicative goals", a qualitative approach appears particularly appropriate as it can illustrate points and highlight tendencies even in smaller corpora.

A potential drawback in such a small-sized corpus is that it cannot provide statistically representative findings in quantitative terms; however, as Sacks remarks, "it may be we can come up with findings of some considerable generality by looking at very singular, particular things, by asking what it takes for those things to have come off" (1992: 298, cited also in Hülmbauer 2007: 13). The same point is made by Cogo and Dewey concerning the adoption of an ethnographic approach in detailed investigation of a small number of cases: their research, as they word it,

> in common with ethnographic methods, does not aim at being fully representative. Instead, we set out to undertake analytic induction, which involves determining to what extent a given case can be regarded as telling. Each case is thus analysed in order to identify what phenomena it illustrates and what issues it gives rise to, the findings from which analysis can be then transported to other contexts to see how they compare (2012: 35).

As we will see, most findings from my study confirm tendencies as emerging from ELF research; furthermore, as noted by Mauranen, "even among hapaxes (words that occur only once) it is possible to discern patters of instances that are similar" (2012: 123). A qualitative approach to the corpus has been deemed as the most appropriate, as it could reveal tendencies that, although not generalizable, could provide significant insights.

The ELF theoretical framework has been my main benchmark in approaching the data; findings have thus been analysed in terms of their functional processes and relevance within an ELF paradigm of research, and interpreted taking into account variation in form, in close connection to the underlying processes and within their contextual contour, not least in their specificity of a CMC setting. When looking at online discourse, a qualitative approach within a sociolinguistic perspective can in fact reveal "how participants in

CMC draw on various linguistic resources in shaping their online personae and in accomplishing various interactional tasks" (Androutsopoulos and Ziegler: 2004: 100). As we have seen in Chapter 2, instances of interaction among participants are not always overtly displayed in Internet modes, blogs included; nonetheless, whenever possible (and relevant), analysis of interactional practices has been a major preoccupation, in that processes of mutual accommodation and co-construction of meaning, which are so central to ELF settings, can be best observed in interactive practices. Indeed, in our context of investigation effective communication, together with self-expression, constitutes one of the main goals of the participants, who are ELF users in all respects, that is, "legitimate users of the language and not deficient learners engaging in interlanguage conversations" (Cogo and Dewey 2012: 38).

As previously mentioned, language in blogs can be considered as naturally occurring and, in the case of personal journals, expression of individual rather than instituzionalized 'identity' (Pölzl 2003: 7). Besides displaying characteristics of informal language, as well as of interactive practices oriented to conversation (cf. § 2.3), my corpus is clearly characterized by linguistic (and paralinguistic) features that are typical of CMC, and in this it differs from spoken discourse, which has been so far more consistently investigated in ELF. Despite the increasingly multimodal content of CMC communication, as Herring argues, "online interaction overwhelmingly takes place by means of discourse. That is, participants interact by means of verbal language, usually typed on a keyboard and read as text on a computer screen" (2004: 1). Since my main research interest has been to investigate how English as a lingua franca is employed in blogs for purposes of online communication among people of different linguacultures, the approach has been essentially linguistically-oriented. The specificities of the setting in which the data was produced have also been taken into account, looking at how the linguistic resources of these ELF multicompetent users are appropriated and manipulated within the 'constellations of interconnected practices' they are part of, and contribute to create and recreate.

4.5. Summary and conclusions

In this chapter the main characteristics of LiveJournal have been outlined, taking into consideration its (young) users, the main features of LJ personal journals and its specifically community-oriented practices, as well as the differentiated locations of LJ users and the languages employed in this web-based blog hosting service. Despite the possibility of creating a journal in 32 languages, and the variegated locations of LJ users, in this cosmopolitan virtual space English appears to be the main choice for LJ bloggers, many of whom non-native, "young, multilingual, geographically mobile" participants (Herring et al. 2007: n.p.).

The methodology of selection of the blogs from which the data included in the corpus of analysis was drawn has been illustrated, together with their characteristics. Data related to the bloggers' experience and use of English and of other languages, as well as their motivations to keep a blog in English as emerging from the questionnaire survey, has been examined, too; English has been part of formal education for all bloggers, many of whom hold an international certification in English, too. The majority can also speak another foreign language: Spanish, French, German or Portuguese, and in four cases Japanese. They all appear to consistently use English for a variety of purposes, from leisure activities to accessing information and communicating for personal and social aims in international contexts, including digital media in blogs, emails and forums.

Finally, salient points related to the ELF paradigm of research have been outlined, as this constitutes the main backdrop for the research questions and the methodological approach to data analysis, that is, investigating how and to what functions English is employed as the lingua franca of communication on LJ by young Italian bloggers and their internationally-oriented audience.

In the next chapters we will deal with the analysis of data and findings, focusing on the ELF traits and their functional underlying motivations in ELF use – as attested in research – within the specific context of blog online language use in the corpus data.

Chapter 5
Using ELF in wider networking: exploiting linguistic resources

> [...] non-conformity of form does not at all preclude functional effectiveness but on the contrary can enhance it (Seidlhofer 2011: 127).

It is widely acknowledged, as discussed in Chapter 1, that English acts as the main lingua franca of the globalized world, and Europe is no exception: English has become an integrated part of the linguistic complexity in the EU – and in many other world contexts – as a consequence of globalization processes: English constitutes an additional linguistic resource for many European citizens in their personal (or professional) networks. This is particularly true for younger generations, whose contact with English takes place both within formal educational and 'outside the classroom' through the media and as a privileged, often default option in international contacts, a point to which I will come back in Chapter 7. It has thus been defined as a "partner language" (Hülmbauer, Böhringer and Seidlhofer 2008: 29), which complements the ways, contexts and functions in which other (national) languages are employed (cf. also Seidlhofer 2003).

As outlined in Chapter 4, in the ELF research paradigm the focus is not set on difference in form when compared to ENL *per se*, but rather on looking at how these 'unconventional', non-standard forms are created, and how they work in successful communication (e.g. Seidlhofer 2011; Hülmbauer 2007: 15). ELF multilingual and multicultural settings are by definition sites where language(s) and culture(s) come into contact, and precisely because of this ELF users have at their disposal a set of entwined linguacultural resources which can be situationally exploited to effective communication and mutually negotiated in meaning construction. Furthermore, it is this "shared non-nativeness in ELF which makes speakers less dependent on adherence to native speaker rules" (Hülmbauer 2009: 325), and which constitutes an additional resource in mutually co-constructing understanding. As Seidlhofer highlights (2011: 101):

> [m]uch of ELF is negotiated ad hoc, dependent on content, purpose, and constellations of speakers and their own linguacultural backgrounds (in terms of

discourse conventions, interactional styles, etc.). ELF discourses are creative local realizations, or performances, of a global resource that continually gets appropriated and re-fashioned in speakers.

One of the main aims of communication in ELF contexts is that of pragmatic clarity; 'getting the message across' and reaching mutual comprehension are most of the time paramount aims for ELF users, for whom English represents a shared lingua franca through which to interact in a (specific) domain or situation, be it academia, tourism or business meetings. Given that English is an additional language for all its speakers, communicative clarity may be achieved via accommodation skills and pragmatic strategies such as repetition or rephrasing, but also exploiting the resources of the (virtual) language to novel functions. Linguistic processes that seem to be regularly employed in ELF interactions include explicitness, enhanced clarity and simplification in terms of regularization (e.g. Mauranen 2012: 56-57). As Seidlhofer points out, "[c]larity can be enhanced by giving prominence to important elements, redundancy added or exploited, explicitness can be increased by making patterns more regular, word classes or semantic relations generally can be made more explicit" (2011: 99).

Indeed, such patterns also frequently occur in many varieties of English, in situations of language contact, and/or are typical of spoken English grammar. To name but a few, different articles usage, a regularized (non) pluralization of nouns, as well as morphological creativity are areas where ELF appears to be employed by its users in non-standard ways, following processes of language innovation which are in some cases similar to the ones observed in other varieties of English, particularly in World Englishes contexts. Many formal and functional properties of ELF can thus be regarded as the result of tendencies towards a regularization of the system, in a process of language change which in ELF appears to be more evident and accelerated than in ENL since it is "freed from the standardizing constraints of a set of norms" (Jenkins, Cogo and Dewey 2011: 7; cf. also Seidlhofer 2004, 2011; Mauranen 2012).

Linguistic innovations in ELF – as probably in any language – can be seen to be motivated by underlying functional processes, as a "a natural tendency for effective communication" realized through processes that involve "*exploiting redundancy, enhancing prominence, increasing explicitness,* and *reinforcement of proposition*" (Dewey 2007a: 339, emphasis in original; cf. also Cogo and Dewey 2012; Mauranen 2012). They are not randomly realized, but rather "familiar processes of language variation in language use, but extended in non-canonical, creative ways" (Seidlhofer 2011: 108). ELF innovations have indeed been shown not to be erratic, but to follow well attested language change processes, with several underlying motives giving way to their appearance (Cogo and Dewey 2012: Ch. 3 and 4; Seidlhofer 2011: chapters 5 and 6; Mauranen 2012: chapter 5). The reasons for their emergence can be traced back to the aforementioned functional motivations, within a more general framework of language contact and language change processes: "ELF is a natural language and can thus be expected to undergo the same processes that affect other natural languages, especially in contact situations – for instance, regularization is already evident in most of the data analysed so far" (Seidlhofer 2004: 222; cf. also Cogo and Jenkins 2019: 277). These motives can at times appear more evident, and in other instances less clearly and transparently identified, or interwoven in a complex set of grounds where several functional motivations may be at work simultaneously, and at times even competing (Cogo and Dewey 2012: 81-82; Seidlhofer 2011: 95-96).

In this and in the following chapter I will deal with the corpus data, taking into examination some among the most salient features investigated in ELF research as emerging from the data. Findings will be presented and organized by looking at the possible common underlying motives underpinning the use of some lexicogrammatical features. My findings include variation at different linguistic levels, from Noun to Verb Phrase, as well as syntax, which all appear in line with ELF research. In the present data analysis I have examined linguistic processes related to lexicogrammar that have been widely researched in other ELF contexts and identified as typical tendencies in ELF usage; my main research aims have been to explore whether they are in line with other research findings, and to which functional motivations they have been employed in the specific context under investigation, that is, online blog communication.

First I will look into regularization processes which may be hypothesized as connected to exploitation of redundancy and economy of expression, to then examine examples related to functional motivations responding to increased clarity and explicitness. Finally, lexical innovations via (overproductive) morphology will be analized. Each section will be preceded by references to literature related both to World Englishes varieties and, more specifically, to ELF research.

5.1. Processes of regularization, economy of expression and redundancy reduction

One on the underlying motives that appear to lead to unconventional forms in ELF is a tendency to regularization, which is often found in combination with economy of expression and exploitation of redundancy. This has been observed at different language levels, from noun to verb phrase, and involves several lexico-grammatical areas, from pluralization of nouns, to the interchangeable use of *who* and *which*, to the loss of the 3rd person *–s* morpheme in present tense singular verb forms, just to quote some areas. The next sections will illustrate and discuss how these processes emerge from my corpus data.

5.1.1. Zero third person singular marking in present tense verbs (3sg Ø)

The zero 3rd person –s marking has been quite extensively investigated in ELF (Breiteneder 2005, 2009a, 2009b; Hülmbauer 2010; Cogo and Dewey 2006, 2012; Seidlhofer, Breiteneder and Pitzl 2006; Dröschel 2011).

The present tense in English is unmarked in terms of aspect and voice, apart from the verb to be and the third person singular *–s* morpheme; in Trudgill's words, "Standard English is unusual among the languages of the world in having marking in the present-tense only in the third-person singular" (2002: 104). Simplification and redundancy reductions related to 3rd person *–s* marking are widely attested in postcolonial Englishes varieties[95] (cf. e.g. Schneider 2007; Platt et al. 1984: 67; Jenkins [2003] 2009a: 29), as well as in pidgins and creoles (Todd 1990; Crystal 2003: 347); it is argued that many English dialects use zero 3rd person marking, particularly in spoken varieties, including East Anglian in the UK, AAVE, English-based creoles of the Caribbean and West Africa, and New Englishes varieties such as Singaporean and Philippino English (Schneider 2011: 163, 204; Trudgill and Hannah 2008: 143). Redundancy reduction in this area, together with superfluous *–s* marking, can be considered "by no means peculiar to ELF talk" (Seidlhofer, Breiteneder and Pitzl 2006: 15); on the contrary, it is said to be a common feature also in proficient ENL speakers informal speech as ellipses

[95] See e.g. Trudgill 1999, 2002 for ENL and other varieties; Svartvik and Leech 2006 and Crystal 2003 for vernacular grammar; Platt et al. 1984 for New Englishes, Crystal 2003 for creoles. Cf. also Kortmann and Schneider's (2004-7) online interactive maps, where "23 out of 46 varieties analysed, present tense zero marking is pervasive or very frequent" (cited in in Breiteneder 2009: 257).

and clipping in interactions are frequently employed (Breiteneder 2005: 11-12). Trudgill indeed refers to the third person singular marking as one of the "[g]rammatical idiosyncrasies of Standard English" (1999: 125), belonging to the "afunctional grammatical devices" (Trudgill 2002: 92), pointing out how in the Norwich area the language contact situation led to non *–s* marking also as "the non-native form had the advantage of linguistic *naturalness* and *simplicity* (Trudgill 2002: 98, emphasis added). As Cogo and Dewey (2006: 88) remark:

> [a]mong the world's languages English then is something of an oddity for its inflection of only one of the present tense verb forms, and especially so for its attachment to the third person singular. The more pertinent and certainly more justifiable question then with regard to 3rd person singular -s is not why the L2 speakers and some speakers of L1 dialects use the zero form, but precisely the opposite – why in standard varieties of English does the 3rd person singular carry morphological marking? Zero marking for first, second, and third person plural makes the use of the singular -s an unexpected irregularity, and surely the phenomenon that most requires explanation.

The missed subject-verb agreement with the 3rd person–s affix can thus be read as "a regularization of the nonnatural system of Standard English" (Seidlhofer, Breiteneder and Pitzl 2006: 16), not least, being English a non-prodrop language, since the categories of person and number are already expressed in the subject. After Cogo and Dewey, it can better be described "as a zero realization as opposed to an omission of *s*" (2006: 76-77; cf. also Cogo and Dewey 2012: 82-84), which is employed by ELF users as more attention is placed on content and economy rather than form. In this perspective the use of the 3rd person *–s* morpheme appears not only redundant, but also detached from the function of social identity and prestige and marker of "in-group-membership" it carries in ENL communities (Breiteneder 2009a: 263; cf. also Widdowson 1994; Seidlhofer 2001). Furthermore, dropping and superfluous *–s* marking have been shown to be triggered by the extra-linguistic environment, too, appearing as natural characteristics of language contact situations where there is a tendency towards the process of regularization and simplification as "economy of expression" (Seidlhofer 2011: 105). This would further support the tendency by ELF users to focus on semantic and functional content of communication, rather than on the form itself, by means of redundancy reduction following "what may be called the principle of appropriate communicative economy" (Seidlhofer 2011: 145).

In ELF 3sgØ occurs across different linguacultural backgrounds, often along with its standard form realization (Breiteneder 2005: 8-9, 2009a: 262, 2009b: 81-84; Seidlhofer, Breiteneder and Pitzl 2006:14-17); as Cogo and Dewey argue, due to the systematicity of this feature in ELF interactions "3rd person *–s* and 3rd person zero are competing variants" (2012: 49). 3sgØ appears to principally occur with main verbs (Cogo and Dewey 2006: 77-82) and in Breiteneder's data (2005: 21) more frequently with some verbs such as *function, want, last* and *ask* probably due to the difficult pronunciation of consonant clusters. These findings appear corroborated in Cogo and Dewey (2006: 81; 2012: 50), whose data registers a high frequency in *–s* affixation with *has, looks, means* and *depends*; according to the authors, this is due to the fact that these forms are part of prefabricated chunks of language (cf. also Cogo and Dewey 2012: 51).

As far as main verbs are concerned, Cogo and Dewey argue that the use of zero 3rd person singular is independent on both the nature of the setting and the first language of the participants, although absence of native speakers appears to be a positive variant for Ø 3sg marking, while more formal settings, such as classroom interactions, appear to trigger *–s* marking (2006: 84-86). Additionally, the 3rd person *-s* appears to be employed primarily when verbs are related to functions of tense and aspect, or to serve as morphological marking in questions and negatives, thus not being perceived as performing "a real communicative function", while the use of the zero marking occurs in relation to efficiency of communication and exploited redundancy (2006: 83).

Dröschel's findings also include instances of unmarked third person verbs (for a total of 0.26 frequency) across Swiss speakers of Italian, French and German linguistic backgrounds (2011: 212-215). The author highlights that her findings appear to point to the fact that "unmarked present tense verbs and hypercorrect *–s* morphemes are deviations from Standard English that are most likely to be a result of regularization processes affecting the target language" and, quoting Sand (2005: 182), that "the suffix for 3rd person singular is typologically marked and therefore becomes a possible target for language change" (Dröschel 2011: 218), thus confirming previous interpretations.

In my data we find 33 occurrences, produced by ten different participants, where the 3rd person verb is unmarked, none of which appears to hinder communicative fluency. All have been realized with main verbs, apart from one instance with the semi-modal *have to* (*she always have to put her mouth in other people's business*); they are all in the affirmative, but one with an auxiliary form (*but she dont know how I feel*). Some regular patterns can be hypothesized in findings, whereby zero 3rd person –*s* marking is employed in conjunction with:

a) it + verb
It's crazy, I know ... but it make me feel better! =); it sound a bit tricky; it always feel like a waste of time; it also fit more the name of this journal[96];

b) the fact/thing(s)/all/something + that (pseudo-cleft sentences)
the fact that they last for only a moment make them so precious...; the thing that make me sad, is that she acted just; a thing that inspire me a fic; check all that apply to you or that you agree with; something that only get worse;

c) V-ing as subject (non-finite clausal subject)
thinking about how much he probably suffered make all this much worse; looking at your works make me want to...; seeing always the same stories [...] make me feel irritated!.

Interestingly, in the above instances the 3rd person singular zero is employed in five cases with the verb *make* followed by an object pronoun (*me*, *them*, see a) and b) above), which could possibly be read in connection with consonant clusters, as well as to a simplification in what may have been perceived as a lexical chunk. The latter functional motivation could also apply to b) and c), where the subjects of the pseudo-cleft sentences, as well as in the case of non-finite clausal ones, could have been perceived as a prefabricated chunk rather than in their 3rd person singularity. One further factor in zero marking may have been the relative distance of these clausal subjects from the verb; *that's where my knowledge of channels and frequencies come from* could also be interpreted in this perspective. A further motivation in some of the exemplifications at point b) above could also be related to the concept of notional concord, a point to which I will come back later.

Eight occurrences have been realized with a personal pronoun (such as for instance, *if she wear that kind of shirt*; *yet he still love J.*; *She likes to watch movies [...] she ask questions about the characters*; *because he just want to stare at Mercury's butt*; *she act like*; *he really care for her!!*; *he still (more or less) follow the story*; *she also befriend a nobleman that shares her interests in literature*).

[96] Underlying has been added in excerpts for language exemplifications under discussion in the relevant section; as to participants, whenever available, location has been specified (e.g., Ger stands for Germany).

In four cases zero 3rd person marking is instantiated with a proper name or a noun (*I'm happy that Subaru make finally his appearance*; *this little guy never let that stop him*; *becomes a model, but quickly becomes a cocaine and heroine addict along with her boyfriend and break all ties with her family*; *when Summer ends and Autumn begin*); in three instances with a noun referring to an object (*the pic look a bit weird; all my body hurt; it's like my brain get disconnected from the rest*), and in two with an abstract noun (*the love for wolves still remain; the government just nods and pass over*).

As it can be noticed in some of the examples cited above, at times marked and unmarked form coexist within the same sentence, a fact that may be due to the variability that this feature still displays in ELF settings (e.g. Breiteneder 2005: 8-9; Cogo and Dewey 2012: 49). In the contextual setting of my data, however, one possibility to be taken into consideration is that some of these forms may also be ascribable to typos.

Finally, a particular case is represented by the example *He ever get angry with you?*, where the unmarked form could also be seen in connection to the dropping of the question auxiliary *does*.

As argued by Breiteneder (2009a: 16; 2005: 15-21), 3sg Ø marking appears to additionally be triggered by three environments in particular: a) a collective head noun; b) coordination; c) an indefinite expression. As to the first, in English collective or group nouns can be agreed according to grammatical or notional concord or proximity, as "singular collective nouns may be notionally plural" (Quirk et al. 1985: 758). While 'grammatical concord' is defined by Quirk et al. (1985: 757) as "the rule that the verb matches its subject in number", in 'notional concord' the choice of verb form is determined by the meaning rather than the form of the subject, and concord is realized "according to the notion of number rather than with the actual presence of the grammatical marker for that notion" (Quirk et al. 1985: 757; cf. also Biber et al. 1999: 187). In notional concord the verb may agree "with the idea of plural in the group noun rather than the actual singular form of the noun" (Leech and Svartvick 1975: 221). The 'principle of proximity', or 'attraction', refers to the tendency for a verb to agree with a noun which is closer to the verb, though not being the head of the subject phrase. According to the principle of proximity, "the verb tends to agree with whatever noun or pronoun closely precedes it, instead of the headword of the subject" (Leech and Svartvick 1975: 221). A singular verb is used when the coordinated elements represent a single entity, and when the noun phrases refer to the same thing (Leech and Svartvick 1975: 222). Notionally collective subjects, which are grammatically singular in ENL (e.g. *ministry*, *community*, *government*) can be interpreted in their notional plural meaning, which is increasingly more common in some types of British textual forms (Bauer 2002: 50). Biber et al (1999: 189) remark that "such clear deviations from grammatical concord are mostly found in speech" due to the pressures of short-term memory and online processing. They also point out that the principles of notional and proximity concord at times operate together, reinforcing each other.

Breiteneder argues that ELF speakers tend to match singular collective nouns with plural verbs in accordance with the principle of notional concord: grammatically singular collective noun heads may be 'notionally' plural in that they can be perceived as a collection of individuals (Breiteneder 2005: 18). On the other hand, coordinated subjects which grammatically count as plural are combined with the 3rd person singular *-s* according to the principle of proximity, meaning that the concord of the verb might be determined by the immediately preceding singular noun constituting part of the coordinated subject phrase (Breiteneder 2005: 19-20). Similar findings, though instantiated only once, appear in Cogo and Dewey (2006: 86), and are interpreted as over-generalisation or hyper-correction on the part of the speaker.

My data includes a few instances of collective nouns with singular verb concord: *staff* (2 instances), *police* (4 instances, all by the same blogger), and *people*, produced by 6 participants, as in *Sometimes I just check if people is still out there! :P; other people that has suffered the same symptoms; it's like the only thing people talks about here ._.; cause there's people who don't know English; I like people who doesn't like me; when people wants help.*

In our case, being the bloggers' L1 Italian, singular concordance could also be ascribable to a transfer process, as *polizia* [police] and *gente* [people] are in Italian singular collective nouns[97]. Instances with *there's people*, *too much people* are also present, as well as *people* preceded by the singular demonstrative *that.*

Another ambivalent area in terms of subject-verb agreement is that of indefinite expressions of amount, where "especially *no*, *none* and *any*, often cause concord problems" (Leech and Svartvick 1975: 221; cf. also Quirk et al. 1985: 763). While with quantifiers followed by noncount nouns the verb concord is in the singular, and with plural countable nouns in the plural (Quirk et al. 1985: 764-765), in informal style *everyone/body*, *someone/body* and *anyone/body* can be replaced with *they*, whereas in formal contexts the substitution tends to be made with *she/he* (Leech and Svartvick 1975: 282).

[97] Duguid (1987 [2001]: 86) indicates the latter as a problematic area for speakers of Italian.

According to the proximity principle, we can have plural concord even with "indefinites such as *each*, *every*, *everybody* and *nobody* (or indefinite phrases with *every one*, *any one*), which are otherwise ambivalently singular" (Quirk et al. 1997: 764; cf. also Biber et al. 1999: 184). Moreover, the plural semantic meaning of the subject, rather than its singular form, may lead to notional concord, an apparently regular feature in ELF European contexts (Breiteneder 2009a: 261; Seidlhofer, Breiteneder and Pitzl 2006: 15-16). In Breiteneder (2005: 19-20; 2009b: 104-106) indefinite expressions such as *everybody*, *somebody*, *anybody* and *anyone* show concord with morphologically unmarked verbs. In my data, along the same lines, quite a few instances by different participants are found, as exemplified in the following instances:

- *Someone* (3 participants):
if someone want to chat a bit [...] I'd be really happy; I hate when someone act like that; someone that deserve this kind of treatment; the moment someone here realize there are more books [...] and starts publishing them XD; probably somebody remember how my desk was set; something that only get worse with constant pressure
- *Anyone* (2 participants)
Have anyone ever loved you that much?; thanks to anyone who find the time; anything that let me creating stories
- *Everybody* (1 participant)
everybody consider her a crazy murderer

To be noticed that in the above exemplifications a range of verb types are employed, and only in one case do we find an auxiliary form (*have*), differently from findings in Cogo and Dewey (2006: 82-83).

As to overuse of 3rd person *–s* marking, this overgeneralization characteristic can be found also in non-standard vernacular grammars of native and non-native varieties of English (Svartvik and Leech 2006: 134; Trudgill 2002: 102; cf. also Dröschel 2011: 215-217), and has been observed in ELF by Breiteneder (2005: 9-10) Hülmbauer (2010: 81), and Dröschel (2011: 213-214, 217-219). In Breiteneder's data, out of 15 instances, twelve are of overtly marked plurals or coordinated subjects; in two cases, morphologically inflected verbs appear after the modal auxiliaries *can* and *have to*, and in one 3sg is found with a third person singular past tense verb. Also Dröschel's investigation (2011: 214) presents several instances of overgeneralization of the *–s* morpheme in the Present Tense, which are produced mostly by French and Italian rather than German speakers in her data, above all with the 3rd person plural form.

In my corpus data, we find only 5 such overgeneralization instances, by 4 different participants; in one case it is combined with the first person singular pronoun (*I'm hungry I says things I don't really mean*); in two instances with a plural subject (*the characters that appears*; *Ancients that doesn't follow the witches that appears*), and in one case it is found in combination with the negative form of the auxiliary *doesn't* (*lol@ B. the hippo (that doesn't actually farts XD)*. Finally, in one instance the *–s* morpheme is redundantly added to the verb in the *make something + V* expression (*You make it seems like*).

To sum up, instances of unmarked 3rd person verb inflection can be said to fit simplification processes of language change, whereby redundancy reduction manifests itself in language contact situations by regularization of lexicogrammar elements that often appear idiosyncratic to Standard ENL. This redundancy reduction is common to many 'non-native' varieties, and can be found also in ENL, especially in spoken language. Instances of zero 3rd person –s marking in ELF can therefore be hypothesized to respond to language change simplification processes, where focus is set on effectiveness of the message rather than on (Standard ENL) form, particularly on occasions where it is communicatively redundant. Findings from my data appear in line with similar ones in other ELF contexts, and can be seen to further reveal the kinds of ongoing modifications in the area of lexicogrammar which are taking place in ELF communicative settings.

5.1.2. This is/there is + plural

Redundancy reduction processes are observable in the data also with reference to other linguistic areas which have been investigated in ELF research. Similarly to the lack of concord in zero 3rd person *–s* marking, the use of the single demonstrative *this* in its singular form also for the plural, which would in ENL require the plural *these*, can be interpreted as an analogous simplification process in terms of redundancy reduction, since the plural is already grammatically and communicatively expressed in the *–s* morpheme of the following noun (Hülmbauer 2010: 84). In some cases the concept of plural may be additionally signalled with the insertion of *all* or a numeral, which in principle makes the use of a plural demonstrative even more redundant (Seidlhofer 2011: 144).

A similar process can be observed in the lack of concord with *there is*: according to normative grammar, with existential *there is* the verb *be* should concord with the noun following it. Biber et al. point out that in spoken conversation "we frequently find a singular form of *be* followed by plural noun phrases" (1999: 186), with the verb often in its contracted form *there's*, (which does however not take place with the past form *was*). ELF speakers are said to interpret subject-verb concordance in its invariable singular form with existential *there is* + plural (Ranta 2009: 97) be the following noun in singular or plural form. This non-standardness in subject-verb agreement in the case of *there is* occurs in English varieties, too, inner circle ones included, as for instance in British vernaculars (e.g. Kortmann and Szmrecsanyi 2004: 1147).

Similarly, in my data we find several instances, produced by different participants where *there is* is followed by a plural (*there's Japanese people*), where plurality is at times reinforced by a quantifier (*there's few interesting places*) or by a numeral (*there's only 20 hours left*; *there's hundreds of years of history and reasons behind his actions*). As Biber et al. argue, "because of the contraction, *there's* tends to behave as a single invariable unit for the purposes of speech processing" (1999: 186), thus not distinguishing anymore between singularity and plurality, an interpretation which is also set forward by Ranta (2009: 98; cf. also Cogo and Dewey 2012: 97). In other cases it is the singular demonstrative *this* which is accompanied by a plural noun, as in: *there's this rules that say*; *happened this days*; *in this past months*; *this awesome colours and this awesome cropping*; *this stupid things*; *why are this things so expensive?*. These cases may be interpreted as processes of redundancy reduction, too, since the plurality is expressed in the noun that follows.

5.1.3. Pluralization of uncountable nouns

The loss of distinction between countable and uncountable nouns, where the latter tend to be pluralized according to regular *–s* morphological rules, has been investigated in different ELF contexts (e.g. Erling 2002: 10-11; Erling and Bartlett 2006: 23; Björkman 2009: 231; Hülmbauer 2010: 82-83). Such regularization processes have also been attested in several World Englishes varieties, such as South Asian Englishes, west African, Nigerian, Indian and Singaporean English (Crystal 2003: 362; Schneider 2011: 204; Trudgill and Hannah 2008: 141; Platt et al. 1984: 50-52). Trudgill and Hannah (1985: 104) refer to this area as "loss of distinction between count and non-count nouns", and Platt et al. (1984: 50) argue that, rather than overgeneralization, the tendency to pluralize uncountable nouns can be seen as "a type of reclassification". Crystal (2003: 362) remarks that countability can be a "tricky area of English grammar" for language learners, regardless of their L1 background, and Carter and McCarthy (2006: 340) point out that in other languages nouns that are non-countable in English are considered countable. Indeed, as Crystal (2000: 3) notes, if this is recognizable as a widespread feature by competent users of English, one may question whether it should be considered an error in a specific contextual setting where it can be diffusely encountered.

As Seidlhofer (2011: 126) underlines, regularization processes as to non-countable nouns have resulted in pluralized forms that "have evolved to meet some functional need. It happens that the need to pluralize *evidence* has not, or not yet at least, arisen in approved NS circles, but there is nothing in the language itself that precludes its production should an occasion arise which makes it conceptually appropriate". Moreover, Seidlhofer continues, "non-conformity of form does not at all preclude functional effectiveness but on the contrary can enhance it" (Seidlohfer 2011: 127): regularization in the pluralization of uncountable nouns can in actual fact also contribute to the clarity of the message, making form less opaque (Hülmbauer 2010: 82).

In line with these considerations, findings from my data include several instances of uncountable noun plural forms with regularized *–s* marking, produced by different participants, which at times coexist with the attested ENL form; exemplifications can be seen in the two occurrences of *advices* (*give me a couple of advices*; *I don't need advices*, which are recurrent also in other findings, cf. e.g. Mauranen 2012: 126), similarly to the 7 instances of *informations* (e.g. *as many visual informations as possible*; *if you need more informations*; *many public informations*; *ask detailed informations about*; *which contains plot-essential informations*; *a lot of unnecessary informations*; *some more infos*). Further instances of regularization processes include *news* (*just a news I wanted to share*; *I have a good news*) and *pliers* used in the singular (*take out my wisdom teeth with a plier*), as well as *resuscitation* (*I need a resuscitation XD*), all employed as countable nouns.

5.1.4. Regularization by analogy

The aforementioned processes can also be interpreted as regularization by analogy. Schendl (2001: 123) defines analogy as a "process by which a form or a pattern becomes more similar to another (usually more regular) one"; analogical formations are generally transparent (Hickey 2006: 157) and as such likely to be understandable. As Pitzl et al. (2008: 36) point out, a relation of analogy can be detected in processes of regularization affecting different levels of the language; in morphology, it may apply to derivational as well as to inflectional affixation, such as the aforementioned *–s* pluralization of uncountable nouns, the zero third person morpheme in the present tense, or in past forms of irregular verbs which are regularized by adding the *–ed* inflectional morpheme. As to the latter, which is well attested in the VOICE (Pitzl et al. 2008: 36) and in the ELFA corpora (e.g. Mauranen 2012: 126), my data includes *teached* (1 occurrence), *stealed*[98] (1), *splitted* (1) and *readed* (2), which can all be found, together with other forms, also in the VOICE corpus. When a double form is possible, as in the case of *burned/burnt*, the first, more regular one appears to be preferred in my data, with 5 instances by three different participants, while the irregular *burnt* counts only twice. By the same token can be regarded *brang* (*I brang here around 75 kilograms of books*) which may have been coined by analogy with other irregular verbs such as *sing: sang :: bring : brang*. Another occurrence which could be interpreted in the same light is the pluralisation of *proof* as *proves*, where the plural form could either have been coined in a process of analogy following *leaf : leaves :: proof : proves*, or through a process of conversion from the verb form.

My data also includes a few occurrences by three different participants where the simple past form of the verb has been employed in combination with the negative *didn't*, both with regular and irregular verbs, such as *I didn't received/phoned/mentioned, I didn't forgot/wrote/saw*; these exemplifications could also be in a way and tentatively regarded as instances of regularization processes in the language.

5.1.5. Non-marking of –s plural in nouns

Non marking of *–s* plural in nouns can also be attributed to processes of redundancy reduction and economy of expression. In ELF contexts (Björkman 2009: 231; 2008a: 38; 2008b: 111) speakers seem to mark the plural meaning in the numeral, adverb or determiner preceding the noun, leaving the latter without inflecting it by the standard *–s* plural morpheme. Together with other features, as we have seen, the de-pluralization of nouns is not unique to ELF: in several New Englishes and creole varieties nouns are indeed not marked for the plural (Crystal 2003: 347; Platt et al. 1984: 47-49), as well as in British vernaculars (Kirkpatrick 2011: 217).

[98] Interestingly, the form *stealed* is also listed in the Urban Dictionary http://www.urbandictionary.com/define.php?term=stealed (accessed 15 November 2013).

Although in some cases the plural morpheme may have been omitted to avoid difficult consonant clusters, such de-pluralization processes can be related to functional processes of exploitation of redundancy and economy of expression since the notion of plurality is already contained in the preceding numeral, adverb or determiner.

My data includes frequent such instances produced by different participants; the following patterns can be hypothesized, according to the determiners preceding the noun[99]:

a) numeral
6 message on my cell phone; *in England for 8 month*; *I did two exam*; *I have three piercing*; *there were two support band*; *six book already read this week*; *at least thirty year older*;

b) a determiner or an expression indicating quantity
loads of/tons of drawing; a couple of cardboard box; *various time*; *how many time I have to tell you*; *how many time a day*; *more scene with A.*; *hope for many many tender scene*;

c) some
some few day; *some professor are busy*; *some friend of mine*; *for some universal rule*; *some interesting item*; *some extra scene*; *some parts were good, some part were bad [...] some important detail*;

d) a demonstrative pronoun in the plural
share those passion; *those Christmas drawing*; *these fundamentalist pull*;

e) one of
one of the guy; *one of my favourite writer*; *one of my dearest friend*; *one of her favorite hobby*; *one of my priority*; *one of the worst part*; *one of my favourite song ever*; *one of my favourite love song*; *how one of my three story will begin*;

f) all
love all kind of animals; *with all genre of books*; *I love slow song.*

This tendency does not appear to hinder effective communication, and – similarly to other ELF variations – can be associated to a "lack of accuracy" (Mauranen 2010a: 18) related to the fact that in ELF effective communication is given priority over grammatical accuracy. Indeed, even though the

[99] Other instances of non-plural marking in nouns in the data include: *BSG and SG-1 are probably my favourite show ever; the left-wing newspaper are.*

plural *–s* morpheme is not provided, in all the above categories the plural-related meaning can be easily inferred from the determiners accompanying the noun.

5.1.6. Interchangeable use of who/which

The principle of economy of expression may be recognizable also in the interchangeability of the relative pronouns *who* and *which*, which appear to be merging in use (Jenkins 2011b). This area is widely present in the VOICE corpus (Seidlhofer 2011: 107; cf. also Hülmbauer 2010: 81). My findings include several examples by five different participants where *which* is used rather than *who*, as in: *journalists and politicians which*; *my ex-classmates (which took this photo)*; *feel so bad for all those people which have lost their family*; *falling in love with someone which is leaving*; *the dumbass which collided with us is ok*; *Christmas with my two cousins, which are 8 and 2 years old*; *A., G. & M. P. WHICH DOESN'T HAVE LJ* .

In all these exemplifications the use of *which* has been extended to include a function normally assigned to *who*, that is, reference to human subjects; such simplification in use, while maintaining the function assigned to the relative pronouns, can be seen in terms of redundancy reduction and simplification (Seidlhofer 2011: 108).

5.1.7. Invariable tags

A further instantiation of regularization and economy of expression can be seen in the tendency to employ in ELF settings one single question tag. Tags are considered a type of yes-no questions (Quirk et al. 1985: 810) with the function to "appeal to the addressee for agreement" (Biber et al. 1999: 139), to express a comment or for confirmation (Biber et al. 1999: 208-9); in Standard ENL, they agree with the verb of the main clause and are mirror-like to it in that the verb changes from positive to negative or viceversa (Crystal 2003: 299, 362).

In New Englishes *is it/isn't it* is often employed as an invariant tag (Crystal 2003: 299, 356, 360; Platt et al. 1984: 128), and attested in several varieties such as West and East African Englishes as *isn't it* (Trudgill and Hannah 2008: 131; Melchers and Shaw 2003: 133), as well as in South Asian Englishes, or as *is it?, or not?* in Indian, Malaysian and Singaporean English (Crystal 2000; Melchers and Shaw 2003: 133; Schneider 2011: 205, 163).

A single question tag is also found in ENL varieties such as Welsh, South African, and Canadian English (Crystal 2000; Schneider 2011: 205; Trudgill and Hannah 2008: 38), or as the invariable *innit/ain't*, particularly among younger speakers (Svartvik and Leech 2006: 237; Biber et al. 1999: 210).

Unsurprisingly, therefore, the use of an invariable tag appears to be an emerging trait in ELF contexts, too: as Seidlhofer remarks, the complexity of tags appears "disproportionate to their relatively simple communicative function" (2011: 161). The use of invariable tags in ELF communication can be seen as part of reduction strategies since meaning is conveyed through the use of forms which are "simpler, and probably even more explicit [and] immediate", "meeting the 'principle of clarity' and the 'principle of economy' at the same time (Hülmbauer 2009: 336). Furthermore, as Hülmbauer continues (2009: 337), in terms of cross-lingual multicompetence, these forms could also be not only easier to produce, but also to be interpreted by ELF interactants, who may not have in their L1(s) structures similar to tag formation in English, such as German (*nicht?*), Italian and Spanish (*no?*). Hülmbauer (2007: 21-22, 2009: 335; 2010: 85-86) indeed illustrates how *no?*, *or?*, *yes?* and *aren't* are successfully employed in her data, with only three instances of 'correctly' concorded tags.

Tag questions are highly typical of interactive casual speech (Svartvik and Leech 2006: 204), and some examples are significantly present in my data, testifying to the interactive nature of posts and comments in blogs; besides instances of *no?* in five entries in Italian, one in Spanish, and two in English (*are you following xx on Twitter? No?; you're curious, I know. No*), *isn't* is employed as a one-purpose tag by five different participants, as in *You draw your own icons isn't? °3°*; *it isn't fair that we have to wait two weeks to know it, isn't it?*.

All the above-illustrated occurrences appear in line with other findings in ELF contexts, and can be regarded as having been created – either consciously or unconsciously – to respond to language change-related functional motivations, where redundancy in the language has been exploited to functional economy of expression. Participants in virtual communicative settings – as the blogs in my corpus are – display in their use of English as a lingua franca the same functional motives that emerge as regular tendencies in other ELF contexts; this can reasonably be related both to the spoken-like interactive characteristics of the medium, as well as to the internationally oriented communicative contexts which characterize the data setting, making them proper ELF contexts.

5.1.8. Zero derivation

Moving towards the lexical level, change of word class by conversion/zero derivation can also be associated to processes of economy of expression. Conversion can be defined as the use of a form from one word class to another "without any concomitant change of form" (Bauer 1983: 227). Zero derivation is a highly productive word-formation process in English, for which there do not seem to be particular morphological constraints as to linguistic items that can undergo this lexical process (Bauer 1983: 226). Conversion takes place principally from noun to verb and viceversa, as well as from adjective to verb (Bauer 1983: 229; Hickey 2006: 159-161; Szymanek 2005: 433), though linguistic items from all word classes – prepositions, adverbs, conjunctions, interjections and affixes included – can in principle be converted (Bauer 1983: 230), and even verbal, prepositional and adverbial phrases can be converted into nouns or adjectives (Hickey 2006: 160). Platt et al. (1984: 99-100) report several instances of grammatical shift in New Englishes, for instance from prepositions (*to under*, *to be aftering something*), nouns (*to friend*, *to barb*) and adjectives to verb (*to nake*), or from verb to noun (*steer*), which could be regarded as processes of change of word class by zero derivation. Being highly economic in word-formation, conversion can reasonably be expected to be part of economy of expression processes enacted by ELF users, too: for instance, function words have been found to be assigned meaning and semantic value, e.g. *I back in Korea next week* (e.g. Jenkins 2011b; Cogo and Dewey 2012: 92-94).

In my data we find several occurrences of novel words coined via zero derivation, employed by nine different participants, which can be said to respond to the functional motivation of economy in form. Findings can be grouped as follows:

a) nouns derived from adjectives
Videogames and electronic; for me and my fellow corregionals; underages; the creatures, non-humans, were portrayed; as always, these are a pile of awesome ; beyond the awesome; she would bring the awesome.

b) nouns derived from verbs
my only 'complain' (frequently found on LJ);

c) verbs derived from adjectives
an Italian website that collects fanfics and I wanted to public mine;

d) verbs derived from nouns
Spain suicides and France is burnt alive; hard to portrait such a believable relationship; I can fangirl about Tony's shower scene.

The most numerous category emerging from the data is that of de-adjectival nouns: in two instances the adjectival *electronic* and *graphic* have been preferred to the nouns *electronics* and *graphics*. In some cases, such as *underages* employed as a noun and *suicide* as a verb, the lexical items appear as acceptable in some online dictionaries, albeit indicated as rare; no instance was however retrieved in the *Corpus of Contemporary American English* (COCA henceforth) and in the BYU-BNC – *British National Corpus*. While all the aforementioned examples of conversion are found in single instances, *awesome* has been converted to a noun by three participants of different L1s. In the first example, *a pile of awesome* was coined by a commenter located in the USA; although no instances are retrievable in the BYU-BNC and COCA corpora, the latter includes one instance of 'a ton of awesome', onto which the expression may have been created by analogy. In the case of *beyond the awesome*, which was produced by a participant located in Spain, it may have been coined by analogy with 'beyond awesome', reported in the Urban Dictionary with the meaning of "achieving a level of greatness that is almost inconceivable"[100]. To be noticed that *awesome* is defined as an adjective also in the Urban Dictionary[101]. The last example related to this lexical item – *she would bring the awesome. And light, maybe?* – was produced by a blogger in a post related to *Stargate Atlantis* and referred to the effects that taking Elizabeth Weir on board the Destiny would have. As to *fangirl* employed as a verb, only the form *fangirling* is included in the Urban Dictionary[102], which otherwise lists *fangirl* as a noun.

In only one case the lexical formation has been flagged by inserting it in single quotation marks (*'complain'*): this may on the one hand be ascribed to linguistic awareness, that is, to signal that the formation is unconventionally used, but also to mitigate the term from a semantic point of view, i.e. to indicate it as a minor side-note rather than a proper complaint. In the case of the noun *portrait* used to perform a verbal function, we find one such

[100] http://www.urbandictionary.com/define.php?term=beyond%20awesome (accessed 15 November 2013).
[101] http://www.urbandictionary.com/define.php?term=awesome (accessed 15 November 2013).
[102] http://www.urbandictionary.com/define.php?term=fangirling (accessed 15 November 2013).

instance in the VOICE corpus. Finally, in graphic *tablet* and graphic *card* the adjective *graphic* has been employed rather than the noun *graphics*, which in ENL collocates with both nouns; in this case, a regularization process may also be detected in the preference for the adjectival form.

5.1.9. Extension in use of verbs with high general meaning

The extension in use of some verbs with a highly general semantic meaning, "especially *make*, but also *do*, *have*, *put*, *take*" (Hülmbauer 2010: 84-5) which appears to characterize ELF use, can be said to respond to the same functional motivation, that is assigning novel functions to existing lexical elements also in terms of new collocations. Erling and Bartlett (2006: 26) include in this area instances that can be interpreted as extensions and transfers of words from German to English, particularly for word pairs that have similar (though distinct) meaning in ENL such as *make/do, listen/hear, speak/talk, study/learn and borrow/lend*. Cogo and Dewey (2012: 95-96.) discuss the case of *make/do*, arguing that this appears as an area of instability and variability also in ENL, as shown by concordance exemplifications from the BNCB.

My data presents quite a few such instances by different participants, particularly as to *make*, as in *making it as a personal favour*, *make a walk in the snow*; *make a test* with reference to educational testing practice; *make* in place of *give*, such as *I decided to make myself a little present*; collocated with *experience* (e.g. *I think I've made the ultimate experience*, *in these weeks I made my first teaching experience*, *mostly because I've made bad experiences*. As to *give*, we find the expression *ask the doctor to give a look*, rather than *have/take a look*.

As previously mentioned, and particularly in the case of lexical innovations, these instantiations cannot always be ascribed to one single functional underlying motive: in many cases more processes are at work simultaneously. In the examples related to general verbs, for instance, influences from Italian can also be detected, as in Erling and Bartlett (2006: 26) for German, for most of the above collocations with *make*. The interweaving of several processes at once applies particularly to certain areas, and a case in point is certainly the use of prepositions, as well as of definite and indefinite articles, which will be discussed in the next sections.

5.2. Increased explicitness

Increased explicitness has also been hypothesized as one of the functional motivations underlying ELF communication. Overdoing explicitness can in fact reinforce clarity, and among the strategies that have been identified to this aim we find that of adding nouns and prepositions (Seidlhofer 2004: 220, 2007a: 145, 2011: 145-147; Cogo and Dewey 2012: 90-92), as well as analytic/double comparative and superlative forms (Björkman 2008b: 110, 112, 2009: 232).

My data includes a few exemplifications where nouns are added when they would not be used in ENL, most presumably to the functional aim of increasing clarity. Two such instances are connected to *colour*, which has been attested also in the VOICE Corpus (Hülmbauer (2010: 87-88; Seidlhofer 2004), and produced by two bloggers: *is all in* *<u>blue color</u>* *with a balcony; it's this* *<u>aqua color</u>* *with this dark fabric*. In one instance the noun *match* has been added to *semi-final*, which according to the *OALD8* is a noun itself (*tomorrow Italy will play the semi-final match of the Fifa world cup*).

When looking at analytic/double comparative/superlative forms, according to Biber et al. (1999: 522) some monosyllabic adjectives can "alternatively take phrasal marking as well as inflectional" (e.g. *fair*, *full*, *proud*, *rude*); the authors argue that a possible explanation for the first alternative is "that it makes the comparison more prominent". Within variation in the comparative choice for bisyllabic adjectives, Biber et al. (1999: 522) include *funny* and *happy*, among the ones which commonly take *-er*/*-est*, and among polysyllabic adjectives (where *wickedest* is to be considered an exception). As to ELF, Björkman (2008b: 110, 112, 2009: 232) has observed a tendency to analytic formations in comparatives and superlatives in her data, which can be ascribed to motives of increased explicitness. This tendency appears to a certain extent instantiated also in my findings with four occurrences by different participants where the comparative/superlative form has been realized respectively as *more funny*, *more happy*, *more smart* and *most wicked*.

5.2.1. Adding prepositions

A typical area of innovation in World Englishes involves the field of prepositions, which can follow verbs (*apologize for*), adjectives (*typical of*), or are part of fixed phrases (*in X's opinion*). A different use of prepositions appears a particularly salient feature in Indian English, either by omitting, adding or using a different preposition (Trudgill and Hannah 2008: 135), and is also attested in South Asian English (Melchers and Shaw 2003: 141, Crystal 2003: 360). L2 users might innovate in this domain by changing the canonical ENL preposition in any of these clusters or even by adding one to verbs that do not usually take prepositions (Mollin 2006: 138).

Prepositions have been shown to be employed not according to ENL norms in ELF data, too (Cogo and Dewey 2012: 52-61, 90-95; Seidlhofer 2004: 220, 2011: 145-147; Mauranen 2010a: 18; 2010b; Kirkpatrick 2011: 217 for Asean ELF). The practice of adding prepositions to increase clarity, or of omitting them following the principle of economy, is a common feature in Hülmbauer's data, too (2010: 87); Erling and Bartlett (2006: 25-26), besides, report a wider use of *to*.

As Cogo and Dewey point out, shifts in preposition use in ELF can be particularly telling: "[p]repositions represent an area of lexicogrammar that is inherently unstable, and therefore particularly open to widespread variation", especially when "a preposition has little or no semantic value, such as with 'dependent prepositions' where the selection of one preposition over another is entirely dependent on its collocation with a preceding lexical item" (2012: 52).

In my corpus data we find both redundant prepositions and patterns of shift in usage, particularly when they follow a verb. As to the first, noteworthy are the five instances where the preposition *to* is added to *ask*, by three different bloggers: *I could ask <u>to</u> Q. E. if she can help; I'll ask <u>to</u> my mother; I should have asked <u>to</u> my flatmate; do you ask <u>to</u> anyone; I am asking <u>to</u> myself.* As Seidlhofer (2011: 147) notes, in this case the preposition, which is similarly attested in the VOICE corpus, may be interpreted as having been inserted to specify that the question or request is addressed to a person.

We also find some cases where the preposition that would be required in Standard ENL has been omitted: in six occurrences by three participants such omission takes place with *wait* where *for* is not inserted (*I'll be waiting it; I'll wait some few days; I had to wait two hours; I wait you have a good birthday; I'll wait you; I usually wait the inspiration*) and in two with *listen* where *to* is left out (*listen those tracks again; listening really loud music*). Both cases occur also in the VOICE corpus, although with a relatively low frequency (5 for *wait* and 6 for *listen*), as well as in Cogo and Dewey (2012: 53). For the latter, the authors convincingly argue that in the case of *listen*, the omission of the preposition could be related also to the fact that in many "Latin derived languages, for example, equivalent verbs occur with no preposition before the object or complement" (Cogo and Dewey 2012: 53), which can be said to apply also to *wait* for French, Italian, and in some cases Spanish. In both instances the preposition may have been perceived as redundant, not least since the semantic meaning is already contained in the verb.

We also have one case in which *for* has been inserted with *need* – *I need for one of them* – which occurs 6 times with the same verb also in the VOICE corpus. In this case, the insertion may functionally have been carried out to semantically reinforce the verb.

Apart from the aforementioned exemplifications, which could be said to be motivated by increased explicitness, a more general shift in the use of prepositions which, as mentioned above, seems to characterize ELF use, can also be noticed in my data. In the case of *about*, which is taken into examination by Cogo and Dewey (2012: 58-61), we find in my data only three occurrences by two different participants where it substitutes *of* (*scared about*, *convinced about*), and once *with* (*at ease about*). In the case of *convinced about*, we find three similar instances in the VOICE corpus, and respectively 21 and 41 in the BYU-BNC and the COCA corpora; it can therefore be seen as a potential ongoing change concerning *about* collocating with this fixed expression; as to *scared about* and *at ease about*, no result was shown in VOICE, but 193 in the COCA and 12 in the BYU-BNC corpora, and 16 (COCA) and 2 (BYU-BNC) respectively.

Regarding *think*, my findings include one occurrence where the preposition has been omitted (*I'm unable to think an interesting plot*), and one where *on* rather than *of* or *about* is employed (*I was also thinking on getting*).

Findings include several other instantiations where prepositions have been employed differently; as to locative expressions, *in* appears to be employed in several cases in place of *to*: *go back in Milan*; *come back in Italy* (with 2 occurrences also in the VOICE Corpus); *a trip in Tokyo*; *go in Tokyo* (with 3 occurrences also in the VOICE corpus). Other shifts in use, always related to place expressions, can be observed in the following, all produced by different bloggers (with Italian as their L1): *I will study Japanese and Korean in Venice University*; *I like the idea of staying in the university* (20 occurrences in the VOICE corpus); *I decided to spend the days to the swimming pool*; *spend a few hours to IKEA*; *I went on holidays at Dublin*; *I have travelled along France*.

Variation also appears in time expressions, as for instance in *in a day like this*; *I get back late at Friday evening*; *In the end of January I went in Sardegna* (4 occurrences with *go/went in* in the VOICE corpus).

As attested in ELF literature, and as my findings show, that of prepositions appears indeed as a highly variable area, in ENL as in ELF, and thus possibly more open to language change processes, at times pointing to simplification (cf. Mauranen 2012: 124); the same can be said for articles, as we will see in the next section.

5.3. Several strategies at work: shift in use of definite and indefinite articles

Generally, in ENL the definite article is used to mark an element as definite or uniquely identifiable/ed by speaker and hearer "in the contextual or general knowledge" they share (Quirk et al. 1985: 265). In ENL, *the* may also be employed to signal the "logical' interpretation of certain words", i.e. "postdeterminers and adjectives whose meaning is inalienably associated with uniqueness" such as ordinals, general ordinals like *next*, *last*, or *same*, *only*, *sole*, as well as superlatives and adjectives (Quirk et al. 1985: 270). Semi-determiners such as *same* and *other*, *former* and *latter*, *last* and *next* may be employed with the definite article[103] (Biber et al. 1999: 280-283).

The indefinite article, on the other hand, is found in ENL when reference is not uniquely identifiable "in the shared knowledge of speaker and hearer" (Quirk et al 1985: 272); it can also be employed to refer to "any representative member of a class" (Quirk et al. 1985: 281).

With plural and uncountable nouns, in ENL we can either have zero article, or, at times, unstressed *some* (Quirk et al. 1985: 274). Zero article is used when reference is generic (Biber et al. 1999: 265), although in certain circumstances we may find it with definite meaning, e.g. when the complement/noun phrase name a "unique role or task" (Quirk et al. 1985: 276).

There appears to be great variability in article usage, both in ENL and in other world varieties such as West and East African (Trudgill and Hannah 2008: 130; Platt et al.1984: 53-59) and Asean Englishes (Platt et al. 1984: 53-59; Schneider 2011: 204; for an overview see Dröschel 2011: 167-169). The same has been observed in different sets of ELF data (Seidlhofer 2004: 220, 2011: 127; Cogo and Dewey 2012: 63-69; Dewey 2007a 339-342, 2009: 62-67; Björkman 2008a: 38-39, 2008b: 111-112, 2009: 232; Hülmbauer 2010:

[103] With singular noun phrases, when the definite article is used to refer to a class as represented by a typical specimen, it is often "formal or literary in tone" (Biber et al. 1999: 282). With plural noun phrases, the definite article is found with national nouns, or with an adjective head refers to a group of people (e.g. the rich); "in other cases, the + plural noun is not used for generic reference; however, when reference is made to a whole group of people collectively (e.g. the Romans) as a generalization, the definite article is employed" (Biber et al. 1999: 283).

82; Mauranen 2010a: 18; Erling and Bartlett 2006: 22-23; Kirkpatrick 2011: 217 for Asean ELF). According to Dewey (2009: 62-65), although the frequency of use of both definite and indefinite articles is similar in ELF and spoken ENL corpora, in English as a lingua franca articles are used in a different distribution (Dewey 2009: 63; cf. also Mauranen 2012: 125): they may be redundantly inserted, or omitted, when Standard ENL would require them, or "just chosen differently" (Mauranen 2010a: 18). As Cogo and Dewey point out for their corpora, "indefinite and definite articles tend to be no less significant in lingua franca spoken discourse than in ENL" (2012: 61).

In terms of redundancy, it has been observed that in ELF articles tend to be employed in patterns which differ from ENL usage, with a tendency to omit definite articles in the presence of ordinals (e.g. *first*, *second*, *third*), superlative adjectives (e.g. *best*, *worst*), or "expressions of singularity" such as *only*, *sole*, *same* (Dewey 2009: 65). In these cases, articles can be said to be "communicatively redundant" (Dewey 2007a: 341) as the notion of uniqueness is semantically contained in the previous stretch of discourse. A preference for zero article when in ENL its usage is idiomatic has also been observed (Dewey 2007a: 341; 2009: 63-65). Similar tendencies have been found by Björkman (2008a: 38-39, 2008b: 111-112, 2009: 232), where articles are either employed when they would be grammatically superfluous, or omitted.

5.3.1. The definite article

Findings from my data show several exemplifications of a shift in the use of articles as identified in ELF research. Omission of the definite article when it may be perceived communicatively redundant occurs in the following cases, by nine different participants:

a) with ordinals
second half of XV century ; difference between first and last photo; *first time I saw them;*

b) with expressions of singularity
none of series I like ended up with romantic; with same interests as mine; the A. fans protests made same effect; Same for The Edge!; same question posted; same goes for (8 instances, 2 different bloggers)*; was too shy to participate in same way; very sorry for your classmate, same happened to me years ago*

As these examples show, the zero article appears more frequently with *same* (cf. Cogo and Dewey 2012: 64) than with numerals. In the case of superlatives, in my data they are accompanied by a determiner – either the definite article or a possessive pronoun – apart from one single occurrence (*worst part is*) and from instances in meme posts where the titles are abbreviated, as in *Worst/Best habit?*; we also find one occurrence where a redundant *the* has been inserted (*I don't know* <u>*the*</u> *most of his roles*).

Omission of definite articles in my data can also be observed in my data with geographical references in the plural (Quirk et al. 1985: 296), such as *to/in US/USA* (9 instances by 3 different participants) and *to Netherlands* (1 instance); in one case the article has been omitted with a specific time reference (*after Christmas holidays*, cf. Quirk et al 1985: 292), and with nationalities (*Germans captured many Italians*).

As to definite article insertion, in ELF it appears to be employed to attach extra importance to a word in a stretch of discourse, thus enhancing its prominence (Dewey 2009: 65; 2007a: 340-342; Cogo and Dewey 2012: 98). Definite articles seem also widely used in generic references, with uncountable nouns (e.g. *the life*, *the child*, *the people*, Dewey 2009: 65) or nouns expressing abstract concepts, where ENL would favour zero article. Therefore, in ELF the use of the definite article is preferred when a word is deemed particularly significant, to convey its prominence and provide additional emphasis (cf. also Cogo and Dewey 2012: 98-101). Dröschel's (2011: 170-180) investigation too has shown that the definite article is often 'overused' with plural and collective nouns with a generic meaning (*the people, the society*), or with nouns related to institutions (*the school, the university*) and abstract nouns (*the identity, the death*) (Dröschel 2011: 172); the latter has also been observed in Erling and Bartlett (2006: 23, *It's the nature's way*). In general, however, Dröschel's findings show an "overall tendency towards the omission of both the definite and indefinite article" (2011: 171).

Findings from my corpus data reveal several instances where the definite article would be omitted in ENL, or a different determiner employed; in these cases the definite article has presumably been inserted to attach prominence to the following noun, thus giving extra importance to the referent, as in the following exemplifications, produced by seven different participants, for which some potential patterns can tentatively be identified:

a) <u>*the lunch*</u> *has been quite boring too; I think* <u>*the things*</u> *will go like you said; in October after* <u>*the graduation*</u>*; thank you for* <u>*the congratulations*</u> *^_^;* <u>*the*</u> *Lucca comic's day*;

b) *and sorry for <u>the English</u>; I study <u>the Ancient Greek</u> ;o;*

c) *I love <u>the licorice</u> XD and <u>the onion</u>; Wonderful, simply wonderful. [...] Thanks for <u>the hard work!</u>; to taste for the first time in my live <u>the sushi</u> and <u>the sashimi;</u> an event dedicated to <u>the manga</u> and <u>the anime</u>.*

In a) references are all to events related to the participants' personal experiences, which may have prompted the use of the definite article to signal their specificity and importance to the participants. In b), we find *the* together with languages – *Greek* and *English*, the latter extremely commonly used in LJ posts in combination with the definite article. In c) the definite article appears to have been employed to enhance the importance of the otherwise general referent. In two further instances (*<u>the earthquake</u> scares me a lot*; *I don't like <u>the advertisement</u> so much*), where in ENL a plural form would probably have been preferred, the singular count noun may have been used due to the prominence given to the referent as conveyed by the accompanying definite article.

As to abstract nouns, in ENL they "tend to be count or noncount according to whether they refer to unitary phenomena (such as events) on the one hand, or to states, qualities, activities, etc. on the other" (Quirk et al. 1985: 286). When they are used generically, abstract nouns tend not to be preceded by an article, either definite or indefinite, unless "the noun refers to a quality or other abstraction which is attributed to a person" or when the noun is pre-/post modified (Quirk et al. 1985: 287).

As outlined above, in ELF there appears to be a tendency for abstract nouns to be preceded by the definite article, of which my data includes the following examples, produced by five different participants, two of which located in the USA: *<u>the love</u> couldn't end* (C, USA)*; I talked about <u>the aestheticism</u>; <u>the over-enthusiasm</u>; Thanks for <u>the loveliness</u>!!* (C, USA; 'the + loveliness' frequently appears on LJ); *<u>the death</u> had been unexpected; a bit disappointed for <u>the Euphi's death</u>*.

Findings also include instances where definite articles are employed with plural and collective nouns with a generic meaning (*they should respect <u>the athletes</u>*; *I think that <u>the females</u> are underestimated*; *<u>the shooting stars</u> aren't stars after all*) and for nouns related to institutions (*the university, the school*). We also find some occurrences related to time references, which in ENL would take zero article (times of the day, days months and seasons, as well as festivals, cf. Quirk et al. 1985: 278), which is instead inserted as in *invited me for <u>the New Year's Eve</u>, perfect for <u>the christmas-time</u>* (C Ger). Other exemplifications of overuse of the definite article by different participants include *listening to the music under the shower*, as well as two instances where it has been inserted after *both*: *both the groups played ballads*; *much much love to the both of them*.

When articles refer to 'sporadic' definite reference, Quirk et al. (1985: 277) note that in some cases this use has "become so institutionalized that the article is not used", as the expressions have become part of idiomatic usage; instances are nouns as complement of *at*, *in* and *on* "in quasi-locative phrases" (Quirk et al. 1985: 277), such as *to be in town/hospital/school* when referring not to the place itself but to the functions associated to it. Possibly the instance in my data *I went to cinema* could be interpreted as an overgeneralization by analogy of such phrases.

As previously outlined, in ELF there also appears to be a tendency to omit the article when it is part of an idiomatic expression: indeed, articles and prepositions are often part of phraseological units "with highly conventionalised schemata" (Mauranen 2010b); in ELF settings, however, such structural elements may vary without affecting communication (Mauranen 2010b). In my data, exemplifications of such variations can be detected in the occurrence where the indefinite rather that definite article is employed (*I'm in a mood for*), as well as in instances (by four different bloggers) where the definite and indefinite articles are omitted: *I never had occasion to finish watching that movie; to play guitar / classic guitar and digital keyboard / if you like playing guitar; totally opposite of what they think*. Regarding the first example, it is worth noticing that a few lines before *I finally had the occasion to watch that movie* had been employed: indeed, in this as in other lexicogrammatical and syntactic areas, variation in ELF usage is found whereby 'standard' expressions often co-exist with other non-standard formations (e.g. Hülmbauer 2010: 61; Seidlhofer 2008: 33.4; Seidlhofer, Breieneder and Pitzl 2008: 24-26).

My findings show a variable usage also concerning (*the) last/(the) next*: the article appears to be widely employed in time references, when it would not be present in standard ENL, as in *I was planning to watch it since the last week*; *the last month I've got my lip pierced*; *the car accident I was involved into the last October*; the definite article tends however to be omitted when *next* is employed to specific reference as in the following exemplifications, produced by six different participants:

(1) *I'm looking forward to next episode; I hope to thank you all in next future; The exam went very well, but now I have to prepare for next one, sigh; last [rainbow] I saw [...] had only the first three colours; (meme) last book I finished was*

/ Ø book I'm reading now; Just one thing about last episode / Last episode was really good /Last episode rocked!; last I heard, she's started writing it tonight

Possibly, in these cases *next* and *last* may have been interpreted as semantically expressing uniqueness of reference, similarly to ordinals and *only, sole, same* in a) and b) above. In the last example, an instance of idiom modification can also be noticed: the ENL idiomatic expression *the last I heard* has been here employed without the definite article, which would instead be part of the Standard English expression. The same could be said for *ask for January book*, where the reference to the month could have been interpreted as sufficient in expressing uniqueness of reference.

5.3.2. Indefinite articles

In ENL the "indefinite article is strongly associated with the complement function in a clause, or more generally with noun phrases in a copular relationship", with "a descriptive role (similar to that of predicative adjectives) rather than a referring role" (Quirk et al. 1985: 273). Zero article may be used instead in the case when the complement/noun phrase refers to a unique role or task (Quirk et al. 1985: 276). The following instances from my data exemplify how the indefinite article in copular descriptive roles appears to be omitted, as in *I'm realist / I'm masochist; I'm agnostic / Catholic/ atheist; if Lippi had waited to become coach*, produced by four different bloggers.

Other instances of omission of the indefinite article can be seen in the following, by 4 participants (2 of which are the same as above): *we are going to leave for short trip to Spain; happy you <u>had wonderful vacation</u>; my sister gave me <u>as present</u>; I have <u>romantic feeling</u>; she's bound to <u>play strong, badass character</u>; it took me <u>one hour and half</u> to work it out.*

In the majority of cases there seems to be a tendency for the omission of the indefinite article, possibly since perceived as communicatively redundant, and only in a few cases do we find its insertion where it would not be employed in ENL (e.g. *despite her lack of <u>a</u> proper training*). Interestingly, my data also contains a few instances where *one* is used in place of the indefinite article (Platt et al.: 56): *You have made me <u>one</u> very happy fangirl!; tonight there had to be <u>a one</u> minute of silence in their memory; having dinner with <u>one</u> group of friends mid-evening – before meeting some other friends for dancing.* As Quirk et al. (1985: 273) point out, "*one* could be substituted as a slightly emphatic equivalent of *a*" in several contexts, with the corresponding meaning of *a single*; the use of *one* could thus be interpreted in the above instances as a way to attach extra-importance to the concept expressed by the noun; in one case *a* and *one* have even been employed together.

Finally, indefinite articles may be "just chosen differently" in ELF talk (Mauranen 2010a: 18), i.e. without taking into account phonological rules in relation to the noun that follows, as exemplified in my data by *an livejournal account, an horrible summer, a old, an helpless character, a hour or so, an happy new year, an year ago, an hard time.*

To sum up, the patterns of variation in article usage in my findings, as well as their functional motivations, appear on the whole in line with what has been so far hypothesized in ELF research. The tendency to omit definite articles when perceived as communicatively redundant since the semantic meaning of uniqueness is provided by other lexical elements, such as ordinals and expressions of singularity, appears to be confirmed, showing that specificity attached to the referent is "by no means lost" (Dewey and Jenkins 2010: 84), but rather expressed differently. Furthermore, in line with other studies, we also have instances of insertion of the definite article with abstract nouns, plural and collective nouns with generic meaning, and more generally to attach extra-importance to a stretch of discourse, as well as a different use in idiomatic and fixed expressions. As Dewey (2007a: 431) points out

> these emerging patterns involve a shift away from distinction between specific and generic reference. A more significant factor determining article selection involves the relative level of importance attached to a noun or noun phrase in a given stretch of discourse. […] This suggests that patterns of article use in ELF are more context dependent and meaning driven than they are in ENL.

This appears particularly relevant when articles are in some way connected to idiomatic usage, and can be seen as a further exemplification of the open-choice principle operated by ELF speakers in language use (Seidlhofer 2011: 128-132). A further observation is that, as in Cogo and Dewey (2012: 62), there appears to be in my findings a higher level of interspeaker variation in article usage: the exemplifications provided above were produced by an overall lower number of participants when compared to other variations illustrated in the previous sections (e.g. zero 3rd person *–s* marking, non-marking of plural in nouns), and in the areas that will be illustrated in the next sections.

As discussed, findings in my data appear in line with ELF research, and show that ELF users – in spoken as in online language use – exploit the redundancies in the language to different functional motivations, in many cases following processes of simplification and regularization that are not random, but part of such processes. What Seidlhofer (2011: 145) remarks concerning zero 3rd *–s* marking in ELF appears also applicable to other strategies as illustrated so far: such variations are "not to be dismissed as a haphazard 'error', but the use of a reductive strategy that follows what might be called the principle of appropriate communicative economy" which, she continues, operates in native as well as in non-native speaker usage, as amply illustrated by ELF research and recognizable in my findings, too. The virtual communicative context in which my data is set may also be seen as a further factor facilitating processes of economy: particularly when interaction takes place in shorter posts and comments – similarly to spoken interaction, attention may be placed more on the message content than on its linguistic 'accurate' form.

5.4. Lexical creativity in ELF: exploiting the virtual language

> Why, in principle, if you have an *uprising*, should you not have a *lifting*? And if we can have the nouns *sickness*, *weekly*, *turnover*, why not the nouns *wellness*, *handy*, *pullunder*? (Seidlhofer 2011: 109).

As in the exemplifications illustrated so far, linguistic innovations in ELF do not appear to be random phenomena, but to follow principles that can be ascribable to processes of regularization, redundancy reduction, economy of expression, and increased clarity. In other words, ELF innovations are not "a matter of arbitrarily replacing a St[andard]E[nglish] pattern with 'just anything'" (Seidlhofer 2011:108); rather, they can be seen as the exploitation of the linguistic resources that are potentially available in the "virtual language, that resource for meaning making immanent in the language which simply has not hitherto been encoded and so is not, so to speak, given official recognition" (Widdowson 1997: 138). The constitutive rules of the virtual language "allow for regulative exploitation that would generally be characterized negatively as 'deviant' or positively as 'creative'" (Seidlhofer 2011: 115; cf. also Seidlhofer and Widdowson 2009b: 98-99). The exploitation of the potentialities inherent in the underlying system – the virtual language – applies to all levels of encoding, from phonology to morphology, whereby new words that are formally possible according to phonotactic or morphological rules can be created and effectively used, though they may not be (yet) codified as ENL usage (Seidlhofer 2011: 115-116). These different realisations represent instantiations of language creativity in use, in that, by exploiting such potentialities, they bring about non-conventional(ized) language forms which are created not arbitrarily, or randomly, but exploiting the constitutive rules of language. Creativity leading to 'exceptional' forms takes place in ENL (e.g. Carter 2004) as in ELF: "a good deal of such non-conformist language is actually produced across the globe" (Seidlhofer and Widdowson 2009b: 101); rather than 'deficient' language output in its non-conformity to ENL since produced by non-native speakers, they ought to be looked at as possible realisations in their own right, and as language usage which is communicatively appropriate and effective (Seidlhofer and Widdowson 2009b). In Seidlhofer's words, "[w]hen people use ELF, they find ways of exploiting and exploring the meaning potential of the language as a communicative resource and realize (in both senses of the word) the significance of the forms they use, their relative functional usefulness. In other words, form and function can be clearly seen as interrelated" (2011: 96).

Lexical innovations constitute particularly striking evidence of how potentially possible words are formed not randomly but following attested word-formation processes. In this section I will take into examination exemplifications of 'unusual' lexical items as emerging from the data. After outlining affixation processes, occurrences will be provided to illustrate how regular and attested word-formation processes are employed to create novel lexical items looking into their functional motives, similarly to other linguistic innovations as the ones illustrated in the previous sections.

5.4.1. Lexical innovations – morphological (over)productivity and ELF

Word formation, together with borrowing, is one of the main ways through which new words are introduced into a language, compounding and affixation being its two most important processes (Schendl 2001: 25-26; Bauer [1988] 2003: 24). Amongst the different ways of creating new words, affixation is described as the most frequent and common (Schendl 2001: 25-26; Bauer [1988] 2003: 24).

Lexical innovation via affixation is the process whereby new words are coined by attaching affixes which add to the meaning of the word, according to regular word formation rules in a language; following the interpretative model of morpheme-based morphology, words are formed through the combination of concatenated linguistic elements – roots and affixes (Plag 2003: 179). According to word-based morphology, on the other hand, new lexical items are regarded as being coined in analogy with existing ones, creating sets of morphologically-related words which share important aspects of meaning (Plag 2003: 179-180). As Bauer explains, occasional complex forms may be coined by analogy, whereby "a new formation [is] clearly modelled on one already existing lexeme" (1983: 95-96). These novel lexical items, though in principle "not giving rise to a productive series", may however become productive (cf. also Clark 1994: 785).

Bauer (1983: 63), following Lyons (1977), distinguishes between 'productivity' and 'creativity' in word formation, defining the latter as "the native speaker's ability to extend the language system in a motivated but unpredictable (non-rule governed) way". Morphological creativity is extremely common in everyday talk: Carter (2004: 97-105) has shown that data from the CANCODE corpus testify to how new words are created using unconventional combinations of stems and affixes. The same concept is underlined in Clark (2004: 785): "speakers are creative. They draw on conventional words whenever these are available, but, when they are not, speakers coin words to carry the new meanings they wish to convey". Specifically mentioning native speakers, Bauer points out how, from a synchronic point of view, the "native speaker has the ability at any time to form a new word"; these new words may remain nonce formations, or become accepted and established in a language, "[y]et they are formed according to specifiable rules in exactly the same way as those formations which, quite by chance, later become established" (Bauer 1983: 64). These observations can be regarded as equally valid for native as well as non-native speakers, in that speakers as language users exploit existing word-formation processes to create novel words, either to fill a temporary, or a permanent, gap in the language (Clark 1994: 785), or by extending the meaning of 'existing' words (Clark 1994: 784). As Seidlhofer remarks, what can be observed in ELF is "the unfolding of familiar processes of language variation in language use, but extended in non-canonical, creative ways" (2011: 108).

The dichotomy between potential, or possible, words and 'actual' ones in terms of word formation is not a simple matter, given that the restrictions concerning the possibility of forming new complex words are "quite often unclear" and not easily determinable (Plag 2003: 45). Furthermore, word-formation rules "are often formulated in such a way that they prohibit formations that are nevertheless attested" (Plag 2003: 45). As Plag points out, a central issue in morphology is thus the differentiation between 'possible' and 'actual' words. A possible or potential word "can be defined as a word whose semantic, morphological or phonological structure is in accordance with the rules or regularities of the language" (Plag 2003: 46); it can therefore be potentially created following word formation rules and regularities, though not necessarily be an existing word, i.e. a word for which usage is attested. On the other hand, defining an 'actual' or existing word is not as straightforward: despite the fact that it is the "overlap between the vocabularies of the individual native [sic] speaker of a language [...] that makes it possible to speak of 'the vocabulary of the English language'", the concept of a word as existing is related also to "variation between individual speakers" and to the individual differences in their mental lexicon (Plag 2003: 47).

In ENL as in ELF, newly-coined (potential) words, as well as low-frequency lexical items, though not stored in the mental lexicon of speakers, can nevertheless be de-codified and understood in that they are coined according to regular word-formation rules (Plag 2003: 53-54; cf. also Pitzl 2012a: 37; Seidlhofer 2011: 103-105, 115-116), resulting in creative, i.e. non-conventional, formations, which are possible though not (yet) encoded in the language (Widdowson 1997: 138, 2003: 48-49, 173). As Pitzl argues, "creativity can also go beyond established norms, subvert existing 'laws' and stretch current conventions, and thereby flout expectations" (2012a: 34).

Thus, "the boundaries between already existent and new, between special vocabulary and so-called 'normal' words are not simple and clear-cut and may vary between different contexts and different constellations" (Pitzl et al. 2008: 39). Words may be coined to respond to the users' expressive and communicative needs in one specific context and moment, but may also be 'taken up' and 'appropriated' either by other participants in the communicative situation, or in other (future) contexts of use. Some of these words may also have already been employed at some point in the past by some other user(s), and have fallen into disuse, or coined and remained a nonce word but recorded in some way on the web, and be thus retrievable through a search engine. Moreover, in the age of the Internet "different uses and usages of English – as a lingua franca as well as a native, second or foreign language – increasingly merge and, in many cases, become indistinguishable if authorship is not explicitly acknowledged" (Pitzl et al. 2008: 39). This seems particularly true in the case of social network websites, and of blogs, where native and non-native use(r)s of the language not only merge, but often cannot be ascribed to a given linguaculture, since this kind of information is not always provided or retrievable. In a way, however, we could say that this aspect makes linguistic investigation of virtual communicative contexts even more interesting – as well as challenging – since processes of innovation and variation in language use can be observed in the making, even going beyond the distinction between whether words have been produced by a native or a non-native speaker, to rather look at processes of effective communication and (cooperative) interaction.

As Pitzl et al. point out, novel words or meanings may indeed have been created and employed "by others following the same natural route. In fact, it would be surprising if no one else followed this line and arrived at the same coinage" (2008: 40): language creativity processes, in ENL as in ELF, can be seen as part of natural language use and may subsequently lead to language change. Thus, looking at how words are created and used, together with other (ELF) elements such as the ones outlined in the previous sections, can provide instances of real language use as well as insights into the processes that underlie the creation and functional motivations of novel language items. Furthermore, since linguistic accuracy and adherence to native-speaker norms can be said to be secondary to intelligibility and communicative effectiveness in ELF, linguistic forms that deviate from ENL cannot simply be considered as errors; rather, they can be seen as successful if the intended meaning and underlying illocutionary act are communicatively effective, that is to say understood by the hearer/reader (Hülmbauer 2007: 10). In other words, the success of an ELF utterance cannot be evaluated according to its correspondence to native norms, but to what the participants in the interaction deem acceptable, and to whether meaning is successfully carried across and negotiated (Hülmbauer 2010: 70-78; cf. also Mauranen 2012).

Among the several innovations at different levels of the language, "processes of lexical innovation that result in words that are not attested in ENL" are among the most "perceptually noticeable" (Seidlhofer 2011: 101). As Mauranen points out, 'morphological overproductivity' "seems to ensue from the nature of morphology, which is highly prolific and held back by convention rather than rule" (2010a: 18). Use of over-productive non-standard morphology and regularisation processes by ELF users appear conventional and creative at the same time, by creating new words, by assigning novel functions to word formation processes (Mauranen 2010b), by ascribing words a new extended meaning, or by collocating them differently. Similarly to the regularization processes illustrated in the previous sections, this phenomenon is by no means confined to ELF: new words are continuously added to any natural language, and "the possibilities the language offers in principle are flexibly exploited when a new communicative need arises, whether or not this results in codified and accepted words/forms" (Seidlhofer 2011: 102).

As in idiomatic expressions, the open choice principle (Seidlhofer and Widdowson 2007, 2009a: 197-198) can indeed be seen at work at various and differentiated linguistic levels; word formation is a case in point, given that free and bound morphemes can be combined to create lexical items which can be 'unconventional' in ENL terms, but which are possible in principle (Seidlhofer 2011: 143). This viewpoint can be seen at work in ELF both in derivational and inflectional morphology, where "users of the language are applying the open choice principle beyond its conventional restrictions as a generally regulative strategy" (Seidlhofer 2011: 144), combining morphemes in such ways to give birth to novel words. As the (working) definition proposed by Pitzl highlights, linguistic creativity "refers to the creation of new (i.e. non-codified) linguistic forms and expressions in ongoing interaction/ discourse or the use of existing forms and expressions in a non-conventional way" (Pitzl 2012a: 37). It can thus involve both creations that are novel in form, and existing expressions employed to new meanings, and can be enacted at all linguistic levels of the language. Moreover, such creative linguistic realizations may result from applying regular rules in the system (which Pitzl defines as *Type-1 creativity*), thus being "conventional, rule-governed, and norm-dependent" (Pitzl 2012a: 37), but at the same time resulting in unconventional linguistic items (*Type-2 creativity*, Pitzl 2012a: 36-37).

Regularization and well-attested word-formation processes are indeed recognizable in most of the new 'unconventional' lexical items created by ELF users. In the VOICE corpus these novel word formations have been tagged as <pvc> (pronunciation variations and coinages) and defined as "[s]triking variations on the levels of phonology, morphology and lexis as well as invented words" (VOICE Project 2007: 4; cf. also Pitzl et al. 2008: 24-26); these words are considered lexical variations as their presence is not (yet) attested in reference dictionaries[104]. Seidlhofer for instance refers to the example of *–ate* verb suffixation as attested in the VOICE corpus, which is applied as a regularization process, or to other suffixation patterns applied to nouns (e.g. *increasement*, *forbiddenness*) or adjectives (e.g. *increasive*) which

[104] In the VOICE Project, the chosen point of reference to define whether a lexical item can be considered as established is constituted by the Oxford Advanced Learners' Dictionary 7th Edition (OALD7, cf. Pitzl, Breiteneder and Klimpfinger 2008). In this study the point of reference was the updated 8th edition Oxford Advanced Learners Dictionary 8th Edition (Seidlhofer 2011).

are coined and employed to similar functions (2011: 103-104). Either in the case where these 'innovative' forms may be employed to increase clarity, or to fill a lexical gap, they appear to have been coined not randomly but exploiting the potentialities of the virtual language, following regular and attested word-formation processes; among these we find analogy, whereby two words bear a proportional relation between them, as for instance *eye : eyewitness :: ear : earwitness* (Plag 2003: 37). "Thus when a speaker coins the verb *examinate*, we can discern an underlying analogy pattern, for example *communication*: *communicate* is like *examination*: *examinate*", and the same for other novel formations in other word classes (Seidlhofer 2011: 108).

To sum up, in ELF processes of language adaptation are particularly evident in the lexical area; not-(yet)-codified words, with a "novel use of morphemes" (Jenkins 2011a: 929), are indeed a common feature in ELF, and seem "to be communicatively effective", "not coined arbitrarily", but following "certain trends or processes" (Pitzl et al. 2008: 22). These language creativity strategies often give way to *approximations* (Mauranen 2012: 101-103) that generally "have recognizable features in common with an item that would meet conventional expectations" (Mauranen 2012: 102). They can also be ascribed to more general processes of language variation and change and serve functional motivations similar to the ones that underlie other variations, such as the ones outlined in the previous sections, i.e. increase clarity, economy of expression, regularization and filling gaps in the lexicon (Pitzl et al. 2008: 40).

5.4.2. Lexical innovations in the corpus data

Pitzl et al. (2008: 28, following Plag 2003) have identified the following broad categories in ELF word formation processes at the word level: suffixation/prefixation/multiple affixation, analogy, reanalysis, backformation, blends, addition/reduction, truncation and compounding; borrowing was also added, taking into account the fact that ELF represents "a multilingual environment and thus a site of language contact" (Pitzl et al. 2008: 28), and it will be taken into examination in Chapter 6. The corpus data was searched taking into account the above broad categories identified in Pitzl et al.'s study; the main focus in analysing occurrences has been set on examining the processes underlying such word-formation processes, as well as on the functional motivations that may trigger these 'unconventional' lexical innovations, as the following sections will illustrate.

5.4.2.1. Prefixation

Prefixes are "bound forms which attach initially to bases" (Adams 2001: 41); differently from suffixes, they are "class-maintaining" (Bauer 1983: 217) and alter or qualify the meaning of the word they are attached to. Like suffixes, they can combine with verbs, nouns or adjectives[105]. In my data, particularly productive prefixes in novel word formations are *re-*, *non-* and *un-*; the first two appear as commonly employed also in Pitzl et al. (2008: 32).

In ENL the prefix *re-* has been shown to be more commonly attached to verbs than to nouns (Bauer 1983: 219; Adams 2001: 44), both with native and foreign-based verbs, generally meaning 'again' (Adams 2001: 44). In my data it can be related to the 'economy of expression' functional motive: it is mostly employed with verbs, with only one instance in which it is attached to a noun, *re-enactment* (which counts in its non hyphenated form 3 instances in the BYU-BNC and 273 in the COCA corpora). The item, *reread* (3) is tagged as <pvc> in the VOICE corpus (cf. also Pitzl et al. 2008: 32), and counts 32 instances in the BYU-BNC and 669 in the COCA corpora. In the majority of cases words prefixated with *re-* are used in the data with hyphenation (e.g. *re-upload*[106], *re-installing*), though in three instances both the hyphenated and the non-hyphenated version can be found (*re-read/reread*; *re-watch/rewatch; re-post/repost*, the latter two not being present in the BYU-BNC and COCA corpora). Interestingly, it can be noticed that many of these words are related to the technicalities of the setting. In three cases, while the non-hyphenated word is listed in the *OALD 8* and frequent in the COCA and, though to a lesser extent, in the BYU-BNC corpora, in my data only the hyphenated form is found (*re-arrange*; *re-organize*; *re-doing*). The preference for the hyphenated version[107] in words created by employing this prefix could be interpreted as revealing of a certain level of consciousness in

[105] According to Biber et al. (1999: 400), the most common derivational affixes attached to verbs in ENL are the following (in order of frequency): *re-*, *dis-*, *over-*, *un-*, *mis-*, *out-*; other less common verbal derivational affixes include: *be-*, *co-*, *de-*, *fore-*, *inter-*, *pre-*, *sub-*, *trans-*, *under-*. When looking at nouns, derivational prefixes are less productive than suffixes (Biber et al. 1999: 323), with the Latinate co- and sub- as the most productive ones (Biber et al. 1999: 324). Biber et al. (1999: 324) point out that, while most suffixes are of Romance or Germanic origin, many prefixes are of Greek origin; however, some among the latter, such as *hyper-*, *mono-* and *poly-*, have been extensively exploited to create words in scientific domains (cf. also Adams 2001: 41).

[106] Not present in the BYU-BNC and COCA corpora.

[107] Incidentally, this is obviously observable in written, but not spoken, data.

word formation, by leaving, so to say, the process leading to the creation of a new lexical item overtly recognizable.

As to the *non-* prefix, in ENL it may be attached either to suffixed or non-suffixed bases (Adams 2001: 47). When attached to adjectives, the prefix *–non* carries a "not-X meaning" (Plag 2003: 100); it is less frequent with nouns (Adams 2001: 49), where it takes on the meaning of "'absence of X' or 'not having the character of X'" (Plag 2003: 101), or bearing a character of unconventionality (Adams 2001: 50). When compared to *un-*, which expresses an evaluative aspect, in ENL *non-* is connected to the negation of the descriptive aspect of the stem (Adams 2001: 48, quoting Zimmer 1964).

Among prefixes realising functions of economy of expression, together with *re-*, *non-* appears common in the VOICE corpus (Pitzl et al. 2008: 32), where we find overall 28 adjectival <pvcs>, such as *non-graduate*, *non-branded*, *non-formal*, *non-christian*, *non-european*; 20 nouns among which *non-production*, *non-meeting*, *non-issue*, *non-belgians*, and one verb (*non-degenerate*).

Also in my data most word formations with this prefix are adjectival (6 occurrences), while three involve a noun (*non-books; non-Japan*; *non-jrock*, the latter listed in the Urban Dictionary). Among the adjectives, *non-existant* (7 instances) can be considered as a spelling deviation form the attested form *non-existen*t (the latter employed twice), while *non-spoken* can be regarded as a novel word created via prefixation. At times the semantic role of *non-* is in my data realized as *not-* or *no-* as in *not-compatible*, *not-Italian* or *no-infected. Non-spoken* in particular, despite the attested ENL form, may have been coined in analogy with other words formed with the same prefix and perceived either as more transparent than the existing *unspoken* form, or having being employed to highlight the negation of the stem. The following extract is a case in point:

(2) B *The book ends with Marianna on the verge of leaving Sicily and its oppressive society, their total aversion to any change, be it political or social, and their <u>non-spoken</u> rules – possibly forever. I cheered for her. Sicily wasn't known for her progressive thinking back then, so a woman openly challenging the society like that must've been truly mad, or made of steel.*

The passage is related to a novel by the Italian writer Dacia Maraini *La lunga vita di Marianna Ucria*, which, as the blogger explains, deals with a mute and deaf girl, Marianna, and is set in XVIII century Sicily, where the social rules are described with the adjective *non-spoken* possibly to enhance its negative meaning.

Another interesting instance, produced by two different participants, is represented by *non-aligned*; although attested as an 'existing word', it has been flagged since in this case it is used in relation to religion rather than with reference to the support provided or received by powerful countries (*OALD8*).

In these examples emphasis appears "placed on the semantic level": both *non-* and *re-* provide "a general, but straightforward and economical, way of expressing the idea of reversal and repetition respectively" (Pitzl et al. 2008: 32), and can thus be ascribed to an economy of expression functional use.

Frequent instances in the data are also those realized through the prefix *un-*, which can be attached to verbs, and at times to nouns, with a reversative or privative meaning (Plag 2003: 101). Although in ENL *un-* with adjectives has restrictions in use and meaning (Bauer 1983: 87-88; Adams 2001: 46-47), it is productive with "derived adjective bases of all kinds, especially verbal bases suffixed by *–able*, *-ing*, *-ed*, and nominal bases in *–ed*" (Adams 2001: 47).

In terms of language change and variation, what Adams points out is worth of note: while in early Modern English pairings of adjectives in both *in-* and *un-* were common, "whether a base now has *in-* or *un-* seems unpredictable", and in some cases an *un-* adjective is acceptable even when its *in-* synonym exists, in others it is not (Adams 2001: 47). Furthermore, Bauer notes that for *in-*, "[t]he negative meaning has lost out to *un-* (e.g. an earlier *impopular* which has now been replaced by *unpopular*)" (1983: 219). Indeed, in ENL *in-* is "exclusively found with Latinate adjectives" (Plag 2003: 100; cf. also Adams 2001: 46), and does not usually occur in new formations (Plag 2003: 100). Negative prefixation with *un-*, even when a word *in-* may already be present in the language, appears thus an area which may be particularly open to novel formations: as Pitzl et al. (2008: 42) point out, the prefix *un-* is probably perceived as less ambiguous in carrying a negative meaning when compared to *in-*, thus enhancing clarity of proposition.

As to my data, instances of words created via the prefix *un-* include *uneffective*, *unsensitive* and *umpractical/unpractical*, the latter occurring also in the VOICE corpus. In these cases, in line with Pitzl et al.'s findings, a novel form has been used despite the fact that a similar one with the *in-* prefix exists in ENL. Other instances of words in my findings which are not listed in the *OALD8* are *unreachable*, *unfound*, *unoriginal*, which are however attested in the BYU-BNC COCA corpora with respectively 21/264, 23/2 and 20/100 occurrences; we find only one instance with the prefix *in-*, *inluckily*.

The reversative/privative prefix *de-* attaches to verbs and nouns (Plag 2003: 99), and is often "in competition with *–dis* and *–un*" (Bauer 1983:

218). In my data we find two instances of words created with this prefix, *de-nuking* and *de-friend(ing)*, which are both verbal and used by two different bloggers. Both lexical items can be said to fill a gap in the lexicon; the second appears commonly employed in social networks, together with *unfriend*, to define the act of removing a friend, and is listed in the Urban Dictionary; in the context of blogs it can be seen as part of in-group jargon at a general level in relation to Web 2.0 practices.

The same function could be ascribed to prefixes such as *super-* and *mega-*, which are commonly employed in young people's language to give additional emphasis to words. *Super-*, together with *hyper-*, *semi*, *sub-* and *ultra-*, combines "with a wide range of gradable adjectives and participial adjective bases to form adjectives current in everyday and specialized registers (Adams 2001: 48) and are seen as productive in English and other European languages (Hickey 2006: 2 as to *mega-*, *hyper-* and *giga-*). In VOICE *super* counts four <pvc> instances, one attached to an adjective (*supernational*) and two to a noun (*supercompact(s); supernarrator*). In my data it appears in combination with a wide variety of adjectives (*sweet*, *bright*, *awesome*, *happy*, *interesting*, *cute*, *busy*, *fantabulous*, *pretty*, *tall*, *lazy*, *late, fantastic, cool, massive*) and is found once with a noun (*super delivery*). It is also largely found in posts and comments in Italian (*super-mega-iper convinta* [convinced], *super mega iper efficace* [effective]; *super scrittona* [someone who writes a lot]; *super eccitata* [excited]; *super nervosa* [nervous]; *super presa* [busy], *superaffaticamento* [fatigue], *la realizzazione è super* [the result is]), together with *mega-* – the latter attached to *abbraccio* [hug]; *allenamento* [training]; *trucco* [trick]; *piano* [plan]; *poster; mega iper efficace* [effective]; *ti faccio un mega in bocca al lupo* [good luck], and may be seen as part of youth language.

Hyper- and *ultra-*, on the other hand, have only one occurrence each in my data: the first (3 instances in VOICE) is the hyphenated *hyper-aggressive*, and the second *ultra-violent* (appearing with 17 instances in the COCA and with 1 in the BYU-BNC corpora). *Hyper-*, together with other affixes such as *anti-*, *meta-*, *-cracy* or *–cide* (Plag 2003: 155-158), are classified as 'neoclassical elements' of Greek or Latin origin and often considered as forming compounds rather than part of affixation processes. However, following Pitzl et al. (2008: 33), many are listed in the *OALD8* as affixes, and we have thus taken them into consideration as such.

The prefix *anti-* can be attached to nouns, verbs and adjectives to carry meaning of 'against, opposing', or to nouns meaning 'the opposite/not having the characteristics of an X' (Plag 2003: 99). In my data we find one instance without hyphenation (*anti anxiety pills*), and two with hyphenation: *anti-possession tattoo*, *anti-Italianism*; the latter may have been modelled by analogy with *anti-Americanism*, also present in the data and produced by one blogger in the same contextual communicative situation; to be noticed that *Italianism* is present once and tagged as <pvc> in the VOICE corpus. In this group of affixes we also find in the data one instance with *meta-* (*fannish meta adaption*), while it is quite common in VOICE in forming <pvc>s (e.g. *metatrend*, *metaperspective*, *metaorganization*, *metalevel*, *metacapacity*, *metaeuropean*, *metaevaluation*). Both *anti-* and *meta-* can be said to be employed to the functional reasons of economy of expression, and the same applies to words created with *over-*, *pre-* and *post-* (Pitzl et al. 2008: 32-33).

Over- can attach either to verbs, adjectives or nouns (Adams 2001: 74), in my corpus data it is employed to form *over-enthusiasm*. As to *pre-*, which in ENL "is productive with both native and foreign bases" (Adams 2001: 44), it appears in the novel formation *preorder*, and in two other words, of which one is listed in the Urban Dictionary (*prebuscent*), while the other can be considered as part of specialized technical musical and video terminology (*prescoring technique*); following Pitzl et al. (2008: 29), these specialized words have also been taken into account, particularly as they appear to be related to the fields of interests of the bloggers, e.g. videos and (fan)fiction. Apart from *post-abduction*, still to technical terminology belong *post-regeneration ep* (Doctor Who), and *post-Entrada* (Fringe fiction), both produced by the same blogger. In the case of *post-raw*, as the following extract illustrates, it appears to have been employed to economically express a nuance in meaning, which could probably be paraphrased as "just after having watched the episode/video":

(3) B *Oh well, "review" is probably too much of a word: I usually just post my thoughts post-raw vision trying to make it sound coherent. Unfortunately, I'm a biased fangirl all the same.*

Finally, one further exemplification of an unconventional prefixed word which has been flagged, presumably to signal its novelty can be seen in the following extract:

(4) B *When activated, the device generated a "sub-audible frequency" which combined with chemical contaminants seeded into the water supply by Sloane.*

To recap, quite a wide range of prefixes are employed in my data to several functions, from economy of expression, to increased clarity, as well as to convey specific nuances in meaning, in line with other ELF findings. Novel lexical items, although not (yet) attested in ENL, have been formed via regular and attested word-formation rules and seem to effectively convey meaning. Noticeably, several among these occurrences are either listed in the Urban Dictionary and thus part of (youth) slang, or related to online Web 2.0 practices and technical affordances of the medium. The same regular word-formation processes apply also to suffixation, as we will discuss in the next section.

5.4.2.2. Suffixation

Suffixes are generally categorized according to the syntactic category the derived word belongs to (Plag 2003: 86; categorization in Adams 2001); we can thus have suffixes deriving nouns (e.g. *–ion*), adjectives (e.g. *–al*) or verbs (e.g. *–ate*). Nominal suffixes "are often employed to derive abstract nouns from verbs, adjectives and nouns […] to denote actions, results of actions or other related concepts" (Plag 2003: 86). Derivational nominal prefixes are less productive than suffixes (Biber et al. 1999: 323); *–tion* appears the most productive one, followed by *–ity*, *-er*, *-ness*, *-ism* and *–ment*, with *–ship* and *–age* as less productive.

The Latinate suffix *–ion*, and its allomorph *–tion* (Plag 2003: 90), denote "events or results of processes" (Plag 2003: 90-91). In my data we have one instance of a word coined with this suffix, as well as one existing word which has been employed in a different context to a novel collocation; both appear to have been formed drawing on the L1 of the bloggers, either in meaning or form. The first is *pression*, in *One minute of tranquillity. One minute without pression. One minute when things go smoothly*, where *pression* has been coined and used to express *pressure*. The second word, *apparition*, has been used in the expression "*in order of apparition*" to list a series of songs among the blogger's favourite, where ENL would rather have "in order of *appearance*". In both cases the words appear to have been respectively employed after the Italian "*pressione*" and "*in ordine di apparizione*": indeed, ELF users commonly draw on their bi- or multilingual repertoires in communicative processes, as will be more extensively illustrated in Chapter 6. In this specific case, whether the coinages are communicatively effective in interactional terms cannot be detected for sure, as in the first instance the post is part of a meme, and the novel word remains quite marginal to the content, not being mentioned in the following comments; in the second case, there are no comments to the post. Nevertheless, the word-formation strategy employed to coin the two items – as well as other exemplifications – appears legitimate in that they can be said to be possible 'potential' words.

As to the productive *–ation*, in ENL many words formed with this suffix "show borrowing from Romance rather than English word-formation" (Bauer 1983: 221). In my data we find two occurrences, *profanation* (33 occurrences in the COCA and 4 in the BYU-BNC corpora) and *humanization* (1 in the COCA and 4 in the BYU-BNC), which may have been respectively created by analogy with the verbs *to profane* and *to humanize*. As to the first, to be noticed that the *OALD8* includes *dehumanization* as a word: *humanization* could thus be also interpreted as an instance of backformation, where words are "analogically derived by deleting a suffix (or supposed suffix)" (Plag 2003: 37; cf. also Algeo 1998: 73). Indeed, as Pitzl et al. argue, assigning a novel word to a word-formation process rather than to another may not always be straightforward, as different interpretations may be possible for the same word (2008: 29), as the example in point illustrates.

The suffix *–er*, and its morphological variant *–or*, can denote performers of actions, instrument nouns or entities associated with an activity (Plag 2003: 89). In the instances retrievable in my data it appears to be employed in all cases to refer to performers of actions, in analogy with similar words from verbs: *granter of indulgences*; *chatterer*; *despiser*, as well as *iconner* (the latter listed in the Urban Dictionary). Particularly interesting appears *plagiarer*: while the previous instances can be said to fill a lexical gap, in this case a "parallel" word, *plagiarist*, is listed in the *OALD8*.

(5) C (Austr) *BUT ARGH. I HATE <u>PLAGIARERS</u>! HAHA. [...] & I spelt <u>plagiarisers</u> wrong. hah*
B *Thank you dear! [...] <u>(don't worry, it can happen to spell a word wrong :D I understood all the same)</u>*

It can be noticed here that the commenter first employs a novel word, *plagiarers*, which may have been formed by deriving it from the noun *plagiarism* rather than adding *–ist* to the (perceived) root *plagiar-*. Immediately afterwards, this novel creation is flagged in the comment, where a new word, *plagiarisers*, is provided instead: this time the word appears to be created from the verb *plagiarise*, to which the suffix *–er* has been added to indicate the performer of the action; both word-formation strategies appear plausible in terms of the process utilized. The blogger's comment which follows is not only reassuring as to the 'mistake' the commenter (who, incidentally, is located in Australia) has signalled in her production; equally importantly, the participant overtly manifests his/her comprehension of the (intended) meaning. This interactive duet nicely exemplifies not only how inaccuracy of form in ELF is secondary to effective communication, but also the supportive and cooperative attitude of ELF users towards their 'inaccuracies' in language use. It is worth noticing also that, though *–ist* is defined as a productive suffix in ENL, "by far the most employed to create lexical items referring to individuals (Adams 2001: 53), we do not find any instances in the data, which, as illustrated above, are albeit present for *–er*. One tentative interpretation could be the fact that *–er* appears productive to derive agent nouns in frequent lexical items such as *teacher*, *singer*, or *footballer*, which are generally commonly presented in teaching syllabuses in early stages of learning; this suffix is thus likely to have become well fixed in memory and therefore exploitable to create lexical items when needed.

One further example of word-formation with *–or* in the data is *procrastinator*, which is employed by two different bloggers and appears a deverbal derivation, coined by analogy with the formation of the noun *procrastination*.

To remain in the area of nominal suffixes, *-ness* is defined as highly productive in current English (Bauer 1983: 222; Plag 2003: 92); it is not particularly restrictive as it can "attach to practically any adjective", as well as nouns and phrases (Plag 2003: 92). In the case of this nominal suffix, a further element to be taken into consideration in its high productivity is the hypothesis that, when compared to *–ity* formations, which are said to be memorized as part of the existing lexicon,

> *-ness* forms are built by rule as they are needed […]. If speakers create *–ness* words on the fly, there is nothing to prevent them from using novel forms. […] It is also reasonable to expect a greater variety in the *–ness* words than in the *–ity* words, because speakers chose the latter form from a defined stored set, but make the former up as they need them (Anshen and Aronoff 1988: 645, as cited in Aronoff and Fudermann 2005: 224).

The suffix *-ness* is indeed widely employed in the data, with overall 16 occurrences of novel formations, most of which appear to have been created and used to "fill a permanent gap in the lexicon" (Pitzl et al. 2008: 31, quoting Clark 1994), and in line with similar occurrences, such as *forbiddennes* in Pitzl et al.'s data (2008: 31). These novel derivative words, which have been produced by bloggers and commenters of different L1s, include in my data *amazingness*, *idiotness*, *gorgeousness*, *lovesickness, wondrous-*

ness, *retardedness*, *crappiness* and *adorableness*, all created by different participants; in three cases the lexical items are defined in the Urban dictionary: *kinkiness* (spelt as *kynkyness*), *aw(e)someness* and *bamfness*. The noun *luckyness*, on the other hand, may be said to have been created by analogy from the adjective *lucky* and employed in place of the corresponding *luck* holding parallel meaning:

(6) B *In the first season he gets a little of luckyness when he is left with his dead grandmother's big house, and starts living there, with his grandmother's helper.*

In one case, as the following example illustrates, the novel word formation has been flagged, testifying once again to the fact that the process of word coinage, albeit taking place via regular word-formation processes, is at times consciously perceived as 'unusual' and thus signalled to the interlocutors by flagging it:

(7) C (no data) ... *look at you and your artistic-ness (that is so not a word, i'm aware XD)*

Flagging, as Firth points out, "appears to occur when the speaker has some cognizance of the unidiomatic 'marked' quality of their speech production" (2009b: 140), thus signalling to the interlocutor(s) "the possibility that their own English language usage *may* be opaque in terms of meaning or intelligibility, and *may* be influenced by the speaker's first, second (etc.) languages" (Firth 2009b: 141, emphasis in original). As previously mentioned for other instances, it is worth noticing that the word is here hyphenated, overtly showing the underlying process which has led to the novel formation, that is then reinforced by the meta-comment in brackets.

Another interesting case in point is *onioness* (Extract 8); the word has been created in a reply to a meme by a commenter in order to describe 'a special talent' the blogger has, and followed by the positive emoticon *^v^* (happy). The word is somehow further clarified in the following lines (*everytime I see an onion I think of you*), and is then jokingly taken up by the blogger further down in the exchange with a direct reference to the word *onion* followed by the emoticon *OwO*, signalling positive surprise.

(8) C (It) *Do I have any special talents: yup! Onioness ^v^ [...] What's your favorite memory of me: evrytime I see an onion, I think of you XDDD (how sentimental of me XDDD)*

[...]

B [...] *I don't have a fave food either... well, maybe the licorice xD and the onion OwO*

This instance aptly exemplifies how English is used in ELF settings 'in situ' and adapted to create meaning which is personal and specific to the language users involved in the interaction, "to carry a certain meaning which has been fixed by the interactants especially for their particular conversation" (Hülmbauer 2010: 77). In this particular case, moreover, the two interactants creatively exploit the resources of the language they are using despite the fact that they share the same native language, Italian: English is their chosen lingua franca in this communicative context, and it is playfully and consciously appropriated to suit their expressive and communicative needs. Despite code-switching and mixing being frequent practices in blogs, as we will see in Chapter 6, in many cases it is the content and the topics which are dealt with that 'call for English', either because of the internationality of the audience the bloggers are addressing, or because the topics have a more global appeal, as they are shared within larger communities – such as manga, anime, icon-making and fanfiction. Furthermore, in the case of meme and quizzes, they are often originally devised in English, and swiftly spread from blog to blog with copy and paste practices. In this sense, the use of English as the commonly shared lingua franca can be seen as being appropriated to suit the participants' communicative needs in ways that are relevant to their "constellations of interconnected practices" (Wenger 1998: 127) as discussed in Chapters 1 and 2.

Moving to the suffix *–able*, it can be either deverbal or denominal (Plag 2003: 94); in the first case, it is extremely productive (Bauer 1983: 224). My data contains several exemplifications where novel words have been created via this suffix, most of which presumably to the function of filling a lexical gap in the lexicon, such as *rentable*, *updateable*, *shippable* and *viewable*; the latter, which bears resemblance by analogy with *readable*, counts 14 occurrences in the BYU-BNC and 109 in the COCA corpora, while the previous three items have significantly fewer occurrences.

Regarding the suffix *–ment*, in ENL it "derives action nouns denoting processes or results from (mainly) verbs" (Plag 2003: 92). In Pitzl et al.'s data, the <pvc> noun *increasement* results formed by adding the suffix *-ment* to the base form *increase*, which in ENL can be both a verb and a noun (2008: 31-32). The fact that a new noun is formed by adding a nominal suffix has been interpreted as increasing its clarity and explicitness: indeed, the nominal suffix makes it clearer that the word is in this case employed as a noun. In my data, the same process can be recognized in "I *refuse to be afraid of changement*", where the addition of the nominal suffix to *change* – either as a verb or a noun – overtly signals its nominal function.

Coming to adjectival suffixes, according to Biber et al. in ENL the most common derivational suffix is *–al*, with *–ent*, *-ive* and *–ous* as "moderately common", and *–ate*, *-ful*, *-less*, *-like* and *–type* being relatively rare (Biber et al. 1999: 531).

The suffix *-al* attaches mostly to Latinate bases (Plag 2003: 95); it is "relatively unmarked semantically, providing adjectival forms with no major change in meaning" from the nouns they derive from (Bauer 1983: 223). Apart from *millennial*, which appears coined in analogy to *biennial*, *triennial* and *centennial*, my data includes one instance of *insurrectional* (37 occurrences in the COCA and 17 in the BYU-BNC corpora), where the *OALD8* accounts rather for *insurrectionary* with the same meaning; its use may have been influenced by the blogger's L1, Italian. We also find one occurrence (*emotion breakdown*, C Canada), where the adjectival suffix has not been added to the noun, which has in this case been employed with an adjectival function without any derivative processes.

The suffix *–ish* can be attached to adjectives, adverbs and syntactic phrases (Plag 2003: 96), and is productive both in ENL and in ELF academic settings (Mauranen 2010a). In my corpus, adjectival forms with *-ish* seem to have been formed by analogy with other similar formations in English: "[n]ew adjectives are readily formed with *–ish* and *–y*, *-ish* in adjectives meaning 'of the nature or character of, resembling NOUN" (Adams 2001: 36; cf. also Plag 2003: 96). The creative formations in the data, to which the above principle applies, have been produced by different participants and include *cartoonish* (which counts 240 occurrences in the COCA but only 2 in the BYU-BNC corpora), *dreamwork-ish*, *odd-ish*, *belt-ish*, *rockish, emoish* (the latter two listed in the Urban Dictionary). As to *fannish*, though listed in the Urban Dictionary, noteworthy that it appears to be employed in my data to a fan-culture in-group meaning, which results communicatively effective as the reply to the comment shows:

(9) C (German) *I was expecting a kind of <u>fannish</u> meta adaption from K.*
B *I know! He's such a fan, he would have made the best adaptation ever.*

Furthermore, the fact that some of the novel creations with *–ish*, like in other instances as shown earlier, are employed in the hyphenated form could be interpreted as a wish to provide evidence of the awareness of the process leading to the formation of such novel words.

In ENL several adjectival forms in *–ic* have a variant form in *–ical*, albeit with a difference in meaning (Plag 2003: 96) or frequency in use (Szymanek

2005: 441-442). In my data we find a few examples when the first has been used where in ENL the second would be preferred (cf. frequencies in the BYU-BNC and COCA corpora), as in *historic novels*, *metaphoric*, *I'm really methodic*, and one where *classical* is used in place of *classic* (*they released a classical pack*). One adjectival form has also been coined, *empathetic*, and used rather than the existing form *empathic* to define friendship and friends' characteristics in a meme. These forms do not appear to be problematic for effective communication, and may be regarded as variations on existing ENL forms. Other adjectival novel formations in the data, produced by different participants, include *utopistic*, which may have been coined after the Italian form *utopistico* and preferred to *utopian*, more common in ENL; we also find *lovelicious, fangirly, piratey* and the expressions *timey-wimey* and *me-likey* (the last four all listed in the Urban Dictionary).

Regarding verbal suffixes, according to Biber et al. (1999: 400), suffixation is less common than prefixation in verb derivational formation, and the following are listed according to frequency as common suffixes in ENL verb formation: *ize/-ise*; *-en*, *-ate*, *-(i)fy*. Plag argues that deverbal formations in *–ate* represent "a rather heterogeneous group" (2003: 92), with several kinds of idiosynchrasies where the suffix *–ate* is "apparently no more than an indicator of verbal status" (Plag 2003: 93). Of the above suffixes, my data includes one instance of a verb created by adding the *–ate* suffix: *prolungate* (*I'm procrastinating and trying to prolungate my student-status limbo as much as possible*). Apart from the deviance in spelling, besides the regularization process involved in this, as in most affixation processes (Seidlhofer 2011: 102), the form may in this case also have been created by analogy with the noun *prolongation*, which could have been perceived nearer to the blogger's L1 (Italian) than the verb *to prolong*.

A case in point is also the expression *renovate my contract*, which in ENL would be expressed as *renew a contract*: here, too, the form *renovate*, which bears a different meaning in ENL, may have been perceived as nearer to the ELF user's L1, Italian. The same may also apply to the adjectival form *determinate*, which would in ENL be *determined* in *Elizabeth, ambitious and determinate to guide the family business – a fashion company*. In all the above three instances, the comments, when present, do not directly address the points where these words are used; we cannot thus say for sure whether in these specific cases the meaning of the unconventionally-created coinages has been successfully carried across. Nonetheless, their analogy with other words with the same affixes is most likely to have fostered comprehension.

My data also contains one instance of multiple affixation, where the noun *over(-)sensitiveness* can be said to form a virtual possible doublet (Plag 2003: 67) with *sensitivity*, the latter being listed in the *OALD8*. This lexical coinage is likely to have been created from the adjective *oversensitive*, which has been first produced in its hyphenated form in a post by a commenter located in the USA, and then taken up in a subsequent comment by two other interactants.

Finally, and more specifically in terms of economy of expression, we find in the data a few formations created with *–like*, such as a *Zabi-like speech* and *weird chair-like stuff*; three similar instances appear as <pvc>s in the VOICE corpus (*objective-like*, *mission-like*, *subject-like*). Quite productive in ELF appears also the suffix –w*ise*, for which 21 <pvc>s can be counted in the VOICE corpus. Derivational formations in *–wise* can work with adjectival or adverbial function, with the latter having become quite common recently (Adams 2001: 39); in my data all four occurrences have an adverbial function: *fansub-wise*, *grammar-wise*, *colouring-wise* and *plot-wise*.

5.4.3. Blends

Blending "involves the analysis of words in new ways" since a blend is constituted by the amalgamation of two words, "one or both of which may be only partially present in the new word (Adams 2001: 138-9). Neologisms are quite common in blending, particularly in technical terminology (Szymanek 2005: 434).

In my data the word f*antabulous* (*fantastic* + *fabulous*), which counts respectively 1 and 13 occurrences in the BYU-BNC and COCA corpora, is an interesting case in point, particularly since in one of its four occurrences in the data it has been flagged and accompanied by a comment questioning whether the word is actually part of the English language: *does this word even exist? XD*. The 'flagging' meta-linguistic comment is in this case accompanied by the *XD* emoticon to indicate a laughing tone; these elements, which are quite frequent in the data, appear to signal awareness in the deliberate choice to employ an unconventional and 'creative' lexical item, which has probably been coined to give a stronger hue to the blogger's emotion, and can in this case be said to fill a lexical gap (Pitzl et al. 2008: 42-43) in terms of 'emotive' and expressive language. The metacomments that follow, of which we have seen a few similar examples in the previous sections, can be said to additionally fulfil the function of 'flagging for markedness' (Firth 2009b: 141-142), a device employed by ELF users "in order to aid their [speaker's] interlocutor in interpreting the meaning of perceivedly opaque, non-standard, unidiomatic or 'marked' usage" (Firth 2009b: 142). As we have discussed in the previous sections, bloggers and commenters frequently flag novel words, or words which they use in novel ways, by different typographical means, often accompanying them with emoticons to affective aims and to signal a light-hearted tone. These strategies, as we have seen in Chapter 3, are peculiar to the virtual settings, where they are employed to orality and compensation functions. Such flagging comments and metacomments are enacted not only for derivational, but also for inflectional morphology, as in *to be there for real was...amazinger (?! does that word exist?!?;P).* In this case the emoticon is accompanied by question/exclamation punctuation marks, too, which can be interpreted as an additional strategy in the participant's flagging aims.

5.4.4. Reanalysis

My data also includes a few exemplifications of lexical items which can be regarded in connection with processes of reanalysis, following which "[w] hen a complex word whose structure is perceived in a certain way is compared to other words to which it can be seen as somehow similar, it may be reanalysed, and perceived as having a different structure, thus paving the way for an abductive change" (Pitzl et al 2008: 37, referring to Adam's definition 2001: 133).

Pitzl et al. cite *medias* and *criterias* in their data as words where the *–s* plural morpheme has been attached to two plural words of Latin origin, *media* and *criteria*, and where the *–a* ending has been reanalyzed to become "the alleged base form in the singular" (2008: 37); cases in point in my data are *datas* and *candelabrums* (the latter commonly found in LJ posts) and can be ascribed to regularization processes. Interestingly in terms of language change, the Oxford Dictionary on line notes that "in practice 'candelabra' is increasingly used as the singular form, with the plural as 'candelabras'. In the Oxford English Corpus these forms are commoner than the traditional ones, and are coming to be regarded as part of Standard English"[108].

Another interesting instance which could be read both as reanalysis and regularization is the word *series*, which is invariable in its singular and plural forms; in my data it has been interpreted in twelve occasions as a plural, for which the singular *serie* has been created, as in the following exemplifica-

[108] http://oxforddictionaries.com/definition/candelabrum (accessed 15 November 2013).

tions produced by five different participants: *the characters are graphically more realistic than in the animated serie*; *I think it's really an interesting serie*; *I'm really excited about the new Naruto serie*; *I bought the first two episodes of the serie*; *a serie of comics I made three years ago*; *it's such an old serie*; *the serie is about a British Prussia* and, with a different meaning, *like a serie of annoying details :P* .

A similar process, though less frequent in the data, may have been applied to *comics*, which may have been re-interpreted and thus employed in the singular form by six different participants: *I want this comic; about the comic--no worries!*; *I'm happy that comic was useful to someone!*; *I promise I will make him appear in a comic*; *this comic, I have it in my Memories. x"D* (C, USA); *one of my friends is writing a comic about it*. It is worth noticing that a web google search produces several instances of *make a comic*.

5.4.5. Addition and reduction

In Pitzl et al. (2008: 38-39), these two processes are related to phonological pronunciation features, as the VOICE corpus refers to spoken data. In my findings we find some examples which could be categorized under reduction, and may at the same time have been influenced by the L1 of the bloggers such as *accidently* (common in LJ) and *devasted*, the latter employed twice by the same blogger (*he would just be devasted over the things he did); how's everyone feeling a week after the finale? I'm still devasted....)* While *accidently* could also be a 'slip of the keyboard', the latter could have been created by eliding *-at-* in *devastated.*

5.5. Discussion of findings

As we have seen in this chapter, ELF users exploit the resources of the linguistic system via processes that respond to functional underlying motives such as regularization, exploitation of redundancy, increased explicitness and clarity and enhanced prominence (Dewey 2007a: 340-342; Cogo and Dewey 2012: Chapters 3, 4). As ELF research findings widely show, exemplifications of non-standard(ized) language use are far from uncommon in ELF settings; therefore, "instead of simply stigmatizing them as deviant forms, evidence of error, we need to consider what the functional motivation for ELF usages might be" (Seidlhofer 2011: 147; cf. also Mauranen 2012: 123). Non-conformity to ENL encoded forms is by no means confined to ELF: several varieties of English show similar processes in all the areas that have been exemplified in this chapter. The unprecedented spread in the use of English as a lingua franca around the world, with the consequent appropriation of the language as a means of communication by non-native speakers, can be seen as a factor contributing to increased language variation which can accelerate processes of language change, particularly in those areas of the system that appear less stable/more idiosyncratic and are thus more susceptible to regularization (e.g. Seidlhofer 2007b: 307, 2011: 70, 73; Dewey 2009: 75-78; Cogo and Dewey 2012). This tendency towards regularization and "alterations" of the "lexicogrammatical subsystems of English" (Cogo and Dewey 2012: 62) has been attested at several linguistic levels in ELF and can be seen as closely connected to the multilingual nature of ELF settings, which are inherently characterized by language contact (Pitzl et al. 2008: 34). Furthermore, such non-conformities are in most cases "non-disturbing" (Bjorkman 2008a: 39) as they do not seem to hinder communication, but may on the contrary even enhance it, either as more regularized forms, or contributing to increase clarity.

ELF users are by definition at least bilingual, and often plurilingual: having more than one language in their linguistic repertoire can certainly contribute to give them a different perspective on language use, as well as in focusing on the semantic nature of the message, rather than primarily on form in order to communicate effectively. This may be reflected also in their use of ELF; as Hülmbauer (2009: 328) points out, also relying on their multi-competence (Cook 2002a, 2010b):

> [n]on-native speakers tend to approach and use an L2 in similar, often strategic, ways. Various communicative strategies involving simplification, regularisation and enhanced explicitness have been shown to be commonly and successfully employed in ELF talk. [...] Thanks to the shared non-native perspective, they can be assumed to understand a great number of linguistic constructions even if or even because they deviate from native speakers norms. They often seem to have the ability to infer the production process of such unconventional constructions. (Hülmbauer 2009: 328)

Indeed, variations at different levels of the language, such as the ones presented in this chapter, appear in line with findings from ELF research and are not random, but realized following regular mechanisms in the system, and/or exploiting its redundancies, within the potentialities of the virtual language (Widdowson 2003: 48-49, 173; Seidlhofer 2011: 109-112).

As we have seen, patterns aimed at increasing regularization can be recognized at different levels of lexicogrammar (e.g. *serie*, *datas*, *candelabrums*, *informations*, *advices*, *teached*, *splitted*), as well as redundancy exploitation which, besides not marking plural nouns, can be observed in the zero 3rd person –s marking and in the use of a single demonstrative *this*, or *there is*, both for singular and plural, and in the shift in use of definite and indefinite articles such as in *difference between first and last photo, with same interests as mine, I'm looking forward to next episode*. The functional motivation of economy of expression can be observed in the tendency to use one single tag question and in processes of zero derivation, as well as in lexical formations like *preorder, non-Japan, reread, anti-Italianism, chair-like*, while novel words like *amazingness, rentable, chatterer* appear to have been coined to fill a gap in the lexicon. To the functional aim of increasing clarity and explicitness can be ascribed *changement, unsensitive, ask to*, and to enhancing prominence *sorry for the English, after the graduation, the love couldn't end.*

In line with ELF research findings in other contextual settings, my data shows that "most of the lexical innovations captured [...] are not erratic, irrational or unmotivated but follow well-attested word-formation processes and in this respect represent a continuation of the long-standing history in the natural development of languages" (Pitzl et al. 2008: 40). Lexical innovations in my data have been created within the range of potential words (Plag 2003: 46), through processes that are not dissimilar to those accepted for native speakers language creativity. Novel words all seem to display a highly communicative function, often also in connection to the need of expressing concepts and nuances related to the interactants' linguacultures and 'communities of interest'. The tendency towards compositionality, whereby the semantic properties of the language are exploited in a bottom-up fashion, that has been observed specifically for idioms and metaphors (cf. Pitzl 2009, 2012a) seems in ELF to be applied to all elements of the language. Following the 'open choice' principle, the selection of linguistic elements can lead to "unconventional combinations" that are possible in the virtual language. As we have seen, it is a "principle that applies to inflectional as well as derivational morphology" (Seidlhofer 2011: 143), and appears particularly noticeable in terms of communicative efficiency in the latter, since lexical items "are comprehensible on an analogical ground, i.e. on account of being rooted in normal word-formation rules" (Mauranen 2012: 131).

Lexical creativity, either when responding to the functional aim of economy of expression, when realized as regularization, or when aimed at increasing clarity or filling a lexical gap, appears in ELF to be "effective and also functional" (Pitzl et al. 2008: 40); unconventional forms are in actual fact created to serve a particular purpose and thus perform pragmatic functions, as "their surface forms are related to underlying functions" (Pitzl et al. 2008: 40). Novel lexical items seem indeed to have been created to fill momentary gaps in the language as "survival words (Carter 2004: 98), or permanent gaps as "there is yet no codified word available to express a certain idea or concept" (Pitzl et al. 2008: 43); they may also be coined to express more subtle nuances in meaning, which are at times personally related and realized 'in situ' as relevant to that specific communicative context – or constellations of interactants. The focus on semantic meaning, in this perspective, applies not only to single words but also to "morphological elements such as affixes" (Pitzl et al. 2008: 42) which are re-employed in non-conformed ways to create new meanings. In their compositional use of elements from the (virtual) language ELF users seem to have internalized its working processes and to use them creatively, exactly as native speakers do (Carter 2004: 97-105; Plag 2003: 46). And ELF speakers do so in their own ways, drawing from all resources in their linguistic repertoires, at times in sophisticated manners (Hülmbauer 2007: 15). In their role of language users, they become 'languagers' (Seidlhofer 2009c, 2011), exploiting the 'language potential(s)' of the code – the possibilities of the "virtual language" not yet codified (Widdowson 2003: 48-49, 173). They thus employ 'deviances' in an authenticating way within their expressive needs and aims, showing that "[n]ot only can the 'incorrect' be effective, it can reveal alternative and creative ways of making meaning in intercultural communication" (Hülmbauer 2009: 324).

Furthermore, findings from my data also show that in virtual environments, such as blogs, common linguistic and functional strategies are often deployed to deal with localized meaning, that is, to express and share content that is relevant to smaller groups – or constellations – of interactants (such as *onion-ess*), or to shared interests, as for instance in *to fangirl, iconner, fannish meta adaption, post-regeneration ep, fansub-wise*. These lexical instantiations can be related to the wish and communicative aim of participating in networks of shared meaning and interests through ELF, where the language is adapted to communicate and express meanings that are globally-set, in ways that are at the same time localized in smaller communities of interaction. The code is thus appropriated and adapted to their purposes of expression and interaction, exploiting it to suit their needs in communicating with the *people* – old and new friends, close and far away contacts – they are interacting with (Seidlhofer 2009c: 243, 2011: 86-87). The fact that in several cases such lexical items are listed in the Urban Dictionary (cf. Androutsopoulos

2011a: 148) can be seen as a further significant element in the use of in-group language which becomes part of a shared pool of (creative) adaptive and adaptable resources. Furthermore, in virtual environments, creating and using unconventional lexicogrammar items can be regarded as common and usual practice – and even more so when English is employed as the lingua franca of communication in across-boundaries virtual environments.

In ELF communication settings, as the findings illustrated in this chapter show, "non-standard usage is mixed with standard usage, with hybridizations, with code-switching (into L1, L3, etc.), neologisms, nonce words and lexical borrowing, but in almost all cases such behaviour is interactionally and artfully rendered 'non-fatal'" (Firth 2009a: 161). As Hülmbauer highlights (2013: 53), as "international speakers" ELF users are "[c]onfronted with a multiplicity of different elements" and "have to develop alternative, more flexible modes of communication", where their different backgrounds "are integral elements of ELF situations and combine to individual constellations which entail a rich linguistic potential beyond English". Hence, Hülmbauer continues, in ELF "the virtuality within the English language is in constant interaction with the multilingual environment in which it takes place and exponentially extended through the resources available from its speakers' plurilingual repertoires" (2013: 53). Intralingual resources thus combine and intertwine with the plurilingual ones "from without" the linguistic system of English (Hülmbauer 2013: 53-54). And in the next chapter we will deal more in detail with how such hybridized and pluri- /polylingual resources are exploited and deployed by the participants in internationally-oriented blogging practices.

Chapter 6
Exploiting and integrating plurilingual resources

> […] proficient ELF speakers emerge from the research as skilled communicators. They innovate in English making full use of their multilingual resources to create their own preferred terms. They code-switch as a means of promoting solidarity with their interlocutors and projecting their cultural identities. They make skilled extensive use of the accommodation strategy of convergence for both affective reasons and to ensure comprehensibility (Jenkins 2011a: 928).

In Chapter 5 we have discussed how ELF users exploit the resources of the linguistic system through processes of regularization, economy of expression and redundancy reduction, as well as to the functional aim of increasing clarity and enhancing prominence of elements which are deemed salient in discourse. They do so by realizing lexicogrammar elements which are 'possible', though not yet encoded, within the potentials of the virtual language. In this Chapter we will examine how the bi-/plurilingual resources of these multicompetent ELF users allow them to draw on different languages to create and negotiate meaning in blog online interaction. After defining the concept of multicompetence in ELF, we will first look at how plurilingual resources are integrated in language usage, and then examine code-switching practices, setting them against an ELF backdrop in the online context where our data is set.

Any language which is part of the repertoire of ELF users can potentially exert influence on the creation of 'unusual' linguistic items, which in ELF constellations can become resourceful (and shared) communicative means (Hülmbauer 2009: 326; 2010: 100 ff.; 2013). New words and expressions may in fact be coined drawing upon the linguistic repertories of ELF speakers, who are by definition bi- or plurilingual (Seidlhofer 2011: 103), and often draw on their variegated linguistic resources either to create new lexical items, to 'bind the code' to their contexts of language use, or to code-switch and mix in processes of "polylingual languaging" (Jørgensen 2008). According to Jørgensen, within a "polylingualism norm" perspective "[l] anguage users employ whatever linguistic features are at their disposal to achieve their communicative aims as best as they can, regardless of how well they know the involved languages" (2008: 163) – that is, of the different (bits of) languages which are part of their linguistic repertoires. Being a multilingual and multicompetent language user represents therefore in ELF settings a "resource for sense-making" (Firth and Wagner 1997: 292) that can be enacted in and towards the creation of meaning and mutually intelligible communication. These resources are locally situated in ways that are peculiar to each specific ELF social setting, since they are carried out "by each set of speakers for their purposes *in situ*" (Firth 2009a: 162). Indeed, "[v]ariability, i.e. the peculiarity of constellations as well as their fleetingness, can be regarded as an inherent feature of ELF communication", which speakers need to come to terms with, using and exploiting all the communicative means at their disposal "in the best possible way" (Hülmbauer 2009: 325). This applies even more to online, virtual spaces, as discussed at length in Chapters 1 and 2. Variation and hybridity, as Firth argues, are inherent to ELF, and ELF users "may borrow, use and re-use each other's language forms, create nonce words, and switch and mix languages" (Firth 2009a: 163) thus adapting, appropriating and shaping the language to their lingua franca needs. Their shared status of non-nativeness often contributes to the exploitation of all the resources in communication and meaning construction; as one ELF user has put it, "we are all on the same boat [...] we are all foreigners" (Cogo 2010: 303).

Novel expressions resulting from cross-linguistic influence may bring about 'true' friends according to the "combination of situational constituents as well as the participants' individual perceptions and subsequent joint handling of these" (Hülmbauer 2011: 142), whereby the plurilingual resources of the speakers' constellations become part of a "*situational resource pool*" in meaning making (Hülmbauer 2011: 142). Novel linguistic forms may be 'taken up' by the interactants in accommodation processes and communally employed to co-construct meaning; (creative) linguistic forms and expressions, which would not be considered standard, or possibly even acceptable, in ENL come thus to constitute a "known-in-common" shared repertoire (Firth 1996: 247) and appear to be treated by ELF interactants as naturally-occurring elements of communication (Hülmbauer 2010: 99, 2013).

Hence, negotiation and co-construction of meaning are main processes at work in ELF, where it is the joint cooperation of the interactants that allows effective communication despite (potential) variation in form (Hülmbauer 2007: 10-12). Even when communicative problems may arise, ELF users' "multilingual backgrounds open up manifold possibilities of dealing with language, which may or may not bring about effective communication" (Hülmbauer 2007: 11). Furthermore, what may be interpreted in ENL terms as deviance from codified norms or ineffective communication, in ELF is often the result of speakers bringing into the communicative act practices from their L1, or of other languages in their repertoires, as well as of other communication strategies such as code-switching and mixing moves (Hülmbauer 2007: 12), which are all enacted to pragmatic functional ends.

A case in point is that of coinages influenced by the speakers' L1, which may not hinder but indeed even facilitate comprehension: in ELF settings, "it is even possible that the ELF speakers share the same perspective towards a 'false friend', i.e. that it carries the same or an overlapping meaning in their mental lexicons" (Hülmbauer 2010: 101). Hülmbauer reports several such exemplifications, such as the term *dictature* which is likely to have been coined under the influence of the speaker's mother tongue *dictadura*, and are at the same time generated according to English morphological rules (cf. also Hülmbauer 2010: 146, 2013). In this, as in other cases, the novel lexical item does not cause any misunderstanding, and may even be processed faster than the standard term 'dictatorship' by the German and Spanish participants, given that the term for *dictatorship* (*Diktatur*, *dictadura*), is in both languages closer in form to the coinage than to the standard English form. A similar instance of 'positive' cross-linguistic influence, leading to the exploitation of a 'false friend' to the speakers' advantage can be seen in *card* (Hülmbauer 2007: 26, 2013: 64-66) employed to express the concept of 'map', which does not result in communicative failure, either, since all the 'constellations' of the participants have in their linguistic repertoire a similar word for that same meaning (as the Greek *chartis*, the German *Karte,* the Italian *carta*). The same can be said for *overfulled* (Hülmbauer 2009: 338): besides bearing closer similarities to other European languages than the ENL corresponding form *crowded*, the newly coined word appears semantically more transparent, too (cf. also MacKenzie 2011: 86-89).

Creativity involving cross-linguistic references in ELF may relate to single lexical items, to shifts in meaning in existing ones (such as the aforementioned *card* as above or *actually* to mean '*now*, *currently*' in place of the British English '*in fact*', Jenkins 2009b: 45), or idiomatic expressions (Hülmbauer 2007: 24-25; Pitzl 2012a). It can also involve unusual word combinations, giving rise to new pairings which have been defined as 'emergent collocations' (Dewey 2007b: 152, quoted in Hülmbauer 2007: 28) or 'emergent co-occurrences' as *psychical illness* instead of the standard ENL collocation *mental illness* (Hülmbauer 2007: 27). This seems to suggest that uncommon combinations might be coined and accepted in ELF, and possibly become increasingly established in these constellations (Hülmbauer 2007: 28). Thus, what would be considered as a glaring lexical error according to ENL norms can be perceived as appropriate and communicatively effective in ELF contexts, where several (and different) linguistic repertoires are at work. Indeed, "for speakers acting outside of their primary lingua-culture, the recourse to first language resources is still a crucial option" (Hülmbauer 2013: 60). Moreover, as we have seen in novel word-formations via affixation, cross-linguistic influences are not randomly employed, but rather they often "exemplify syntactic patterns and semantic properties more consistently than some of the standard ENL forms they were replacing" (Dewey 2007b: 9, quoted in Hülmbauer 2007: 29).

6.1. Multicompetence and ELF users

Non-nativeness and plurilingual multicompetence constitute natural elements in ELF settings, since they are prompted (and supported) by the linguacultural backgrounds of the participants taking part in these interactions; unconventional linguistic items arising from cross-linguistic creativity processes, rather than constituting 'negative transfer', are exploited as further resources in meaning-making (Hülmbauer 2009: 337-341, 2013) and most often result in intelligible, effective communication (Hülmbauer 2007: 25-26). The negative aura which is traditionally associated in SLA and ELT to cross-lingual phenomena can in this perspective rather be seen as a positive 'non-native' communicative resource (Firth and Wagner 1997: 762), whereby meaning is co-constructed thanks to shared plurilingual resources, too. In other cases, where (and if) this may not happen, possibly because of the varied and varying constellations of speakers involved in ELF interaction, the 'new' meaning of novel terms may be clarified in negotiation moves (cf. e.g. Vigo 2012). As Hülmbauer points out, what makes 'false friends' communicatively effective in ELF settings is not so much their formal relationship in meaning with the original code, but "the subjective perceptions of sameness based on plurilingual and other cues" (2011: 147).

Indeed, ELF users are by definition at least bilingual, being thus multi-competent L2 users, i.e. "the compound state of a mind with two grammars" (Cook 1991: 103) or having "knowledge of more than one language in one mind" (Cook 2005b: 2, cf. also Cook 1994). The two, or more, languages which are part of their linguistic repertoire do not work separately in the user's mind, but as holistically integrated along a continuum: "[t]he L2 user stands between two languages, even when apparently using only one, having the resources of both languages on tap whenever needed" (Cook 2002a: 5) since "neither of the two lexicons is ever completely off-line but always present at some level of activation whichever language is actually being used" (Cook 2005b: 9, cf. also Grosjean 2010). Differently from monolinguals, multi-competent L2 users have the possibility of drawing upon the resources of more languages on an integration continuum, which operates at different levels, from phonology to lexis and syntax (Cook 2002a: 4-7); this does not only concern balanced bilinguals, but "the mind of any user of a second language at any level of achievement" (Cook 2010b: 4). Rather than deficient native speakers, or permanent language learners, multi-competent L2 users can thus be regarded as individuals skilfully employing the multiple resources available to them to communication, who "have the right to speak English as L2 users rather than as imitation of native speakers" (Cook 2005a: 50; cf. also 2005b: 4; Jenkins 2006a: 154-155, 2009b: 47-55). This appears particularly relevant to ELF settings, where "[t]he hybridity of language forms which are e.g. based on cognates – as well as the existence of the cognate phenomenon itself – can be taken as a sign for the permeability of what have been assumed to be separate language entities" (Hülmbauer 2011: 154). Cook's construct of multi-competence may therefore be seen to relevantly include "skills like the exploitation of available linguistic resources and their flexible integration into the production and reception process whenever appropriate and potentially effective in a given communicative context" (Hülmbauer 2011: 154). This exploitation of all the resources available to the purposes of effective communication also resonates with the definition of "good English" set forward by Greenbaum (1996, quoted in Björkman 2011b: 90), which does not necessarily correspond to "correct English", nor to a specifically defined level of proficiency in the language, as in ELF communication "using the language effectively takes precedence over language complexity" (Björkman 2011b: 90-91).

In the following section we will discuss how the participants in our corpus data skilfully exploit their multicompetence as ELF users, integrating their multilingual repertoires to meaning making, from borrowings to expressing specific elements related to their culture(s), to adaptation and appropriation of idiomatic expressions.

6.1.1. Borrowings

Vocabulary is particularly permeable to the influence of languages in language contact situations; indeed, a characteristic feature of World Englishes is the use of culturally-specific lexical items and expressions, which can be realized in the form of borrowings, or translation from local languages, by modifying the meaning of Standard English words (Kirkpatrick 2011; Jenkins [2003] 2009a), or assimilating different idiomatic expressions into one (Platt et al.1984: 107-110).

This appears a common feature in ELF contexts, too: the linguacultures that are involved in ELF communication are in most cases variegated, making language (and cultural) contact a prominent and consistent characteristic of such settings. What Hülmbauer defines as 'incorrect semantics', i.e. the use of unusual words or expressions, appears to be often influenced by the speakers' L1 with the "transfer of L1-constructions into English" (2010: 77), that can be enacted either by literally translating them into English or by code-switching, as we will see in the second part of this Chapter.

Pitzl et al. (2008: 34-5) in their analysis of word-formation processes in ELF have in fact included borrowing as a language contact phenomenon. As in Hülmbauer's data (2007, 2009), their findings from the VOICE corpus include several instances where words have been coined drawing on the linguacultures of the speakers involved in the interaction, as *decreet* from Dutch or *inscenation* from German, resulting nonetheless in 'English-looking' words (cf. also Seidlhofer 2011: 104).

Similar instances are present in my data too; in the previous chapter we have illustrated how the bloggers' L1 may have played a part in the formation of some 'unusual' words, such as *pression*, *in order of apparition*, *renovate my contract* or *utopistic* (cf. § 5.4.2.2). We will now look at further occurrences of lexical items whose coinage seems to have been influenced by the multilingual repertoires of the participants. As noted for the exemplifications discussed in Chapter 5, more than one process can be traced in many such novel formations (Pitzl et al. 2008: 29), and resources "from within" are at times mingled with resources "from without" (Hülmbauer 2013).

Findings present quite a few instances of such coinages, produced by different participants, some of which have been flagged, i.e. signalled as 'unusual', and others taken up and/or clarified during interaction. Instantiations of borrowings that can be said to represent examples of 'true' friends include: *implied* as in *they're surely implied in that murder*[109], where the term is likely to have been coined after the Italian '*implicato*' with the ENL meaning of *to be implicated in*; *in my head was turning this idea* which may have been inspired by the Italian idiomatic '*idee/pensieri che girano per la testa*', and could correspond to the ENL 'thoughts whirling around someone's mind'; *they tell me [...] I'll remain without friends*, where in ENL we would probably rather have *to be left without friends*, or *friendless*. In the case of *Elizabeth does her best to emarginated Caitlin at home and in the private school they attend,* apart from the *–ed* past participial suffixation, *emarginated* can be seen as being coined from the Italian '*emarginare*' in place of the ENL standard form *marginalized* or *isolated*. All these instances are likely to be comprehended as largely similar in meaning, despite their "incorrect semantics" (Hülmbauer 2010: 70).

At times a word existing in ENL is employed with an extension in meaning (e.g. Hülmbauer 2013: 61), which can often be detected as derived from the bloggers' or commenters' L1, as in the following exemplify for Italian:

(10) B *I've inaugurated my christmas present!*

(11) B *the book is very well-written and the story proceeds fluidly, following them from childhood to adult age*

(12) B *Fortunately that zone wasn't very foggy when we got there; the area [...] is famous for its incredible fog!*

In the first example *inaugurated* much resembles the Italian '*inaugurato*', and *christened* would probably have been a standard choice in ENL; in the second example the Italian '*procede*', which collocates with '*storia*' [story], can be detected, while *flows* or *unfolds* would possibly be preferred collocations in ENL. In the third example *area* would possibly be preferred to *zone* in standard ENL, while '*zona*' in Italian would be a reasonable alternative in this context.

We also find instances where the shift in meaning is related to the extension of the socio-cultural connotations of the words in the bloggers' L1, as *I was impressed by his culture*, where the semantic meaning corresponding to *culture* would rather be expressed in standard ENL as *knowledge* or *education*, and appears to have been influenced by the Italian '*cultura*', which can be used to refer to someone's knowledge. In *I think I have the best company in*

[109] Underlying has been added in excerpts for language exemplifications under discussion in the section; as to participants, whenever available, location has been specified (e.g. Ger stands for Germany).

[...] *Italy! =)* the semantic connotation of '*compagnia*', which in Italian is related to a group of close friends who usually spend time together, has been extended to the English term *company*. In these latter examples, the concepts expressed appear closely related to the participants' primary linguacultures and may thus result less easy to grasp in their connotative implications.

In two other cases we have a standard and a non-standard lexical item which are employed alternatively to refer to the same concept. In one case, the accepted standard form *conservatives* to indicate people who are favourable to tradition rather than change, is found alongside *conservators* to refer to the same concept; influence from the Italian word '*conservatore/i*' can be detected in the latter, while this term has a different meaning in ENL in that it refers to people taking care of buildings or other works of art which have a cultural value (*OALD8*). Nevertheless, the context in which the term is employed, i.e. an overview on politics, does not seem to create problems in interpreting the word in its intended meaning as the discussion flows smoothly.

In *an architectural heredity /Art Sciences and Cultural Heritage,* in one case *heredity* is used in place of *heritage*, while in another post the second is 'correctly' collocated.

Similarly to other cases discussed in Chapter 5 (§ 5.4.2.2), two occurrences of 'unusual words' have been flagged; the first is illustrated in the following extract, which is part of a discussion following a meme about reading habits:

(13) B *pagans and polyteists (hope that's the right word) didn't want or need to be baptized*

Entries in the *OALD8* include the noun *polytheism* and the adjective *polytheistic*, but no instance of a noun describing a person who believes in polytheism; the singular and plural form of the word count respectively only 2/5 in the BYU-BNC and 3/12 the COCA corpora[110]. The term seems to have been coined following a regular word formation process by adding the *-ist* suffix, and is likely to have been created by analogy with the Italian term *politeista*. The comment is then followed up, and the word does not seem to interfere in any way with the discussion which flows smoothly. As we will see in Chapter 7, these flagging practices related to the participants' perceptions

[110] The word 'polytheist' is however listed in the Ragazzini 2013 online version dictionary (G. Ragazzini. Il Ragazzini 2013. *Dizionario inglese-italiano, italiano-inglese.* Bologna: Zanichelli) http://consultazione.zanichelli.it/catalogo-e-novita/inglese/ (accessed 15 November 2013).

of their non-nativeness often lead on the one hand to expressing insecurity as to language use, while on the other hand they point to a creative exploitation of the 'liminalities' of the language system.

Another occurrence is illustrated in the following extract, where the blogger flags his/her use of the word *morale*, which is then clarified by the interactact:

(14) B *You MUST see Avatar, it's amazing: it has action, romance, morale (hope that's the right word) and it's very funny and interesting :)*
C (no data) [...] *Morals, I believe. Morale is good spirits & morals are right vs wrong. It looks really good. Really creatively done.*
B [...] *Yep, that's morals :D It is very creative... I'm going to watch it for the third time tonight! XD lol*

The extract nicely exemplifies how co-construction of meaning takes place in interactive turns, not least from a meta-linguistic point of view: the meaning of the word, flagged in the meta-comment *hope that's the right word*, is then discussed and cooperatively constructed by the two participants in a totally natural way without disturbing their main topic of discussion, i.e. showing appreciation and exchanging opinions about a film. These flagging practices, which can also be seen as explicit references to the status of non-nativeness (Firth 1996: 254), show once again how language-awareness appears to characterize these multicompetent ELF/L2 users – a point that will be further discussed in Chapter 7. Indeed, as Hülmbauer remarks, "ELF speakers do have something in common, namely their status as non-native and intercultural users of English and the communicative resources they can draw upon through this situation" (Hülmbauer 2009: 324).

6.1.2. ELF and 'expressing culture(s)'

Plurilinguality is exploited in my data also to refer to concepts which are connected to the specificities of the participants' primary linguaculture(s), and/or to the 'cultures' related to the interest-based groupings they are part of (and wish to show affiliation to). At times, as we will see in § 6.4, this is done via code-switching and code-mixing, but there are occasions when specific cultural references are rendered in/through English, so as to address the bloggers' broader audience.

As Alptekin (2010) has argued, the notion of multicompetence set forward by Cook should in ELF embrace aspects related to cultural dimensions and identities brought to the interaction by the participants: "[t]he language experienced in these encounters provides ample input not only for the participants' language knowledge to expand but also for their cultural horizons to broaden" (2010: 102). Given the variety of settings in which ELF is employed, and the variable range of linguacultures involved in ELF encounters, "English-knowing bilinguals are likely to become familiar with multiple cultures" (Alptekin 2010: 103), including opportunities to reflect on aspects related to their primary culture, too, which are likely to be shared via ELF with other participants in international audiences.

The complex relationship between language and culture has been a widely debated issue (cf. e.g. Baker 2009 for an overview in relation to ELF), which goes beyond the scope of this study. As to ELF, given its translocal, hybrid and fluid nature that is by definition not tied to one (Anglophone) community of reference, ELF encounters can be said to be characterized by the complex and interweaving linguistic and cultural resources of participants. As Baker words it, "the cultural content or meanings of English language use will vary greatly depending both on the users and on context of use, and will range from more stable professional or specialist use to highly variable individual meanings and communicative practices" (2009: 573). These resources will include the participants' linguacultures, which can be seen as tied to one's primary language (and language of socialization), as well as to one's personal history (Risager 2006); they will also comprise experiences with other languages, as well as the participants' engagement in different communities of practice, and constellations of interconnected practices, each with their own discourse and communicative shared linguistic and 'cultural' resources. ELF encounters can thus be said to be characterized by a continuous and contingent complexity resulting not least from the interweaving variegated range of linguistic and cultural resources that the participants bring to communication. With Baker, "linguistic and cultural forms expressed through ELF are likely to be hybrid, dynamic, and continuously adapting to local needs, global influences, and the demands of communicating across cultures" (Baker 2009: 574).

It has been argued that ELF cannot represent a culture-free language, but rather a "native-culture-free code" in that it is not associated by default to Anglophone NS culture (Pölzl 2003: 4-5). In ELF settings participants bring to the communicative acts "their own unique cultural history which results in particular communicative behaviours and expectations" (Baker 2009: 588), thus creating a mosaic where several linguacultures, personal cultural histories and identification aspects – including affiliation to different communities of practice – intersect and entwine. ELF is thus adapted to the aim of sharing different cultural aspects, cultural identities and affiliations, with (in) and across communities.

In my corpus data several linguistic devices and strategies can be hypothesised to be employed to the aim of expressing concepts and references related to the participants' primary culture (and L1), from affixation to adaptation of lexical items to convey ideas which are specific to a certain linguaculture. A case in point is represented by the term '*regione*', which can be defined as culture-laden[111] (Pölzl 2003: 18-20): it is indeed typical to the Italian political and territorial structure, since the country is organized into 20 regional areas which are granted a certain level of political and local executive autonomy. In six occurrences, appearing in different posts by the same blogger, the term has been translated into English with *region* (e.g. *my beloved region*); in three occurrences by other participants it is accompanied by its name in Italian (e.g. *the region Marche, region of Abruzzo*) and once by the location (*a region in North-Eastern Italy*). In two instances (*Piedmont, Lombardy)* the geographical reference has been provided in English, and in one case the term has been code-switched as *regione*, and flagged by means of inverted commas, albeit followed by the explanatory *district* in brackets:

(15) B *Tuscany is [...] a wonderful "regione" (district) full of history and nature. Come see Modena too :D it's in Emilia-Romagna.*

In this example, the names of the two regions have been provided once in English (*Tuscany*) and once in Italian (*Emilia-Romagna*). The above exemplify how linguistic strategies are enacted in ELF settings by adopting and adapting words which have a more general meaning, like *region*, or an extended use of affixation as in *Lombardian* (which may have been created from the English version of *Lombardia*, i.e. *Lombardy*), to express concepts that are closely related to geographical and historical local settings, and therefore to the participants' linguaculture. As to the names of Italian 'regions', the fact that for some, such as Lombardy or Tuscany, an English translation is available (though not listed in the *OALD8*) has most probably played a part in the lexical choices illustrated above. However, given that the chosen lingua franca of communication in these online spaces is English, the lexical adaptation and the explanations provided in English seem effective in conveying the specificities of territorially-connected aspects, as the com-

[111] It is worth noticing that various occurrences appear in the VOICE corpus, some of which related to discussions about what can be defined as a region.

menting activities, when present, indicate. These instances appear to confirm that "ELF is flexible enough to allow its users to signal not only their group membership, but also their individual cultural identity which is part of the ELF interculture" (Pölzl 2003: 20).

Quite interestingly, in the above-illustrated instances flagging is rarely used (in fact only once to signal the code-switch in *regione*); other culturally-specific concepts are however signalled as 'unusually specific', as in the case of *civil education*, which has been employed to refer to the area of beliefs and behaviours connected to '*Educazione Civica*', a subject that is part of most school curricula in Italy and that in standard ENL would correspond to *civics*. These exemplifications can also be interpreted as instantiations of special(ized) registers (Hülmbauer 2010: 111), in which speakers have to deal with the additional challenge to employ terms that are specific to the field being described. Indeed, an area where we find several instantiations of borrowings with reference to culturally-specific terminology is that of education, particularly in relation to school and university evaluation procedures. For instance, in a post related to the Italian university marking system in exams, the blogger explains that '18 out of 30' can be expressed as '6 out of 10': *6 means 'sufficient' and 5 means 'insufficient'! That's the Italian method.* The terms '*sufficient*' (pass mark) and '*insufficient*' (fail) have been expressed following the Italian terms and flagged to signal their peculiarity to the contextual setting. Similarly, references to subjects are at times flagged, as in *Medioeval Archaeology and Computer Science (I think it's called like this)*, or expressed drawing on Italian-like terminology, as the following extract exemplifies:

(16) B *I did an exam today and took 25/30 [...], I went to register the vote [...] My usual grades are 30, 30 w/ praise, 28 at minimum...*

The need to deal with procedures related to the Italian university system can here be detected in the lexical choices: *took* rather than *got* with reference to the mark, the noun *vote* in place of *mark* or *grade*, and possibly in *register*, which appears however in use in American English. The effort to give account of the Italian higher education marking system has also led to the expression *w/praise* meaning "with full marks/top grades", which has however in ENL a different collocation. Finally, the expression *at minimum* has been employed in place of *at lowest/the lowest mark*, possibly reinterpreting the linguistically similar, albeit collocating differently, *at a minimum*.

These lexical 'adaptations' create no comprehension problems: for instance the discussion concerning the latter example, which involves four different commenters, one located in the Philippines, one in Australia, one in the USA and one for which no data are available, continues for several turns, discussing both the specificities to the system and the blogger's good marks.

ELF is used by these participants to share their cultural identities, which may be related to their 'native' primary linguaculture, or to other kinds of groupings, as code-switching practices will later illustrate. These exchanges, as Alptekin argues, often lead to "a unique type of multilingualism and multiculturalism: ELF users contribute to the linguistic and cultural content of the exchange and, simultaneously, receive linguistic and cultural feedback" (2010: 106). In some cases ELF is also employed among speakers of the same L1 (Italian mostly in our corpus), at times to accommodate the participant(s)' choice of language in interactions, in others to keep with the purpose of communicating with their internationally-located friends; in this sense participants "appear as comfortable addressing each other in English in intracultural communication, as they are using it for intercultural communication" (Baker 2009: 586). In their flexible communicative practices our ELF users create a "third space" (Kramsch 1993; Jenkins 2006a: 155) of communication where different cultural identities intersect and new meanings are created through a code which is adapted and appropriated to suit their communicative purposes, not least in expressing several culture-related affiliations.These online ELF users appear to be intercultural speakers (Byram 1997: 21, 70) and citizens (Byram 2008), transcultural speakers (Risager 1998, 2007) who easily move across different cultures, cultural identities/ indentification and affiliations, "using ELF to express and construct individual, local, national and global cultures and identities in dynamic, hybrid and emergent ways" (Baker 2011: 46).

6.2. Appropriating and adapting idiomatic and fixed expressions

Idiomatic expressions are closely interrelated to cultural aspects of a language: following the cooperative imperative, native speakers rely on these semi-preconstructed phrases as part of their commonly shared knowledge, not least since they can reduce the speaker and hearer's processing load and thus ease communication. Following Sinclair (1991a, b), Seidlhofer argues that "[t]he idiom principle can be seen as a means whereby users of a language accommodate to each other by conforming to shared conventions of established phraseology" (Seidlhofer 2009a: 197). Among members of the same linguaculture, idiomatic expressions function also as "territorial markers of social identity and group membership", since they are naturally acquired and become part of commonly shared knowledge (Seidlhofer 2009a: 198; cf. also Seidlhofer and Widdowson 2007).

ELF settings, however, are radically different in that participants belong to many linguacultures; for them English is not a native but an additional language, and they "are not using the language to qualify for membership of a pre-defined community" (Seidlhofer and Widdowson 2007: 368). Rather than a set of commonly-shared native knowledge to 'imitate' and conform to, it is their bi- or multilingual language competence ELF users bring to communicative acts. Thus, in ELF contexts "the idiom principle can only realize its cooperative (and possibly also territorial) function [...] if the users are able to develop their own idiomatic realizations as appropriate to the particular interactions they are engaged in" (Seidlhofer 2009a: 201). Furthermore, in ELF setting ENL idiomatic expressions, particularly when used by one interlocutor and not known to other participants, may potentially lead to non- or misunderstanding since they can represent realizations of what Seidlhofer defines as "unilateral idiomaticity", whereby "metaphorical language use, idioms, phrasal verbs and other fixed native speaker expressions" (2004: 220) are employed uncooperatively, that is regardless of the interlocutor's knowledge or familiarity with them (cf. also Seidlhofer 2011: 134-137).

Therefore, in ELF contexts idioms and fixed expressions constitute a particularly interesting area in terms of language appropriation: expressions that in ENL are perceived as fixed, may be analysed semantically, decomposed and recomposed (cf. also Kecskes 2007: 201-204, 212) in a process that Pitzl (2009, 2012a) defines as "re-metaphorization", whereby in ELF "metaphoricity is reintroduced into otherwise conventionalized idiomatic expressions" (Pitzl 2009: 306). Using a bottom-up process, novel forms are thus created applying the 'open-choice principle' – in ways that in terms of variation have indeed been investigated and shown in native speaker language production (e.g. Moon 1998). As Pitzl argues, a 'varied' idiom "is deconstructed and reassembled in order to create a new or different meaning which relies on the semantic properties of the individual linguistic components and is thus compositional, although not literal" (2009: 303-304) creating "figurative expressions which are compositional, semantically transparent and can be interpreted as metaphors" (2012a: 48).

Idiomatic expressions appear not to be avoided, but rather employed by ELF users in a variety of forms to fulfil a mosaic of communicative functions, from more transactional to interpersonal ones (Pitzl 2012a: 46-47). Metaphorical and idiomatic language thus constitutes integral part of the linguistic resources speakers can draw upon to effective communication: "ELF is not about simplification, as speakers do not avoid idiomatic language; instead they use expressions they are more familiar with or create idiomatic expressions that are more appropriate and understandable in their contexts" (Cogo 2012a: 103; cf. also Kecskes 2007: 201-202). ELF is, in this respect too, not a 'neutral' language: users bring along to ELF their linguacultural values, and their multilingual backgrounds "provide them with invaluable resources and strategies, which they can draw upon to achieve their communicative purposes" (Cogo 2012a: 103). Novel expressions may in fact be created by modifying an ENL idiom in (one of) its components (e.g. *head and tails*, *draw the limits*, Pitzl 2009: 310-311 313; *in my book*, *in my observation* Seidlhofer 2009a: 202, 204). Idioms may also be entirely new, "with a metaphorical image being created ad hoc by a speaker" (Pitzl 2009: 317), or produced by bringing in the ELF participants' linguacultures (e.g. *we should not wake up any dogs*, Pitzl 2012a: 45). At times "these instances appear as normal metaphors in the data" (Pitzl 2012a: 45); other times they are code-switched in the original L1; in some occasions their multilingual provenance is overtly signalled (e.g. *money in the sock*, Pitzl 2009: 315), or meaning is jointly co-constructed (e.g. *fleur bleue*, Cogo 2010: 300-302, 2011: 118-120).

Particularly concerning the latter, as in novel words and expressions created via borrowing, the shared non-native status of ELF participants can in actual fact contribute to a commonly constructed (pragmatic) meaning, as well as to the creation of a "shared affective space" (Seidlhofer 2009a: 206). Hülmbauer (2009: 327; 2010: 97-98) points out how new expressions (such as *feed woman* in her data) or coinages can be seen as a 'special' ELF phenomenon in terms of creativity, highlighting how unconventional forms, as in the case of novel words and expressions coined exploiting the multilingual repertories of ELF users, are not problematic but may even "foster the effectiveness of communication in ELF" (Hülmbauer 2010: 98) inasmuch as meaning is mutually constructed and interpreted. Moreover, the creative non-standardness of these forms does not appear to be in any way questioned by ELF participants in non-nativeness terms, nor to undermine their status as successful ELF users (Pitzl 2012a: 46). On the contrary, these unconventional creations are mostly treated as 'effective marked' elements, and become part of the natural flow of conversation. While on the one hand ELF users are often aware of the variegated sources they employ in these processes (Cogo 2012a), on the other hand co-negotiated language variations in meaning construction become a shared resource: as we have seen in the previous section and in Chapter 5, they are most often "made normal" (Firth

1996: 245) in that they become part of the natural flow of conversation, their aim being effective communication rather than strict adherence to ENL form (Seidlhofer 2009a: 205- 211). Or, as MacKenzie remarks, "in a hybrid variety and speech community, there is no need to use standardized NS formulaic sequences, and every reason to calque or translate useful expressions and idioms that you think will be understood (i.e. not totally lexicalized or opaque ones" (2011: 88), or to adapt them – as well as existing ones – making them more transparent.

Also phraseological units, according to Mauranen (2006: 155) are frequently used by ELF speakers; in the ELFA corpus they often appear in non-standard formulations; deviations at the lexicogrammatical level do not seem to hinder comprehensibility (Mauranen 2010a: 19; 2010b). There also appears to be greater variability in ELF as to collocations for fixed expressions referring to metadiscursive organizers, where ELFA speakers seem to show preference for some 'variational' patterns, which are nevertheless used as unmarked choices, e.g. *a couple of words about*, *some words about* (Mauranen 2010a: 21). At times two forms close in meaning are blended, e.g. *in my point of view* (Mauranen 2009: 230); such instances can be seen as processes of "approximation", where ELF speakers tend to "latch on to salient features of a phraseological unit, which they use in its established sense, but without exactly reproducing the standard form" (Mauranen 2009: 230; cf. also Mauranen 2012). Like idioms, rather than being seen as L2 learner errors, deviations in phraseological units produced by ELF users may be regarded as the product of compositional processes where the unit may be broken down into smaller chunks and, so to say, re-interpreted, albeit generally playing the same function (Mauranen 2010a: 25-6; cf. also Mauranen 2005: 290). For instance, *in my point of view*, rather than resulting from a simplification process, could thus be seen as the result of blending from the two ENL expressions *in my view* + *from my point of* view, which have been broken up, reinterpreted and assembled by ELF speakers, thus generating variation and "new phraseological preferences" (Mauranen 2010b). As Mauranen points out, although "phraseological units get their meaning from the whole rather than just single items", discourse reflexive expressions tend to "appear as partly fixed, partly varying phraseological units", and "seem to follow Sinclair's (1991b) 'idiom principle'" (2007: 8) – which is in line with the observation that in ELF contexts idiomatic expressions which are fixed in ENL can be, and often are, de-codified and re-interpreted in their compositional, semantic units (cf. also Seidlhofer 2011: 143).

As we have seen, ELF communication is generally oriented primarily to meaning making rather than accuracy in form, and in the overwhelming majority of cases unconventional language forms do not hamper effective communication, which is jointly negotiated and constructed. Metadiscursive linguistic units and phraseological expressions, as well as non-standard language usage in other areas such as articles or prepositions (see Chapter 5), in ELF discourse are often "approximate rather than accurate", "aiming at communication rather than form" (Mauranen 2007: 14). Such approximation has been noticed by Mauranen particularly in the choice of prepositions (either missing or employed differently from ENL).

According to Pitzl (2012a: 42), creative variation in idiomatic expressions can be enacted at the lexical, syntactic and morphosyntactic level, and may also take place simultaneously, as well as involve more that one process. My data includes quite a few exemplifications of idiomatic variation at different levels; following Pitzl, these instances have been categorized into three main types, that is a) lexical substitution, b) syntactic variation, c) morphosyntactic variation (Pitzl 2012a: 42), and will be illustrated below.

(a) Substitution of (lexical) elements

In *Young is apparently keeping his married foot in two shoes again* the second element in the ENL *to keep a foot in both camps* has been substituted with *in two shoes*; possibly, in this case the change has been modelled on the L1 of the blogger, as in Italian it would be expressed as "*tenere il piede in due scarpe*". Moreover, an extra lexical element has been inserted (*married*) to contextualize the idiomatic expression to the specific situation which is being described, that is a Stargate Universe episode. In the several comments following the post, though the modified idiom is not taken up, the conversation flows smoothly discussing the episode contents. Another instance can be noticed in the following extract, which is part of a post about a series of short films adapted from a videogame, related to Italian history:

(17) B *I think I'll love this series* [...] *They respected the Italian history* <u>*adding some 'pepper'*</u> *in all the right places.*

Here the expression *add some pepper*, where the noun has been flagged by means of inverted commas signalling its markedness, could be interpreted as an adaptation of the ENL *add spice*, with the substitution of the nominal lexical element *spice* into *pepper*; in Italian, indeed, pepper is connected to expressions denoting liveliness and zing.

In these modified figurative expressions elements of the ELF users' linguacultures appear to have been transplanted into English, thus connecting them to the participants' linguacultural repertoires, similarly to what has been observed in this and in the previous Chapter for some novel lexical items.

Another exemplification, though not strictly an idiomatic expression, appears in the substitution of one element in *play with phrases* rather than *play with words*, resulting in a different collocation.

Lexical items, which can be considered as 'existing' in ENL, are at times employed with a different, possibly extended, semantic function as exemplified by *inaugurated* or *zone* in § 6.1.1. with reference to borrowing. In *Just remember to "recharge" yourself" from time to time and you'll be just fine*, common also in other LJ posts, the ENL figurative expression *recharge one's batteries*, which is included in the *OALD8*, has been slightly modified by substituting *your batteries* with *yourself* and results thus similar to the Italian semantically analogous reflexive verb '*ricaricarsi*'. Significantly, this extract is part of a personality test related to manga characters, and the verb *recharge* has been flagged by means of inverted commas, thus potentially indicating awareness of its unusual connotation.

(b) Pluralization

We find three exemplifications of idiomatic expressions, some related to phrasal verbs, which have been modified by three participants by pluralizing a noun which would be expressed in the singular in the 'original' ENL version. In the emote **bursts into laughters** a process of regularization can be hypothesized, as the idiomatic phrasal verb *burst into* is followed by a plural noun in *burst into tears* and *burst into flames* (*OALD8*), which could thus have been applied by analogy to *laughter*. The idiomatic *they'll get us into troubles* may on the other hand have been influenced by the equivalent expression in Italian, which is in the plural ('*mettere nei guai*'). In the case of *they have the tendency on trying to put their noses on matters that are NOTHING TO dO WITH THEM* (C Spain), we find pluralization of the noun *nose* in combination with lexical substitution (*put* rather than *poke* or *stick*) and a flexible use of the preposition (*on* rather than *into*). In the first case we can infer that the expression has been communicatively effective from the several *XDDD* emoticons in the following comments; in the other two cases, however, there is no interactional activity following the post or comment.

(c) Flexible use of determiners
Three instances, produced by two participants, can be related to variation in the determiner: in *Such a luck* (C Germany) *luck* has been considered countable with the omission of *a bit/stroke of.* The second relates to a proverbial saying – *Third time is the charm*, which the *OALD8* relates to American English, and has been employed in my data with the indefinite rather than the definite article: *ready for another round of job-hunting. Third time's a charm, or so people keep saying to me XD Fingers crossed, y/y?*. In the third instantiation, *all of sudden*, the indefinite article has been omitted.

(d) Prepositional variation
Findings show five occurrences of prepositional variation in idiomatic expressions, all produced by different bloggers; in one case, *I already made my mind anyway*, the prepositional part of the idiomatic expression *make up one's mind* has been omitted. In the other four occurrences, we have instead a varied preposition: *in* rather than *to* for *In my mind, it makes sense*; *as* in place of *in* and/or *for* rather than *of* in *as exchange for*; *on* rather than *of* in *I'm still in awe on*, and *on* rather than *in* as to *We're on the same boat*. It is worth noticing that the latter is also employed in Cogo's data (2010: 303), and several occurrences can be retrieved on LJ, too.

(e) Internal modification – insertion of adjectives, adverbs, nouns
The instance *OMG, I don't even know why the* […] *song came to my mind...* could either be interpreted as a variation where one element (*my*) has been added to the ENL *come/call/bring something to mind*; it could however also be seen as the *to my mind* expression employed in an unusual collocation

Do we have to make fools of us (C France) can also be interpreted as internal modification, where the reflexive pronoun element in the ENL idiomatic *to make a fool of oneself* has been substituted with the object pronoun. In *my head is splitting up*, the idiomatic ENL *a splitting headache* has been somewhat reinterpreted and the phrasal verb *split up*, which has a different meaning and collocation in ENL, is employed to create the figurative expression. In neither case do we have any interactional activity.

In the case of *he has a total crush for M.* two strategies can be detected: on the one hand the insertion of an adjective (*total*), and on the other a change in preposition, with *for* in place of *on*.

A modification which appears to have been determined by blending an ENL expression with an Italian one is illustrated in *when you start reading for passion*: the ENL *have a passion for something* seems here to have been modified, possibly after the Italian *per passione*, which in Standard English could be expressed as *out of passion*[112].

At times cross-linguistic influence can be detected also in instances such as *Good work!* or *How's the weather*; expressions like *Have a nice reading*, on the other hand, may have been created in analogy, resulting in an extension in the collocational field (which in ENL would possibly be expressed as *have a great read/enjoy the book/have fun reading this*).

Finally, the following extract is part of quite an intense interactive activity, with more than 100 mostly brief comments related to a *Supernatural* episode; the comments are partly in Italian and partly in English following to a post in English where some teasers (related to icon-making) were shared by the blogger.

(18) C (Mexico) *Ohhh, this episode riped [ripped] out my heart of my chest too... I cannot wait for the season finale... I want to know what is gonna happen to Castiel,*
B *that consoled me watching and rewatching this epi was the thought that I wasn't alone in this...*

The idiomatic *tear/rip the heart out of something* (*OALD*8) has been here modified in the determiner *my* in place of *the*, as well as in the shift in the position of the preposition *out*, which has been placed directly after the verb. These modifications do not appear to hinder the effectiveness of the idiomatic form, as the reply by the blogger exemplifies.

To conclude, the variegated uses of idioms in my data can be seen to support the fact that ELF users do not shy away from the use of figurative language, but rather employ idiomatic expressions often adapting them and creatively mingling their compositional elements with their (pluri)lingual resources, first de-idiomatizing and then re-metaphorising the components. They do so in order to express their intended meaning and fulfil different pragmatic and communicative functions (Pitzl 2009: 317, 2012a: 40-41; Seidlhofer 2011), at times to emphasize a concept, or to give it a particularly expressively subjective hue, other times to express idiomatic meaning from their linguaculture, fully exploiting the expressive means of the code as creatively as they would probably do in their own language. They can thus be said to appropriate English to all nuances of expression, exploiting

[112] In the BYU-BNC and COCA corpora we find respectively 6 and 60 occurrences of *for passion*; however, in the BYU-BNC none appears to be employed to this meaning, and only 2 in the COCA corpus.

resources both for self-expressive purposes, and to communicate with their international old and new (potential) friends, not least to the affective aim of creating rapport (Pitzl 2012a: 47).

The findings illustrated so far show that ELF participants in blogging discourse draw on the variegated resources of their plurilingual repertoire, and do so in creative ways, exploiting the potentials of the virtual language – as findings in other contexts of spoken ELF discourse have shown.

We now turn to practices where English is mixed with other languages, particularly with the participants' L1, in digital blog spaces. After an outline of literature on code-switching related both to ELF and to virtual settings, we will take into examination how language alternation and heteroglossic practices are employed in the data, analysing their communicative functions in ELF terms.

6.3. Code-switching

Code-switching can be broadly defined as "the ability on the part of bilinguals to alternate effortlessly between their two [or more] languages" (Bullock and Toribio 2009: 1), or, in a classic definition, "the alternative use by bilinguals of two or more languages in the same conversation" (Milroy and Muysken 1995: 7).

Code-switching (CS henceforth) has been an extensively studied area of research since the 1950s; early conceptualizations saw CS as expression of interference and imperfect language proficiency, or as "deficient knowledge of language, a grammarless mixture of two codes" (Bullock and Toribio 2009: 9). As discussed in Chapter 1, the construct of monolingualism is rooted in the nation-state belief, and does not represent any longer the norm in modern societies, characterized by high interconnectedness and mobility both of people and resources in linguistically more and more "super-diverse" contexts (Vertovec 2007; Cogo 2012b). In Bailey's words, a negative orientation to bilingualism "simply mirrors the dominant Western language ideology of monolingual speech as normal and code-switching as a mixed-up jumble that reflects speakers' inability to speak properly" (2007: 264; cf. also Auer 2007; Milroy and Muysken 1995; Auer and Wei 2007). Since the 1970s, however, and particularly since Gumperz' seminal work (Blom and Gumperz 1972; Gumperz 1982), a shift in research has shown how code-switching represents a rule-governed, systematic and skilful manipulation of two or more language repertoires, which is exploited to a diversity of communicative functions, representing thus an (additional) communicative resource for bi/plurilinguals.

CS as a language contact phenomenon has been approached over the years from different theoretical perspectives. The structural approach has focused on the study of patterns at different linguistic levels in order to uncover mechanisms about language structure; the psycholinguistic approach has investigated CS from a cognitive and neuro-anatomical point of view in terms of bilingual production, perception and acquisition processes. The sociolinguistic approach, on the other hand, has investigated the social factors behind CS at a macro-level (community behaviour) and, most of all, at a micro-level, i.e. the individual motivations and mechanisms underlying CS and its discursive and identity functions (Bullock and Toribio 2009: 15-16 *passim*). Interactionist approaches, as Heller points out, aim to "explore more directly the ways in which bilingual resources could be involved in the construction of social meaning, both in terms of the construction of social categories" primarily in connection to ethnolinguistic identity, but also to "local social roles, such as speaker and addressee" (2007a: 13). As Klimpfinger underlines, what these fairly recent different approaches "have in common is that they each look at the involvement, influence and/or relation of two or more languages" (2007: 36), which are frequent practices among bi/plurilingual individuals. While in earlier studies, or within theoretical orientations such as Second Language Acquisition, bilingualism was perceived as related to imperfect (bi)lingual proficiency, more recently it has been regarded as the natural expression of plurilingualism: Heller, for instance, point out that "[t]he constant emergence of traces of different languages in the speech of individual bilinguals goes against the expectation that languages will neatly correspond to separate domains, and stay put where they are meant to stay" (2007a: 11). As discussed in Chapter 1 and shown in earlier sections of this chapter, particularly for English as a translocal lingua franca, multiple linguistic resources are drawn upon in communication, and languages mixed in translingual practices (Pennycook 2010). The deployment of multiple resources by L2 multilingual users also resonates with Cook's theory of the "integrated continuum" (2002a: 18): languages in bi- and plurilingual users are not separated entities, which are activated 'one-language-at-a-time'; rather, multicompetent L2 users "draw on linguistic resources which are organized in ways that make sense under specific social conditions" (Heller 2007a: 1) and "'jump' spontaneously back and forth from one language of their repertoire to another" (Lüdi 2005: 341). CS practices can thus be seen as the exploitation by L2 users of the different linguistic repertoires they have at their disposal, and upon which they can draw to meaning-making construction.

Following the well-known early functional categorization by Blom and Gumperz (1972), in *situational* code-switching the different codes are employed stemming from a change in the communicative situation and to the wish/need to accommodate other speakers, while *metaphorical* switches are enacted to achieve a special communicative effect, often bearing socially indexical meaning (cf. also Bailey 2007: 264-265). The broader category of *conversational* code-switching was developed by Gumperz (1982), suggesting that CS may also serve several different local discourse strategies and management contextualization functions (see below), as well as group membership. As Heller points out, these initial categorizations introduced the ideas of "looking at bilingual speakers as social actors within social networks, engaged in the practice of making meaning, and those concerned with conversation, or discourse, itself, as a site for meaning making" (2007a: 12). Code-switching can indeed fulfill different functions in interactions; it may be an unmarked, i.e. expected, choice, or a marked – unexpected – one; language choice is usually connected to the expression of different social identities (Myers-Scotton 1993, 2000) and to their negotiation (Gumperz 1982).

Since the 1980s, following Auer's pioneering work (1984, 1988, 1998a, 1999), research has focused on the function and meaning of CS as a discourse management tool enacted by speakers in a contextualized way (Bailey 2007: 265; Androutsopoulos 2013a: 662). In this perspective, CS practices are seen as locally meaningful in that language choice can be related to the situation (discourse-related switching), or to the participants, and act as a *contextualization cue* in the ongoing process of interaction.

CS can involve the use of single words, phrases or sentences; code-alternation has traditionally been observed at different linguistic levels, and defined with varying terminology, often according to the approach undertaken in analyzing this phenomenon. Generally, within sociolinguistic and discourse analysis perspectives distinctions between "classic", or alternational/intrasentential code-mixing and inter-sentential code-switching (Bullock and Toribio 2009: 2) are foregrounded. Furthermore, according to the syntactic organization of the switches, the approach to their categorization can be made distinguishing, for example, switches that involve the insertion of an exclamation or a tag, or taking place at clause or sentence boundaries (inter-sentential), or within word, clause and sentence boundaries, including single lexical items. However, CS can also be perceived "as a continuum ranging from whole sentences, clauses and other chunks of discourse to single words, which could be inserted into a grammatical structure" (Klimpfinger 2009: 350 citing Romaine 2001: 124), including both inter-sentential and intra-sentential code alternation.

6.3.1. Code-switching in ELF

The continuum perspective is the one taken up in ELF research on CS phenomena, which include "word-fragments, single words, and clauses up to whole passages" (Klimpfinger 2009: 351); 'code-switching' is employed in ELF research as an inclusive umbrella term to include different code-mixing, borrowing and code-switching phenomena (Klimpfinger 2007, 2009; Cogo 2009, 2011).

CS in ELF is seen as an integral part of the plurilingual repertoires ELF users can draw upon: as we have seen in the previous sections, ELF speakers make use of all the linguistic resources in their repertoires in order to communicate, of which code-switching is but one instantiation, together with cross-lingual 'positive transfer (Hülmbauer 2007, 2009, 2010, 2013); as Böhringer, Hülmbauer and Seidlhofer (2008: 16) point out:

> cross-linguistic influence is an inherent and essential feature of lingua franca communication. As effective ELF talk does not depend on native-like performance but rather on situational factors determined by the lingua-culturally diverse speakers themselves, plurilingual resources can be exploited as appropriate in the communicative context. Approached from this perspective, 'transfer' phenomena, which have tended to be regarded negatively in traditional applied linguistics, can appear in a new light when observed in an ELF way.

In ELF research, a sociolinguistic interactional approach appears to be prominent also in examining CS, looking into its social dynamics at the micro level, related to the choices speakers make at a discourse level, the functions it performs in communication, and how social meaning is generated. Investigations of CS in ELF follow Auer's Conversational Analysis approach (1984, 1988), at times combined with ethnographic methods as to identity aspects (Cogo 2011: 108). Following Auer (1998a; 1998b, 2011), code-switching is seen to act as a contextualization cue for the participants' social identity to emerge, and at the same time as an organizational *we-code* aimed at creating in-group solidarity (Gumperz 1982; Cogo 2011: 119). Language alternation, or insertional code switches, are also considered, in Auer's terms (1999: 309-312) as locally meaningful to the participants in interaction, i.e. in their function of creating interactional meaning.

Far from a traditional SLA perspective, where CS is regarded as a compensatory strategy learners resort to when their linguistic means are limited, in ELF bi- or multilingual speakers are viewed as having a range of linguistic competences they can exploit in a skilful way (cf. Cogo 2009: 263 citing Gross 2000, Myers-Scotton 2000). As implied in Gumperz' (1982) notion of conversational code-switching, choices about which code to employ retain for bi- and plurilingual speakers important discourse functions, and social meaning is cooperatively constructed "assigning different functions to different codes", from referential meaning to signaling social identity (Cogo 2009: 263-4). Cogo also significantly refers to the distinction made by Wei (1998) between "brought-about" and "brought-along" meaning: while the first can be seen as more general, macro-level symbolic references associated to codes, indexing the participants' "individual associations and values", the latter refers to meanings, values and views which are negotiated "through code-switching in conversation, with new meanings created as a result of the negotiation itself" (Cogo 2009: 264).

Research into code-switching has mainly regarded "bilingual speech communities with two or more languages in more or less regular contact" (Klimpfinger 2009: 349). However, as we have seen, ELF settings are much more fluid both in terms of contexts and of the number of languages potentially present and, differently from bilingual communities, "involve *ad hoc* groupings of speakers of different first language background who then establish a 'shared set of norms and rules for the use of language' (Romaine 2000: 23)" (Klimpfinger 2009: 349). CS, as other strategies, is thus a locally situated and complex phenomenon in the multilingual framework of ELF, where speakers are at least bilingual by definition and have to deal simultaneously with English, their first language and, possibly, other languages, and may potentially code-switch into all of them. In fact, in a typical ELF interaction the languages involved are at least three: the speakers' L1s and English (Klimpfinger 2009: 348), and the number increases if there are more than two speakers interacting, or more languages in the speakers' repertoires. Moreover, a further factor to be taken into consideration in ELF is that speakers may have different levels of proficiency in English, and may thus need to accommodate to each other also in this respect (Cogo 2009: 265).

In ELF communicative contexts it is therefore not always easy to make a clear-cut distinction between what function(s) are assigned to which code(s), and the interpretation of CS, despite the acknowledged importance of the association between certain codes and the social values connected to them, is neither simple nor unidirectional. Particularly relevant to ELF communication is thus Auer's remark that "often, and in many ways, the verbal interaction between bilingual speakers is open to local processes of language negotiation and code selection" (1998b: 3). In fact findings from several ELF studies highlight how the local context and cultures play a significant role in the construction of (social) identities, which are locally realized and expressed through different codes according to the context (cf. e.g. Pölzl 2003; Pölzl and Seidlhofer 2006). Pölzl for instance maintains that ELF users consciously choose to export their L1 into ELF either due to personal preference, to the context, or to their communicative goals. ELF speakers have thus "the freedom to either create their own temporary culture", transferring their individual primary culture into ELF, or to reinvent their cultural identities "by blending into other linguacultural groups" (Pölzl 2003: 5). This can take place either in the participants' L1, or with any other (bits of) language that may happen to be part of their repertoires. Participants may switch into their L1 mainly aiming to display cultural membership and consciously show their 'loyalty' to their linguaculture; at the same time ELF users may wish to act politely and co-operatively with the other participants and thus take up their participants' L1 using it as their LN language, or may insert other (bits of) languages part of the participants' repertoires (e.g. Baker 2009; Cogo 2010, 2011). Despite these differentiations and specificities, findings from several studies tackling the role and function of CS in ELF have shown that ELF speakers, among other accommodation strategies, make frequent and successful use of code-switching for various communicative aims.

The six discourse strategy functions of CS identified by Gumperz (1982), i.e. quotation marking, addressee specification, interjection, reiteration, message qualification, and personalization vs. objectivization, have been found in Klimpfinger's findings from the VOICE corpus; CS appears to be employed by ELF speakers above all to specify an addressee, to introduce another idea, to appeal for assistance, and to signal culture (Klimpfinger 2007: 38-58; 2009: 359-366). The latter in particular is performed either in "emblematic switches" to "implicitly give a linguistic emblem of this culture" through "tags, exclamations, pause fillers, or function words" (Klimpfinger 2007: 40-1). It may however be employed at a more conscious level to "explicitly refer to concepts associated with a specific culture" to "stress the named elements as a signal of cultural identity", which can be seen to correspond to Gumperz's personalizing function (Klimpfinger 2007: 41). In many cases a code-switch serves more than one function: as Klimpfinger (2007: 57) summarizes:

> ELF speakers switch to another language to direct what they say to one or more specific addressees, they switch to get assistance of another speaker, or because they feel another language is more appropriate to express a certain idea. Furthermore, ELF speakers switch languages to communicate their bi-/multilingual identity and show group membership.

Instances of CS appear widely present in Klimpfinger's data, and from diff ferent languages; they mostly involve single words, short idiomatic phrases, fillers and function words, that are all easily employed in the interaction without causing problems of intelligibility and understanding, confirming that code-switching is commonly and effectively deployed in ELF interactions.

Cogo has highlighted that CS, together with repetition, represents in ELF communicative contexts an accommodation strategy; both are not used as "[c]ompensatory actions taken by learners in a problematic exchange or helping strategies to make up for non-understanding" (Cogo 2009: 259), as they have traditionally been viewed in communication strategies or language learning theories. On the contrary, in ELF they seem to be genuinely deployed as "[a]ccommodation strategies whereby speakers adapt to the speech of their interlocutors in the conversation, i.e. strategies they use to sound similar to the interlocutors or to align to their strategic use" (Cogo 2009: 259). Moreover, both repetition and code-switching operate "[m]ultiple and overlapping" purposes as "[t]hey are used to acknowledge understanding, ensure the smooth development of the conversation, the synchrony of its delivery, and alignment", and are employed to suggest affiliation and membership in the multilingual community of ELF speakers (Cogo 2009: 259). The switch between languages, and the consequent language diversity it generates, does not necessarily work in ELF as a social identity marker, but rather a resource speakers make use of "[t]o represent aspects of their identity or membership in their community" (Cogo 2009: 259), or communities, according to the affiliation and identification aspects they wish to foreground in a specific setting, situation or communicative act. CS can thus be used to accommodate diversity, and/or the interlocutor(s), and it represents a positive expression of the participants' multilingual competence, often deployed to greater nuances of expression (Cogo 2009: 268). Furthermore, in Cogo's data CS is infrequently flagged (2009: 268, 2011: 116), even when performed in a third language, testifying to how for ELF speakers it represents an unmarked choice, used "with expertise, a certain nonchalance and playfulness, typical of speakers who habitually accept and make use of this strategy in their conversation" (2009: 266). The example in Cogo's data (2010: 301-302, 2011: 118-120) is a case in point, where code-switching involves an idiomatic expression in English (*cheesy*), for which the richer French expression (*fleur bleue*) is provided by another participant in the conversation; the meaning is then negotiated first by translating the expression into French, and then by explaining it. This instance well exemplifies how meaning is explored and co-constructed by the participants in mutual collaboration through interactional supportive work, not least via pragmatic strategies of negotiation also when CS is involved.

To briefly recap, in ELF multilingual settings CS represents a commonly employed strategic communicative resource, serving different functions among which displaying affiliation to one or more communities and /or constellations of interconnected practices, as well as expressing cultural and identity aspects, which are realized drawing upon the bi/plurilingual repertoires of ELF users as integrated communicative resources.

6.3.2. Code-switching and web practices

Given the multilingual nature of participants and interactions on the Internet (see Chapter 1), it is hardly surprising that code-switching is a frequent feature in interactive web modes (e.g. Crystal ([2001] 2006: 234; Dorleijn and Nortier 2009; Androutsopoulos 2013a; Leppänen at al. 2009; Georgakopoulou 1997; Seargeant and Tagg 2011). Indeed, "the internet has produced a large additional space, relatively free from normative constraints, in which speakers can practice multilingualism in written, computer-mediated communication" (Sebba 2011: 5; c.f. also Sebba 2002). As discussed in Chapter 2, the hybrid nature of the language on the Internet, despite its 'physically' medium-determined written form, grants it overall characteristics of speech-like informality and immediacy. As Androutsopoulos maintains, "[w]hile CS in CMC obviously qualifies as written in terms of the written representation of linguistic signs, it also bears resemblance to spoken conversational CS, most obviously in terms of its dialogic contexts and its discourse functions" (2013a: 675). Relevant aspects are thus on the one hand the hybrid nature of CMD, which, as we have discussed in Chapter 3, can be defined neither as written not as oral, and on the other hand the differentiated modes in CMC, each with their different (language) characteristics. Furthermore, writing in digital media "is dialogical, i.e. oriented to particular addressees, and often embedded in multi-party conversational sequences; it also is often vernacular, i.e. located outside of educational professional and other institutions, and it is often simultaneously used together with other semiotic resources" (Androutsopoulos 2013a: 675). Thus, the fact that "CMD is unscripted, dynamically unfolding communication in its own right" (Androutsopoulos 2013a: 674) represents a salient feature in multilingual CS practices, too.

In principle, synchronous Internet genres appear more suitable to be analysed for CS practices, as they display characteristics which make them closer to colloquial language (Dorleijn and Nortier 2009: 128-133); however, as discussed in Chapter 3, the distinction between synchronous and asynchronous modes is becoming increasingly blurred as new technological affordances develop. Moreover, even asynchronous modes, generally considered nearer to the written end of the continuum, can constitute an interesting setting of investigation in terms of orthography, as well as more structural aspects and different patterns of CS (cf. Androutsopoulos 2013a: 667): for instance, the role of spelling in signalling CS, particularly for non-Roman alphabets, can constitute an intriguing area of analysis in terms of pragmatic meaning. Thus, written modes could be seen "not as a limitation, but as a new set of conditions for the deployment of multilingual resources in discourse" (Androutsopoulos 2013a: 674).

Indeed, research into CS in written online discourse is attracting growing academic interest (see e.g. Kytöla 2012; Lee and Barton 2012; Leppänen 2012; Leppänen and Peuronen 2012; Barton and Lee 2013). Approaches to CS in CMD data have been predominantly pragmatic and sociolinguistic, with the main aim to "understand the pragmatic functions, social purposes and interactional dynamics of CS online" (Androutsopoulos 2013a: 660) – an approach which is shared by ELF research, too. A prominent issue in conversation-analytic approaches to CMD, either in general or when investigating CS, is that, despite the fact that in CMC "important dimensions of the interactional co-construction of meaning are altered or restricted", the sequential organization of CMC discourse remains (Androutsopoulos 2013a: 662) and can thus be investigated within a Conversation Analysis approach[113] (cf. Chapter 3). Furthermore, as literature has revealed, in online discourse several strategies are deployed to integrate the lack of face-to-face elements, and "CMC interlocutors use code-switching, style shifting

[113] Even though Androutsopoulos (2013a: 663-664) questions whether in Web 2.0 environments all comments in a different language should be considered as CS, arguing that, to qualify as such, they should be "dialogically interrelated by responding to previous and contextualised subsequent contributions" (Androutsopoulos 2013a: 664).

and other manipulations of written signs in order to accomplish pragmatic work that would be accomplished by phonological variation, prosody, gaze, posture and other cues in ordinary spoken conversation" (Androutsopoulos 2013a: 662; cf. Chapter 3).

The Internet and digital media appear therefore a fertile terrain of investigation of CS practices not least in virtue of their increasingly multilingual characteristics: "given the importance of multilingualism and the pervasiveness of digital media worldwide, it seems safe to assume that digitally mediated communication (including networked computers and mobile networked devices) offer opportunities for written CS at an unprecedented scale" (Androutsopoulos 2013a: 659). Language alternation in digital spaces can indeed be seen to constitute an additional resource to identity, community and meaning creation, and "[p]articipants in various modes of CMD have been shown to draw creatively on multiple languages and to appropriate them to their communicative purposes" (Leppänen and Peuronen 2012: 392).

As Dorleijn and Nortier (2009: 133-135) point out, CS research in CMC environments is quite a recent field of research, and has so far mainly investigated the presence of different languages on the web (Danet and Herring 2007b), migrant/minority/ethnic groups' (for an overview see Androutsopoulos 2006a) and young people's language choices (e.g. Leppänen et al. 2009; Androutsopoulos 2013a); Web 2.0 spaces such as Flicker.com (Lee and Barton 2012), YouTube (Barton and Lee 2013) and fanfiction practices (Leppänen 2012) have been looked into, too. The use of code-switching in virtual diasporic communities has also been a largely investigated area[114] (e.g. Paolillo 1996; Fialkova 2005; Androutsopoulos 2006b, 2007).

[114] Paolillo (1996) researched a Usenet group of Punjabi expatriates living in Canada, the UK and the USA, where English was the unmarked-chosen language, and Punjabi was employed to conversational, expressive functions and to group-identification needs. Androutsopoulos' (2006b) investigation of linguistic diversity in diaspora groups websites in Germany has shown that several linguistic resources are employed: besides utilising the home languages and German, English frequently plays the role of an 'emblematic' linguistic choice as a "popular resource for formulaic expression and performance" as in singing, website styling and users self-presentation (Androutsopoulos 2006b: 541). On the whole, "[s]ome studies document dense conversational code-switching and mixing across or within turns at talk, whereas others report a rather minimal use of home languages in settings of English-language dominance" (Androutsopoulos 2007: 218). Warschauer (2002) looked into online code-CS between Egyptian Arabic and English, where the latter was predominantly used in work-related communications and the first to in-group functions; these findings appear confirmed in other studies: in Warschauer, El Said and Zohry

In general, studies of CS in online practices show how English is usually employed for information rather than personal identity and communication, a function the latter which is generally performed by the minority or first language of the interactants. Càrdenas-Claros and Isharyanti's investigation among students of different linguacultural backgrounds has shown a "tendency of bilingual speakers to use the language they identify the most with to express personal thoughts and topics that convey a degree of intimacy", and thus a preference to employ their L1 rather than English for content related to personal thoughts and feelings (2009: 73; cf. also Ho 2006).

A different perspective appears to emerge from Tsiplakou's study of e-mail messages, where English is used to express affect and in evaluative comments, and Greek to convey more factual and referential information; language alternation is nevertheless employed as an "idiosynchratic linguistic bricolage" strategy to signal "symmetrical participant alignment and ingroup solidarity" (2009: 382, 385). CS may also be employed to signal nationality, also in regional terms, as shown in Hock for Outer Circle speakers (1995, cited in Yates 1996: 132-33).

As discussed in Chapter 1, on the web communication is realized at translocal and transnational levels, where English constitutes on the one hand the lingua franca of communication, and on the other it is constantly mixed with other linguistic (as well as semiotic) resources as frequently employed in heteroglossic practices. Multilingualism in these new communicative environments mostly takes place between the local language(s) and English, either in productive or in receptive forms, at times through chunks and formulaic routines (Androutsopoulos 2013a: 668; 2004, 2006b). Particularly for young people, online CS practices are often associated with music and media culture, as well as with aspects related to a young, Internet-related and international identity (Huang 2004).

In Leppänen (2007) and Leppänen at al.'s study (2009) Finnish young people's CS practices range over differentiated online settings, such as writing fanfiction and weblogs; in the latter especially, English is the predominant code into which cultural references and expressions in Finnish are inserted in

(2002) for Arabic/English in e-mail professional communication, in Goldbarg (2009) for Spanish/English interactions, in Georgakopoulou (1997), where style- and code-switching were employed as an in-group alignment strategy to enhance intimacy and solidarity, and in Durham (2007) for a Swiss mailing list. English appears to be the favoured lingua franca in professional online settings, although a multilingual localized policy is increasingly chosen by global brands (Kelly-Holmes 2005; Dor 2004).

different measures. Drawing from Bakhtin's notion of heteroglossia (1981) as "the cohexistence, combination, alternation and juxtaposition of ways of using the communicative and expressive resources language/s offer us" (Leppänen at al. 2009: 1082), the study shows how Finnish young people draw on their multilingual and heterogeneous resources to actively engage in a variety of translocal practices on the web, employing English, or English-mixing with their L1, as their most often preferred communication style. Indeed, as the authors argue

> the actors in new media environments often operate in a multidimensional linguistic and discursive universe where they simultaneously make their choices interlingually – drawing and combining resources from more than one language – and intralingually – selecting and combining features associated with registers, genres and styles of one language (Leppänen at al. 2009: 1082).

As discussed in Chapter 2, the expressive and interactive practices operated in these virtual, translocal spaces are often related to commonly shared interests more than strictly to national identity aspects. However, the differentiated semiotic – linguistic as well as multimodal – resources from the participants' repertoires are frequently creatively employed to appropriate and localize 'the global' in discursive modes, in ways that go beyond traditional categorizations of languages as separate entities, language varieties and similar categorizations (Seargeant and Tagg 2011), but are rather heteroglossic practices in that they draw upon several linguistic (L1, Ln) and multimodal resources to express different voices and identities (cf. also Leppänen and Peuronen 2012).

Androutsopoulos (2006b: 541) significantly argues that the formulaic use of English in diaspora websites in Germany is often emblematic and "part of a wider tendency to exploit minimal amounts of multilingualism (or 'other-languagedness') for emblematic purposes". Such findings are comparable to those in multilingual advertising, where the use of English-mixing can often be interpreted as a symbolic "linguistic fetish" (Kelly-Holmes 2005: 22-25) pointing to the values of modernity and progress associated to English in its role of an international language (e.g. Piller 2001, 2003; Kelly-Holmes 2005). According to Androutsopoulos, such 'bits of language' (Blommaert 2010) can also be tied in to localization processes of non-native English use in youth-cultural discourse: "[r]ather than drawing on undifferentiated 'global English', forum users selectively appropriate social styles of English from the global flow of media discourse" to their aims (Androutsopoulos 2006b: 541; cf. also Androutsopoulos 2012).

When looking at blogs, their potentially interactional characteristics make them particularly suitable to the investigation of CS within a sociolinguistic, micro-level perspective. As discussed in Chapter 2, asynchronous modes, such as blogs, potentially allow a higher level of planning than face-to-face or synchronous genres, which could result in less spontaneous linguistic production. Yet, this may also "enable participants to use language mixing in creative and sometimes masterful ways that might not have occurred in speech" (Androutsopoulos 2013a: 673), as well as to employ CS strategies, particularly in replying to different participants in the interaction by differentiating addressees – a discourse organization that is "uniquely digital" (Androutsopoulos 2013a: 673).

According to Montes-Alcalà, codeswitching is a common feature in personal blogs produced by young people. Most switches in her data are related to lexical items, an area where, as the author points out, switches "under no circumstances should thus be interpreted as a lack of language proficiency, but rather as the lack of an exact equivalent in the other language", a choice which is "related to the biculturalism of the subjects" (2007: 167). Switches due to emphatic reasons, realized either by code-switching or by repeating a concept in two languages, are also very common in her study, together with elaborations aimed to further explain an idea, and switches with no obvious interpretable reasons (free switches), while tag-triggered switches and quotes are less common. The author hypothesizes that "while code-switching has often carried a social stigma in oral production, such stigma does not seem to obtain in informal written expressions, especially in such a democratic forum as the internet" (Montes-Alcalà 2007: 169). Moreover, the bloggers in her study appear to have "sufficient linguistic and cultural knowledge of the nuances both of Spanish and English in order to manipulate the two languages both for stylistic and communicative effects" (Montes-Alcalà 2007: 169). Similar findings as to CS practices emerge in Carey's investigation of academic blogs part of the WrELFA corpus[115] (2013), both in terms of language choice with routine words from other languages than English (e.g. *hola*, *merci*, *ciao*), and more extensively in comments and replies.

The use of CS in web-mediated ELF settings can thus be said to be common practice, and to be deployed by plurilingual Internet users to a diversity of communicative functions, as a linguistic resource to be exploited in interaction, rather than a sign of lack of proficiency, interference and imperfect language. These practices can indeed be seen as an instantiation of "polylingual languaging" (Jørgensen 2008), and/or translanguaging and hetero-

[115] www.helsinki.fi/elfa/wrelfa (accessed 15 November 2013).

glossic practices, which form integral part of the manifold semiotic resources deployed by L2 plurilingual ELF users to achieve effective interpersonal communication and self-expression. As Androutsopoulos remarks,

> social appropriations of new communication technologies are extending the public visibility of bilingualism, in both societal and impersonal settings. […] Although the new media do not constitute *per se* sites of language revitalization and maintenance (Sperlich 2005), spaces of online discourse allow for practices of conversational switching and mixing that are qualitatively different from traditional forms of bilingual written discourse, and provide opportunities to establish such practices as the default case (Androutsopoulos 2007: 227).

This often happens beyond traditional categorizations of code-switching and other language manipulation practices as displaying distinct characteristics in written and spoken media (Androutsopoulos 2013b: 5). The exploitation of different language resources in web-related settings has been defined by Androutsopoulos as "networked multilingualism", characterising "multilingual practices that are shaped by two interrelated processes: being *networked*, i.e. digitally connected to other individuals and groups, and being *in the network*, i.e. embedded in the global digital mediascape of the web" (2013b: 4, emphasis in original). And indeed, as we will see in the next sections, these two paradigms most often intersect in my findings, too, whereby English and other languages are entwined yet selectively chosen according to the audience bloggers wish to address, the interaction with their participants as developing *in-situ*, as well as the topics being expressed and discussed and the affiliations to the primary linguaculture(s) or to other interest-based communities the participants wish to express.

6.4. Code-switching in blogging practices

As we have discussed, in ELF communication settings, as well as in online Web 2.0 contexts, code-switching is regularly employed to a diversity of pragmatic functions, testifying to the participants' multilingual competence and to the common practice of exploiting all the linguistic, as well as semiotic, resources at their disposal while communicating with a multilingual, internationally-oriented audience.

In looking at how CS is employed in my data corpus, these instances will be considered as part of the participants' potential range of code choice(s) – English in its lingua franca function, L1, Lns, either in single posts or, whenever present and relevant, as part of comment threads seen as conversational events in dialogic interaction. While taking into account the specificities of the web context in which the data is set and contextualized, since the ELF research paradigm constitutes the main backdrop for this study, my approach to the analysis of findings will be set within the orientation adopted in previous ELF literature in analysing CS (see above), investigating to which functions CS is employed within Gumperz' categorisation (Klimpfinger 2007, 2009), and within an analytical framework that takes into account organizational and identity-based approaches in combination (Auer 2011: 32-38; Cogo 2011: 110-111). In particular, in categorising and analysing the findings, Klimpfinger's (2007: 38-58; 2009: 362) identification of the main purposes characterizing code-switching strategies in ELF, that is, specifying an addressee, appealing for assistance, introducing another idea and signalling culture will constitute the main point of reference, as the following sections will illustrate. At the same time, although tentatively – particularly with reference to CS – findings will be contextualized in relation to linguacultures and other affiliations the participants seem to relate to. As illustrated in Chapter 4, apart from the questionnaire survey, a limitation of this study can be seen in the fact that it does not include a full set of ethnographic-based data, which could of course provide deeper insight on the participants' perspective. Furthermore, the fact that all bloggers are Italian entails that findings in this section in particular are naturally more exemplificative of specificities connected to this linguaculture. Nevertheless, findings can to some extent be potentially seen as exemplifying processes that could, by analogy, be found for other linguacultures, too (cf. e.g. Barton and Lee 2013).

Overall, code-switching appears common practice in my corpus data. Given the bloggers' native language, switches into Italian are widely present, although other languages are can be found, too, either as they may be the participants' L1 (e.g. Spanish), or be part of their multilingual repertoires. Japanese, for instance, is employed primarily in connection to the manga and anime fan communities, which is a frequently shared interest in these blogs, and can be interpreted as a sign of affiliation (cf. Franceschi 2014); Latin and Greek appear in the form of fixed, often integrated chunks (such as in *ex-novo*, *dulcis in fundo*, *vidi vidi*, *mea culpa*) or in quotations; German and French are occasionally present, too, generally to refer to specific linguacultural concepts (e.g. *Österreichische Küche (Austrian cookbook): this is the book that introduced me to the proper recipes of Vanillekipferl, Kartoffelnsalat and Frittatensuppe*), a point that will be further discussed in Chapter 7.

6.4.1. Appealing for assistance

CS seems to be employed by the participants in my corpus for all the aforementioned functions, apart from appealing for assistance, whereby a speaker resorts to another language to ask for help as to words or phrases. The lack of instances of CS to this function can presumably be connected to the characteristics of the medium, that is to say the fact that asynchronicity would not allow for immediate response to such appeals for help. However, when seeing this function within a broader communication strategy paradigm (Klimpfinger 2007: 39; cf. also Hynninen 2013: 92-94), other strategies specifically afforded by the medium, like resorting to hyperlinkis to provide visual exemplification of 'lacking' words, are in some cases employed to a similar functional aim, as the following extract shows:

(19) B (meme) […] *a good pair of shoes with these (sorry I don't know their name in english)*

The extract is part of a meme including a few questions about favourite artstyles and outfits. In the answer related to the latter, the blogger has here inserted a hypertextual link to a picture of the intended lexical item – a pair of shoes with white spats – accompanying it with a meta-comment overtly signalling he/she does not know the English corresponding term. In such cases in spoken, face to face conversation, or in synchronous online modes, speakers would possibly resort to code-switching to appeal for assistance to the interlocutors. Using a multimodal hyperlink could here be interpreted as an alternative strategy afforded by the medium and skilfully exploited to make up for lack of specific terminology, as well as of how the participants as ELF users strategically resort to the specificities and affordances of the online context to express their intended meaning.

6.4.2. Specifying an addressee

When looking at the first function of code-switching in ELF interactions as identified by Klimpfinger (2007: 46-47, 2009: 359-360), ELF speakers use CS to direct their speech to a specific addressee, inviting him/her to participate in the conversation. In my corpus data several instances employed to this function can be observed. In general, as the bloggers' purpose is to communicate with an international audience, English is used, either with a *you* pronoun, or with proper nouns and other appellatives (cf. Myers 2010:

76-77). CS to this function is in most cases employed to address their Italian-speaking friends, as the following extracts exemplify:

(20) B *Per gli italiani interessati, la Y. svende la collezione completa di U. (10 DVD) a meno di 40 euro :D. Mentre io penso a quanto l'ho pagata, voi approfittatene, se siete incuriositi XD.*
[to the Italian people who may be interested: Y. is selling off the complete U. collection (10 DVDs) at less than 40 euros :D While I think about how much I paid for it, you can take the opportunity if you are intrigued XD]

(21) B *I had to post it in my blog as well, so here it goes. Anybody volunteers to fill in one for Akira Ishida?:P Sugitan? Anybody else you love/like? Potete farlo anche in italiano , per me :D.* [you can do it in Italian, as far as I am concerned]

In Extract (20) the switch into Italian is preceded by a few lines in English commenting on how good the plot in one Naruto anime episodes is; Extract (21) relates to a meme, wholly in English apart from the above code-switch, about female *seiyuu*, that is, Japanese voice actors[116]. The fact that the code-switches refer to a specific group of people in the audience is overtly signalled in the first extract by addressing the Italian audience (*Per gli italiani interessati*), and covertly in the second, where the switch specifies that the request for contribution for two *seiyuu* (*Akira Ishida, Sugitan*) that was expressed in English in the previous line, may be carried out in Italian, too. These two examples may also be seen as an instantiation of how the participants' language resources are continuously intermingled, and how naturally code-switches are carried out within and across turns.

CS may also be employed to address an even more restricted audience, by specifying the nationality (e.g. *per gli amici italiani*), or addressing specific people/friends by their names or by affective appellatives (e.g. *lovve* for close friends), mixing codes within the same sentence, as in (22) and (23):

(22) B […] *Ed un messaggio finale alle mie lovve* [names follow] *VI AMOOOOOOOOOOOOO <3 <3 <3* [and a final message to my lovve. I loveeeeeeee you]

(23) B […] *ITALIANI! Aspettatevi una sorpresa da me dopo il 30 giugno :3 Le lovve anche prima XD.* [Italian people! Expect a surprise from me after June 30th! And the lovve even before that XD]

Here the blogger directly addresses a group of interactants by using their

[116] Cf. e.g. http://www.urbandictionary.com/define.php?term=seiyuu (accessed 15 November 2013).

first names in (22) and by reiterating the affective, in-group appellation "*lovve*" in the second. In both cases, the first part of the post reports in English an experience related to a trip and a live concert, which is then followed by comments in Italian, presumably by the group of the close friends the blogger is addressing in the code-switch into Italian, thus possibly testifying to the in-group function to which the native language has been employed (Klimpfinger 2007: 48).

In other cases, the comments are produced in a language that is different from the one used in the post, to which most often the blogger, or other commenters, accommodate by showing preference for the same language (Auer 1984; Garafanga 2007). These accommodation-oriented CS practices have also been noticed in another Web 2.0 multilingual environment, that of Flicker, where, "[w]hen responding to comments in different languages, many users write their replies according to the language used by the comment posters; if they do not know the language concerned, they would respond in English" (Lee and Barton 2012: 141; cf. also Barton and Lee 2013: Chapters 4 and 5). As Androutsopoulos highlights referring to multilingual networking practices on Facebook walls by Greek-German students, "both languages [German and Greek], and also English, can serve as a 'we-code' depending on context" and "bilingual talk might be recontextualized as an index of intimacy in network language practices" (2013b: 19).

These 'LN duets' are extremely common in my corpus data, particularly but not only with Italian, both in shorter and longer stretches; besides performing the function of accommodating the interactant in mirroring the language he/she used in the replies, they can also be seen in their phatic function to create an 'intimate' atmosphere (cf. Klimpfinger 2007: 48; Appel and Muysken 1995). Such interactive duets, in this case with intersentential CS, can be observed in the following exemplifications, both taking place in a longish thread commenting on icon (and video) sharing:

(24) C (GB) *I love the icons! Molto bella!* [very beautiful] *The animation is* ♥
B *Ahah, Grazie! :D* [thank you]

(25) C (Portugal) *Uh-Oh some more videos!! *flaps hands** <u>*Grazie mille*</u> [thank you so much] *for sharing!!!* ♥
B *You're welcome!! Love the icon by the way [...] LMAO*

Interestingly, the switch into Italian has been here performed by participants located in countries other than Italy (Great Britain in the first extract and Portugal in the second extract), in small language chunks (or 'bits') which are almost formulaic. In these examples, all related to posts about icon making, CS can all the same be said to be enacted to affective accommodation by using the language which is the L1 of the interactant (Cogo 2011:116-117). To be noticed also that in these excerpts affective in-group aspects are reinforced by the use of the heart icon '♥' (cf. also Androutsopoulos 2013b: 12). As in the exemplifications provided earlier on, these code-switches are unmarked and inserted in a natural way, without interrupting the conversational-like exchanges, which continue in English. Such natural switches between languages appear common practice in the data, either accommodating to the code overtly employed by the interlocutor, or switching to one which is supposedly known by the interactant, as shown in the next extract where both participants are located in Italy and share an interest in icon-making:

(26) C (Italy) ♥♥♥♥♥♥♥♥♥♥♥♥♥♥♥♥♥♥ *I love all of them!!!!! ^_^ [...] XD*
B <u>*Grazie*</u> [thank you] ♥ *again.*

While of course the participants' (declared) location may not necessarily be inductive of their L1, and even more so on the web, it is nevertheless worthy of notice that English constitutes the language most frequently employed even in small exchanges like the ones exemplified in extracts (24)-(26), where switches into another language are inserted; this is most probably due to the internationally-oriented 'constellations' these exchanges take place in, and are easily employed also by participants who presumably share an L1.

Finally, it is noteworthy that code switches related to routines, such as thanking practices, frequently involve 'bits' of different codes besides English, such as Spanish (*Gracias*, C, no data), *Muchas muchas muchas muchas gracias! :D*, C, no data), Japanese (*Arigatou, ne, onegai*, several participants), or elaborations recalling spoken informal language (*kyuuuu!*).

As previously discussed, speaker constellations in ELF settings are variable in nature, and blogs are no exception to this, where variability in participants fluctuates from blog to blog, and in some more 'populated' ones even from post to post (see Chapter 4). Therefore, also the languages that constitute the participants' plurilingual resources differ, as several of the extracts that have been illustrated in this section exemplify. Common practice in my data is also intertextual switching into another language for quotations (Androutsoupoulos 2001: 5, 2004: 88), most often to share songs lyrics, but also poems, often providing a translation of the texts when they are not in English (e.g. Japanese or Italian). In the case of Japanese, references to cultural elements are also given, at times in relation to manga and anime, and thus to one of the thematic threads running across these interconnected practices, or to more general culturally-specific notions (e.g. *hitsuzen*[117] from Japanese). At times, particularly in the case of songs, they are reported both in the original Japanese *Kanji/hiragana* characters, in their Romaji/Romanized transliteration and in the translated version into English (only at times into Italian).This appears a common practice in fanfiction, too, where "the use of token Japanese phrases and lyrics was a way for these youth to index their insider status within the anime fan fiction community and to affiliate with the Asian origin of the media" (Black 2009: 414; cf. also Leppänen et al. 2009).

In our case, too, CS into Japanese can be seen as closely connected to the personal interests of the participants, either in cultural aspects, in language(s), or both, around which blog posts and, when present, interaction with other participants revolve. Such fan-related interconnections can be seen as situated at a global level, and are at the same time indexed and appropriated in these smaller constellations as a sign of bond and commonality (see Chapter 2, cf. also Franceschi 2014). As Pennycook notes for hip-hop, in global "circles of flows" of practices and languages, we find a "constant mixing, borrowing, shifting and sampling of music, languages, lyrics and ideas" (2007: 126), which in my data is instantiated also via CS into different languages, presumably to the aim of sharing these affiliations. Particularly in the case of Japanese this is frequently done through the use of Japanese *Kanji/hiragana* characters, but at the same time engaging in transliteration and translation practices both for their audience's sake and out of interest in languages (cf. § 7.4). In one occasion, in a meme related to favourite lyrics, lines in Celtic from a song by Kila are quoted: in this perspective this could be read as mirroring the mix of global and at the same time local linguistic and cultural identity of the participant(s), who is in this case located in Northern Ireland.

CS practices may also be employed to emblematic purposes "to exploit minimal amounts of multilingualism" (Androutsopoulos[118] 2006b: 541), as instantiations of those 'bits of language', part of 'truncated' language repertoires in multilingual competence and practices, which are common in global, transnational and translocal flows – and involve translingual and transcultural practices (Blommaert 2010). Such instances may also be related to pop culture – e.g. bits of songs, at times in relation to posts of

[117] http://www.urbandictionary.com/define.php?term=hitsuzen (accessed 15 November 2013).

[118] Referring to non-native English in diaspora websites and forums as a "popular resource for formulaic expressions and performance" (Androutsopoulos 2006b: 541).

videos or other music-related material, such as lyrics (Androutsopoulos 2013b: 12-13); as Androutsopoulos remarks, such practices create "a sort of dialogue between networked actors and global networked resources, which demonstrates the participants' flexibility with languaging as much as the diversity of cultural discourses to which they orient" (2103b: 19). As to my data, the bloggers' plurilingual repertoires – which in many cases include at least another language beside Italian and English (cf. Chapter 4), together with the differentiated linguacultures of their international interactants – may also further explain the inclusion of even small chunks of several languages in their messages. These small chunks may relate to their interests, to youth (e.g. songs, films, videos and TV shows) and fan-related (manga and anime for Japanese) cultures, but always seem to emerge as part of their wish to express complementary sides of their bloggings acts, "*to be networked*" and "*in the network*" (Androutsopoulos 2013b: 4, cf. § 6.3.2). As Barton and Lee put it, Web 2.0 practices "are no longer confined to the local sphere. People are using these spaces consciously and deliberately to tell the world something about their personal experiences or local life" (2013: 151), and they do it by deploying different sets of intermingling communicative resources. Once more, the variegated sources for CS point to the plurilingual and multicultural repertoires of these ELF users, which can be simultaneously related to their linguacultures or to other (indentification) aspects part of their interests they wish to share. Indeed, as Klimpfinger points out, an "interplay of languages" is at work in ELF, thanks to the variety of cultures and languages they have "at their disposal to switch into" (2007: 51; cf. also Cogo 2012b). As discussed earlier, this applies particularly to online environments and to my data, where language alternation is frequently found as part of translingual and heteroglossic practices that are inherent to the communicative environment, being embedded and exploited by the participants as naturally occurring 'polylingual languaging' communicative and expressive acts, as will also be seen in the following sections.

6.4.3. Introducing another idea

When looking at the function performed by CS to introduce another idea, whereby a different language is used to imply that it is thought to be more appropriate to discuss a particular new topic (Klimpfinger 2007: 49; 2009: 364; Appel and Muysken 1995), a few instantiations are present in my corpus data. At times the change in language, and topic, is overtly signalled, for instance by tagging it as '*Italian comment*', or signalling the shift in the title, as in the following, where the switch takes then place halfway through the post:

(27) B *DVDs are home^^ -plus Italian-only bit-*
In the end they came sooner than expected, and now I'm holding the precious Terra e... Limited Edition DVD1 in my hands, as well as the ~~BL~~ extra fan-disc with wonderful SaigaXSugitan rambling. Much, much love to the both of them, for the manga reading session and the priceless Wakamoto impersonation by Sugita.
[...]
*Oh! And if you were wondering (of course you were **), DVDs are also equipped with Japanese subtitles, something I'd basically never seen XD,and discovered by mistakingly playing with the remote.*
[...]
*Allora, i sub sono pronti fino alla puntata 14, 15 entro questa settimana, ma quel che piu' conta è che, essendo una versione da DVD-rip pensavamo di encodarlo come HD 264 anzichè come semplice XviD. Tuttavia, si pone il problema della lettura dei file da parte di PC particolarmente vetusti oppure dei lettori DVD/DivX stand-alone, che non supportano questo formato. A questo proposito, preferireste quindi un formato agile, leggero e leggibile, ma di minore qualita', o il formatone definitivo e strafigo, ma piu' pesante e difficile da visualizzare con macchine non aggiornate? Ah, questo dilemma si presentera' anche per il F. presumo, quindi esprimete liberamente il Vostro eccelso parere *_* e trasmettero' le opinioni ai Grandi Capi XD*[119].

In this case a double function can be identified in CS: besides a change in topic, in that the switch to Italian signals more 'technical' matters, we also have a direct question to the audience ('*preferireste quindi*' [would you then rather have]), that can be related to the 'specifying an addressee' purpose; the latter is also recognizable in the English part of the post, where the blogger addresses his/her implied audience directly in the comment *And if you were wondering (of course you were **)*. Noteworthy that all comments that follow are in Italian, and refer only partially to the English part of the post,

[119] [So, the subs are ready up to episode 14, 15 by this week, but the most important thing is that, since it is a DVD-rip version, we were thinking about encoding it as HD 264 rather than a simple XviD. However, it may be a problem for old PCs, or for stand-alone DVD/DivX players, which may not support this format. On this point, would you rather have a quick, light and readable format, although of a lower quality, or the final and extra-cool big format, but heavier and difficult to be read by older machines? And I guess this dilemma will arise also for the F., so feel free to express your highly-valued opinions and I will pass them on to the Big Bosses XD. My translation].

as they mainly answer the question – in Italian – related to the preferred format, and thus provide an instantiation of the effectiveness in communicative terms of the code-switch in both its functions. On a different level, it is worth noticing that both parts of the post contain English lexical items which are technology-specific, a characteristic that is widely present in these types of topic-related posts (cf. e.g. Leppänen 2012: 243), as well as in-group jargon related to icon-making sharing practices such as *banner*, *header*, *texture*, *spoiler*, *icon(s)*, *fandom*, *season finale*. Hybrid lexical forms are widely employed in my data, too, and can be ascribed to in-group, technology or online-related language use (cf. Androutsopoulos 2011a: 148), as for instance *snaggare*, *ranteggiare*, *handcuffare*, *stalkare*, *friendare*, *addare*, *straquotare*, *fangirlamente*, *kittosa*, which can be interpreted as a further exemplification of how a creative use of the pluringual resources these blogging ELFers have at their disposal may be carried out to affectively signal in-group affiliation.

6.4.4. Signalling and sharing (lingua)cultural affiliations

As we have seen, ELF contexts are characterized by a multiplicity of linguacultures, which intersect with the participants' personal (linguacultural) histories, with their affiliations and interests. English is employed in Web 2.0 environments, and similarly in blogs, as the lingua franca allowing communication to take place at a global level with the wish '*to be networked*' and '*in the network*' (Androutsopoulos 2013b: 4), and to share with old or newly made friends personal experiences and interests (see also Chapter 2). CS may be employed to signal a "special bond" (Klimpfinger 2007: 41) to fan (e.g. manga and anime) and Web 2.0-related practices, such as icon-making or fanfiction, around which blogging practices are created and maintained; in this case, switches usually take place in an additional language (Ln). When code-switches are performed in the participants' L1, they may be closely related to their primary linguacultures. As we have seen in the previous section, CS may serve to index in-group affiliations, as well as to refer to more localised aspects that are reckoned as peculiar to a specific linguaculture. In this case, and in its complexity, "language choice can be a semiotic strategy through which participants seek to distinguish themselves and to create voices of their own in a multilingual online setting. Language choice can thus serve as a particular resource for the creation of stylistic and cultural effects, and for the negotiation of identity and community" (Leppänen and Peuronen 2012: 390).

Looking at code-switching as a means to signal cultural affiliations, in ELF settings the switch to a different code may be realised either to give a linguistic emblem of primary linguacultures, or to refer to concepts associated with a specific cultural context. In the first case switches appear 'emblematic, unintentionally performed and not specifically related to content; they may consist in tags, exclamations, pause fillers, conjunctions or affirmatives, and express the L2 user's multicultural identity (Klimpfinger 2007: 55); this aspect will be dealt with at the end of this section. In the second case, switches generally represent references to cultural concepts and serve also to highlight aspects related to the participants' cultural identity/ies, linguacultural background as well as group membership(s) that are deemed particularly relevant by the participants (Klimpfinger 2009: 361; cf. also Cogo 2011). In my data occurrences of CS related to the interactants' cultural identity include references mainly in relation to food, geography, titles of songs, books and films, in most cases concerning the bloggers' linguaculture, that is, in our case, Italian-based. As to geographical references to "homelands" (Klimpfinger 2007: 55), we often find mention of specific, smaller locations the participants are familiar with and they wish to share with their international friends. When the references are related to more internationally (or globally) well-known locations, both translations and code-switches to the 'original' language of these places are included, as in the following extract, part of a longer post describing a one-day trip to Venice:

(28) B *Venice, Ponte di Rialto, Ponte dell'Accademia*
[...]
Asian Way or Life, a Biennale collateral event
[...]
It started with a bridge... [picture of bridge] and it ends with one :) This is the most recent bridge in Venice, Ponte della Costituzione, or Calatrava Bridge (after the architect that made the project), as everyone calls it. Hope you like it! Cookies for everyone that made it till the end XD

It can be noticed in the extract that, while *Venice* is reported in English (differently from the instance in Klimpfinger's data where Rome is referred to as *roma*, 2007: 55), other 'territorial' references are inserted in the 'original' language (*Ponte di Rialto*, *Ponte dell'Accademia*); as to the *Ponte della Costituzione*, it is reported combining the L1 and English (*Calatrava Bridge*); an explanation for the name of the bridge is given, as well as for the popularity of its *Calatrava* name. A possible interpretation could be that either English or Italian are employed for references which are well known as they tourist or artistic sites, and English is used when the need for further specification (e.g. *bridge*) is perceived in order to fully share the cultural reference. In the long post example (28) is part of, which describes a trip to Venice with pictures consistently added to the narration, the comments are all in English; two participants are located in Italy, one in the USA, one in Russia and one in Singapore, and thus represent a varied audience from a linguacultural point of view; some interactants appear to have first-hand experience with the *Calatrava* bridge, and some also comment on its aesthetic qualities. This may lead us to infer that the blogger's personal experience has been successfully partaken, not least in affective terms, both thanks to the use of English and in its more specific linguacultural terms as expressed through the participant's L1.

Another exemplification can be detected in *Mantova is Mantua for foreigners*, where a similar care for the potential international audience can be detected in the fact that the English version of the name of the city is provided together with its Italian equivalent term; in the example we can also notice a metacomment related to what seems a perceived 'across-languages' function the English version of the geographical reference plays (*for foreigners*), while at the same time 'localizing' it by means of yielding the name of the city in Italian.

CS into the participants' L1 is also frequently employed in conjunction with references to films or books which specifically belong to the Italian cultural scene. In several cases, as in the following extract (29), the titles are also translated into English; the extract is part of a post related to the books the blogger read over an entire year; apart from the titles of the books in Italian (and one in German), the post is wholly in English, and includes literature both in English and in Italian.

(29) B *I segreti della jungla nera/I pirati della Malesia* (The mysteries of the Black Jungle/The Pirates of Malaysia)– *Emilio Salgari: I grew up with Salgari's novel. Sandokan, the Tiger of Malaysia, is my childhood's hero and the story of his doomed love for Marianna, the niece of his sworn enemy, British colonialist Lord Guillonk, one of my favorite love stories ever. These are my mandatory bedtime summer readings.*[…]
La lunga vita di Marianna Ucria (The long life of Marianna Ucria) – *Dacia Maraini: I don't think this book is known outside of Italy, and it's a shame* [plot in English follows].

Besides providing the translation of the book titles into English, the blogger in this case explains their relevance to his/her personal history in the case of Salgari, who has indeed represented a must-read piece of children literature for whole generations in Italy. The reference to this, as well as to the following book where the blogger specifies that it is probably best known only in Italy, can also be read as an act of cultural 'identity'-sharing with the audience, which is recognizable both in the use of the title in the original (Italian) language, and of the description of the two plots in English. A very similar process is detectable in the frequent practices of intertextual CS by quoting (and translating), above all in memes, titles of songs and films, at times accompanying them with a hypertextual link where additional information can be retrieved in English; this too could be seen as a wish to index affiliation to their linguaculture, making it at the same time internationally understood through English. This hyperlinking strategy is deployed in another case for a local event, accompanied by an overt comment about it yielding information in English, which, as in the previous examples, has been most likely provided with the blogger's international audience in mind:

(30) B *Friday night I went with some university to Recco (a little town near Genoa) to see a fireworks show for the "Sagra del fuoco" (I have found a little article about the event in English here). It was the first time I saw a show so good*

References to the participants' primary linguaculture in terms of food are also quite common in the data; the name of different dishes are generally provided in the 'original' language, and then translated or explained in English, as in memes about favourites – *FAVORITE PIZZA TOPPING? Quattro formaggi (which should be cheese pizza I think), and Margherita (tomato sauce and mozzarella, a Italian cheese* – and even in whole menus on special occasions, such as food eaten on New Year's Eve, where we find specific cultural reference to Italian traditions (*Lenticchie e Cotechino*); in this case, too, a hyperlink to a picture is provided as a multimodal resource, and an explanatory comment is added as to its good-luck wish connotative meaning, once more confirming the care skillfully taken in providing support to ease understanding by an audience that may not necessarily be familiar with such specific linguacultural references. Resorting to English to explain the cultural elements which are perceived as relevant in terms of the participants' linguacultures can thus be seen as a way to make them become from (potentially) unknown into 'known-in-common' resources – a cooperative strategy frequently found in ELF environments. Indeed, the interactants' positive and emphatic comments to these entries show appreciation towards such sharing and localizing practices, carrying across not merely transactional but also affective meaning.

A somewhat different connotation can be noticed in a post containing a reference to Halloween which, despite its origins in the Anglo-American world, has in the last decades spread over Europe and, albeit not free from criticism, is celebrated in native as in non-native countries. This reference is in this case explicitly connected to *Risotto con la zucca*, a typically seasonal dish, especially in Northern Italy, for which a translation and a hyperlink to the recipe are also provided.

Similarly, a rather detailed explanation is provided for a local practice related to mobile phones habits in the following example, part of a post related to a personal experience:

(31) B *Because you see, I gave him a rang (uno squillo donnine belle)* [a ring my dear ladies] *it's a common practice in Italy, when you need to tell something and you don't have money you make the other person's cellphone ring only once (it can mean "yes" or "I received your message" or another 100 things depending on the context).*

In the above extract, rather than a translation, a longer explanatory comment is given, most likely since a 'mere' translation of the lexical item would not convey in full the nuances related to the social practice of a *squillo*; the comment that follows – *it's a common practice in Italy* – may be said to represent a contextualisation cue to the explanation similar to the "we say" highlighted by Cogo (2011: 119), also in socio-identity terms.

It could be argued that some of the above-quoted instantiations of CS in terms of lexical borrowings, such as types of pizza or pasta, have become part of international (globalized) cuisine and can therefore be understood as 'bits of language' even by people with no familiarity with the blogger's L1; the same could be maintained for other references such as the ones mentioned in a meme about favourite food: *oh man this is tough. Lasagne if it's Italian. Mansaf if Arabic, sushi and tofu if it's Japanese ^__^ Least favorite: pasta al pesto.* However, what appears relevant in the use of these elements in ELF contexts, such as the blogs in my corpus, is on the one hand the linguistic choice operated to refer to elements connected to primary linguacultural identity in the 'original' language, thus localising them as 'brought along' meaning(s), values and views (Wei 1998; Cogo 2009: 264). These strategies also resonate with Lee and Barton's findings, where a participant who simultaneousy employs bilingual practices on Flicker remarks that, as "English wasn't good enough to explain" the complex cultural connotations embedded in a Chinese character, both codes were used: "I tried my best to share all these information I found with my flicker friends who may have an interest in that" (2012: 137; cf. also Barton and Lee 2013). Similarly, the bloggers in my corpus can be seen to employ their L1 to express nuances in meaning that are part of their expressive wishes.

Thus, when dealing with cultural events that are 'specifically and typically tied to the bloggers' primary linguaculture, either English, the bloggers' L1, or a mix of both, are employed. A general tendency in the data appears that of using the mother tongue to address a specific group of people a blogger has in mind, similarly to the functions of CS to specify an addressee, and English/code mixing when speaking to a more varied, international audience, which may then respond either in Italian or in English. The following extracts nicely illustrate the point:

(32) B
WORLD CHAMPION!!! ITALY WON THE FIFA WORLD CUP!!!!

Yes!!! I'm so happy and now it's time to celebrate!!!!
C1 (Italy) *E chi ci sperava?*________* Alla fine non ho capito nemmeno che avevamo vinto e sono rimasta davanti alla tv basita, con un'espressione piu' scimunita del solito. Fantastici, fantastici!!! ^_^ -me abbraccia tutti*
C2 (UK) *YAY!! i was celebrating all night!*

Here the blogger's affiliation to 'Italianness' can visually be detected in the flag; the post, despite dealing with a 'typically' Italian event, is in English, once more most probably for the sake of the bloggers' friends whose L1 is not Italian. The comments, one in English and one in Italian, exemplify how language(s) alternation is a naturally occurring feature in these internationally-oriented blogs, constituting an additional linguistic resource to communication, which is 'unmarkedly' employed. Similarly, in the next extract by a different blogger both the post and the comments are in English, although in this case we find an instantiation of CS in the form of an exclamation:

(33) B *Italy won! Italy-Germany 2-0!!!! Yes!!! Jump for joy in my room*
We won!!! I'm so happy!!! after a very long match, when they were left only a few minutes of the second extra time, thanks to goals from Grosso and Del Piero (Go Alex!!!!) we are in the Final!!! The next match will be sunday versus the portugal team or the french team. GO ITALY!!!!!!!!!
C1 (Italy) *I'm sooo Happy too!!! FORZA AZZURRI!!!*

C2 (UK) *You don't know how happy i was that we won! ^_^*
B *I can guess your happiness (probably similar to mine when the match ended) ^^! Here in Italy, after the match, the streets were full of people celebrating our victory!!*

Again, English is likely to have been employed by the participants located in Italy (blogger and first commenter), and an inclusive *we* can be noticed as to the commenter located in the UK. This and the code-switch in the first comment, *FORZA AZZURRI!!!*, have most probably been inserted to signal affiliation to the participants' linguaculture in this international sports event.

In the exemplifications illustrated so far, several strategies have been deployed alongside CS to the aim of sharing locally-set aspects, either culturally or practice-specific. These resources are both linguistic and non-linguistic – e.g. multimodal uploads and hyperlinking – as typically afforded by the technicalities of the mode. The interactionally-oriented imagined audience of the bloggers can be clearly perceived in their use of English as the commonly shared means of communication with their diversely-located interactants. At the same time, resorting to another language in code-switching often contributes to indexing either the specificities of the 'local' culture (L1), or affiliation to shared interest-based communities of practice (L1, Ln), such as the use of Japanese for a transnational group of interest, in our case predominantly manga and anime. Such a skilful and entwined use of linguistic resources can be seen to exemplify how, in virtual spaces in particular, territorial and linguistic boundaries as traditionally conceived of are continuously crossed, trespassed and interwoven with linguistic resources from English and other language(s), moving liminally in areas that are at the same time global and local, related to the participants' linguistic 'personal histories' and to other affiliations they wish to signal, thus testifying to the complex intermingling of codes in the pluri- and polylingual practices ELF users deploy to their communicative and self-expressive aims (cf. e.g. Cogo 2012b: 291).

The use of explanatory comments or communicative strategies such as the ones exemplified above – more or less specific to the medium – draw attention to how bloggers are highly considerate of their international audience, and 'plurilingually flexible' in combining different codes: by using English alongside their L1, and other Lns, often pre-signalling these 'local' elements, they comply to the wish to politely co-operate with participants (Pölzl 2003: 13, 15) in making meaning more accessible. The two strategies do not appear to be in contrast – i.e. privileging the local vs. the global, or vice-versa; on the contrary, they can rather be regarded as exemplifications of how English in its role of lingua franca can be fluidly employed alongside other languages to relate to aspects of linguacultural identity and broader cultural affiliations that are part of these multilingual ELF users' repertoires when addressing an international audience. Code-switches, as well as borrowing, can thus be seen to represent instantiations of local elements which are re-localized into English, in this case to be shared with an audience that may, or may not, be familiar with them. With Montes-Alcalà, we may say that "switching for lexical items [...] is closely related to the biculturalism of the subjects rather than to the lack of proficiency in any of the languages involved", particularly when such elements are 'culturally-bound' (2007: 167).

Moreover, the exemplifications also point to how CS is by no way random practice, but constitutes integral part of the participants' polylingual repertoires, that are employed alongside English to signal more specific affiliations. In this light, nor can it be seen as a sign of a lack of proficiency in English, but rather as a further indication of these multicompetent ELF users' language awareness, as we will discuss more in detail in Chapter 7, as well as of their care to make more specific references 'sharable' with an international audience. As for Barton and Lee's informants, "[b]y accommodating their language choice to different audiences, Flickr members [...] actively present themselves as global citizens through their constant switches between languages and selecting the most suitable form of language for their intended viewer [...], even though not all of these languages are used in their offline lives" (2013: 48).

A multiplicity of voices appear thus to emerge from such heteroglossic practices, which are deployed for several functions. Particularly when dealing with events that are closely connected to the participants' primary culture, posts and comments are characterized by Italian-only, such as, for instance, in posts related to celebrations of the centenary of the Unification of Italy, or including references to the 25th April celebration of post-war liberation. The participants' choice of employing their L1 may indexically signal intimacy and feelings of group belonging to and by one part of the community of their interactants, i.e. one particular constellation of participants, as well as shared linguacultural identity.

As to the other function of CS, that is, to emblematically signal cultural affiliation in ELF encounters, only a few occurrences are instantiated in the data, such as informal exclamations by swear words in Italian, closing greetings in a message (such as *ciao ciao*), or occasional tags (e.g. *right?*). In terms of multilingual in-group language practices related to commonly shared interests, we find the *ne* interjection borrowed from Japanese, that may thus be related to manga and anime in-group affiliation, and is employed in combination with English in five instances by different participants, in its tag function as an intersential code-switch, and once with Italian and English (*Arigatou, ne* *__________* *Buon divertimento a Lucca!!*[120]) [enjoy Lucca]. On the other hand, the informal interjection *meh*, which is listed in the Urban Dictionary[121] as implying indifference, is employed by six participants, possibly to a similar in-group function feature, in this case related both to Japanese and non-standardness in language use. Thinking about the 'constellations of interconnected practices' the participants are often engaged in, these instances could also be seen as exemplifications of how the multilingual repertoires of the participants are drawn upon to create "an even stronger cultural association for the interlocutors" (Klimpfinger 2007: 55).

Intersentential and intrasentential code-switches are also widely present across turns, which in the data do not frequently overlap (cf. Herring 2001), but rather most often take the form of interactional duets, resembling adjacency pairs in spoken conversation, as exemplified in the following:

(34) C (Spain) G*razie mille! :)* [thank you so much]
B *Prego eheh! :D*

(35) C (USA) *Thank you thank you thank you!!!!!!!!*
B *your welcome your welcome!! xD*

These extracts are part of a long stretch of brief comments related to icon-making, and instantiate language alternation in two different interactional pairs; the second extract also provides an example of accommodation in language style, where the blogger affectively, both verbally and via the *xD* emoticon, mirrors the commenter's repetition at the previous line. Indeed, as in these cases, emoticons very frequently seem to retain an affective and emotive function, either to emphasize verbal meaning, or to add in tone and mood, representing an integral part of the message (Crystal [2006] 2001: 38-39; Huffaker and Calvert 2005: 4-5, 12-13, Baym 2010: 60) working as a conversational feature (Myers 2010: 78-79). In the following example, the interactive turns with code-alternation are longer, illustrating once more how CS is employed to 'bind', so to say, participants together, without at the same time disrupting the conversational flow.

---

[120] Referring to the International Festival of Comics, Animation, Illustration and Games, http://www.luccacomicsandgames.com/it/2013/home/ (last accessed 15 November 2013).

[121] http://www.urbandictionary.com/define.php?term=meh&f=1 (accessed 15 November 2013).

(36) C1 (Italy) *Bellissime <3* [very beautiful]
C2 (Croatia) *Beautiful :) Love the GG ones of course*
C3 (USA) *GG ones are lovely! I miss CSINY a little bit when I see icons like these...*
B *Thanks :D You should watch CSI:NY again. It's good* ♥
[...]
C4 (Italy) *[...] oO Ma cosa non sono queste icone *__* [...] Mi piacciono quelle di GG, ma quelle che amo alla follia sono quella della season finale di GA *___** [wow, these icons are so beautiful. I like the GG ones, but the ones I'm crazy about are those of the GA final season]
B *Grazieee. [...]*[thank youuuuu]
C5 (UK) *I love the DL ones. :)*
C6 (Australia) *I snagged #x and #x. I love them and will credit you. Nice work :)*
B *Thanks ^_^*

The alternation of languages as exemplified in the above extract can be ascribed to accommodation, as well as to enhancing intimacy and solidarity among the participants taking part in the interaction. Indeed, thanking practices as to sharing materials, particularly for multimodal (remixed) ones, are common in Web 2.0 environments (cf. e.g. Lee and Barton 2012; Barton and Lee 2013). In the blogs in my corpus when the focus is on shared interests, e.g. icon-making, in the overwhelming majority of cases such multimodal postings give way to a high number of comments, where languages are mixed and alternated, not necessarily in connection to the L1s of all the participants. In these, as in longer stretches of discourse, the combination of different linguistic codes can be seen as a retextualization "of globally disseminated popular cultural products", where English is employed to address a wider, global audience, and the L1 a more local one, who is assumed to understand both linguistic codes (Leppänen et al. 2009: 1092).

On several occasions English lexical elements are entwined with the bloggers' L1 in intra-sentential code-switches, often in interactions including speakers of Italian: despite the availability of a common L1, these insertions can be seen as pointing to how "the use English appears to have become an intrinsic element of their online interactive practices" (Seargeant and Tagg 2011: 509; cf. also Leppänen et al. 2009: 1097-9; Androutsopoulos 2001: 10), as exemplified in: *awwwesome!!!!!!!!! ^^ senza parole come sempre!!!! :D* [speechless as usual] (C, Italy); *no words davvero* [indeed] (C, Italy); *davvero fantastiche! Great job!! : D* [really fantastic] (C, no data); *Io sono spoiler-free* [I am spoiler-free] (B); *brave as always, aspetto le prossime 1500 canzoni XD* [clever as always, I'll be looking forward to the next 1,500 songs] (C, Italy). In these cases English can also be seen to have become a natural part of verbal routines (Androutsopoulos 2004: 89-90) characterising these online practices.

All in all, code-switching and the language choices operated in these virtual community spaces appear not to be in opposition, but complementary: on the one hand, the wish to share more locally-situated primary linguacultural identity aspects via English with a wider international audience, which emerges from the corpus data as the most frequent practice. On the other hand, findings seem to show that the choice of communicating via a different language – either the L1 of the bloggers and of some of their friends, or an Ln – is carried out to signal in-group belonging and affilitation to certain 'constellations of interconnected practices' stemming from the participants' shared interests, as well as linguacultures.

6.5. Discussion of findings

The exemplifications provided from my data clearly show that the exploitation of plurilingual resources, both in adapting the code and in code-switching, is common practice in these internationally-oriented blogs, where English is used as the main lingua franca of communication. Bloggers and participants draw on all their linguistic and semiotic resources to fulfil their communicative aims, using linguistic items that, although they may be unusual in form or collocation, are created in accordance with the rules of the virtual language. Whether in the creation of novel words, in using 'existing' ones by shifting their meaning, or in adapting idiomatic and fixed expressions, these multicompetent L2 users adapt the code in skilful ways to express meaning and content that they deem salient to their interactional and self-expressive purposes. At the same time, they draw on their plurilingual repertoires, using linguistic elements from their L1 and other languages they are more or less familiar with, and have different levels of proficiency in. As in Cogo's study, participants in these blogs "demonstrate themselves to be skilled languagers that cross, mix, and play with their resources, which assume different meanings in the contexts in which they are used and with the niterlocutors with whom they are negotiated" (2012b: 308).

The use of languages other than English appear to fulfil three out of the four main functions identified for CS in ELF by Klimpfinger (2007: 35-38, 2009: 359-366), i.e. specifying an addressee, introducing another idea, but above all signalling different cultural affiliations. Code-alternation, either when constituted by single lexical items, by short phrases or longer passages, when occurring in isolation or as part of a sequence of switches (cf. Klimpfinger 2007: 56), is naturally and easily incorporated in the flow of discourse for a diversified set of communicative and socio-cultural aims and effects.

Both CS and the exploitation of plurilingual resources appear to represent an integral part of the multifaceted repertoires these ELF users have at their disposal in creating meaning, which are deployed to express aspects related to their cultural and multicultural identities, as well as common interests, so that they can be shared with the audience. On the one hand, locally situated primary linguacultural elements may be represented in non-standard linguistic forms, thus sharing local meaning in internationally-oriented practices. This can be enacted through strategies such as hypertext linking to online resources, translation or explanations in the commonly shared code – English – in order to make them 'sharable' with internationally-located interactants. At the same time, affiliation to more globally set interest-based fan communities is made locally meaningful in blogs also by resorting to CS as a 'binding' tool in these 'constellations of interconnected practices'. As in other web-based collaborative modes, such as fanfiction writing, young people "mobilize a set of heterogeneous linguistic and textual resources which quite explicitly position and link up their discourses as both local and translocal" (Leppänen et al. 2009: 1092; Barton and Lee 2013: 114). As noted by Cogo (2012b: 309),

> the distinction between the local and the global, the international and the domestic is certainly blurred in ELF contexts, with the resulting increased variability of linguistic repertoires. ELF is also unquestionably a hybrid phenomenon, or a 'pluralized English' (House 2012: 173), though the plurality or hybridity are not a sum of different and bounded linguistic systems, but are of a fluid, variable and shared nature, which rely on use.

The naturalness and nonchalance (Cogo 2009: 266, 2011: 166) with which languages are mixed in ELF discourse point to "polylingual languaging" as a preferred style of communication (Jørgensen 2008: 170). As Leppänen and colleagues have shown for young people's media practices, CMC environments and the new media encourage bilingual practices with English, whereby linguistic resources are appropriated and employed to communicative and community practices, and "participants seem to treat English-language elements as an integral part of their communicative mode", which is intrinsically characterized by language mixing (Leppänen et al. 2009: 1097). As discussed at length in Chapter 1 (§ 1.3), this is confirmed by findings as to blogging practices in several studies: bloggers signal their being "comfortably cosmopolitan" (Myers 2010: 54), travelling "from one language to another" (Leppänen and Peuronen 2012: 391) through the use of different languages, and choose codes according to the audience and communities they want to interact with, as well as the linguacultural or interest-based identity they wish to express and affiliate to. Indeed, as in Leppänen's study, for these bloggers "English is becoming one of the languages with which they can express themselves and communicate with other – Finnish and non-Finnish – bloggers" (2007: 166). "In this respect, the use of English on Finnish blogsites can be seen as one example of the increasing popularity of English as the lingua franca of the web which allows bloggers with varied linguistic backgrounds to communicate with one another" (Leppänen 2007: 166.). At the same time, the use of code-switched elements, especially in the participants' L1, "contributes to a sense that the writer[s] and the world depicted in the blog" are perceived as locally relevant, too (Leppänen 2007: 166).

In CMC studies about CS and minority languages, the function of the latter was often shown to be of affirming "in-group intimacy and familiarity, contrasting with a more standard or formal lingua franca, which in each case was English" (Negrón Goldbarg 2009: 3). In my data, English and other languages do not appear to be employed according to this distinction, but rather to differentiated communicative practices and purposes. Affective attitudes are often (creatively) expressed in English, or Englishized and hybrid linguistic forms, such as *lovve, lovva, addata, friendata, snaggata, stalkare, handcufferemo* (cf. Tsiplakou 2009: 379-380 for similar findings), which are in most cases related both to the technological characteristics of the setting and to the shared interests of each constellation of practice. What Leppänen points out for young Finnish people web practices in her data can also be said to apply to the participants in my corpus; they are "generally fairly proficient in English" and "choose to use English for their own purposes, rather than English choosing them as channels through which it unidirectionally spreads into Finnish [or other European countries] society and culture" (2007: 167).

To sum up, these blogging participants draw upon their linguistic resources and repertoires to engage in communication, skilfully gauging when and how to employ them according to the setting (e.g. in accommodation to the different comments within a thread), to the linguistic and sociocultural characteristics of their interlocutors (the participant(s) to the discussion in comments), as well as to their self-expressive, affiliative and communicative aims, in languaging practices that are often polylingual in their natural mixing of several resources, including shorter or longer bits of language(s). These blogging ELFers thus seem to

> use the language at their disposal to negotiate meaning and personal relationships and so co-construct mutual understanding and establish the common conceptual and affective ground of a 'third space'. They engage in banter and troubles-telling and language play, the very linguistic 'abnormalities' of ELF talk in reference to ENL norms draw attention to the essentially normal functions they realize as a natural and actually occurring use of language (Seidlhofer 2010a: 158).

The way in which plurilingual resources are integrated in ELF use in my findings appear to be effective, creative and attuned to the expressive and interactive purposes of these internationally-set bloggers. As Ferguson points out,

> [...] many learn English not to interact with native speakers but with other lingua franca users, and the importance of English in their lives is such that it constitutes an element in their personal identity; and these bilingual users deserve to be identified not as deficient speakers of a British or American native-speaker English but as competent, authoritative users of their own self-sufficient variety (2006: 175).

Even though they believe their English at times 'sounds weird', as we will see in the next chapter, these ELF participants are in actual fact language-aware, effective language users and communicators, who stretch and put into practice whatever English they have learnt, within and outside school.

Chapter 7
Learning, using and appropriating the language

> The teaching of foreign languages must be made relevant to social life, where people need to communicate with each other in order to set the stage for possible mutual understanding. (Kramsch 1993: 240)

In the last two chapters we have explored and discussed how the young participants in this study communicate in their personal blogs with people of different linguacultures through English, which constitutes the commonly shared code in such internationally-oriented settings. We have exemplified how communication is effectively carried across, appropriating English to its lingua franca function and exploiting the potentials of the virtual language. This is done not least by drawing upon the repertoires which are part of these plurilingual ELF users. Findings from the data appear in line with ELF research in other contextual settings, also for the functional motivations that underlie 'non-standard' instances of language use. English certainly appears to play a consistent part in the bloggers' lives; besides having learnt it for at least five years in formal education, they have consistent experiences with English in outside-school contexts, and consciously employ it in its lingua franca function to reach out to an internationally-oriented audience (see 4.2.3).

Given the relevance of contacts with English both in formal education and in the environment, in this chapter we will first explore the presence of English in the European context, particularly in bottom-up terms, to then examine how the roles of L2 learner and user increasingly complement each other in ELF contexts. The self-perceived negative competence in English displayed by the ELF users in my data, which is at times set against a native-speaker backdrop, will also be dealt with, as well as their language-aware use of ELF and of other languages as emerging from the data. Finally, implications of findings for ELT practices will be discussed.

7.1. English "from above", English "from below"

As in most parts of the world, English functions as "the *de facto* 'extra-territorial' lingua franca throughout Europe" (Seidlhofer 2010b: 355), serving as a common communication language in an array of domains, across territorial boundaries, with speakers who may be located within or outside Europe. Together with national and other (local) languages, most Europeans come into contact with English, and/or have it as part of their repertoires: as Graddol points out, this contact "can be extensive or minimal" and can take place in professional and private lives, or both. "'Having English' in Europe has thus become a bit like having a driving licence: nothing special, something that most people have, and without which you do not get very far" – that is, it has become a basic skill (Graddol 2006: 359).

In European countries English is learnt as a foreign language (EFL), which means that "Europe is an example par excellence of the Expanding Circle. Its history of contact with English, its uses of English, its goals for learners of English, and the range of users across social groups is unique and thus distinguishes it from exponents of either the Inner or Outer Circles" (Berns 2009: 194). At the same time, this uniqueness also presents significant diversities, since its role and presence are differentiated across European countries (cf. Berns 1995): societal bilingualism with English appears a stronger reality in some more than other countries, particularly in Northern but also in Central Europe (e.g. the Netherlands, Germany, Luxembourg), where English can be said to act more and more as a second rather than a foreign language[122] (Jessner 2006: 49). As a consequence, it proves increasingly difficult to apply traditional EFL/ESL categories in the European context as a whole (Mollin 2006: 86-87) since such a distinction is becoming more and more blurred (Berns and de Bot [2005] 2008: 212).

Although in different measures, it is nonetheless undeniable that English is highly present in the lives of all Europeans and particularly so for younger generations. According to the 2006 Special Eurobarometer *Europeans and their Languages*, English stands out as the most widely spoken foreign language in Europe with a 38% figure, reaching 89% for Sweden and 87% in the Netherlands; other languages follow at much lower rates: for instance, German and French at 14%, Spanish and Russian at 6%, Italian with a 3% and Polish at 1%. In 2001, 53% respondents in the survey said that they could hold a conversation in a language additional to their mother tongue and

[122] Although such realities also question the notions of 'first' and 'second' language, since, particularly in Outer Circle countries, "English is one language among many, functioning for most speakers within a multilingual repertoire" where language hybridity resulting from mixing of these linguistic resources is extremely frequent (Dewey and Leung 2010: 8).

in 2006 the figure increased to 56%[123] (for earlier data cf. also Mollin 2006: 59-64; Labrie and Quell 1997). Younger generations in particular reveal a good degree of competence in English, with 69% in the 15-24 age and over 58% in the 25-39 age ranges. The 2012 Special Eurobarometer *Europeans and their Languages* confirms that English is the most widely spoken foreign language; 25% respondents state that they can read articles and follow the news on the media in English, and 26% use it to communicate online (European Commission 2012: 6).

In most EU countries English is part of formal instruction since primary school; according to the *Eurydice* 2005 report data, in 2002 it was learnt by 66.17% pupils in Europe; in the 2008 *Eurydice* edition figures for secondary education raised to at least 90%, and to 50% or more for primary school pupils (cf. also Enever [2005] 2008: 179-180; Graddol 2006: 88-89; Mollin 2006: 69-71). In the 2012 edition, 73% primary school pupils learn English, and more that 90% in secondary education (EACEA/Eurydice/Eurostat 2012: 11). English has acquired a place in all curricula becoming the first foreign language in formal instruction, often replacing other less spoken languages, as it is otherwise often chosen as a preferred option (Berns et al. 2007: 24-25). It is also increasingly introduced as a vehicular language in education through CLIL provision (e.g. Graddol 2006: 86; Seidlhofer 2010b: 358; Dalton-Puffer 2007; *Eurydice* 2006, 2012), and as a medium of instruction in tertiary education within internationalisation measures (e.g. Graddol 2006: 74-79; Berns et al. 2007: 27-29; Berns 2009: 195; Jenkins 2011a: 926-927, 2014; Gnutzmann and Intemann [2005] 2008: 18; Björkman 2011b).

This prominent role in FL education is also acknowledged in the public opinion: the 2006 Special Eurobarometer *Europeans and their Languages* reports that 77% of the EU citizens reckon that English should be the first language learnt at school by children (2006: 9) starting from the age of six, together with a second language[124]. According to the 2012 edition, 79% Europeans deem English is the most useful foreign language for children to learn (European Commission 2012: 75). Thus, despite EU policy and declarations positioning all languages on equal status, in practice English has become the most commonly employed code across different domains (cf. e.g. Seidlhofer 2010b: 357-359; House 2003: 561-562, van Els 2005).

---

[123] 28% in at least two languages (26% in 2001), 11% in at least three languages, though a still significant percentage of 44% in none, and language skills seem to be not evenly distributed both in terms of territory and of socio-demographic groups.

[124] French gained 33% responses, followed by German with 28%, Spanish 19%, Russian 3% and Italian 2%.

Indeed, several EU language policy documents have repeatedly stressed the importance for European citizens to learn more than one foreign language for mutual comprehension, as well as to appreciate the complex linguistic and cultural richness of Europe. Just to quote one example, in the EU Action Plan 2004-2006 *Promoting Language Learning and Linguistic Diversity*[125] we read that for EU citizens

> a *lingua franca* alone is insufficient […] to integrate into the local community. And whilst a *lingua franca* may help with basic transactions, real mutual understanding and a rich appreciation of other cultures comes through direct contact with people in other countries – by attempting to speak their language. […]. The goal for every European [is] to have meaningful communicative competence in at least two other languages, not necessarily native-like fluency (European Commission 2003: 45).

However, European policies towards multilingualism have often been criticized, particularly on the ground that support to multilingualism is often confined to the level of intentional declarations rather than encompassing actual implementation (e.g. Ammon 1994; Modiano 2009; Phillipson 2003; House 2003). Although in principle recognizing respect for linguistic diversity as a founding principle, and thus acknowledging the complex plurilinguistic European reality (e.g. Balboni 2004), EU language policies in their call for multilingualism can be seen as "an attempt at reconciling fundamental contradictions underlying the very idea of the EU, namely unity that is coexistent with diversity" (Studer et al. 2010: 257). The two are not easily reconcilable in practice, and represent a complex challenge from several points of view: the historical-ideological construct of one-language-one-nation as deeply entrenched in the construction of European nation states (cf. e.g. Wright 2004; Anderson 1983), with a still pervasive bias towards monolingualism and homogeneity in how language, and (national) language communities, are perceived (e.g. Canagarajah 2007, see also Chapter 1). Moreover, the underlying human rights discourse in which the promotion of multilingualism is set emerges as increasingly "mingled with socio-economic ideologies" (Studer et al. 2010: 258) – a factor the latter which is also visible in the increasing demand and implementation of English in school curricula since an early age, and as a vehicular language in tertiary education. Nonetheless, and not least, the fact that English constitutes the main language of

[125] http://eur-lex.europa.eu/LexUriServ/LexUriServ.do?uri=COM:2003:0449:FIN:en:PDF (accessed 15 November 2013).

wider – intranational and international – communication in Europe cannot be ignored: as Seidlhofer acutely points out:

> 'Turning' linguistic diversity into a social and economic advantage is an ambitious objective indeed, especially when this linguistic diversity appears not to be high on the list of priorities of the citizens themselves, who predominantly go for English if given a choice, plus a few other 'big' languages. (2010b: 360)

And indeed, English has constituted for at least a decade the main language for international contact among European citizens, whether for professional, educational or personal communication aims. Despite the acknowledged role of lingua franca it plays in numerous European contexts, its significance as detached from the variety(ies) of its native speakers appears as yet not to have been officially recognized. One of the central factors can certainly be seen, as Seidlhofer suggests, in the still prominent position that the constructs of nation, national languages and "independent national lingua-cultural identity" play in the European context (Seidlhofer 2010b: 356, cf. also Cogo and Jenkins 2010: 274; Berns 2007a: 2-6, 12-13; Phillipson 2003).

Given the de-facto role ELF plays across Europe, several calls have been made for its formal recognition in EU documents and policies, which would detach it from the association to the national language and culture of its native speakers, and dissociate it from it being their 'exclusive property', taking into account the role that non-native speakers have in shaping it through use. Such recognition could also promote on the one hand a "democratisation of English" (Ferguson 2006: 176), distinguishing its appropriation as ELF from what have been defined as 'linguistic imperialism' impositions (e.g. Phillipson 1992), or Anglo-American linguistic and cultural hegemony and 'Mcdonaldian' homogenization (Phillipson 2003; Block 2004). On the other hand, rather than 'displacing' other less-widely spoken languages in Europe, giving recognition to ELF would set it 'alongside' other codes in its role of "partner language" (Hülmbauer, Böhringer and Seidlhofer 2008: 29; Seidlhofer 2003: 10-11), and could effectively promote awareness of plurilingualism, as well as support the EU commitment to multilingualism (cf. e.g. Cogo and Jenkins 2010: 279, 289-290; Lichtkoppler 2010: 192-193, 210; Seidlhofer 2010b: 362-365; Berns 2007: 9; Modiano 1999, 2001).

Indeed, as Hasebrink et al. (2007: 118) point out, the use of English as a common means of communication among young people in Europe, across national boundaries and language communities

> serves as a marker of a social identity, of group relations, but does not replace the identities established in the first language or the language of the home. Instead, a new identity is drawn from what English offers as a linguistic and cultural resource, one that individuals have at their disposal to communicate effectively in the lingua franca context that is Europe.

Furthermore, opportunities of contact with several languages, as well as multilingual acquisition (Cenoz and Jessner 2000) are increasingly becoming part of the linguistic and social scenarios in many European countries, first of all in relation to globalization processes, increased mobility, as well as migration flows, leading to linguistic "super-diversity" (Vertovec 2007). Encounters with 'bits and pieces' (Blommaert 2010: 43) of language are also becoming common experience, often resulting in forms of truncated repertoires as they are learnt and employed to different functions and in different contexts of use (Blommaert 2010). Even within Expanding circle contexts, in global(ized) communication language repertoires act as "truncated complexes of resources often derived from a variety of languages, and with considerable differences in the level of development of particular resources" (Blommaert 2010: 106). As we have seen, ELF involves by definition at least three languages: the speakers' L1s and English; "many Europeans are capable of understanding a large amount of cognate lexis, as a result of either multilingualism or what Franceschini (2009) calls 'unfocussed acquisition' – picking up a language through direct contact without any overt, conscious effort" (MacKenzie 2011: 86).

The same point is made by Jørgensen, who maintains that "[t]he young urban language users have contact with speakers of a wide range of different languages. The young speakers become acquainted with many different features from these languages, and they use some of them in their speech without learning all the other parts of the languages involved", and frequently insert them in speech, particularly in in-group interactions, without necessarily connecting these language 'bits' to the specific languaculture they 'originally' come from (2008: 168-9). This common practice is noticeable also for young Italians, whose linguistic repertoire is rapidly changing also due to fast tranformations in society, and to the role of the new media. Their linguistic repertoires increasingly include forms of language mixing: "il multilinguismo si estende rapidamente, sino ad interessare una percentuale altissima degli scambi comunicativi; nella stessa frase si incrociano e si sommano italiano formale, italiano colloquiale, usi scherzosi e usi pensosi, dialetto e italiano regionale, espressioni inglesi e formule burocratiche, ecc.[126]" (Sobrero 2010: 27; cf. also Miglietta and Sobrero 2007: 150, 157). As for English, Tosi reports that in Italy "the situation reflects the more general picture of the contacts between national languages and English" with the latter employed in official "government, commercial and scientific organizations" (2001: 205), which is influenced by the spread in availability of US commodities, as well as by the role of lingua franca this language has come to play. A natural consequence is also the increasing presence of borrowings and word-formations involving English in different domains, particularly in advertising, in the linguistic landscape (e.g. Tosi 2001; Ross 1997; Coluzzi 2009; Vettorel and Franceschi 2013), as well as in computer and electronic music related fields (Tosi 2010: 219-223). Indeed, the influence of English can more and more frequently be found in many European languages at several linguistic levels, above all in the lexicon, either through borrowings that become nativized, or hybrid forms (e.g. Hoffmann 2000; Androutsopoulos 2004, 2005; cf. also papers in Görlach 2002; Tosi 2001), whereby (young) users adapt the language to their own uses and contexts, "incorporating it into their national languages by borrowings and codeswitching" (Cheshire 2002: 32). This is frequently done according to the (perceived) relevance to youth (sub)cultures, whereby these linguistic elements representing at the same time expressions of globalized cultures and local identities (e.g. Androutsopoulos 2004; Pennycook 2007). Significantly, for young Europeans English also seems to be assuming an "emotional" role (Cheshire 2002: 29-32), bearing connotations of internationalism that are often connected to in-group solidarity within international youth culture and subcultures, which are "no longer necessarily associated with a specific English-speaking country" (Cheshire 2002: 31).

Therefore, for younger Europeans, competence in English can be said to be acquired via both 'top-down' processes in formal education, and 'bottom-up' contact thanks to the everyday pervasive presence of English, especially in pop culture and the media – what Preisler terms "English from below" (1999: 242-246; cf. also Mollin 2006: 74-79; Seidlhofer, Breiteneder and Pitzl 2006: 3-5; Phillipson 2003). Music and computers, personal networks with family and friends (the latter created and maintained also via the Internet), increased mobility and travelling constitute above all for younger generations significant and consistent opportunities of contact with English

[126] "Multilingualism is rapidly extending, to the point of affecting an extremely high percentage of communicative exchanges; formal and colloquial Italian, 'thoughtful' and joking usages, dialect and regional Italian, English expressions and bureaucratic formulae – they all cross and add up within in the same sentence" [my translation].

(cf. e.g. Berns and De Bot [2005] 2008: 198-202, 208-209; papers in Berns, De Bot, Hasebrink 2007; Grau 2009: 161-164; Ranta 2010: 159, 167). As Mollin points out (2006: 79):

> [i]t is a given that in Europe contacts between individuals from different states have substantially multiplied in the last decades. Town twinnings, school exchanges, programmes such as Erasmus and, simplest of all, holidays, as well as increased general mobility, have all created situations in which Europeans meet and need to find a common medium of communication", which is in most cases represented by English as the most widely known language.

When looking at the media, the situation appears varied across European countries particularly as to dubbing and subtitling practices for TV products (Berns et al. 2007: 32-33; Berns and de Bot [2005] 2008: 200-201). However, generally English is largely present through popular music on TV, on the radio and on CDs/cassettes, and more recently in downloading practices from the web, as well as in advertising, the latter not least in the printed media (Berns et al. 2007: 34-35; cf. also Martin 2002, 2008, Piller 2001, 2003; Gerritsen et al. 2007; Tosi 2001; Vettorel 2013b). Significantly, young people across Europe appear to "selectively choose" the media that become part of their environment, also in correlation to different levels of competence in English, which "underscores that proficiency may not be conceptualized as a one-dimensional construct"; consequently, "[t]he particular level of proficiency and the particular communicative competence in English they acquire will depend on concrete needs" (Hasebrink 2007: 109-110; cf. also Berns and de Bot [2005] 2008: 207-209). Younger generations' use of English appears thus to be correlated to functional needs, according to the different settings in which it is employed – professional, private or the globalized mass media – developing into "a multi-dimensional means of expression and communication" (Hasebrink et al. 2007: 114).

As discussed in Chapter 1, the Internet undoubtedly represents a prominent opportunity of contact with English, both in passive and in active terms, often in combination with more traditional media (Hasebrink 2007: 90-93). Together with music, the web consistently seems to be the medium through which younger people's contact with the global language takes place across several European countries (Berns and de Bot [2005] 2008: 195, 208-209; Hasebrink 2007: 92; Hasebrink et al. 2007: 113; Mollin 2006: 79-82) and, more generally, across territorial geographical boundaries. As Bolton well summarizes, "[t]oday, the linguistic experiences of young people in particular are becoming increasingly diverse, and, in this context, their linguistic worlds are not simply defined through physical space, but also through electronic space, educational travel and migration, global travel, media awareness and usage, popular culture and the virtual spaces of the internet" (Bolton 2012: 33). These uses encompass both global and localized functions, where English is consciously chosen in its lingua franca role; as in Leppänen's study, we could say that they "choose to use English for their own purposes, rather than English using them as channels through which it unidirectionally spreads into Finnish [and European] society and culture" (2007: 169).

Indeed, what Erling reports for German students could well apply to other contexts in Europe, at least for universities in major cities: "[s]tudents of English at the FU[127] are proficient in the language by the time they go to university, and for most of them, English plays an important role in their lives, both inside and outside the classroom" (Erling [2005] 2008: 218). Furthermore, the main motivation provided by 99% respondents to why they learn English is "communicating with people from other countries has become important to me and *English is our bridge*" (Erling [2005] 2008: 220, emphasis added). English emerges thus as a significant presence, and is extensively used also as a means for intercultural communication in the students' environment, as well as in international contexts either through mobility or via the web (Erling and Bartlett 2006: 14-18; cf. also Erling 2007: 116-121). Furthermore, many respondents in Erling's study openly connect English to its function of an international means of communication, without identifying themselves with any specific Anglophone linguaculture or native linguistic variety, but rather as "'good' English or a mixture of varieties depending on the context" (Erling 2007: 127).

In Ranta's study (2010) related to Finland, 62% respondents say that their active use of English had taken place in lingua franca contexts, either at home or abroad, while a minority of 25% use it to communicate with native speakers; more than half (56,5%) predict that in the future they would use English to interact with other non-native speakers. An overwhelming majority (70%) state that they do not keep to a specific variety of English in their use of the language, but rather to "'their own personal variety'" (2010: 163); yet, 23% express a preference for American English due to its prevalence in the media, in contrast with British English as the most widely taught school model (Ranta 2010: 161-163). The majority also show positive attitudes towards the use and intelligibility of non-native English speakers in the media, favouring diversity and variety. Similarly, secondary school and Erasmus

[127] Freie Universität Berlin.

participants to the LiNEE project, in relation to their perceptions of ELF in European settings highlight how English is generally used in a variety of contexts such as "student exchanges, school trips, family holidays" as well as work experiences (Cogo and Jenkins 2010: 282; cf. also Cogo 2010: 308), positively valuing the language skills of multicompetent ELF users. The same appears to emerge in a parallel study with Erasmus students in Prague, who, albeit acknowledging NS English as "real" and "correct", do not think of it "as an appropriate goal in ELF contexts" but rather value "strategies of accommodation, negotiation and cooperation as a key to successful communication" (Kalocsai 2009: 40).

The above-outlined situation points to the fact that "school is but one source of contact with English – and at least for some groups not the most important one" (Hasebrink et al. 2007: 115). However, an important element to be taken into consideration is that the increasingly prominent presence of English 'from below' seems to be perceived and kept separated from the school context by learners/users, also in their teachers' perceptions. Grau's (2009) study related to the presence of English in German youngsters' lives, particularly in outside-school contexts, has shown that in their free-time activities such as TV, music, computer games, Internet and travelling, teenagers are considerably exposed to English. Teachers, while showing awareness of some among these practices, such as listening to music, surfing the web and computer games, appear on the whole not fully aware of their relevance, particularly as to the active involvement in language use they entail. Interestingly, although expressing the desire for a stronger connection in the classroom with their 'real-life' outside-school contacts with English, given that it is frequently related to personal interests these young people also show a wish to keep them separated from the classroom "to avoid the risk of their English teachers 'exploiting' them for pedagogical purposes" (Grau 2009: 169). Teachers, on their side, either for lack of time or as they are doubtful about the appropriateness of content and (in)formality of language in school contexts, are not particularly keen on their inclusion in classroom activities. Significant however is the fact that students appear unsure and doubtful about the relationship (and possibly usefulness) of "school English" with the language as "actually used by competent users of the language" (Grau 2009: 170).

A more encouraging picture emerges in Ranta's study with Finnish students (2010): while 67% point out that in school more attention is given to grammatical correctness than to communication skills to be used in outside school, real-life contexts, 79% respondents state, somehow contradictorily, that English instruction provides students with "good abilities to use the language independently after school" (2010: 165-166). This perception can possibly be interpreted as appreciation of training in 'formal' varieties of English, also in relation to final exams (Ranta 2010: 167), as well as to the perceived predominant 'focus on grammar' in classroom teaching practices (Ranta 2010: 175). Differently form Grau's study, the teacher respondents in Ranta's research are well aware of the substantial presence of English in the students' environment, and the majority display knowledge of its international role, with reference to the students' future needs, too; 74% also show appreciation towards non-native varieties in the media (2010: 168ff.). Positive evaluations towards exposure to different varieties are also expressed (79%), and 52% teacher respondents lay stress on "encouragement to communicate without worrying too much about errors" (Ranta 2010: 169). Despite this growing awareness of the consistent presence of ELF in the student's environment, many teachers "showed fairly mixed feelings about the models and goals that should be present in the classroom": the native-speaker model was in many cases still perceived as an "appropriate yardstick for measuring their students' skills", and a consequent perception of "a division into 'school English' and 'real-world English'" (Ranta 2010: 174).

A somewhat similar picture emerges in D'Andrea's study related to the Italian secondary school context: on the one hand the teacher respondents acknowledge the role that ELF interactions play in the students' everyday life (including international exchanges) and express favourable attitudes towards the inclusion of different varieties of English in didactic terms. On the other hand, however, the models of language they mostly refer to in classroom practice are ENL, traditional ones. Furthermore, as the author points out,

> [a]s to the students' roles as learners or users of English, the teachers' views converge more towards the former which keep a prevailing position in their perception of the students, to a disadvantage of their role as users. To be more precise, these teachers tend to keep the role English should retain for the learners within the school walls, and separate from that it has for the users outside school (D'Andrea 2012: 212)

D'Andrea relates this stance to "the great importance teachers tend to give to form correctness, which is seen as a fundamental step in the process of acquiring the model of language to be provided within the educational path, which happens to be a prevalent NS one learners are expected to conform to" (D'Andrea 2012: 212). Similar findings as to perception of correctness of form emerge also in Vettorel (2013c).

As we will discuss in the following sections, these perceptions bear significant relevance in terms of the extent to which ELT practices could be reconceptualized in order to take account of the pervasive presence and changed role English currently plays in actual contexts of use. Whether in 'passive' exposure or active use, indirectly in the students' environment or in their direct first-hand experience, as we have seen in relation to blog online communication, such exposure undoubtedly represents a substantial part of their contact with English.

7.2. English and ELF users

In the previous sections we have outlined how English is being used for an increasingly wide range of communicative purposes and, despite variation across European countries, its presence in the media, in the linguistic landscape and the environment in general, as well as in educational contexts, has been rapidly growing.

Together with exposure to the language in its written (e.g. the media, advertising, the linguistic landscape, computer communication) and oral forms (e.g. songs, advertising and non-dubbed media products), English is more and more actively employed in practices 'from below', which are in the case of young people frequently connected to "Anglo-American oriented youth subcultures" (Preisler 1999: 244; cf. also Mollin 2006: 74-78). Such contact with English is generally mainly related to American and British varieties, the former preferred by younger people (although British English is considered more suitable for teaching by 68% respondents in Preisler's research). In Preisler's study the widespread presence of English in the Danish society is perceived in most cases as a practical consequence of internationalisation (92%), which is deemed pragmatically useful as "it helps improve people's English" (89%) and "widens people's cultural horizon" (69%) (Preisler 1999: 247). According to Preisler, while young people's active use of the code may at time mirror the informality of native non-standard features, their contact with other non-native speakers of English is frequent, and ought thus to be taken into account in formal instruction, too, together with exposure to both American and British English.

Educational mobility programmes constitute an increasingly significant factor in the active use of the language in international contexts, which can in most cases be characterized as ELF communicative settings. These range from EU partnership and exchange projects involving schools since/from nursery and primary level (such as eTwinning, cf. e.g. Crawley, Gilleran et al. 2010; Crawley, Gerhard et al. 2010; Vettorel in preparation), to secondary education (e.g. James [2005] 2008; D'Andrea 2012), and in higher education both with the Erasmus programme (cf. e.g. Kalocsai 2009) and internalization measures in Universities (e.g. Jenkins 2011a, 2014; Mauranen 2012). Together with new technologies and the Internet, this increased mobility via EU-funded programmes, as well as at a more personal or family level in tourism, has made transnational communications among Europeans (and more generally at an international level) easy and widely common. And it is English in its lingua franca role that is in most cases employed to interact in such settings. Hence, language learners have multiple opportunities to simultaneously take on the role of ELF users all along their language learning process (Seidlhofer 2011: 189-190), either at a personal level or within educational mobility contexts.

7.2.1. Language learner, language user, language learner-user

In ELF settings L2 speakers are conceived of as language users who employ the language to the aim of effective communication, and their "status depends on the language functions rather than on the language forms involved" (Hülmbauer 2007: 15; cf. also Hülmbauer 2009: 328-329). Traditionally, on the other hand, in SLA and ELT non-native speakers of English are considered as 'permanent' learners, within a deficit perspective that regards any deviance from ENL norms as part of interlanguage and as 'language errors' (Hülmbauer 2007: 6; cf. also Jenkins 2006a, 2007: 239-240; Seidlhofer 2007a: 147, 2011: 186-187). The term 'language learner' sets thus emphasis on the process of learning a language for later use, and "it concentrates attention on how people acquire second languages rather than on their knowledge and use of second languages" (Cook: 2002a: 3); furthermore, the term bears connotations of deficiency as it is positioned against a native speaker idealized model within a SLA paradigm (Firth and Wagner 1997; Firth 1996; 241; cf. also Mauranen 2011: 159; Seidlhofer and Widdowson 2009b: 94-95; Kramsch and Whiteside 2007: 911-912).

An L2 user can be defined as "any person who uses another language than his or her first language" (Cook 2002a: 1); bi- and multilingual speakers are an increasingly widespread reality world-wide (e.g. Jenkins [2003] 2009a: 163-165), and L2 users can be said to represent the norm and not an exception. Rather than within a deficit perspective as measured against native-speaker proficiency, the concept of L2 user is set within a paradigm of difference: consequently, L2 users would be best compared with other successful L2 users, i.e. members of the same group, "not with a native speaker – a member of another group the L2 user could not belong by definition" (Cook 2007: 9 and *passim*). As Bassetti and Cook put it (2011: 171):

> [f]rom the multicompetence perspective, using a native speaker standard for measuring L2 users is like describing apples in terms of pears; it may yield some insights – there are cone-shaped apples called Worcester Pearmains – but it distorts the picture considerably and it never yields the distinctive qualities of apples that make them different from pears.

ELF users, or Bilingual English Speakers/users of English, can be positioned along a differentiated level of proficiency continuum (cf. Jenkins 2006a: 141, [2003] 2009a: 90; McKay 2002: Chapter 2). As Canagarajah, points out, even people with a limited proficiency in the language can successfully communicate in ELF (or LFE, as he defines it) contexts, and "[t]his facility is no doubt attributable to the language awareness and practices developed in other contexts of communication with local languages. Multilingualism is at the heart of LFE's hybrid community identity and speaker proficiency", and LFE speakers' "competence for cross-language contact and hybrid codes derives from their multilingual life" (2007: 925).

Language learners may therefore be at the same time L2 users once and when the language is employed as a means of communication; as Cook puts is, "[s]ome of these L2 learners become L2 users as soon as they step outside of the classroom" (2002a: 3). Furthermore, as Firth argues, "[l]anguage learning is a ubiquitous social activity" and, being communicative competence a continuously evolving and dynamic process, "any language users, (including both L1 and L2 users) will always be 'learners' (or 'acquirers') regardless of the social setting" (2009b: 130). Hence, "[n]otions of language use and language learning are not only conceptually inseparable, they are also context sensitive and context dependent" (Firth 2009b: 130). This position is also part of Seidlhofer's argumentation that "language learning and using are *not consecutive but simultaneous* processes", whereby, taking into account their experience with their mother tongue and possibly of other languages in their repertories, "language learners are already language users and will quite naturally be inclined to exploit the foreign language as they exploit the one they are familiar with" (Seidlhofer 2011: 189; cf. also Widdowson 2012).

Given the global presence of English in a diversified array of domains, and the wide range of settings where it is employed as the lingua franca of communication by more non-native than native speakers (Crystal [1997] 2003: 62-71; Graddol 1997: 10-11), the role of learner and user do undoubtedly often overlap (cf. Cook 2007: 241-242). As outlined in the previous sections, English is a consolidated presence in top-down as in bottom-up contacts; new technologies and electronic media have come to constitute a salient space for across-boundaries communication, where English is most often employed as the shared lingua franca. International mobility has in the last decade immensely increased the range of opportunities for young people of all ages, from primary school to tertiary education, to come into contact with people of variegated linguacultures, and in these contexts, which encompass both educational and non-educational communicative settings, English is often the only in-common code of communication. In these – as in other – ELF contexts participants may be (still) learners, but can at the same indeed be conceived of as users in that they employ ELF in contexts of communication which are authentic (cf. Mauranen 2011: 162-3).

In such settings ELF speakers as L2 users exploit "whatever linguistic resources they have for real-life purposes" (Cook 2002a: 2); as widely shown by ELF findings, and exemplified in Chapters 5 and 6, a variety of skills and strategies are commonly put into practice and strategically employed in order to communicate with other (native and) non-native speakers, and it is this set of skills that clearly and positively distinguishes L2/ELF users from monolingual speakers (e.g. Cook 2009b).

7.3. L2 learners, L2/ELF users and self-perceptions of proficiency and competence in English

Teacher attitudes towards ELF has been a widely investigated area both in terms of intelligibility and acceptability issues (cf. Jenkins 2007 also for an overview of previous studies; Llurda 2005; 2009); other researchers have looked into learners' stances towards ELF and non-native varieties (c.f. e.g. Jenkins 2009c: 203-206; Erling 2007: 121-127, [2005] 2008: 221-226; Hynninen 2010), while relatively fewer studies have incorporated views on how ELF speakers perceive their competence in English when used in ELF contexts (Cogo and Jenkins 2010; Kalocsai 2009; Cogo 2010; Hynninen 2010, 2013; Kontra and Csizér 2011). As discussed above, given the increasingly frequent opportunities in which English can be employed as a lingua franca, drawing a clear-cut line between the roles of L2/ELF learner and user is becoming a challenging and debated/able issue. Students participating in international mobility measures, for instance, are at the same time learners and users of ELF, since in such contexts communication takes place most often with other participants who belong to different linguacultures; the same applies to digital settings, such as the interactants in internationally-oriented social networks, forums and blogs who use English for self-expression and interpersonal communication (cf. e.g. Berns 2009). Perceptions about ELF as expressed by students, and by Erasmus exchange students in particular, can to my mind be seen in this double light since their role and experience include the dimension of *user* as well as that of *learner*.

Participants in the previously cited LINEE research study with European secondary school and Erasmus students' experiences of English in international contexts reveal overall a positive orientation towards ELF, both in its function of LF allowing communication across different L1s, and towards ELF speakers' "good communicative skills", where non-nativeness is not negatively perceived (Cogo and Jenkins 2010: 282-283). The communicative and language skills of multicompetent ELF users are valued positively also in Kalocsai's findings, where they are even compared against NS students' lack of appropriate communication skills (2009: 40-43). Thus, experiencing the role of *learner-user* (D'Andrea 2012: 82-83) in such settings can provide that kind of direct, first-hand contact with ELF which can contribute to a change in stance towards the role it plays as an effective and real lingua franca of interaction. As Cogo remarks,

> the participants' backgrounds, their coming from different socio-cultural contexts and possibly their everyday exposure to cultural and linguistic diversity, may influence their positive orientation towards ELF, as itself born out of language contact and diversity, and displaying similar creativity and meaning negotiation to the ones they are familiar with. (2010: 308)

However, other studies have pointed to the other side of the coin, i.e. how ELF speakers often feel "incompetent" and overtly express and share the opinion that the English they "produce is 'flat' and thus deficient in nature" when compared against ENL norms (Hülmbauer 2007: 4; cf. also Hynninen 2010, 2013; Jenkins 2007). Furthermore, both in Kontra and Csizér (2011: 148) and in Hynninen (2010: 37), despite acknowledging the changing and international role of English and displaying awareness of its plurality, students identify native varieties – and mostly with reference to the idealized native speaker conceptualization – as the most appropriate, correct model. Even in the overall positive evaluation of ELF expressed by Cogo's informants quoted above, a "reference to the native speaker ideal is present" throughout the interviews and focus groups (2010: 306). This sense of "linguistic insecurity" (Jenkins 2007: 247-250) appears common to many participants in my corpus data, too, and is detectable particularly in meta-comments related to their self-perceived inadequate level of proficiency in English. As discussed at length in Chapter 4, the people with whom these bloggers interact are diversified and most often include speakers of different linguacultures. Their use of ELF is in most cases not merely informative or transactional, but aimed at establishing interpersonal relationships and exchanging ideas in relation to common interests, which, as we have seen, are frequently shared by the participants in these online communities. English is their chosen language of communication since, in its lingua franca role, it allows to reach out to an interactional and linguaculturally diversified audience and to interact with old and newly-made friends across territorial and language boundaries.

By definition, ELF does not have any native speakers to it, and constitutes an additional language for all ELF users – native and non-native speakers of English – who thus share a common status of non-nativeness. As Hülmbauer (2009: 325) highlights, in ELF "[c]ommunicators from different lingua-cultural backgrounds face the challenge of establishing mutual intelligibility through a language which is not their mother tongue". ELF is therefore a common code through which to co-construct meaning, establish relationships and share worlds, interests and thoughts that may be either personally or professionally oriented, in a variety of different settings. Shared non-nativeness is inherent to the role of ELF users and, as shown by ELF research and discussed in previous chapters, it works as a resource in communication rather than a hindrance to it.

Participants in my corpus data often overtly express their lack of confidence and 'linguistic insecurity' frequently feeling the need to apologise about their 'poor' English, as the following exemplify: "*I apologize for my bad English* xD I hope *I'm understandable* <ç<"; "*Well, I'll try to improve my english. I've never written a blog in english* […]. *However I hope you'll understand what I'm written*. Xxx"; "*Non capisco neanche perchè scrivo nel mio inglese* °_° " [I don't even understand why I am writing in *my English*, my translation].

The language they effectively use to communicate is thus in their self-perception "*bad*", at times a sort of personal 'variety' (*my English*, emphasis added), about which the hope that it will be comprehensible to their audience is expressed. As in Barton and Lee (2013: 119), on the one hand they seem to claim "ownership of such 'poor' English", while at the same time expressing their preoccupation to be communicatively effective and understood (Barton and Lee 2013: 120), at times connecting it to identity issues ("My poor English is part of me", French informant quoted in Barton and Lee 2013: 121). This self-perceived inadequate proficiency is at times overtly set against a native speaker standard, which is clearly seen as 'the' model of reference: comments like *I'm not an English mother tongue* or *English is not my first language* appear frequent, and even a simple web-search with these keywords can reveal how widespread this kind of perception is. Other times the feeling of low competence is specifically associated to grammar (*wow, great grammar XD Ok, must I repeat that I can't write in English?*), or to language skills as in the following extract:

(37) B *[...] my English is horrible, so I force myself to write in this language sometimes You might call this masochism... and you were completely right! I don't like English, I only like the fact that I understand perfectly this language, even if I can't speak (or talk) properly. It's so frustrating!*

This comment, besides the above-mentioned perceptions of linguistic insecurity, also exemplifies how writing in English on the web is frequently perceived by participants in my corpus data as practice to improve their language skills (Hynninen 2013: 185-186), also collaboratively (Barton and Lee 2013: 118); furthermore, the feeling of frustration expressed in the last line in relation to the blogger's competence in 'passive' and 'active' language skills may be interpreted as a sign of awareness as to the usefulness of this language to communicate on the web; on the other hand, it can also be related to beliefs connected to the difficulties in using it "*properly*", i.e. according to ENL norms. The following extract nicely summarizes the points discussed above:

(38) C (Belgium) *[...] my English is very bad [...] and generaly I don't understand question and answer ^^ Sorry English is Not my mother tongue ^^*
B *English isn't my first language too, and unluckily I have also some problems in writing correctly, but I try to make people understand what I write ^^. I'm italian where are you from?*
C *Yes I try people understand me ^^ I'm belgian. My mother tongue is French ^^ Nopt far of you LoL bisous*
B *Yes, I really would like to be your friends too (A new friend! a new friend! I'm happy when I meet new people), and as you I'm also interested in Sesshomaru-sama, see-saw, full metal alchemist, roruouni kenshin and TM revolution.*

> *I had seen that you are a fanfic writer, I really like read fanfic in english but I can't write one because my english is really pathetic and also I'm unable to think an interesting plot (this is the main reason^^).*

Here the two interactants, whose mother tongues are respectively French and Italian, overtly declare their non-native status, at the same time apologising for it. The blogger, in commenting upon his/her interactant's statement, adds that she/he too has "*problems in writing correctly*", presumably referring to spelling and grammar. Significantly the purpose of making "*people understand*" what he/she writes is stated and taken up by the interactant immediately after; in the next turn the blogger expresses her/his enthusiasm at making new friends and meeting new people, then stressing the interests he/she and his/her 'new friend' share. Their 'incompetent' English appears to perfectly serve their communication and online friendship aims. It is noteworthy too that these statements of self-perceived poor non-native English are here consistently accompanied by a *kaomoji* smiling emoticon, which can be read as an affective means to underline that the participants' non-English-nativeness is a shared status; laughing emoticons are present in similar statements also in the extracts above, further testifying to their mitigating, empathic and affective social function in CMC. In the last extract (38), besides, in the last line the "^^" emoticon is added to the comment about the fact that the blogger's "*pathetic English*" is not the main reason not to engage in writing fanfiction, thus further mitigating the previous statements and creating in-group 'we-are-all-on-the-same-boat', bonding ties (cf. also Barton and Lee 2013: 121-122).

While pointing out that the target model of the native speaker seems to be still much alive in teaching (and learning) models, Cook (2005a: 54), referring to the insecurity feelings we have outlined above, poignantly remarks that

> I couldn't count how many times a perfectly fluent L2 user has apologized to me for their level of English; yet they were doing something I could not possibly do in their language […] People who have spent their language learning lives trying to speak as much like native speakers as possible become upset when you say that such a target is meaningless: what they want to hear is praise that they have almost got there and could be mistaken for natives.

Similarly, many among Hynninen's informants overtly express their insecurities about 'their own' English (2013: 102-109), although acknowledging that in ELF communicative settings ENL correctness is not a major issue

(2013: 182-184, 189). According to Barton and Lee, this "self-deprecating metalanguage", as they define it (2013: 114), is commonly found on the web, and NNSs seem once more to hold an authoritative voice, both for English and other languages (such as Arabic, Barton and Lee 2013: 115). Similarly to my findings, Barton and Lee's Flickr informants appear to downplay their linguistic competence in English through the use of "some typical affective adjectives such as 'good', 'bad', 'terrible', 'poor'" (2013: 117), often accompanied by apologetic expressions. And indeed, as Mauranen notes, bivalent attitudes as the ones shown in the data are commonly expressed in interviews, even among academic ELF users, and "to some extent they may also reflect speakers' awareness of the transition that English is currently undergoing", which has been very fast (2012: 25).

Somewhat more comfortingly, rather than a hindrance to communication, non-nativeness is at times overtly seen in my data as a commonly shared status and a communicative resource, as the following extract exemplifies:

(39) C (Canada) *And sorry for the English* *[...]*
B *hey Thanks so much X3 Of course it's ok, I love making new friends! I added you back ^^*
Don't worry, your English is fine, anyhow I make mistake too, since English is not my first language either XD

Here the blogger's reply to the apology expressed in the previous comment shows a supportive attitude, which emphasizes both participants' common non-native status of ELF users, as well as the adequacy of their English to their aims: in the previous line, "*making new friends*" is indeed indicated as a salient purpose, which does not appear to be hampered by their "making mistakes" in their lingua franca use of English.

As shown in Chapters 5 and 6, despite their 'declarations of linguistic incompetence', the participants in my corpus appear to effectively draw upon all their linguistic resources to self-expression and meaning making, as well as to establish relationships in their blogs. Their non-nativeness is actually exploited as a common, binding and shared resource "for sense-making" (Firth and Wagner 1997: 290), creating a sense of commonality in interaction; similarly to Barton and Lee's findings, in these online interactive spaces, "talking about English skills allows participants to build rapport, to ensure mutual intelligibility, and to negotiate identity in the Flickr world. It is also clear that the very act of talking about one's own language skills is an act of opening themselves to the global Flickr world, an act of positioning themselves as active participants" (2013: 121).

As in the above extracts and as emerging from other ELF research findings, in my corpus data participants often "make their non-native status, and a (perceived) lack of competence, explicit" in their talk (Firth 1996: 254), either by flagging 'unusual' words or expressions, or by openly declaring their non-nativeness. Indeed, what Hülmbauer remarks appear to be as valid for the participants in this study: "ELF users are very often very conscious of their special status as non-native language speakers. As they all share this position, there is a great deal of identification with each other. Sometimes, the lack, or insecurity in 'correctness of form', in terms of linguistic knowledge is even foregrounded by the interactants themselves" (2010: 103) – and, we would add, cooperatively resolved, as illustrated by findings in Chapters 5 and 6 (cf. also Barton and Lee 2013: 121-122).

The bloggers and their interactants establish mutually fruitful and effective exchanges about a number of topics, ranging from their interests, such as icon making, manga and fanfiction, to commenting activities on more 'serious' issues; they effectively employ a language that is not their own to their communicative aims. As in Firth (2009a: 152), despite the variety of linguistic features that would not be considered 'standard', these bloggers and their interactants are effective communicators and "enjoy and cultivate personable and in many cases long-standing acquaintances with one another". In a variety of ways, they are "'doing not being an L2 learner'", and their primary focus is not on form but on "accomplishing transcendent interpersonal meaning" (Firth 2009a: 156). Although the participants in these online interactions may have no notion the code they are using is a 'lingua franca' as defined in research(ers') terms (Firth 2009a: 161), they employ English to the aim of communicating internationally with people of different linguacultures, to establish relationships with (new) people they wish to interact and communicate with. As Lee and Barton put it for language practices and language choice on Flicker, "[w]ithout an imagined global audience, our informants would not have translated their content info in English, nor would they have wanted to socialize and interact with the wider world" (2012: 141). Interestingly, also Lee and Barton's participants display a sense of self-perceived inadequacy as to their proficiency in English, which they – as the bloggers and commenters in my corpus – nevertheless use alongside their native language, in this way "positioning themselves as 'active' members of the site, thus attracting visitors from different parts of the world, regardless of their level of English proficiency" (Lee and Barton 2012: 142, 2013: Chapter 8). Lee and Barton's informants also often express awareness of the global role of ELF in their metalinguistic comments (ibid.), similarly to most bloggers in my corpus who stated they employ English to this aim (cf. § 4.2.3).

The above-illustrated negative self-perception about their inadequate competence in English – which is consistently voiced in my data – can be related to the "linguistic schizophrenia" Jenkins (2007: 214, 231) refers to in terms of accent and identity issues. While on the one hand their ability to appropriate the code for their communicative aims is noticeable in my data, on the other, their perception of linguistic 'foreigness' is somewhat hanging in the background, as seen in the extracts above and as the following summarizes:

(40) B *Sorry but I have to write this quote in Italian. I've already got a blog, where I write in Italian, and I didn't have the inspiration to write here, too in a language that is not mine and that I can't speak it and write it well. I'll try to find them in english but I think I will write some of them in Italian (especially italian songs)*

In this case the feeling of non-"ownership of the language" (Widdowson 1994, 2003: 35-43) is overtly mentioned, and can be related to a sensation of foreignness as "associated to concepts such as 'alienness', 'unfamiliarity' and 'strangeness', with an additional associative meaning of 'not belonging'" (Dewey and Leung 2010: 4). Such self-perceptions can most likely be explained as deriving from the conceptualization of English as a *foreign* language (EFL) in ELT practices (Dewey and Leung 2010: 4; cf. also Jenkins 2007: 149; Hynninen 2010: 34-37, 2013: 184 and Chapter 7), where the native speaker still constitutes the main point of reference and attainment in language learning, and is brought along also in language use: with Hülmbauer, "ELF speakers may feel incompetent particularly because they are used to making comparison to ENL" (2007: 4-5). Or, in Piller's terms, to "ideologies of passing" for a native speaker (2002: 198), that appear to be widespread for successful L2 users; developing "fuller descriptions of high-level L2 ability and the linguistic practices it entails […] would help to set up more realistic goals, and support SLT teachers by presenting students with realistic role models of successful L2 users rather than the monolingual native speaker they can never be" (Piller 2002: 201).

To recap, despite the negative self-perceptions associated with non-nativeness in terms of language competence, the shared non-native 'condition' in meaning negotiation is nevertheless most often exploited positively by interactants who are "*on the same boat*" in their shared status of 'foreigness'; and yet, "it is this drawing on being non-native speakers that facilitates their communication and enhances understanding" (Cogo 2012a: 101).

Despite their active involvement in communication via ELF, the SLA view that "NNSs are perforce deficient communicators, who are perpetually agonizing chronically struggling, like Sisyphus and his stone, to ascend the steep incline of their 'interlanguage', the goal being the promised land of 'target competence'" (Firth 2009a: 151) appears to be 'ghostly hanging' in their self-perceived competence as ELF users. Perhaps an increased awareness of the legitimacy of their effective use of English as a lingua franca could bring about new, more positive perceptions, like, for instance, the feeling of liberation which is perceivable in the comments expressed by the students in Seidlhofer and Widdowson (2003) when confronted with conceptualizations of ELF. And it would possibly help in overcoming the sense of "linguistic schizophrenia" Jenkins registered in her investigation of accents by non-native English teachers (2007, 2010) which similarly emerges in my study in relation to the participants' non-nativeness (cf. also Vettorel 2012).

7.4. Language-aware ELF users

Multilingual L2 users – or Bilingual rather than Monolingual English Speakers (BES, MES, Jenkins [2003] 2009: 90, 163-165, 2010: 111) – have "a different awareness of language itself" (Cook 2009b: 15), which, among other skills, often encompasses meta-linguistic awareness (cf. also Jessner 2006, [2005] 2008). Language awareness can be seen as "the development in learners of an enhanced consciousness of and sensitivity to the forms and functions of language" (Carter 2002: 64), or "the ability to consciously reflect about the structure and functions of language, about what it can and it cannot do, as opposed to competence in using a language as an instrument of communication" (Seidlhofer 2002: 293; cf. also Seidlhofer 2003: 22). That is, an ability not only to reflect on language, but also to consciously exploit its virtual potentialities, realizing them in language use. In my data, instantiations of language-awareness can be detected at different levels: for instance, the flagging practices illustrated in Chapter 5, in their signalling awareness of 'unusual' expressions, also by means of metalinguistic comments, constitute salient and telling examples. As we have seen, these multilingual and multicompetent ELF users frequently incorporate such comments and reflections in the natural flow of the interaction, mutually co-constructing meaning despite (or precisely because of) their non-nativeness to the language.

Such flagging instances and their negotiated 'resolution' in interactive activity (when present) are generally dealt with in a natural way in the data: responses from the interactants are supportive and content-oriented, and in some cases the meaning of the flagged word is cooperatively negotiated or co-constructed, too, making "the abnormal become normal" in a shared pool of resources (Firth 2009a: 163-164, 2009b: 144-148). In so doing, as illustrated in Chapters 5 and 6, not only do participants 'pragmatically' exploit the inherent possibilities of the virtual language creating 'unusual' words and expressions and actualizing these possibilities "in their own way" (Seidlhofer and Widdowson 2009b: 102); they also reveal – e.g. by drawing on regular word-formation processes – that they are language-aware users in their exploitation of the "language they have acquired as learners" (Seidlhofer and Widdowson 2009b: 103; cf. also Seidlhofer 2011: 186-190).

Further instantiations of language-aware use of English, as well as of other languages, can be detected in the frequent practices of translation participants engage in as part of their online sharing practices, such as poems from Italian into English, or songs from English, and Japanese into Italian, English, or both – and at times even transliterating practices from Japanese *Kanji/hiragana* to *Romaji* characters. These translation practices are at times accompanied by meta-linguistic comments, or by reflections about translation processes, where help, support or advice is asked for and/or offered by interactants, as exemplified in the following extract:

(41) B *I passed all the evening trying to translate my old fics from English to Italian, because I had found an Italian website that collects fanfics and I wanted to public mine even there but... ...I didn' succeed. Oh yes. Even if I'm italian I wrote my fics thinking in English and I discovered that the translations I made this evening simply SUCKED! Or better, it seems that in English the stories have a meaning while in Italian they are TOTALLY meaningless and there's NO way to make they become interesting. How weird. And now my question is: are the fics stupid in itself or I'm not able to write in my own mother language??*
C (no data) *It's not you, it's the languages. There are ways of phrasing things that don't translate well at all. Like in German there's the word Schadenfreude, which means taking delight in the misery of others. There isn't an actual word equal to it in English, so in a way it loses some of its meaning when translated. There's a better example, but for some reason I can't think of it right now*
B *I think I love you for your comment. (You know? even this sentence in italian doesn't have any meaning!) I'm so happy you think this thing too, because it was my first explanation, but you know, it sounded more like an 'excuse'... :)*

The interactive duet shows how the two participants share their reflections on translation practices, in this case specifically related to fanfiction writing (which is commonly carried out in English), and on how concepts expressed in one language are often awkward to be rendered into another. Here the commenter also cites a specific lexical exemplification from another Ln language, German (*Schadenfreude*), providing a supportive interpretation to its language-related uniqueness. These interactive language-related practices are particularly common in the data, not only with translations into and from English, but also for other LNs part of the participants' repertoires, as extract (42) exemplifies for Japanese; the extract is part of a post reporting the lyrics of a song first in Kanji and then in Romaji characters, followed by a translation into Italian and by the comment reported in the next extract:

(42) B *1.* […] *Traduzioni in inglese varie, come anche le mie interpretazioni. Questa mi è stata suggerita da C., ma comunque non abbiamo idea se sia corretta o meno. […] Vedete un po' voi.*
2. intraducibile. Ci sono due versioni "cring" o "crying". Contando che Gackt[128] *usa queste frasi in inglese come se fossero in giapponese, ho deciso che quella rimane così com'è XD*
[…]
C (It) *[…] Cmq, visto che alla fine hai scritto "guardiana" non è meglio mettere al femminile anche il resto?* […] *Brava!!!! ^^*
B *Sì metterò tutto al femminile! Ma diamine, sai che non ci avevo pensato? XD*[129]

In this case the comment to the original post provides a cooperative suggestion to the translation doubts expressed by the blogger, which is then positively taken up in the subsequent turn. Noteworthy also the collaborative practice in translation (*this has been suggested to me by C.*), and the direct address to the audience to evaluate the resulting translation ("*Vedete un po' voi"* [you are free to evaluate, my translation]).

Another common practice in the data is to publish posts both in Italian and in English, where the English version is most likely provided for the sake of the non-Italian speaking friends in the audience. In some cases, the two languages are mingled, possibly to the aim of intentional language-play or even

[128] A Japanese musician, singer-songwriter and actor, cf. http://en.wikipedia.org/wiki/Gackt (accessed 15 November 2013); the difficulty of translating lyrics from Japanese singers is also mentioned by other bloggers.

[129] [Several translations into English, as various as my interpretations. This has been suggested to me by C., but we have no idea whether it is correct […] you are free to evaluate 2. cannot be translated. There are two versions "cring" or "crying". Reckoning that Gack uses these sentences in English as if they were in Japanese, I have decided that this stays as it is. (B) […] In any case, seen that in the end you wrote 'guardian' in the feminine, wouldn't it be better to put all the rest in the feminine, too? (C). Yes I will set it all in the feminine! Of course, I had not thought about it, you know? (B). My translation].

ironic effect. An exemplification is provided in the next extract, which is part of a longer post related to the blogger's familiarity with Japanese:

(43) B *I found this italian group on facebook and I'd like to share with everyone. This is my life, everyday...*
[...] questo non significa che io conosca TUTTI i kanji in cui ti capita di imbatterti, che il 99% delle volte sono scritti in modo osceno e che immancabilmente ti portano a chiedermi "ma cosa vuol dire?"
[...] this doesn't mean that I know EVERY kanji you run into, that 99% of the time are written in an horrible way and that, without fail, make you wonder "what does it mean?"

In other cases, typical Italian sayings are introduced by a lingua-cultural marker "*in Italy/in my language we say*" (cf. Cogo 2010: 302) and given either in English or in both languages, as for instance in *we have a saying in my mother tongue which roughly translates as wear it with health* (C, no data), or *in Italy we say "God helps the ones that help themselves"* (B).

English, indeed, appears to play a consistent part in these bloggers' lives: they often watch TV series and read books in the original language (*now I want to read it in English XD oh well, I'll buy the English version when I'll have the money XP*), write, and read fanfiction in English (*I practically only read fics in English).* The common practice among fans to watch series in the original language, or with subtitling, is at times exploited in language-awareness, too, for instance in comments where the quality of dubbing in TV programmes is critically commented upon (e.g. *can you cope with the dubbing on Italian TV* (B), *Yes I manage to watch my shows, the dubbing is terrible at times I know, but I'm used so... Besides It's great when they say something in Italian, different from the real sentence in English lol,* C, France).

In other cases awareness of different varieties of English is displayed, too, in relation to World Englishes, as in the following:

(44) B *translating GW was a pain because of the strained audio and extremely questionable Englishese (Chinglish?:P) subs, so i had to do it all on my own, and withut a Japanese script it's very next to impossible, but still... Ganbarimasu*[130]*!!*

[130] *Ganbarimasu* is defined by the Urban Dictionary as follows: "Its a play on words of the Japanese word gambaru -gambarimasu, a succinct word best translating to 'I will do my best'". http://www.urbandictionary.com/define.php?term=Gambarimasu (accessed 15 November 2013).

It is interesting to note the wording in "*extremely questionable Englishese*", and the pejorative *Chinglish*, in this case possibly referring specifically to intelligibility problems. In the next extract, differences between British and American English are discussed, also in their relation to the connotations related to the terms 'football' and 'soccer' in the Italian context :

(45) C (no data) *I get confused when I see the word football these days because I know two kinds and I think, "Which one?!"* ლ(´﹏`ლ)
But then I reminded myself that M. is Italian and probably means the kind of football I just watched with y'all this summer.
[…]
B *ffff I'm sorry /7\ I don't like so much the word "soccer" and it comes easier to me saying "football" (also because in Italian we say football = american football and calcio = British football so we don't get Confused!).*
[…]
B *And I'm trying to use the more British words I can remember, since we aren't learnt any specific type of English at school, so I'd like to stick with either British or American...and British, I'm sorry to say, has a sexier pronunciation ;3;*

Apart from the personal, 'emotive' evaluation towards English varieties expressed in the last line (cf. Jenkins 2007: Chapter 6), as well as the preference to consistently employ either American or British English, noteworthy is in this case the reference to the "*type of English*" provided for in formal education, which is interestingly perceived as unidentified/able in terms of variety. Generally, in European – as well as Italian – curricula British English has traditionally been given prominence (e.g. Gnutzmann and Intemann [2005] 2008: 17; Cogo and Dewey 2012: 172; D'Andrea 2012: 170-177), although other varieties, American English above all, have increasingly been introduced in ELT materials, not least in vocabulary and listening activities (e.g. Matsuda 2012a; as to the Italian context cf. e.g. Vettorel 2010a, 2010b; Vettorel and Corrizzato 2012; Vettorel and Lopriore 2013).

As these extracts illustrate, interest in languages in general appears widespread for these bloggers who, as we have seen in Chapter 4, often speak, or are studying, at least two foreign languages, in some cases including Japanese or Chinese. At times even 'bits of language' (Blommaert 2010: 43) become an opportunity for participants to reflect upon translation practices and how concepts can be expressed in different languages, as in the following extract:

(46) C (Germany) *[...] What's the literal translation of the Italian title of 'girl with the dragon tattoo'? My Italian is crappy at best but it seems to be saying something different.*
B *[...] It does! The Italian title is 'Uomini che odiano le donne', and it's the exact translation of the Swedish title. I really don't understand why the title got changed in the English version.*
C *[...] Oooh, see, I didn't know the English title isn't the exact translation of the Swedish title(don't know the Swedish title), I just knew the German one was different from the English one and the Italian one didn't sound like it meant something with 'tattoo'. ;) I'm giving this too much thought apparently. LOL*
B *Män som hatar kvinnor is the Swedish title. I know this because I play 'Spot the Millennium Trilogy' every time I visit IKEA :) [...] What's the German title?*
C *LOL That's one way of keeping busy. The German titles are Verblendung (1st book), Verdammnis (2), Vergebung (3).*

Besides the curiosity about, and the meta-linguistic reflection upon, the different versions of the title of a well-known book in Italian, Swedish, English and German, this extract also hints at how bits of different languages are well present in the linguistic landscape, from book titles to videogames in Swedish, as specified by the blogger in the last turn. Their presence 'from below' becomes integrated in language use, and can be said to visibly represent how 'truncated' multilingualism is taken up and naturally deployed in these discursive practices.

Finally, and always in relation to language awareness, I would like to briefly explore a few exemplifications of language play. In my data, manipulative and language play practices are often based on the exploitation of deviant spelling to reproduce pronunciation, for instance in *tho*[ough], *becuz*; *forevaH*; *sparklus* [sparkles]; great *emosciòn* [emotion], *seekret fangirl*; *ughei* [OK] (cf. also Negrón Goldbarg 2009: 10-11; Tsiplakou 2009: 331 for similar findings, Thelwall 2009: 64, 68 as to social networks, and Androutsopoulos 2004 for media discourse). Such non-standard usage of orthography appears intentionally employed, in some cases to a humorous effect, contributing to create in-group solidarity, too. CMC discourse is indeed characterized by several deliberately creative devices, among which deviant spelling (cf. Chapter 3; Herring 1999, 2011) serving different functions, that are often locally created and deployed as a commonly shared 'code'. As Tsiplakou points out with reference to online discourse:

> generalized language play [is] performed through the construction of a genuinely mixed, hybrid code, that not only reflects the inherent hybridity of the di-

> scourse mode, but is further implemented *locally* to mediate in particular types of social negotiation in which the participants are socially aligned in virtue of sharing, and collectively constructing and performing, hybrid linguistic/discursive norms (2009: 380, emphasis added; cf. also Kramsch 2009: 165-166).

Language play also appears characteristic to ELF communication, where "[p]layfulness and creativity in spoken interaction show the richness of the language as well as the positive attitudes to being non-native" (Cogo 2012a: 102). In ELF settings the interplay of languages is, or becomes when shared in interaction, part of the linguistic resources deployed in communication; as Cogo points out, we frequently find an "atteggiamento ludico, dove il creare, giocare, e modificare le norme delle lingue standard è permesso e anche apprezzato dai partecipanti[131]" (Cogo 2011: 113). Language play for ELF speakers can thus be seen as related on the one hand, more in general, to an intrinsically creative use of the language, and on the other to meaning co-construction which is locally enacted – both being central elements to ELF. In my data playful creativity in deviant spelling related to pronunciation is at times exploited in interactional terms, to co-construct an 'intimate' atmosphere, showing "involvement in the interaction" (Hülmbauer 2010: 66 quoting Brkinjač 2005: 95). In CMC discourse, deviant spelling is one of the means that can be skilfully deployed to the creation of lighthearted humour, fostering intimacy and solidarity among participants; in this perspective can be seen other instantiations in the data, such as the variable ways of expressing gratitude, from *thanky thanky* to code-switched lexical elements such as *arigatou*, *graccie* and *muchas gracias*; in this light can also be interpreted the onomatopoeic *cliccheti clicheti* used to refer to a blogger's intense translation work in typing, or *ghì, guh gah* to express admiration for another participant's visual work, or the appellative *gurl/garl* used to affective purposes.

It is also worth noticing that phatic exclamations are frequently instantiated in the corpus: besides emoticons (cf. e.g. Herring 1999), we find instances such as *pleeeease* (3 occurrences), *aww(www)* (126), *OMG* (135), *wow* (149). Positive backchannels (e.g. *uhm*, *uhu*, *haha*) are also present, as well as other verbal routines and discourse markers signalling interaction such as *well* (203 occurrences) or more rarely *well well well*, *you know* (122), *I mean* (73), *BTW* (60) and *by the way* (26) (cf. de Geerdes 2005: 118-120; Myers 2010: 77-79; Puschmann 2013: 92; Androutsopoulos 2004: 89-90).

---

[131] "A ludic attitude, where creating, playing and modifying the norms of standard languages is allowed and appreciated by the participants" [my translation].

Such interactive and playful practices can be seen in their dual local function: on the one hand they are inherent to the mode (CMC), on the other hand they are drawn from the variegated repertoires of these multicompetent ELF users, and are locally realized in the creation of a mutually cooperative and in-group atmosphere. As Lichtkoppler (2010: 208) summarizes, ELF users

> use their multilingual competence and create a context-related community in which the linguistic and cultural backgrounds of their interlocutors are included and valued. They use a language they learned [or are learning] at school, add their intercultural knowledge to it, mould and re-form it, and still – or therefore – achieve mutual understanding.

As we have sought to illustrate, the ways in which English is employed in these interactive virtual spaces encompass language-aware attitudes that are enacted in the (plurilingual) exploitation of the code at different levels, in word-formation processes as well as in meta-linguistic comments, and more generally in the interest participants show in language and language practices related to the several Lns part of their repertoire(s), thus "doing not being" foreign language learners and users (Firth 2009b).

7.5. Implications for ELT pedagogical practices

> So how can learners become the authors of their own words beyond just mouthing the sentences from the textbook, imitating the utterances of their teacher, appropriating for themselves the phrases of other speakers? […] [i]t is through dialogue with others, native and non-native speakers, that learners discover which ways of talking and thinking they share with others and which are unique to them (Kramsch 1993: 27).

As discussed in earlier chapters, communicative practices involving English increasingly take place in ELF settings. Widespread mobility at different levels on the one hand, and new technologies on the other, have substantially contributed to creating opportunities for interaction among speakers of different mother tongues, for whom ELF constitutes in most cases the only commonly shared means of communication.

In this extended scenery English has become part of people's everyday life, above all for younger generations, who experience it not only in formal education settings since an early age, but also in outside-school contexts. This takes place both in its consistent presence in the linguistic landscape at large, and actively in interactions among ELF users. Increased mobility, transnational communication, as well as digital computer mediated settings such as forums, blogs and social networks, are prominent spaces where ELF is employed to carry out communicative acts that cut across territorial boundaries, and represent, particularly for 'digital natives', a natural ground for ELF use.

As illustrated in § 7.2, among other issues, that of drawing clear-cut distinctions between the role of English language 'learner' and that of 'user' has become increasingly problematic and debatable: first of all, the notion of complete and perfect competence in (any) language has been questioned on several parts (cf. e.g. Seidlhofer 2011: 89); secondly, the two roles of *learner* and *user* often overlap into that of *learners-users* (D'Andrea 2012), since communication via English as a lingua franca has become extremely frequent in everyday practices in an array of contexts. The problematicity inherent in this distinction, which directly derives from the significant and profound changes in the settings, circumstances and functions in which English is nowadays employed, clearly bears momentous implications for language pedagogy, too (cf. Jenkins et al. 2011: 16-17). As MacKay points out,

> [t]he growing number of bilingual users of English suggests that a productive theory of EIL[132] teaching and learning must recognize the various ways in which English is used within multilingual communities. Typically these bilingual users of English have specific purposes for using English, employing their other languages to serve their many additional language needs. Often they use English to access the vast amount of information currently available in English, and at times to contribute to this knowledge base. One purpose they all share, however, is to use English as a language of wider communication, resulting in cross-cultural encounters being a central feature of the use of EIL. (2006: 126)

Taking into account such experiences of ELF as encountered in 'real life' outside-school contexts could be not only beneficial in ELT in order to foster the development of communicative strategies to effective communication, but could also provide a substantial contribution to move away from the target-native speaker model which still appears to constitute the main point of reference in ELT beliefs and practices. As argued by Leung, together with the

[132] For a discussion on the use of EIL, ELF see e.g. Seidlhofer 2003: 8-9; 2004: 210-211; Jenkins 2007: 3, 2006b; Jenkins et al. 2011: 2

native-speaker of English idealization, "the reduction of the social to mean classroom interaction have effectively insulated the concept of communicative competence from the developments in English and the myriad ways in which it is now understood and used in different contexts" (Leung 2005: 139; cf. also Berns 2006). Considering these diversified uses and contexts as relevant for ELT pedagogy, rather than separate, distant and unworthy-of-notice, would allow "to reconnect with the social world" (Leung 2005: 139) beyond the narrowly-rendered "guided social practice" often represented in CLT models (Leung 2005: 136; cf. also Kramsch 1999: 132-135; Jenkins 2006a: 147-148; McKay 2002 Chapter 5, 2006: 122-125; Alptekin 2002). It would also contribute to reconsider the notion of communicative competence in the light of the diversity inherent to language use, rather than to an abstract and reified notion of language as a set of fixed (ENL) norms (cf. also Cook 2002b: 335-337; Widdowson 2012: 19-22). Ethnographic sensitiveness, epistemological relativity, reflexivity and critical consciousness "would potentially enable the ELT professional to re-engage with the socially dynamic uses of English and to continuously re-work the contextualized meanings of the concept of communicative competence" (Leung 2005: 138), which cannot any longer be related to one native-speaker variety but to the hybrid, locally emerging forms inherent to the current uses of English. Moreover, as Seidlhofer argues, in ELF settings and communities parameters for what is (grammatically) possible, feasible, appropriate and actually performed in terms of Hymesian communicative competence are bound to be different from native speakers conventions: "these aspects that Hymes [1972] identifies can be related not to the definition of some fixed communicative competence, but to the ways language functions in the communicative process itself" (2011: 91) in actual contexts of ELF use. This notion is further explored by Widdowson, who highlights that

> [u]se of the language in ELF, as research has amply illustrated, provides abundant evidence of how its users relate these factors. The possible is generally subordinated to the feasible and the appropriate, and what is, or more strictly has been, actually performed becomes irrelevant. It does not matter, in other words, whether the language conforms to established code rules or usage conventions so long as it is intelligible and pragmatically effective. […] ELF users develop their own construct of the possible as a function of what is feasible and appropriate for their purposes, by exploiting the potential for meaning making inherent in the language", as well as its redundancies and (potential) regularities. (2012: 21)

In pedagogical terms, Widdowson continues, this would entail looking at *how*, rather than *how much*, learners know the language (2012: 23, emphasis in original), how they have learnt "how to mean in English" and "what they *make* of the language" (2012: 24, emphasis in original). Such a shift in focus in EL teaching would allow promoting what Widdowson defines as communicative language *learning* (2012: 22, emphasis in original) and a "genuine learner-centred approach" (2012: 24) in that, rather than focusing on what is to be corrected as not conforming to NS norms, it would encourage effective and strategic use of the language in different contexts, as well as the development of learners/users' capability to develop their abilities in *languaging* (Seidlhofer 2011: 189-90) and in exploiting the potentials of the virtual language. As Seidlhofer and Widdowson (2009b: 102) point out, "ELF usage makes it clear that what learners learn can be put to usage as an end to itself": the constraints set in pedagogical settings for learners to conform to ENL usage do not "prevent them from learning something of the essential meaning-making potential inherent in the virtual language. [...] They may not be playing or performing English in the approved way, but they are nevertheless conforming to constitutive rules of the game". And indeed, "what is achieved, and put to use, in ELF, is clearly not the English that has been *taught*, but the English that has been *learnt*" (Seidlhofer 2011: 186, emphasis in original, cf. also Hulmbauer 2009: 328; Widdowson 2012: 22-24; cf. also Kohn forthcoming).

Taking into account in ELT practices the new roles and functions developed by English would undoubtedly mean to acknowledge the increasing complexities brought about by the actual uses of English around the world; this diversity, which includes ELF, has become a (if not the most) substantial part in everyday practices, since in the majority of cases English is employed to communicate with a diversified array and range of ELF users around the world. As Firth (2009b: 150) points out,

> [l]anguage teachers should [...] provide their students with opportunities and resources to record their everyday interactions outside the confines of the L2 classroom. To do so would be to further complicate the picture of what it means to use and learn an L2 in modern societies, where notions of 'learning', learnership', 'competence', 'proficiency', and 'performance', are intricately tied to contextual exigencies, and always, emergent within the micro-details of social interaction.

Acknowledging findings from ELF research in pedagogical practices would thus imply "a radical shift in the way language is understood as a concept, and then positioned in the curriculum" (Cogo and Dewey 2012: 172; cf. also Dewey 2012: 166-167; Jenkins et al. 2011: 16-17), which does not appear to have substantially, let alone extensively, taken place so far (e.g. Jenkins 2007: Chapter 8, 2010: 101-102; Seidlhofer 2007a: 146, 2011: 56), above all in classroom practices. However, some recognition of ELF research findings and of the differentiated roles that English plays in world contexts seems to have been acknowledged to a certain extent in teacher training programmes, such as the well-known DELTA UCLES scheme (cf. Cogo and Dewey 2012: 171, Dewey 2012: 144-148), as well in other institutional teacher training contexts (e.g. Matsuda 2009; papers in Matsuda 2012b; Lopriore 2010: 73-79; Jenkins et al. 2011: 17; Pitzl 2012b). ELT materials have also started to include a broader representation of the diversity of English(es) (e.g. Alptekin 2010: 100-101, 104; Vettorel 2010a, 2010b; Vettorel and Corrizzato 2012), thus providing opportunities to foster awareness of several varieties in classroom contexts. Nevertheless, and despite CLT and other methodological approaches giving priority to aspects other than grammatical structures such as task-based teaching (e.g. Willis and Willis 2007) and the lexical approach (e.g. Lewis 1993), language syllabuses in ELT materials still seem to be widely centred on ENL language models, most frequently British and American English. As Cogo and Dewey underscore, "the notion of grammatical accuracy still remains central to the way in which language is represented in ELT material" and "the language syllabus in ELT is almost entirely oriented towards presenting the lexical and grammatical items found in standard ENL varieties. The primary goal of many English-language classrooms remains the imitation of native-speaker-like grammar and lexis, often with emphasis on accuracy and the eradication of non-standard forms, which are usually perceived unequivocally as 'errors'" (Cogo and Dewey 2012: 173; cf. also Dewey and Leung 2010: 11-12).

Since communication in ELF contexts does not rest merely on native-like accuracy but rather entails the deployment of a range of accommodation and communication strategies and skills, as well as the ability to effectively exploit the resources of the 'virtual language' and of plurilingual repertoires, it would seem of primary importance for ELT pedagogic practices to take such a shift in perspective into account. Rather than prioritize a focus on ENL varieties and norms, this would imply to foster the development of skills which can make communication effective – or, as Sifakis suggests, embracing a C-bound rather than an N-bound approach, which "would mean to concentrate on and get learners involved in the creation of understanding of NNS communicative discourse that is comprehensible" (2004: 244-245). Indeed, as research has shown, ELF is highly variable and context-dependent, and meaning is locally constructed by the participants in ways that rely primarily on the deployment of communicative pragmatic and strategic strategies. ELF research findings and ELF corpora can inform SLA "by showing how L2 actually works in ordinary life outside educational contexts and what might be worth focusing on in teaching" (Mauranen 2011: 164).

As argued by numerous ELF scholars (e.g. Seidlhofer 2006: 45, 48; Cogo and Dewey 2012: 182-183; Jenkins 2007: 120, 2010: 106-107; Dewey and Jenkins 2010: 74; Jenkins et al. 2011: 17), acknowledging ELF research in ELT would not in any way imply applying a prescriptive pedagogic model, namely 'teaching ELF features' as derived from ELF corpus findings. Neither would it mean imposing an 'ELF language model': "[u]sers of the language will naturally be required to adjust and extend their language to make it appropriate to a purpose; and where in their communicative interests to conform to ENL convention, they will, of course, seek to conform" (Seidlhofer 2011: 199). Jenkins et al. state very clearly that ELF research "is not about determining what should or should not be taught in the language classroom. Rather, ELF researchers feel their responsibility is to make current research findings accessible in a way that enables teachers to reconsider their beliefs and practices and make informed decisions about the significance of ELF for their own individual contexts" (Jenkins et al. 2011: 17).

Rather – and in broader terms, aspects that appear of foremost relevance in pedagogic practices, first of all in teacher education, would be fostering awareness of language variation, of the hybrid and fluid nature of ELF interactions, and therefore of the salient role communication strategies and accommodation skills retain in such settings (e.g. Seidlhofer 2003: 22; 2007a: 147; Jenkins 2007: 250; Ferguson 2012: 179; Dewey 2012: 166; Canagarajah 2007: 936; Kontra and Csizér 2011: 145), as well as the importance of the contextual deployment of all linguistic and pragmatic resources for a successful cooperative construction of meaning and the achievement of "comity" (McKay 2002: 127-128).

As Canagarajah points out, the notion of competence should not refer "so much to the mastery of grammar or sociolinguistic systems, as to the *strategic capacity* to use diverse semiotic items across integrated media and modalities" (2008, cited in Pennycook 2010: 129, emphasis added), developing a "grammar of multimodality", that contains "rules that account for how language meshes with diverse symbol systems, modalities of communication, and ecological resources to create meaning" (Canagarajah 2007: 932). This appears to be even more relevant in language-use terms in CMC modes, where communication encompasses the deployment of linguistic as well as non linguistic, multimodal elements. Indeed, as we have seen, CMC constitutes a prominent space of interaction for ELF users and ELF communities. As Kramsch puts it, "[t]eaching the spoken language is teaching resourcefulness, imagination, and effective poaching on all levels of meaning available" (1993: 246). That is, "making do with words" (Kramsch 1993: 246), hence focusing not only on Norm-bound aspects, but promoting a Communication-bound perspective in classroom practices (Sifakis 2004, 2006), one that gets "learners involved in the creation and understanding of NNS communicative discourse that is comprehensible" (Sifakis 2006: 161) and develops awareness of the differentiated competences needed to effective interaction in ever-changing, ever-anew ELF contexts (Sifakis 2006: 159).

Firth remarks that, "given the quotidian nature of L2 use in innumerable social settings, not least in our age of globalization, the Internet, mass tourism, mass migration and employment mobility [...] one of the main goals of L2 classroom activities is to prepare learners to use their L2 *outside* the classroom" (Firth 2009b: 129, emphasis added). Given the variety, not least in demographic terms, of the contexts in which English as a lingua franca is used today, pedagogically-wise it would therefore seem fundamental to take account of the ways in which English is employed, appropriated and deployed to effective communication by language users in ELF settings. In this perspective, rather than the unattainable goal of native-like proficiency, "the purpose of teaching becomes the development of a capability for effective use which involves the process of exploiting whatever linguistic resources are available, no matter how formally 'defective'" whereby "learners are not learning *a language* but learning *to language* (Seidlhofer 2011: 197, emphasis in original). This implies that prominence ought to be given not to form *per se*, but to all those strategies which are so essential in the cooperative co-construction of meaning in ELF interactions, as well as to the exploitation of the (pluri)lingual resources of the virtual language – in an orientation to process rather than product (Canagarajah 2006: 210). Such an approach could foster attitudes and skills of language-awareness at different levels (variation/variety, successful meaning-negotiation strategies, cross-linguistic similarities and differences, cf. Ferguson 2012: 179; McKay 2002: 125-126; papers in Matsuda 2012b; Alsagoff et al. 2012; Rubdy and Saraceni 2006: 209-210; Tomlinson 2006; McKenzie 2011), as well as consciousness of how linguistic 'mobile resources' may take on different meanings in differentiated contexts of use (Ferguson 2012: 179, referring to Blommaert 2010). Canagarajah points to the need of developing competences needed to negotiate meaning, and grammar, in LFE contexts: “language awareness that enables speakers to make instantaneous inferences about the norms and conventions of their multilingual interlocutors; strategic competence to negotiate interpersonal relationships effectively; and pragmatic competence to adopt communicative conventions that are appropriate for the interlocutors, purpose and situation” (2007: 928). A further interrelated goal in this perspective would be that of fostering strategies aimed at developing comity, that is “friendly relations – when English is used with speakers of other languages” (McKay 2002: 127; cf. also Aston 1993). This would be related to the development of appropriate pragmatic competence in settings that involve by definition speakers of different linguacultures, where effective communication entails to “mutually seek ways to accommodate to diversity” (McKay 2002: 128), which, as we have seen, is a prominent trait in ELF interactions (cf. also Baker 2011).

Hence, rather than focusing primarily on near-nativeness unattainable goals, what ought to be fostered is the students’ ability “to be able to use both the L2 and the L1 in the appropriate situations and for the appropriate use” (Cook 2005a: 55), taking advantage of the specificities of L2 users, whose mind functions differently from monolinguals, exploiting and supporting such specificities (Cook 2010a: 5-8) both in plurilingual and in pluricultural terms (Alptekin 2010: 106). Among other aspects, the coexistence of different languages in a multicompetent speaker’ repertoire has been proved to positively result in increased “communicative flexibility and sensitivity as well as metalinguistic awareness” (Jessner [2005] 2008: 235). Indeed, English constitutes in many cases a third language for many European – and ELF – speakers; just to quote a few, Spanish speakers of Basque and Catalan, Dutch speakers of Frisian, of German and Italian in South Tyrol, as well as for immigrants’ L1s (cf. Jessner 2006). Besides, since classrooms, as a consequence of – and similarly to – societal modifications are increasingly becoming multilingual settings, teaching practices can build on such differentiated and variegated competences, too: “L2 users have different language abilities and knowledge and different ways of thinking from monolingual native speakers. Rather than encouraging the students to get as close to the native speaker as possible, teaching should try to make them independent L2 language users who can function across two languages with mental abilities the monolingual native speaker cannot emulate” (Cook 2005a: 53; cf. also Cook 2009a: 151-155, 2009b: 13-16; McKay 2002 Chapter 2; Jenkins [2003] 2009a: 163-164: Alptekin 2002).

Such a perspective could also promote a shift from a focus on ‘languages’ as separate entities (and as an ideological and institutional construct) to that of resources as "the actual and observable ways of using language" (Blommaert 2010: 102; cf. also Lüdi and Py 2009; Blommaert et al. 2005), reformulating questions such as "what is it to 'know' a language, to 'speak it well' or to 'be fluent'" (Blommaert 2010: 102), reflecting on the unattainable model of the native speaker, as well as on the actual relevance of the still rooted native/non-native dichotomy, as the self-perceptions of albeit successful interactants in my corpus has shown, too.

If we recognize that polylingual language practices constitute such an important part of today's communicative modes, particularly for younger generations (cf. Jørgensen 2008; Kramsch 2009), and that language(s) users' repertoires are more and more multilingual, "acquiring these resources (a process usually called 'language learning') would in effect be the construction of a multilingual repertoire" in its different aspects (Blommaert 2010: 105-106). Hence, as Canagarajah argues, an extended, broader notion of competence is needed to account for language use in multilingual and ELF contexts, one encompassing multiple resources and languages and "always in the state of becoming" (2007: 933); such resources derive not only from educational settings, but from everyday practices of multilingual users and usage, acknowledging that "learning is more meaningful in actual contexts of language use and practice" (Canagarajah 2007: 933). As the author remarks, "in the case of LFE, there is no meaning for form, grammar, or language ability outside the realm of practice. LFE is not the product located in the mind of the speaker; it is a form of social action" (2007: 928). It is therefore of primary importance to acquire skills to align "one's language resources to the needs of a situation", particularly in plurilingual ELF contexts where successful interaction is based on "intersubjective construction, something achieved by two or more people, based on strategies they bring to the interaction" (Canagarajah 2007: 928). And indeed, we have seen that in ELF meaning is socially and cooperatively constructed locally, *in situ* in each specific contextual setting, and depends not so much on the normative/non-normative use of grammar, but on the functional meaning which is jointly ascribed to (innovative) unconventional forms. In the case of virtual communication in particular, this often depends on the networks that are created and recreated within each 'constellation of interconnected practices', transcending physical boundaries but being nonetheless communicatively significant to the participants.

As Kramsch highlights, "[t]raditionally, language acquisition defines success as the ability of the learner to produce target-like forms of the language, in all dimensions of communicative competence. Language socialization, by contrast, defines success as the ability to communicate in the language of a particular community and to act according to its norms" (Kramsch 2002a: 24). This naturally resonates with Firth and Wagner's 1996 and 2007 seminal articles where they set forward a critique of SLA in calling for its reconceptualization "as a more theoretically and methodologically balanced enterprise that endeavours to attend to, explicate, and explore, in more equal measures and, where possible, in integrated ways, both the social and cognitive dimensions of S/FL use and acquisition" (Firth and Wagner 1997: 286). Such an objective cannot be reached without taking into account the contextual and interactional dimension of language in use – a point which is further stressed in their 2007 contribution, where the authors remark the need to include in SLA research a socially-based perspective of language learning as encompassed within socio-cultural theory (Lantolf 2000; Lantolf and Thorne 2006; Pavlenko and Lantolf 2000), constructivist and social-interactional approach to learning. As to the latter, Firth and Wagner point out that "[l]earning is an inseparable part of ongoing activities and therefore situated in social practice and social interaction [...] a ubiquitous social activity, as an interactional phenomenon that transcends contexts while being context dependent" (Firth and Wagner 2007: 807). Indeed, as the authors highlight with reference to social views of learning within a community of practice perspective (Lave and Wenger 1991; Wenger 1998; Gardner and Wagner 2004), "L2 speakers are not interactional dopes. They show perseverance and ingenuity in interacting with others. They produce not so much 'language forms': rather, they engage in complex, multimodal, finely tuned co-participation" (Firth and Wagner 2007: 807). Incorporating a social-interactional approach would then help to uncover what L2 users actually *do* with language in social interaction, moving away from "the construct of a linguistic system or a competence that serves all the speaker's purposes" to take account of "the development of social relations, the mutual constituency of linguistic resources and tasks, and the linguistic biography of the language learners" (Firth and Wagner 2007: 812; cf. also Cook 2009c).

Jenkins (2006a: 147-148, 151), discussing correlations between socio-cultural theory and ELF, identifies some common points of concern between the two approaches: besides the detachment from a native-speaker perspective, the notions of learners – and users in ELF – as legitimate agents in transforming the language as they are using it, in socially situated settings, as well as the possibility that "L2 learners may wish to create for themselves 'new and distinct linguistic and ethnic identities, or even communities'" (quoting

Pavlenko 2002) outside a native speaker model (cf. also Pennycook 2007; Seidlhofer 2011). Indeed, Widdowson (2009: 214) poignantly points out that

> what is actually performed in foreign language communication is a realisation of what has been learned. Foreign language communicators are not borrowing someone else's language but using the language of their own learning. Their communication is their learnt language put to use. This being so, a description of foreign language communication as the achievement of a goal would also provide indications of what learning processes are involved in achieving it, what aspects of the language taught, and what strategies, are carried over, exploited and extended in contexts of communicative use.

A rethinking of the strict separation into which the notions/constructs of L2 learner and ELF user as conceived of in ELT, particularly in the case of English, would bring about significant effects both to teaching and learning, not last taking into account that, given the highly complex and diversified nature of ELF interactants and settings, in order to attain successful communication "acquisition and use go hand in hand [...]. Meeting different speakers from the vast, diffuse and virtual community of LFE, one always has to learn a lot – and rapidly – as one decides which receptive and productive resources for a context", as well as which pragmatic strategies, that could then be effectively re-employed in similar situations (Canagarajah 2007: 927). "In this sense, learning never stops in LFE. If there is no language use without learning, there is also no language learning without its use" (Canagarajah 2007: 927).

7.6. Concluding remarks

As widely testified by ELF research findings, and as detectable in my corpus data, English is actively employed as a common means of communication in an array of situations, whether in face to face or virtual online settings, serving pragmatic as well as interpersonal aims. In these contexts ELF speakers are most often at the same time *learners* and *users* of English as a lingua franca, who actively employ the language in their communicative acts intersecting these 'real-life' usages with their language learning experiences. In web-based communities, such as blogs, English is appropriated and suited to its users' communicative aims and is effectively deployed in internationally-oriented virtual spaces despite – or possibly because of in its being appropriated – its differences from standard(ized) norms – or even, we may say, as it is different from "school English" (Androutsoupoulos 2001: 9-10). In the imagined communities "based on people's mental images of their affinity" (Mauranen 2012: 18) globally-projected practices entwine with locally-set meaning, which is created and negotiated through a commonly shared code within each 'constellation of interconnected practices'.

This complex but vital reality cannot any longer be left out of the classroom walls, dismissively ignoring that (and how) ELF use does take place in everyday and daily contexts; rather, its relevance and pervasiveness ought to be acknowledged to constructively build on it. In my data, as we have discussed, ELF is enacted both to global (in its role of internationally shared lingua franca) and localized aims, expressing and addressing the different (sub)cultures and linguacultures involved. Kramsch (2009: 191) to this point significantly remarks that

> [t]eaching the multilingual subject means teaching language as a living form, experienced and remembered bodily, with a relation to an Other that is mediated by symbolic forms – an experience that an increasing number of students nowadays have already had at home or by living in multilingual neighbourhoods. Learning another language in an academic environment can give them words to understand that experience.

As argued in ELF research, ELF emerges thus as a hybrid, moving, fluid language realization in communication, that is locally realized in each specific setting by its participants. At the same time, common tendencies responding to functional motivations appear to emerge, motivations that are not unique to ELF, but can be found in any natural language evolutionary paths. Indeed, increased mobility, both physical and virtual, together with the inherent changeability of networks where English serves as a lingua franca, are likely to accelerate language change processes and make them more visible (Mauranen 2012: 27). Furthermore, ELF is spoken in complex linguacultural settings, where the multilingual and hybrid repertoires of speakers mingle (e.g. Mauranen 2012: 29; Hülmbauer 2013).

The resistance to the acknowledgement of this matter-of-fact reality in the ELT world, despite some openings, still appears widespread and persistent. As maintained by Ferguson (2006: 177):

> […] gaining acceptance [of ELF] is a formidable obstacle that can probably be overcome by convincing teachers, students and the wider public not just that English is sociolinguistically in a different position from all other languages, which is obvious, but that this sociolinguistic uniqueness justifies the abandonment of a popular assumption that by and large holds sway for most

> languages; the assumption, namely, that native-speaker-like proficiency, and conformity to native speaker norms, is the truest measure of achievement in second language learning.

The traditional tenets of SLA and language teaching, i.e. "monolingual native speakers, homogeneous national standards, pure standard national languages, instrumental goals of education, functional criteria of success" (Kramsch 2009: 190) do not appear to hold any longer in our "super-diverse" globalized times: the pervasive presence, as well as the changed role of English, together with the reality of multilingualism and polylingual practices, are all factors calling for a shift in perspective, so that pedagogy would be able to "prepare the new generations adequately for the complexities of a multilingual world" (Kramsch 2009: 190). And indeed, young people's continuous and consistent contact with English, not least as active ELF users, testifies to how what is learnt in the language classroom is actually and effectively (in both senses of the word) put into use. Independently from whether educational agents recognize and acknowledge it, this has by long become a matter-of- fact reality; this is true for the first generation of ELF users (Mauranen 2010b; 2012: 33), and it will be even more real for the ones to come. With Tomlinson (2006: 135; cf. also Pennycook 1994; Kramsch 1993),

> [w]hat is needed is both a curriculum and a methodology for teaching English for global communication which identifies what its learners need and want to do in that language, which predicts the contexts in which they will need and want to do it, and which helps them to learn to do so in ways which will facilitate both language acquisition and the development of a global and personal voice.

It would thus be important for ELT pedagogic practices to "accommodate to the modes of communication and acquisition seen outside the classroom" (Canagarajah 2007: 936), connecting learning classroom practices to the *learners-users'* worlds, to their linguistic as well as affective and self-expressive needs and aims, devising curricula which are more significantly based on these communicative needs. Besides, this would allow a reconsideration and appraisal of *learners-users'* self-esteem towards their language skills while communicating in diversified contexts, and thus support their effective and actual capability to "shuttle between communities" (Rubdy and Saraceni 2006: 211), developing "a readiness to engage with a repertoire of codes in transnational contact situations" (Canagarajah 2007:

936). Possibly, such a shift in perspective would also be advantageous in terms of motivation: as we have outlined in the previous sections, teachers are not always fully aware of the consistent and persistent role that English plays in their students' lives, which is infrequently acknowledged for also in ELT materials, still much centred around native-speaker language models, and integrative notions of culture. As several research studies have shown, a traditional, restricted view of integrative motivation may no longer be adequate for the widespread and different uses of English at a global – as well as local – level, primarily since it cannot any longer be associated solely to NS culture and communities (e.g. Dörnyei and Csizér 2002; Csizér and Dörnyei 2005; Dörnyei 2005; Csizér and Kormos 2008). Rather, it has been argued, the spread and differentiation of English calls for an enlarged view of integrativeness, which includes the notion of the Ideal L2 Self (as well as the complementary Ought-to Self), and "can be used to explain the motivational set-up in diverse learning contexts" and "would be suitable for studying the motivational basis of language globalization, whereby international languages, and World English in particular, are rapidly losing their national cultural base ad are becoming associated with a global culture" (Dörnyei 2005: 104). Despite Dörnyei not referring specifically to ELF as such, but rather to plurality in World Englishes, the intermingling of instrumental and attitude components in the Ideal L2 Self, as well as of the relevance of the L2 Learning Experience (cf. Dörnyei 2005: 105-106; 2009: 217-218), suggest that the L2 Motivational self-System conceptualized in this way could also bear significant relevance to ELF-oriented pedagogical practices, in that other aspects in motivation related to personal language use, perception and relevance in terms of experience could be taken into account (cf. e.g. findings in Csizér and Lukacs 2010). And indeed, young people's practices related to the media and to virtual spaces "develop a global identity that gives them a sense of belonging to a worldwide culture and includes an awareness of the events, practices, styles and information that are part of the global culture" (Lamb 2004, cited in Dörnyei 2005: 97). Motivation is thus driven by instrumental reasons (e.g. participation in technologically-afforded spaces) but also by the desire to be part of these global 'imagined communities' and imagined selves (Norton 2001, quoted in Dörnyei 2005: 97, 108; cf. also Black 2009; 420-423; Mauranen 2012: 18-19).

In pedagogical terms, this may imply connecting ELT practices to uses of English outside the school walls, either in real or in virtual mobility; indeed experiences based on virtual resources as a site for language learning constitute pedagogically feasible and salient moments where to explore language use which is socially and individually meaningful (cf. e.g. Lam 2000, 2004; Kramsch 2009; McKay and Bock-Hurst 2008; Vettorel 2013a). Telecollaboration projects, for instance, are increasingly developing as a relevant pedagogical tool in this sense (e.g. Guth and Helm 2011; Kohn forthcoming; Grazzi 2012, 2013). Or, in more general terms, "[s]uch global discourse communities are useful resources for EIL [English as an International Language] teaching because they offer possibilities of imagined communities and hybrid identities that allow EIL learners to explore and engage with English in truly authentic EIL contexts outside the classroom" (Alsagoff 2012: 112).

Yet, to my mind it is not only a matter of including in classroom practices opportunities for ELF communication in (virtual) international contexts: they would for sure constitute salient moments of (and for) language experimentation and appropriation, and bridge out to real contexts of use which, as argued, are such a salient and consistent part of *learners-users'* everyday life. As Androutsopoulos remarks, "the use of English as an international 'lingua franca' in media discourse is diversified in accordance to particular 'ecologies', i.e. audience communities" and is often different from 'school English'" (2001: 10). What would be most needed in my opinion is the acknowledgment of the room that these varied, plurilingual and heteroglossic language practices have in the *learners-users'* experiences of the language. Rather than focus primarily on accuracy and "seek to replicate 'authentic' contexts of reality and rehearse learners in native speaker performance" (Widdowson 2003: 179), they should be taken into account in terms of reflection, as well as of development of communicatively-oriented capability, which of course resonates with 'ecological' language perspectives within a complexity framework, that sees language and language learning in continuous adaptive flux, flow and transformation (e.g. Larsen-Freeman 2002; van Lier 2002; Kramsch 2002a, 2002b; Kramsch and Whiteside 2007).

As we have sought to show, encounters with English*es*, ELF included, in 'the world out there' are widespread and common, in different settings and to variegated aims; leaving these experiences of language use out of educational worlds would mean both downplaying the socially interactive and creative resources in language teaching, and impoverishing occasions for (socially situated), relevant and meaningful language learning. Rampton remarked already in 1997 that:

> [a] lot of the time at school, students are pushed towards standard languages of international communication relevant to work, and their capacities for

> physical expression are channelled into script. But it is very hard to ignore the comic, exotic or dangerous representations of other ethnolinguistic groups that students meet outside their textbooks, and how well they do at school is itself very much dependent on how they manage the tension between school on the one hand, and a whole vernacular aesthetic on the other (1997: 332).

This is something which, as we have seen, is so much part of 'real life' in socially-set virtual communication. Taking these and other similar experiences of language use into account would entail embracing "an ecologically oriented pedagogy that approaches language learning and language use not just as an instrumental activity for getting things done but as a subjective experience, linked to a speaker's position in space and history, and to his or her struggle for the control of social power and cultural memory" (Kramsch 2009: 190). Or, with Pennycook, engaging in micropractices where

> classrooms might be seen as language ecologies, that students might be seen to have language rights, and at the very least, we should explore the possibilities of multilingual classrooms. […] These perspectives, therefore, suggest different possibilities, such as language awareness for diversity, multilingual education, and policy decisions to oppose the imperialism of English (Pennycook 1999: 153; cf. also Sifakis 2004).

Indeed, Widdowson argues for the need to develop a "capability which would serve as an investment for subsequent learning", intended as a strategic ability and "knowledge of how meaning potential encoded in English can be realized as a communicative resource" (2003: 177). It would therefore seem of primary importance to connect the English as experienced by its users to what takes place within the classroom walls both in terms of setting goals for the language as a subject, and in relation to the processes of learning. As to the latter, Widdowson remarks that rather than "simplistic notions of authenticity", what should be explored is "how the language can key into the learners' reality so that they can be induced to engaging with the language in their own terms, and learn from it" (2003: 178). And the English classroom can in this perspective be(come) a place where contexts are suited to local realities, meaningful to different groups of *learners-users*, as in EFL the language is "'foreign' in very different ways to different groups of learners" (2003: 179), who in any case do appropriate what they have learnt to make it their own to their communicative aims. And should the provision of effective tools to *communicate* not be a/the primary goal of/in the foreign language classroom?

Conclusions

Findings from my empirical research, despite the small-sized corpus, appear in line with current ELF studies both in terms of form and function. Blogging practices as the ones emerging from my investigation reveal that English, when employed in wider networking to communicate in international, multilingual and multicultural contexts, works as the lingua franca across territorial boundaries and beyond nativeness paradigms to the main aim of enhancing communication among participants belonging to different linguacultures. As in other ELF research studies, findings emerging from my empirical study show that linguistic innovations follow well-attested word-formation processes and display a highly communicative function, often related to the need of expressing concepts connected to the interactants' linguacultures. At times these innovations are overtly flagged as such, and/or exploited in terms of language play within a plurilingual repertoire framework, creating a lexico-cultural shared repertoire among the participants.

The same appears true for most instances of code-switching, where a language other than English is frequently employed to relate to ideas and nuances peculiar to that linguaculture, or to signal affiliation to groupings and constellations, as well as to address a specific audience. Code-switching and code-mixing practices are employed by the participants in my data as a naturally occurring linguistic practice, whereby codes are entwined and intermingled in polylingual and translingual ways; English emerges as the shared lingua franca working as a common denominator in addressing and interacting with the blogger's international audience and friends. As in Androutsopoulos' findings concerning Facebook status updates, "users with an L1 other than English and international 'friends' networks' often select English [...] in order to make them available to their entire audience" (2013b: 7).

CMC spaces indeed constitute increasingly widespread settings for internationally-oriented communication, where a commonly shared code is needed – and employed – to allow interaction: this code is most frequently English. When looking at how English is used in these diversified and heterogeneous CMC settings, questioning whether 'traditional' approaches to such transnational and translingual practices of language use are (still) appropriate unsurprisingly constitute common concerns in ELF and CMC and CMD research (see e.g. Androutsopoulos 2013a, 2013b). As Seargeant and

Tagg (2011: 511) cogently point out as to CS practices in their data

> [i]f significant amounts of English use around the world today resemble in some form or other the nature of this discourse (i.e. if much worldwide English usage is of a similarly 'mixed' nature to these examples), does the category of the 'variety' simply become an instrumental way of describing aspects or features of the discourse, or does it still have a phenomenological reality?

The authors then argue that a shift in conceptual methodology which focuses "from the outset on the diverse semiotic discourses employed, and examines the way the various features respond to specific contextual influences, offers an opportunity for a more nuanced understanding of the ways in which the spread of English manifests itself in online communicative encounters in the era of globalization" (Seargeant and Tagg 2011: 511). One of the tenets of the ELF paradigm of research is that "description in ELF research should mean 'describing, and therefore building an understanding of what speakers who do not share a first language do when using English'" (Baird 2012: 12). And indeed the communicative practices which are enacted thanks to and within the specificities of online interactive media, including those emerging from the data in my study, appear to share several salient points with the ELF paradigm of research, and with ELF findings in other contexts:

- all the linguistic resources available to participants are exploited for their communication purposes; their use stretches beyond traditional categorizations of languages as separate entities, emerging rather as translingual, translocal and polylingual languaging practices;
- codes – and ELF in particular – are appropriated and adapted to suit the participants' self-expressive and communicative aims, which in the case of the on-line participants in my corpus are to communicate with an internationally-oriented audience of old and newly made friends, with whom English is in most cases the only commonly-shared language;
- meaning (co-)construction is generally privileged over (standard) form. Indeed, in online spaces such as the setting of my corpus data, digital practices may often lead to 'vernacular' exploitations of the code (Androutsopoulous 2011a; Seargeant and Tagg 2011: 510), whereby the language is appropriated and tweaked to its users' aims and by means of all communicative, linguistic and heteroglossic resources at their disposal;
- English works as the in-common lingua franca, and is often localized

to express meaning that is peculiar to the participants' national, local or personal identity and affiliation, as well as to the 'constellations of interconnected practices' they partake in.

As we have seen in Chapter 1, Internet practices are increasingly widespread on the European scene, as well as on the Italian one, especially for younger generations, for whom the Internet largely represents a way to be socially connected. Despite the increasing presence of other major languages on the web, and in the blogosphere too, English still retains a primary role, particularly in its lingua franca function. Non-native English speakers in Europe – as elsewhere in Western societies – frequently surf the web to access content in English, and use it most often to communicate with other web users of different L1s. Although preference for accessing the Internet in one's native language is expressed, and the mother tongue and English are often used in combination, English represents nonetheless the most widely employed code in internationally-oriented web-related practices, particularly by younger and frequent Internet users. The blogosphere, similarly, is an increasingly multilingual virtual space, where language choice is mostly related to the audience participants intend to address: English constitutes the lingua franca that allows communication in virtual, beyond-territorial boundaries settings, with elements of the participants' L1s and of other languages often serving 'more localized' functions. In the wish to communicate in international networks, ELF enables Internet users to create and maintain connections in socially-based networks according to common interests, across languages and (speech) communities as traditionally conceived of.

What Black (2009: 420) remarks for online fanfiction communities, also appears true for other Web 2.0 based environments, among which blogs: "new media and ICTs can open up potential for strengthening ties with existing friendship groups, as well as for establishing communication with a wider group of friends at the local, national and international level" and "provide youth with opportunities for connecting and exchanging perspectives with individuals whom they otherwise would be unlikely to ever meet due to geographic distance".

And indeed, "wider networking needs a lingua franca" (Seidlhofer 2011: 86); in these spaces we do not find a single, homogenized (and imperialistic) English, but rather a lingua franca which appears to be skilfully employed for communicative purposes, often to promote interaction among *people* who share common (multicultural) interests, wish to exchange ideas on trivial or more 'serious' topics, and share either globally or more locally-set cultural and identity aspects, or both. Notions of nativeness, ownership, standardness, national-language boundaries and speech communities as traditionally conceived of are significantly challenged in virtual spaces, not least since communicative practices are afforded by the peculiarities of the medium and at the same time shaped by the aims, experiences, interests and linguistic repertoires of its participants (cf. also Androutsopoulos 2130b: 6). As in other ELF contexts, they are realized *in situ*, combining (pluri)linguistic and non-linguistic, multimodal codes. In these highly fluid and mobile realms communication takes place by definition beyond territorial boundaries, communities are not related to geographical proximity and cohesion, but rather to "*constellations* of interconnected practices" (Wenger 1998: 127) which are built around and according to the participants' global interests, but also in more locally set interactive encounters. Blogging practices on social networking sites like LiveJournal indeed offer "the possibility for individuals to use their own 'friends list' as a means to bring different spheres of their social lives into a single online space" (Hodkinson 2007: 640) – spaces which are created, maintained and re-created through the deployment of an array of linguistic and semiotic communicative resources.

As seen in Chapter 2, blogs are an easy-to-use, flexible and hybrid Internet mode which has rapidly spread within participatory Web 2.0 practices, constituting a preferred self-expression and communication mode particularly for younger generations. Among the main motivations to blog we find self-expression and connecting with like-minded people, who can either be old or newly-made friends. Despite the difficulty in defining clear-cut boundaries in blog typologies, due to the hybrid and highly flexible characteristic of this CMC mode, personal journals are the most common, especially in that connections between people are afforded by their potential interactivity via hyperlinks and, above all, comments to posts. Indeed, in personal blogs, as in other social networking websites, the sense of belonging to a virtual community is defined and built through interactivity and participatory sharing practices rather than by geographic or linguistic boundaries, wherein common interests and friendship – or, better, 'friending' – are central elements. It is thus the diversified set of communicative functions allowed by blogs, from self-expression to social interaction, which makes them a hybrid mode that can be flexibly exploited to its users' needs. And, when addressing an international audience, English in its lingua franca role is largely chosen as the code that allows communication in these "wider networking" practices.

In Chapter 3 we have seen how recent approaches to CMC have moved beyond the written-oral categorization, to consider linguistic features in the light of "socio-technical modes" that is, in their own specificities and dual characteristics as afforded by the medium, but also shaped by situational and social factors (Herring 2007). Web 2.0 practices in particular have deeply influenced the way in which discourse is constructed, particularly – though not only – how language(s) and multimodal practices are interwoven by digital users (Herring 2013: 5-7). More recent research has indeed aimed at investigating how the complex array of linguistic and semiotic resources are employed by the participants in CM-situated discourse, and to which communicative functions (Thurlow and Mroczek 2011a, 2011b; Androutsopoulos 2010, 2011b).

Innovative language features in CMD can be related to the dimensions of orality, compensation and economy (Androutsopoulos 2011a), and are typical of the *e-grammar* of English, as well as of other languages, particularly at the lexical level (Herrinng 2012a). Personal journals in particular are characterized by an immediacy which, together with the aforementioned interaction-oriented affordances, makes them potentially conversational in genre despite their asynchronicity. Indeed, in personal blogs participants most often aim at reciprocal exchanges, deal with topics that are related to their personal life and interests, where monologic and dialogic modes – as well as linguistic and other multimodal codes – are mixed according to the bloggers' and to the participants' communicative purposes.

The corpus data, the theoretical framework of reference and the methodology adopted in my empirical study have been dealt with in Chapter 4. After illustrating the main characteristics of LJ as a blog-hosting service, of its (young) users, of LJ blogs and LJ community-oriented practices, we have looked into LJ language(s) practices. Despite the possibility of choosing from 32 languages, and the variegated locations of LJ users, in this cosmopolitan virtual space English appears to be the main choice for bloggers, many of whom are non-native, "young, multilingual, geographically mobile" (Herring et al. 2007: n.p.). And in my corpus data English emerges as a consistent presence in the bloggers' lives for a variety of purposes, from leisure activities to accessing information and communicating for personal and social aims in international contexts; all participants state that they have chosen to write their blog in English to the aim of addressing an international audience, and many are well aware of its lingua franca function among people of different linguacultures and in virtual spaces where common interests are communicatively shared.

The main focus of this study has been to investigate how and to what functions English is employed as the lingua franca of communication in internationally-oriented personal journals, that is, how ELF is deployed in these digital 'constellations of interconnected practices' to suit the participants self-expressive and communicative aims. Within the ELF paradigm of research, this study has been guided by four main research questions:

- RQ1: which ELF lexico-grammatical elements, as attested in relevant literature, are present in the corpus and at which linguistic levels?
- RQ2: in which self-expressive and interactional processes and to which function are they employed?
- RQ3: how are plurilingual repertoires exploited to meaning making, both in terms of exploitation of linguistic resources and as code-switching practices?
- RQ4 given the specificities of the research setting, not least in terms of 'constellations of interconnected practices', are the above characteristics employed to the same (or to different) functions as attested in ELF findings for oral data?

Findings in relation to the above research questions have been specifically dealt with in Chapters 5 and 6. In Chapter 5 we have seen how ELF users in the corpus exploit the resources of the linguistic system via processes that respond to functional underlying motives such as regularization, exploitation of redundancy, increased explicitness and clarity, as well as enhanced prominence. As to RQ1, variations and innovations in my findings appear in line with those of ELF research in other contextual settings, and we have discussed how regularization processes can be recognized at different levels of lexicogrammar in the data. For example, exploitation of redundancy is instantiated in non-marked plural nouns, use of zero 3rd person *–s* morpheme, of a single demonstrative for singular and plural, and in the shift in use of definite and indefinite articles. The functional motivation of economy of expression can be observed in the tendency to use one single tag question and in processes of zero derivation, as well as in several lexical formations via affixation. Other novel lexical items and expressions can be ascribed to the functional aim of increased clarity and explicitness, and the frequent instances in the use of the definite article to that of enhancing prominence.

As in other ELF research findings, my data suggests that such lexico-grammatical innovations are not created randomly: rather, regular mechanisms responding to one or to several among the aforementioned underlying motivations can be detected, and appear "effective and also functional" (Pitzl et al. 2008: 40). In their compositional use of elements from the (virtual) language these ELF users seem to have appropriated the working processes of the language and to use them creatively, exactly as native speakers do, but in their own ways, drawing from all resources in their linguistic repertoires, at times in sophisticated manners (Hülmbauer 2007: 15). In their role of language users, they have become 'languagers' (Seidlhofer 2009c, 2011), exploiting the 'language potential(s)' of the code – the possibilities of the "virtual language" not yet codified (Widdowson 2003: 48-49, 173). In relation to RQ2, 'deviances' are thus authenticated within the users' expressive needs and aims, and may fill either momentary or permanent gaps in the language when "there is yet no codified word available to express a certain idea or concept" (Pitzl et al. 2008: 43). These novel creations may also respond to the wish to express more subtle nuances in meaning, which are at times personally related and realized *in situ* as relevant to the participants – and the participants' constellations – in a specific communicative context. My findings also suggest that common linguistic and functional strategies are often deployed to deal with localized meaning, i.e. to express and share content that is relevant to smaller groups of interactants, or to the interests they share in these virtual (blog) communities. In such cases ELF is adapted to express meanings which are globally-set, in ways that are yet at the same time localized to these (smaller) communities of interaction: unconventional elements pertaining to e-grammar, as well as the use of in-group language, become thus part of a shared pool of (creative) communicative resources.

In ELF, the exploitation of the potentials of the linguistic system of English are often entwined with other languaging practices, which draw on the participants' plurilingual repertoires (e.g. Hülmbauer 2013; Cogo 2012b); this appears to emerge from my findings, too. As to RQ3 and RG4, findings in Chapter 6 have shown how plurilingual resources and code-switching and mixing represent an integral part of the multifaceted repertoires these ELF users have at their disposal in creating meaning, and they are deployed to express and share aspects related to their cultural and multicultural identities, as well as to common interests. Code-switching practices are frequently employed in the data mainly to fulfil three out of the four main functions identified by Klimpfinger (2007: 35-38, 2009: 359-366), i.e. specifying an addressee, introducing another idea, but above all signalling cultural affiliations both to primary linguacultures and to shared in-group interests, identification and practices.

On the one hand, awareness of how linguacultural elements are locally situated may lead to adaptations resulting in non-standard linguistic representations. On the other hand, specifically to online settings, strategies such as hyperlinking, translation or explanations in English as the in-common code are frequently provided in order to make such localized elements 'sharable' with the participants' internationally-located interactants. As we have discussed, in these digital communities the deployment of such multiple heterogenous linguistic and multimodal strategies plays a major role in making the local global. Blogging participants draw upon their expressive resources and repertoires to engage in communication, skilfully employing them according to the setting, to the linguistic and sociocultural characteristics of their interlocutors, as well as to their self-expressive and communicative aims, not least in linguacultural terms. These languaging practices are often polylingual in their natural mixing of resources, be it shorter or longer bits of language. The naturalness and nonchalance (Cogo 2009: 266, 2011: 166) with which languages are mixed in ELF discourse in the data also shows how "polylingual languaging" (Jørgensen 2008) appears to emerge as a preferred style of communication in media practices (Leppänen et al. 2009) and in blogs (Myers 2010: 54) whereby codes are chosen according to the audience and communities participants wish to interact with, or to affective attitudes, as well as in consonance with the (lingua)cultural identity/ies they want to express and affiliate to.

Thus, with reference to the research questions in my study and despite the relatively small-sized corpus, we can say that my findings are in line with those of ELF studies in other settings. Although further research would be needed, findings in this study can potentially be seen to confirm that ELF users exploit the code through their linguistic and plurilingual resources for their self-expressive and interactive purposes, in online as in face-to-face settings. Furthermore, in Web 2.0 environments these appropriation practices intersect with CMD communicative and linguistic traits that are often non-standard and deployed to meaning-making purposes. The widespread availability (at least in the Western world) of access to the Internet can be said to have made language contact with "super-diverse" linguacultural repertoires even more visible, potentially accelerating language change processes – not least involving English – too. However, rather than an indifferentiated and homogenous 'global English', findings for online practices such as the ones illustrated in this study, seem to show that the code is appropriated to the aims of the participants to express meanings that are personally- related, either within more globally-set (sub)cultures, or more localised ones. What my findings seem to point to is that, in a constantly interconnected world, and in parallel with the spread of English at different levels and in an array of domains, (online) ELF users, rather than being 'passively appropriated' by a global, uniform English, can transform its ubiquitous presence by combining repertoires – whether their L1, L2, an Ln or other heteroglossic practices – and by drawing on the not-yet encoded possibilities of the virtual language.

The increasingly widespread presence of English in the lives of young Europeans entails that the roles of *learner* and *user* often intersect, as we have seen in Chapter 7. Despite their effective and language-aware use of ELF as emerging from the data, the participants in my corpus often display negative self-perceptions as to their 'non-native' English – an attitude which is albeit at times exploited in more positive and affective sharing of their in-common status. As widely testified by ELF research findings, and as detectable in my corpus data, too, English is employed as a common means of communication in an array of face-to-face and virtual settings, either for essentially pragmatic or for interpersonal and affective aims. In these contexts participants actively employ the language in their communicative acts intersecting 'real-life' usage with their learning experiences, hence often being at the same time EFL *learners* and ELF *users*. The ELT world, however, has been so far largely resistant to acknowledge this matter-of-fact reality, at times dismissively ignoring that (and how) ELF is part of our daily experiences. Young people in particular, who can be defined as the "first generation" of global ELF users (Mauranen 2010b, 2012: 33), have a continuous and consistent contact with English, not least as active users, actually and effectively (in both senses of the word) putting into use what they have learnt – and are learning – in the EFL classroom. As we have illustrated, digital media have come to constitute spaces of interaction in which English is commonly employed to reach out to the world, and where pluri- and polylingual are common, almost constitutive practices.

As discussed in Chapter 7, it would thus appear important for ELT pedagogy to "accommodate to the modes of communication and acquisition seen outside the classroom" (Canagarajah 2007: 936), connecting learning classroom practices to the *learner-users'* worlds (D'Andrea 2012: 82-83), to their linguistic as well as affective and self-expressive needs, as widely encountered and employed in out-of-school contexts. In motivational terms, it has been argued (cf. Dörnyei 2005, 2009) that the notion of the Ideal L2 Self may be much more relevant and appropriate than traditional integrative conceptualizations: in a globalized interconnected world motivation is driven both by instrumental reasons (e.g. participation in technological-afforded spaces) but also by the desire to be part of 'imagined communities' and imagined selves (Norton 2001, quoted in Dörnyei 2005: 97, 108; cf. also Black 2009) which play such a consistent part in *learners-users* face-to-face and virtual worlds. It would thus seem of primary relevance to raise awareness of the consistent and persistent role that English plays in today's *learners-users*' lives and personal worlds. This issue is however still not frequently acknowledged in teacher education, as well as in ELT materials, as yet much centred around native-speaker language (and cultural) models, where accuracy and integrativeness continue to be deeply rooted and to constitute major instructional goals.

Promoting a more 'ecologic' approach to language learning and teaching would allow to acknowledge the considerable role these heteroglossic language practices have in the *learners-users*' experiences of the language, first of all by including in ELT reflection on plurality and difference, as well as the development of truly communicatively-oriented skills and strategies. Excluding from educational contexts encounters with English*es*, ELF included, in the outside-classroom world would mean both downplaying socially interactive and creative resources in language teaching, and impoverishing occasions for (socially situated), relevant and meaningful language learning. To my mind including in ELT practices the way in which today's *learners-users* experience ELF would not only be a matter of 'practically' setting up opportunities for ELF communication in (virtual) international contexts, such as international exchanges and partnerships (Vettorel 2013a), classroom blogs or telecollaboration projects (e.g. Guth and Helm 2011; Kohn forthcoming; Grazzi 2012, 2013) – no matter how relevant and important they are. Rather, it would have to entail acknowledging that *learners* are in actual fact also *users* of the language, looking into how they actually and effectively appropriate it in their communicative acts, to express and co-construct meaning that is subjectively meaningful to them (Kramsch 2009). Indeed, as Seidlhofer puts it, "'[f]ailed' learners can (be)come effective users of English" (2011: 197) – as my research findings show, many of the participants indeed downplay their effectiveness in language use, highlighting instead their self-perceived 'bad English' as non-native – and thus non-legitimate – users to it.

Connecting English as experienced by ELF users to what takes place within the classroom walls both in terms of setting goals for the language as a subject, and in relation to learning processes, would seem of primary importance, in order to explore "how the language can key into the learners' reality so that they can be induced to engaging with the language in their own terms, and learn from it" (Widdowson 2012: 178). As shown by ELF research and as emerging from my findings, too, learners do appropriate what they have learnt to make it their own, suiting it to their communicative aims in their active experiences of the language. They indeed engage in languaging practices, putting *into use* what they know of the language for their communicative aims, not least through a "strategic exploitation of the linguistic resources of the virtual language that characterize the use of ELF" (Seidlhofer 2011: 198). When engaging in such skilful practices, "they are fully involved in the interaction, whether for work or for play. They are focused on the purpose of the talk and on their interlocutors as people, and emphatically not on the code itself" (Seidlhofer 2009c: 242; cf. also Cogo 2012b). As a result, unusual forms may derive from the way in which different linguistic resources in their plurilingual repertoires are combined and exploited. Whether they may or may not "correspond to the regulative conventions of standard English" (Seidlhofer 2011: 198), these instantiations of language use are most often motivated by functional reasons and by "the communicative purposes and the interpersonal dynamics of the interaction" (Seidlhofer 2009c: 242) – and seem indeed to work effectively.

These acts of appropriation by ELF users, who deploy and tweak the expressive resources in their (pluri)lingual repertoires to accommodate their communicative purposes, makes them potential and direct agents of language change processes. This appears particularly evident in digital settings, where, as we have seen, adapting the language(s) to suit the users' expressive and interactive purposes is common practice. Therefore, rather than feeling 'foreign' to the language they frequently and effectively use to communicate with the world, with the native speaker idealized model continuously hanging as a somewhat ghostly presence (cf. Chapter 7), participants in internationally-oriented communicative settings ought to be regarded as legitimate language *users*. In this sense "nativization can also be understood as the appropriation of the language by individual speakers, who make it their own for particular purposes and conditions of use so that *they are 'at home' in it*" (Seidlhofer 2011: 96, emphasis added). Numerous ELF researchers have indeed argued that "[t]he use of English as the international lingua franca should be accompanied, for all its speakers, by a sense of ownership of the language. This should include access to the full ranges of its communicative functions, including creative functions in all their variety" (Carter 2007: 604). As suggested by my data, too, English is not only employed to transactional purposes, but increasingly serves as a means for self-expression and relational practices: as Carter continues, "learners in many contexts around the world relatively quickly pass from purely utilitarian motivations towards goals associated with expressing their social and cultural selves and seek that kind of liberation of expression which they enjoy in their first language, especially in the form of language play" (Carter 2007: 604). And, as I have sought to illustrate, this well emerges from the internationally-oriented blogging practices in my data, too.

ELF research has amply shown that ELF is a hybrid, moving, fluid language, which is locally realized by the participants in each specific setting – and this is suggested by my findings, too. At the same time, ELF appears to be characterized by common tendencies responding to functional motivations, which are also part of language change processes that are not unique to ELF, but can be found in any natural language, and are indeed characteristics that can be found in many varieties of English in the world. The language contact settings which are peculiar to ELF use may indeed accelerate such processes of language change, and make them more evident (e.g. Cogo and Jenkins 2010: 277). Findings from my corpus data suggest that we are in the presence of not 'one' monolithic 'English' (e.g. Seargeant and Tagg 2011: 509-512), but of 'an' English that is appropriated and localized within specific ELF speaker constellations, suited to their self-expressive and communicative needs, often deployed in combination with semiotic and heteroglossic resources as afforded by the medium itself. CMC digital modes can indeed be seen as sites of 'appropriation', where an array of (linguistic) resources is put into use for self-expressive and interactional aims. With reference to Europe, it has been suggested that in public spaces, "[i]t is the internet and the English language which provide the most appropriate form of communication […]. Within these spheres and among the users, it is likely that quite different kinds of English will evolve to serve the primary function of the respective groups" (Berns and de Bot [2005] 2008: 212) – that is, English will most likely be localized to serve the specific communicative needs of its speakers. Thus, rather than having a globalizing and homogenizing effect, "English would serve, instead, as the minimum communicative condition which would allow people from different countries and cultures to develop their *specific* ways to communicate" (Berns and de Bot [2005] 2008: 212), emphasis added) via ELF, that is, to appropriate and adapt it to their communicative contexts as a "multidimensional means of expression and communication that is linked to the professional sphere as well as to the private sphere, to globalized mass media entertainment as well as to private communication" (Berns and de Bot [2005] 2008: 210). Be they native or non-native, it will be their expertise (Rampton 1990) as Bilingual English Speakers (Jenkins [2003] 2009a) that plays a major role in meaning construction and effective communication, rather than birth-to-language.

Furthermore, it can forcibly be argued with Kramsch that although "[g]lobal access to English, like global access to the Internet, facilitates communication, it does not necessarily facilitate understanding. In fact, it requires an additional effort in discursive reflexivity and linguistic circumspection to overcome the illusion of sameness created by the use of a common language" (Kramsch 1999: 142). Therefore, an ELF-oriented pedagogic perspective would firstly have to take into account the diversity and complexities inherent in ELF contexts of communication, not least in intercultural terms: as Kramsch continues, "a pedagogy of English as a global language can capitalize on the outsideness of the local, non-native speaker to foster an understanding based not only on orate uses of language but on a critical reflection that can only be acquired through literacy" (Kramsch 1999: 142). As argued by Kramsch elsewhere (2009: 166), in virtual spaces such as chat rooms – as well as blogs:

> the taboos of language learning are suspended: grammatical and spelling errors, code-switching, code-mixing, non sequitur slip in, that foreground signifiers and weaken the links between utterances and their intentionalities, thus bridging semiotic 'play', or looseness, into the system. In the moving, fluid, relational realms of cyberspace, there seems to be an increased temptation to exploit the transitional contact zones between languages, between spoken and written language, between authoring and animating words [...] and to use these contact zones for greater manoeuvre and creativity. As such, it seems to offer particularly interesting possibilities for the construction of a multilingual subject if reflected upon later in class.

To conclude, further investigations of how ELF works in virtual online settings can indeed represent a significant complementary area to that of spoken interactions; it would contribute to uncover how English in its lingua franca function is normally and naturally used to interactional as well as self-expressive aims in non face-to-face, but equally meaningful and widespread communicative settings. I believe that the fact that most findings from this study are consistent with current ELF research may suggest that the potentially interactive nature of blogs – as well as of other social networks which are consistently used by younger generations as personal communication spaces (Seidlhofer 2007b: 315, 2011: 86) may certainly be worth of further ELF investigation. Moreover, research in the fields of CMC and Web 2.0-based virtual settings has shown interesting overlapping areas in terms of epistemic and methodological approaches, as well as data analysis and findings. Both research areas, for instance, are based on similar problematizations of notions and phenomena related to post-modern conceptualizations of language(s), communities and plurilingual repertories. These significant interrelations could be further explored by combining the two approaches in more consistent and overtly interrelated ways. Indeed, digital interactive settings will most presumably continue to represent significant communicative arenas for multicompetent and plurilingual ELF users who wish to connect to larger, globally-oriented virtual communities, as well as participate in smaller, yet not necessarily locally-bound, groupings. As we have seen, these practices, which are typically afforded by Web 2.0 digital spaces, often give way to different 'constellations of interconnected practices', some having a broader orientation and others with more 'intimate' characteristics, as my findings in relation to personal blogging suggest. Furthermore, broader and narrower spaces frequently intersect in and through "networking audiences" (Androutsopoulos 2013b: 6), and it is here that English is most often chosen in its lingua franca connecting function, together with other linguistic and semiotic resources. Investigating and exploring CMC interconnected practices in ELF-related terms could thus complement research findings for spoken data, uncovering the way in which ELF is appropriated and the functions to which it is employed in digital self-expressive and interactive spaces by first, and future second and third generations (Mauranen 2012: 33) of ELF (digital) users.

Appendix A – Questionnaire

Dear Blogger,
Thank you very much for having accepted to cooperate in this research project.
I kindly ask you to complete the following questionnaire and send it back to paola.vettorel@univr.it

1. Live Journal username: ____________________

2. Age:_____

3. Gender: [ ] Male [ ] Female

4. Level of education:
[ ] secondary school
[ ] undergraduate degree
[ ] post-graduate degree
[ ] PhD
[ ] other ______________________

5. Are you still a student? [ ] Yes [ ] No
5a. If your answer to the previous question is *yes*, in which context?

____

____

6. What is your mother-tongue?

____

7. Do you speak any other languages beside your mother tongue and English? [ ] Yes [ ] No

8. If your answer to the previous question is *yes*, which ones?

Language	Level
1.	A1 [ ] A2 [ ] B1 [ ] B2 [ ] C1 [ ]
2.	A1 [ ] A2 [ ] B1 [ ] B2 [ ] C1 [ ]
3.	A1 [ ] A2 [ ] B1 [ ] B2 [ ] C1 [ ]

9. How long have you studied English at school? _____ years (please specify)

10. Have you ever lived in an Anglophone country? [ ] Yes [ ] No

11. If your answer to the previous question is *yes*, where?

___

12. How long? Months [ ] (please specify) – Years [ ] (please specify)

13. Have you ever received English-medium education? [ ] Yes [ ] No

14. If your answer to the previous question was *yes*, at what school level did you receive English-medium education?
[ ] Primary education [ ] Secondary education [ ] University

15. Was it partial (one or more subjects / workshops) or full-time?
[ ] Partial [ ] Full-time

16. In what context?
[ ] In my home country [ ] Secondary education [ ] University

[ ] In an Anglophone country (specify which ____________________)
[ ] Secondary school [ ] University

17. Do you have any English language certification? [ ] Yes [ ] No
17a. If your answer to the previous question was *yes*, which one?
[ ] Cambridge [ ] TOEFL [ ] Trinity
[ ] other_______________ (please specify)
17b. What level?
[ ] A2 [ ] B1 [ ] B2 [ ] C1 [ ] C2

18. What do you use English for? (tick the one/ones that apply)
[ ] school/studies
[ ] leisure activities (reading books, watching TV/DVDs, travelling, etc.)
[ ] accessing information (news, articles, etc.)
[ ] communication for personal/social purposes in international contexts
[ ] communication for professional purposes in international contexts
[ ] other ____________________________________

19. If you have ticked 'communication for personal/social purposes' in the previous question, do you use English mostly for: (cross the one/ones that apply)
[ ] oral communication [ ] written communication
Other ____

Online:
[ ] e-mail [ ] newsgroups [ ] blog [ ] chat [ ] forum [ ] gaming
[ ] other____

20. Why do you use English in your blog?

____
____
____
____
____
____

e-mail contact: ____

Thank you! ☺

References

Adami, Elisabetta. 2008. Blogs: life writing on the net. In Angelo Righetti (ed.), *The Protean form of life writing: auto/biography in English, 1680-2000*, 251-270. Napoli: Liguori.

Adams, Valerie. 2001. *Complex words in English*. Harlow: Pearson Education/ Longman.

Adamic, Lada & Natalie Glance. 2005. The political blogoshere and the 2004 U.S. election: divided they blog. *LinkKDD-2005 Conference*, Chicago, Illinois. http://citeseer.ist.psu.edu/viewdoc/download?doi=10.1.1.59.9009&rep=rep1&-type=pdf (accessed 15 November 2013).

Algeo, John. 1998. Vocabulary. 1776–1997. In Suzanne Romaine (ed.), *Cambridge histories online*, Vol. IV, 57-91. Cambridge: Cambridge University Press.

Ali-Hasan, Noor F. & Lada A. Adamic. 2007. Expressing Social Relationships on the Blog through Links and Comments. *Proceedings of the international conference on weblogs and social media. (ICWSM)*. Boulder: Colorado. http://www.icwsm.org/papers/paper19.html (accessed 15 November 2013).

Alptektin, Cem. 2002. Towards intercultural communicative competence in ELT. *ELT Journal* 56(1). 57-64.

Alptektin, Cem. 2010. Redefining multicompetence for bilingualism and ELF. *International Journal of Applied Linguistics* 20(1). 95-110.

Al-Sa'Di, Rami A. & Jihad M. Hamdan. 2005. "Synchronous online chat" English: Computer-mediated Communication. *World Englishes* 24(4). 400-424.

Alsagoff, Lubna, Sandra Lee McKay, Guangwei Lu & Willy A. Renandya (eds.). 2012. *Principles and practices for teaching English as an international language*. London: Routledge.

Alsagoff, Lubna. 2012. Identity and the EIL learner. In Alsagoff, Lubna, Sandra Lee McKay, Guangwei Lu & Willy A. Renandya (eds.), *Principles and practices for teaching English as an international language*, 104-122. London: Routledge.

Ammon, Ulrich. 1994. The present dominance of English in Europe. *Sociolinguistica* 8. 1–14.

Ammon, Ulrich, Norbert Dittmar, Klaus J. Mattheier & Peter Trudgill (eds.). 2005. *Sociolinguistics/Soziolinguistik. An international handbook of the science of language and society / Ein internationales Handbuch zur Wissenschaft von Sprache und Gesellschaft*, 2. Aufl., Vol. 2. Berlin & New York: Mouton de Gruyter.

Anderson, Benedict. 1983. *Imagined Communities*. London & New York: Verso.

Androutsopoulos, Jannis. 2001. Switching from national language to English in media discourse: some findings from German youth-cultural media. Presentation given at *Language, the media and international communication conference*, Oxford. Retrieved at http://www.ids-mannheim.de/prag/sprachvariation/tp/tp7/Oxford-draft.pdf (accessed 15 November 2013).

Androutsopoulos, Jannis. 2004. Non-native English and sub-cultural identities in media discourse. In Helge Sandøy (ed.). *Den Fleirspråklege utfordrings/The multilingual challenge*, 83- 98. Oslo: Novus, http://www.setav.org/ups/dosya/10388.pdf (accessed 15 November 2013).

Androutsopoulos, Jannis. 2005. Research on youth-language/Jugendsprache-Forschung. In Ulrich Ammon, Norbert Dittmar, Klaus J. Mattheier & Peter Trudgill (eds.), *Sociolinguistics/Soziolinguistik. An International Handbook of the Science of Language and Society / Ein internationales Handbuch zur Wissenschaft von Sprache und Gesellschaft*, 2. Aufl., Vol. 2, 1496-1505. Berlin & New York: Mouton de Gruyter.

Androutsopoulos, Jannis. 2006a. Introduction: sociolinguistics and Computer-Mediated Communication. *Journal of Sociolinguistics* 10(4). 419-438.

Androutsopoulos, Jannis. 2006b. Multilingualism, diaspora and the internet: Codes and identities on German-based diaspora websites. *Journal of Sociolinguistics* 10(4). 520-547.

Androutsopoulos, Jannis. 2007. Bilingualism in the mass media and on the internet. In Monica Heller (ed.), *Bilingualism: a social approach*, 207-230. Basingtoke & New York: Palgrave-Macmillan.

Androutsopoulos, Jannis. 2010. Localizing the global on the participatory web. In Nikolas Coupland (ed.), *The handbook of language and globalization*, 203-231. Oxford: Wiley-Blackwell, pre-print copy http://jannisandroutsopoulos.files.wordpress.com/2010/09/localizing_preview.pdf (accessed 15 November 2013).

Androutsopoulos, Jannis. 2011a. Language change and digital media: a review of conceptions and evidence. In Kristiansen Tore & Nikolas Coupland (eds.), *Standard languages and language standards in a changing Europe*, 145-161. Oslo: Novus. http://jannisandroutsopoulos.files.wordpress.com/2011/11/language-change-and-digital-media-preprint.pdf (accessed 15 November 2013).

Androutsopoulos, Jannis. 2011b. From variation to heteroglossia in the study of Computer-Mediated Discourse. In Crispin Thurlow & Kristine Mroczek (eds.), *Digital discourse: language in the new media*, 277-298. Oxford & New York: Oxford University Press.

Androutsopoulos, Jannis. 2012. English 'on top': Discourse functions of English resources in the German mediascape. *Sociolinguistic Studies* 6(2). 209-238. *Pre-print copy* http://jannisandroutsopoulos.files.wordpress.com/2009/12/english-on-top-pre-print-april-2011.pdf (accessed 15 November 2013).

Androutsopoulos, Jannis. 2013a. Code-switching in computer-mediated communication. In Susan C. Herring, Dieter Stein & Tuija Virtanen (eds.), *Handbook of the pragmatics of CMC,* 659-686. Berlin & New York: Mouton de Gruyter. [version December 2011] http://jannisandroutsopoulos.files.wordpress.com/2009/12/code-switching-in-computer-mediated-communication_v3_12-2011.pdf (accessed 15 November 2013).

Androutsopoulos, Jannis. 2013b. Networked multilingualism. Some language practices on *Facebook* and their implications. *International Journal of Bilingualism*, online version June 2013, http://ijb.sagepub.com/content/early/2013/06/07/1367006913489198.abstract (last accessed 25 April 2014).
Androutsopoulos, Jannis & Evelyn Ziegler. 2004. Exploring language variation on the Internet: Regional speech in a chat community. In Britt-Louise Gunnarsson, Lena Bergström, Gerd Eklund, Staffan Fridell, Lise H. Hansen, Angela Karstadt, Bengt Nordberg, Eva Sundgren & Mats Thelander (eds.), *Language variation in Europe*. Papers from ICLaVE 2, 99-111. Uppsala: Uppsala University Press.
Anshen, Frank & Mark Aronoff. 1988. Producing morphologically complex words. *Linguistics* 26(4). 641-655.
Appel, René & Pieter Muysken. 1995. *Language contact and bilingualism*. London: Arnold.
Aronoff, Mark & Kirsten Fudeman. 2005. *What is morphology?* Malden: Blackwell.
Aston, Guy. 1993. Notes on the interlanguage of comity. In Gabriele Kasper & Shoshana Blum-Kulka (eds.), *Interlanguage Pragmatics*, 224-250. Oxford & New York: Oxford University Press.
Auer, Peter. 1984. *Bilingual conversation*. Amsterdam & Philadelphia: John Benjamins.
Auer, Peter (ed.). 1998a. *Code-switching in conversation. Language, interaction and identity.* London: Routledge.
Auer, Peter. 1998b. Introduction: bilingual conversation revisited. In Peter Auer (ed.), *Code-switching in conversation. Language, interaction and identity*, 1-24. London: Routledge.
Auer, Peter. 1999. From code-switching via language mixing to fused lects: toward a dynamic typology of bilingual speech. *The International Journal of Bilingualism* 3(4). 309-332.
Auer, Peter. 2007. The monolingual Bias in bilingualism research, or: why bilingual talk is (still) a challenge for LInguistics. In Monica Heller (ed.), *Bilingualism: a social approach*, 319-339. Basingtoke & New York: Palgrave-MacMillan.
Auer, Peter. 2011. Code-switching. Conversational structure and social identities. In Raffaella Bombi, Mari D'Agostino, Silvia Dal Negro & Rita Franceschini (eds.), *Atti del 10 Congresso dell'Associazione Italiana di Linguistica Applicata [Proceedings of the 10th Conference, Italian Association of Applied Linguistics]*, 27- 45. Perugia: Guerra.
Auer, Peter & Li Wei. 2007. Introduction: multilingualism as a problem? Monolingualism as a problem? In Peter Auer & Li Wei (eds.), *Handbook of multilingualism and multilingual communication*, 1-12. Berlin & New York: Mouton de Gruyter.
Baker, Will. 2009. The cultures of English as a lingua franca. *TESOL Quarterly* 43(4). 567-592.
Baker, Will. 2011. Culture and identity through ELF in Asia: fact or fiction? In Alasdair Archibald, Alessia Cogo & Jennifer Jenkins (eds.), *Latest trends in ELF research,* 36-51. Newcastle-upon-Tyne: Cambridge Scholars.

Bakhtin, Mikhail. 1981. *The dialogical imagination.* Austin: University of Texas Press.
Balboni, Paolo E. 2004. Transition to Babel: the language policy of the European Union. *Transition Studies Review* 11(3). 161-170.
Bailey, Benjamin. 2007. Heteroglossia and boundaries. In Monica Heller (ed.), *Bilingualism: a social approach*, 257-273. Basingtoke & New York: Palgrave-MacMillan.
Baird, Robert. 2012. English as a lingua franca: the study of language practices. *English in Practice. Working papers of the Centre for Global Englishes, University of Southampton* 1. 3-16.
Baron, Naomi. 2000. *Alphabet to Email. How written English evolved and where it's heading*. London: Routledge.
Baron, Naomi 2003. Language of the Internet. *In* Ali Farghali (ed.), *The Stanford handbook for language engineers*, 59-127. Stanford, California: CSLI. Retrieved at http://www.american.edu/cas/lfs/faculty-docs/upload/N-Baron-Language-Internet.pdf (accessed 15 November 2013).
Baron, Naomi. 2008. *Always on. Language in an online and mobile world*. Oxford: Oxford University Press.
Barton, David & Carmen Lee. 2013. *Language online. Investigating digital texts and practices*. London: Routledge.
Basset, Elisabeth H. & Kathleen O'Riordan. 2002. Ethics of Internet research: ConO testing the human subjects research model. *Ethics and Information Technology* 4(3). 233-247.
Bassetti, Benedetta & Vivian Cook. 2011. Relating language and cognition: the second language user. In Vivian Cook and Benedetta Bassetti (eds.), *Language and bilingual cognition*, 143-190. New York / Hove: Psychology Press – Taylor & Francis.
Bauer, Laurie. 2002. *An Introduction to international varieties of English*. Edinburgh: Edinburgh University Press.
Baym, Nancy K. 2010. *Personal connections in the digital age*. Cambridge: Polity Press.
Bell, Brandi. 2007. Private writing in public spaces: girls' blogs and shifting boundaries. In Sandra Weber & Shanly Dixon (eds.), *Growing up online*, 95-111. New York & Houndsmill: Palgrave MacMillan.
Berns, Margie. 1995. English in the European Union. *English Today* 43(3). 3-11.
Berns, Margie. 2005. Expanding on the Expanding Circle: where do we go from here? *World Englishes* 24(1). 85-93.
Berns, Margie. 2006. World Englishes and communicative competence. In Braj B. Kachru, Yamina Kachru & Cecil L. Nelson (Eds.), *The handbook of World Englishes*, 718-730. Oxford: Blackwell.
Berns, Margie. 2007. The presence of English. Sociocultural, acquisitional, and media dimensions. In Margie Berns, Kees de Bot & Uwe Hasebrink (eds.), *In the presence of English: media and European youth*, 1-14. New York: Springer.

Berns, Margie. 2009. English as a lingua franca and English in Europe. *World Englishes* 28(2). 192-199.

Berns, Margie & Kees de Bot 2008 [2005]. English language proficiency at the secondary level: a comparative study of four European countries. In Carl Gnutzmann & Frauke Intemann (eds.), *The globalisation of English and the English language classroom*, 193-213. Tübingen: Gunter Narr Verlag.

Berns Margie, Kees de Bot & Uwe Hasebrink (eds.). 2007. *In the presence of English: Media and European youth*. New York: Springer.

Berns, Margie, Marie-Thérèse Claes, Kees de Bot, Riet Evers, Uwe Hasebrink, Ineke Huibregtse, Claude Truchot & Per van der Wijst. 2007. English in Europe. In Margie Berns, Kees de Bot & Uwe Hasebrink (eds.), *In the presence of English: media and European youth*, 15-42. New York: Springer.

Biber, Douglas. 1988. *Variation across speech and writing*. Cambridge: Cambridge University Press.

Biber, Douglas, Stig Johansson, Geoffrey Leech, Susan Conrad & Edward Finegan. 1999. *Longman grammar of written and spoken English*. Harlow: Pearson.

Björkman, Beyza. 2008a: 'So where we are': spoken lingua franca English at a Swedish technical university". *English Today* 24(2). 11-17.

Björkman, Beyza. 2008b: English as the lingua franca of Engineering: the morphosyntax of academic speech events. *Nordic Journal of English Studies* 7(3). 103-122.

Björkman, Beyza B. 2009: From code to discourse in spoken ELF. In Anna Mauranen & Elina Ranta (eds.), *English as a Lingua Franca: studies and findings*, 225-252. Newcastle-upon-Tyne: Cambridge Scholars.

Björkmann Beyza. 2011a. Pragmatic strategies in English as an academic lingua franca: ways of achieving communicative effectiveness?. *Journal of Pragmatics* 43. 950-964.

Björkmann Beyza. 2011b. English as a Lingua Franca in higher education: implications for EAP. *Ibérica* 22. 79-100.

Black, Rebecca W. 2008. *Adolescents and online fan fiction*. New York: Peter Lang.

Black, Rebecca W. 2009. Online fanfiction, global identities, and imagination. *Research in the Teaching of English* 43(4). 397- 425.

Block, David. 2004. Globalization, transnational communication and the internet. *International Journal on Multicultural Societies* 6(1). 22-37

Blom, Jan-Petter & John J. Gumperz. 1972. Social meaning in linguistic structures: code switching in Northern Norway." In John J. Gumperz & Dell Hymes (eds.), *Directions in sociolinguistics: The ethnography of communication*, 407-434. New York: Holt, Rinehart & Winston.

Blommaert, Jan. 2010. *The sociolinguistics of globalization*. Cambridge: Cambridge University Press.

Blommaert, Jan, James Collins & Stef Slembrouck. 2005. Spaces of multilingualism. *Language and Communication* 25. 197-216.

Blood, Rebecca. 2000. Weblogs: a history and perspective. *Rebecca's Pocket*. 07 September 2000, 25 October 2006. http://www.rebeccablood.net/essays/weblog_history.html (accessed 15 November 2013)

Blood, Rebecca. 2002. *The weblog handbook. Practical advice on creating and maintaining your blog*. Cambridge, MA: Perseus Publishing.

Boase, Jeffrey, John B. Horrigan, Barry Wellman & Lee Rainie. 2006. *The strength of internet ties: The internet and email aid users in maintaining their social networks and provide pathways to help when people face big decisions*. The Pew Internet and American Life Project, Pew Research Center, Washington, D.C., 25 January 25 2006, http://www.pewinternet.org/~/media/Files/Reports/2006/PIP_Internet_ties.pdf.pdf (accessed November 2013).

Böhringer, Heike, Cornelia Hülmbauer & Barbara Seidlhofer. 2008. RT4.2, *Dylan Working Paper 3*. http://www.dylan-project.org/Dylan_en/dissemination/page102/page101/page101.php (accessed 15 November 2013).

Bolton, Kingsley. 2012. World Englishes and linguistic landscapes. *World Englishes* 31(1). 30-33.

boyd, danah. m. 2006a. A blogger's blog: exploring the definition of a medium. *Reconstruction* 6(4). http://www.danah.org/papers/ABloggersBlog.pdf (accessed 15 November 2013).

boyd, danah m. 2006b. Friends, friendsters, and mySpace top 8: writing community into being on social network sites. *First Monday* 11/12.

boyd, danah m. & Nicole B. Ellison, 2007. Social network sites : definition, history and scholarship. *Journal of Computer-Mediated Communication* 13(1). Article 11.

Brady, Mark. 2005. Blogging: personal participation in public knowledge-building on the web. *Chimera Working Paper 2005-02*. Colchester: University of Essex.

Brala, Marija. 2008. Language, policy and identity: perceptions of and expectations for (non)anglicized language on the web. The case of Croatian blogs. In Daniel Perrin & Eva L. Wyss (eds.), Perspectives de la Linguistique des Médias: Multiplicité des Langues et Mondialisation Médiatique en Europe. *Bulletin Suisse de Linguistique Appliquée* 87. 73-94. http://doc.rero.ch/lm.php?url=1000,20,4,20111202120004-ZZ/bulletin_vals_asla_2008_087.pdf (accessed 15 November 2013).

Breen, Michael P. (ed.). 2001. *Learner contributions to language learning: new directions in research*. Harlow: Longman.

Breiteneder, Angelika. 2005. The naturalness of English as a European lingua franca: the case of the 'third person -s'". *Vienna English Working PaperS* 14(2). 3-26. http://anglistik.univie.ac.at/fileadmin/user_upload/dep_anglist/weitere_Uploads/Views/Views0502ALL.pdf (accessed 15 November 2013).

Breiteneder, Angelika. 2009a. English as a lingua franca in Europe: an empirical perspective. *World Englishes* 28(2). 256-269.

Breiteneder, Angelika. 2009b. *English as a lingua franca in Europe. A natural development*. Saarbrüchen: VDM Verlag Dr. Müller.

Brkinjač, Tina. 2005. *Humour in English as a lingua franca*. University of Vienna unpublished MA thesis.

Bruns, Axel & Joanne Jacobs. 2006. Introduction. In Axel Bruns & Joanne Jacobs (eds.), *Uses of blogs*, 1-11. New York: Peter Lang.

Bruckman, Amy. 2002. Studying the amateur artist: a perspective on disguising data collected in human subjects research on the internet. *Ethics and Information Technology* 4. 217-231.

Bullock, Barbara E. & Almeida Jacqueline Toribio. 2009. Themes in the study of code-switching. In Barbara E. Bullock & Almeida Jacqueline Toribio (eds.), *The Cambridge handbook of linguistic code-switching*, 1-17. Cambridge: Cambridge University Press.

Byram, Michael. 1997. *Teaching and assessing intercultural competence*. Clevedon: Multilingual Matters.

Byram, Michael. 2008. *From foreign language education to education for intercultural citizenship*. Clevedon: Multilingual Matters.

Canagarajah, Suresh. 2007. Lingua franca English, multilingual communities, and language acquisition. [Focus Issue]. *The Modern Language Journal* 91. 923-939.

Canagarajah Suresh. 2008. Foreword. In Angles Clemente & Michael J. Higgins (eds.), *Performing English with a post-colonial accent: ethnographic narratives from Mexico*, ix-xiii. London: The Tufnell Press.

Càrdenas-Claros, Monica Stella & Neny Isharyanti. 2009. Code switching and code mixing in internet chatting: between 'yes', 'ya', and 'si' – a case study. *The Jalt Call Journal* 5(3). 67-78.

Carey, Ray. 2013. "Sorry if I were incomprehensible": Language regulation in academic ELF blog discussion. Presentation given at the Colloquium "ELF in Combputer-Mediated online Communication: characteristics and implications", *ELF6 Conference, Intercultural Communication: new perspectives for ELF,* Rome, 4-7 September 2013.

Carter, Ronald. 2002. Language awareness. *ELT Journal* 57(1). 64-65.

Carter, Ronald. 2004. *Language and creativity. The art of common talk*. London: Routledge.

Carter, Ronald. 2007. Response to: Special Issue of *Applied Linguistics* devoted to *Language creativity in everyday contexts*. *Applied Linguistics* 28(4). 597-608.

Carter, Ronald & Michael McCarthy. 2006. *Cambridge grammar of English: a comprehensive guide. Spoken and written English grammar and usage*. Cambridge: Cambridge University Press.

Cenoz, Jasone & Ulriche U. Jessner (eds.). 2000. *English in Europe: The acquisition of a third language*. Clevedon: Multilingual Matters.

Cherny Lynn. 2005. Gakking memes: LiveJournal 'conversations'. *The Math-Works*, Report.

Cheshire, Jenny. 2002. Who we are and where we're going: language and identities in new Europe. In Paul Gubbins & Mike Holt (eds.), *Beyond boundaries. Language and identity in contemporary Europe*, 19-34. Clevedon: Multilingual Matters.

Clark Eve V. 1994. Creativity in language use. In Ron E. Asher (ed.), *The encyclopaedia of language and linguistics* Vol.2, 784-765. Oxford: Pergamon Press.
Cogo, Alessia. 2008. English as a lingua franca: between form and function. *English Today* 94/24(2). 58-61.
Cogo, Alessia. 2009. Accommodating difference in ELF conversations: a study of pragmatic strategies. In Anna Mauranen & Elina Ranta (eds.), *English as a lingua franca: studies and findings*, 254- 273. Newcastle-upon-Tyne: Cambridge Scholars.
Cogo, Alessia. 2010. Strategic use and perceptions of English as a lingua franca. *Poznań Studies in Contemporary Linguistics* 46(3). 295-312.
Cogo, Alessia. 2011. Identità e appartenenza nell'inglese come lingua franca [Identity and sense of belonging in English as a lingua franca]. In Raffaella Bombi, Mari D'Agostino, Silvia Dal Negro & Rita Franceschini (eds.), *Atti del 10 Congresso dell'Associazione Italiana di Linguistica Applicata*, 105- 123. Perugia: Guerra.
Cogo, Alessia. 2012a. English as a Lingua Franca: Concepts, Use, and Implications. *ELT Journal* 66/1. 97-105.
Cogo, Alessia. 2012b. ELF and super-diversity: a case study of ELF multilingual practices from a business context. *Journal of English as a Lingua Franca* 1(2). 287-313.
Cogo Alessia & Martin Dewey. 2006. Efficiency in ELF communication: from pragmatic motives to lexico-grammatical innovation. *Nordic Journal of English Studies* 5(2). 59-93.
Cogo, Alessia & Martin Dewey. 2012. *Analysing English as a lingua franca*. London/New York: Continuum.
Cogo Alessia & Jennifer Jenkins. 2010. English as a lingua franca in Europe. *European Journal of Language Policy* 2(2). 271-294.
Coluzzi, Paolo. 2009. The Italian linguistic landscape: the cases of Milan and Udine. *International Journal of Multilingualism* 6(3). 298-312.
Cook, Vivian. 1991. The poverty-of-the-stimulus argument and multicompetence. *Second Language Research* 7(2). 103-117.
Cook, Vivian. 1994. UG and the metaphor of access. In Nick C. Ellis (ed.). *Implicit and explicit learning of languages*, 477-502. London & New York: Academic Press.
Cook, Vivian. 1999. Going beyond the native speaker in language teaching. *TESOL Quarterly* 33(2). 185-209.
Cook, Vivian. 2002a. Background to the L2 user. In Vivian Cook (ed.), *Portraits of the L2 user*, 1-28. Clevedon: Multilingual Matters.
Cook, Vivian. 2002b. Language teaching methodology and the L2 user perspective. In Vivian Cook (ed.), *Portraits of the L2 user*, 327-343. Clevedon: Multilingual Matters.
Cook, Vivian. 2005a. Basing teaching on the L2 user. In Enric Llurda (ed.), *Non-native language teachers. Perceptions, challenges and contributions to the profession*, 47-61. New York: Springer.

Cook, Vivian. 2005b. *Multi-competence: black hole or wormhole*? http://homepage.ntlworld.com/vivian.c/Writings/Papers/SLRF05.htm (accessed 15 November 2013).

Cook, Vivian. 2007. The goals of ELT: reproducing native-speakers or promoting multi-competence among second language users? In Jim Cummins & Chris Davidson (eds.), *Handbook of English language teaching,* 237-248. Norwell MA: Kluwer Academic Publishers. http://homepage.ntlworld.com/vivian.c/Writings/Papers/EFLGoals.htm (accessed 15 November 2013).

Cook, Vivian. 2009a Developing links between second language acquisition research, In Karlfried Knapp & Barbara Seidlhofer (in cooperation with Henry G. Widdowson). *Handbook of foreign language communication and learning*, 139-161. Berlin & New York: Mouton de Gruyter.

Cook, Vivian. 2009b. Questioning traditional assumptions of language teaching. *Nouveaux Cahiers de Linguistique Française* 29. 7-22.

Cook, Vivian. 2009c. Language user groups and language teaching. In Vivian Cook & Li Wei (eds.), *Contemporary applied linguistics, Volume 1, Language teaching and learning*, 54-74. London: Continuum.

Cook, Vivian. 2010a. Who is the L2 user? Multicompetence and foreign language teaching. Shiko Language Education Society. http://homepage.ntlworld.com/vivian.c/Writings/Papers/Kochi2010.htm (accessed 15 November 2013).

Cook, Vivian. 2010b. Multi-competence. http://homepage.ntlworld.com/vivian.c/Writings/Papers/MCentry.htm (accessed 15 November 2013).

Cook, Vivian & Li Wei (eds.). 2009. *Contemporary applied linguistics, Volume 1, Language teaching and learning.* London: Continuum.

Crawley, Christina, Anne Gilleran, Donatella Nucci & Santi Scimeca (eds.). 2010. *Voices of eTwinning: teachers talk.* Brussels: European eTwinning Unit. http://desktop.etwinning.net/library/desktop/resources/5/55/955/43955/etwinning_book_voices_of_etwinning_en.pdf (accessed 15 November 2013).

Crawley, Christina, Paul Gerhard, Anne Gilleran & Alexa Joyce (eds.). 2010. *Building the community for schools in Europe.* Brussels: Twinning European Unit/European Schoolnet http://resources.eun.org/etwinning/25/EN_eTwinning_brochure.pdf (accessed 15 November 2013).

Crystal, David. 2000. *The future of global English grammatical identity.* Paper given to the Symposium on 'Grammar and Lexis', 40th anniversary of the Survey of English Usage, University of London. [adapted for the 2nd edn. of English as a Global Language]. http://ww.davidcrystal.com/DC_articles/English19.pdf (accessed 15 November 2013).

Crystal, David. 2003 [1997]. *English as a global language.* Cambridge: Cambridge University Press.

Crystal, David. 2003. *The Cambridge encyclopedia of the English language.* 2nd Edition. Cambridge: Cambridge University Press.

Crystal, David. 2006. [2001]. *Language and the internet.* Cambridge: Cambridge University Press.

Crystal, David. 2011. *Internet linguistics*. London: Routledge.
Csizér, Kata & Zoltàn Dörnyei. 2005. The internal structure of language learning motivation and its relationship with language choice and learning effort. *The Modern Language Journal* 89(i). 19-36.
Csizér, Kata & Judit Kormos. 2008. Modelling the role of inter-cultural contact in the motivation of learning English as a foreign language. *Applied Linguistics* 30(2). 166-185.
Csizér, Kata & Gabriella Lukàcs G. 2010. The comparative analysis of motivation, attitudes and selves: the case of English and German in Hungary. *System* 38. 1-13.
Dalton-Puffer, Christiane. 2007. Outcomes and processes in content and language integrated learning (CLIL): current research from Europe. In Werner Delanoy & Laurenz Volkmann, (eds.) *Future Perspectives for English Language Teaching*, 139-157. Heidelberg: Carl Winter. http://www.univie.ac.at/Anglistik/Dalton/SEW07/CLIL%20research%20overview%20article.pdf (accessed 15 November 2013).
D'Andrea, Maria Luigia. 2012. *English as a lingua franca: examples from students' production and teachers' perceptions – A case study in the Italian school context*. Verona: University of Verona Unpublished PhD dissertation.
Danet, Brenda & Susan C. Herring. 2007a. Introduction. Welcome to the multilingual internet. In Brenda Danet & Susan C. Herring (eds.), *The multilingual internet. Language, culture and communication online*, 1-39. Oxford: Oxford University Press.
Danet, Brenda & Susan C. Herring. (eds.). 2007b. *The multilingual internet. Language, culture and communication online.* Oxford: Oxford University Press.
Davies, Mark. (2004-) *BYU-BNC*. (Based on the British National Corpus from Oxford University Press). Available online at http://corpus.byu.edu/bnc/ (accessed 15 November 2013).
Davies, Mark. (2008-) *The Corpus of Contemporary American English: 425 million words, 1990-present*. Available online at http://corpus.byu.edu/coca/ (accessed 15 November 2013).
de Gredes, Marta. 2005. Englische Weblogs (US). In Peter Schlobinski & Torsten Siever (eds.), *Sprachliche und textuelle Merkmale im Weblogs. Ein internationales Projekt*, 86-130. Hannover: Net.Workx.
Dewey, Martin. 2007a. English as a lingua franca and globalization: an interconnected perspective. *International Journal of Applied Linguistics* 17. 332-354.
Dewey, Martin 2007b. *English as a lingua franca: an empirical study of innovation in lexis and grammar*. London: King's College unpublished PhD dissertation.
Dewey, Martin. 2009. English as a lingua franca: heightened variability and theoretical implications. In Anna Mauranen & Elina Ranta (eds.), *English as a lingua franca: studies and findings*, 60-83. Newcastle-upon-Tyne: Cambridge Scholars.
Dewey, Martin. 2012. Towards a *post-normative* approach: learning the pedagogy of ELF. *Journal of English as a Lingua Franca* 1(1). 141-170.

Dewey, Martin & Jennifer Jenkins. 2010. English as a lingua franca in the global context: interconnectedness, variation and change. In Mukul Saxena & Tope Omoniyi (eds.), *Contending with globalization in World Englishes*, 72-92. Bristol: Multilingual Matters.

Dewey, Martin & Constant Leung. 2010. English in English language teaching: shifting values and assumptions in changing circumstances. *Working Papers in Educational Linguistics* 25(1). 1-15.

Dor, Daniel. 2004. From Englishization to imposed multilingualism: globalization, the internet, and the political economy of the linguistic code. *Public Culture* 16(1). 97-118.

Dorleijn, Margreet & Jacomine Nortier. 2009. Code-switching and the internet. In Barbara E. Bullock & Almeida Jacqueline Toribio (eds.), *The Cambridge handbook of linguistic code-switching*, 127- 141. Cambridge: Cambridge University Press.

Dörnyei, Zoltàn. 2005. *The psychology of the language learner*. Mahwah/NJ & London: Lawrence Erlbaum Associates Publishing.

Dörnyei Zoltàn. 2007. *Research methods in applied linguistics*. Oxford: Oxford University Press.

Dörnyei Zoltàn. 2009. *The psychology of second language acquisition*. Oxford: Oxford University Press.

Dörnyei Zoltàn & Kata Csizér. 2002. Some dynamics of language attitudes and motivation: results of a longitudinal nationwide survey. *Applied Linguistics* 23(4). 421-462.

Dresner Eli & Susan C. Herring. 2010. Functions of the non-verbal in CMC: Emoticons and illocutionary force. *Communication Theory* 20(3). 249-268.

Dröschel, Yvonne. 2011. *Lingua franca English. The role of simplification and transfer*. Bern: Peter Lang.

Duguid, Alison. [1987] 2001. Italian speakers. In Michael Swan & Berbard Smith (eds.). *Learner English. A teacher's guide to interference and other problems*, 73-89. Cambridge: Cambridge University Press.

Durham, Mercedes. 2007. Language Choice on a Swiss Mailing List. In Brenda Danet & Susan C. Herring (eds.), *The multilingual internet. Language, culture and communication online,* 319-361. Oxford: Oxford University Press.

EACEA/Eurydice/Eurostat. 2008. *Key data on teaching languages at schools in Europe 2012*. Brussels: Eurydice.

EACEA/Eurydice/Eurostat. 2012. *Key data on teaching languages at schools in Europe 2008*. Brussels: Eurydice.

Efimova, Lilia & Aldo de Moor. 2005. Beyond personal webpublishing: An exploratory study of conversational blogging practices. *Proceedings of the 38th Annual Hawaii International Conference on System Sciences (HICSS'05)* (p. 107). IEEE Computer Society.

Ehrenreich, Susanne. 2009. English as a lingua franca in multinational corporations. In Anna Mauranen & Elina Ranta (eds.), *English as a lingua franca: studies and findings*, 126-151. Newcastle-upon-Tyne: Cambridge Scholars.

ELFA 2008. The Corpus of English as a lingua franca in academic settings. Director: Anna Mauranen. http://www.helsinki.fi/elfa/elfacorpus. (accessed 15 November 2013).

Enever, Janet. 2008 [2005]. Europeanisation or globalisation. In Carl Gnutzmann & Frauke Intemann (eds.), *The globalization of English and the English language classroom*, 177-192. Tübingen: Gunter Narr Verlag.

Erling, Elisabeth. 2002. 'I learn English since ten years': the global English debate and the German university classroom. *English Today* 18(2). 8-13.

Erling, Elisabeth. 2008 [2005]. Who is the 'Global English' speaker? A profile of students of English at the Freie Universität Berlin. In Carl Gnutzmann & Frauke Intemann (eds.), *The globalization of English and the English language classroom*, 215-230. Tübingen: Gunter Narr Verlag.

Erling, Elisabeth. 2007. Local identities, global connections: affinities to English among students at the Freie Universität Berlin. *World Englishes* 26(2). 111-130.

Erling, Elisabeth & Tom Bartlett. 2006. Making English their own: the use of ELF among students of English at the FUB. *Nordic Journal of English Studies* 5(2). 9-40.

European Commission. 2003. *Promoting language learning and linguistic diversity: an Action Plan 2004-2006*. COM/2003/449. http://eur-lex.europa.eu/LexUriServ/LexUriServ.do?uri=COM:2003:0449:FIN:en:PDF (accessed 15 November 2013).

European Commission/Eurydice/Eurostat. 2005. *Key data on teaching languages at schools in Europe*. Luxembourg: Office for Official Publications of the European Communities.

European Commission. 2006. *Special Eurobarometer 243. Europeans and their Languages*. Brussels. http://ec.europa.eu/public_opinion/archives/ebs/ebs_243_en.pdf (accessed 15 November 2013).

European Commission/Eurydice. 2006. *Content and Language Integrated Learning (CLIL) at school in Europe*. Brussels: Eurydice. http://bookshop.europa.eu/en/content-and-language-integrated-learning-clil-at-school-in-europe-pb-NCX106001/ (accessed 25 April 2014).

European Commission/The Gallup Organization. 2011. *User language preferences online. Analytical Report. Flash Eurobarometer 313*. http://ec.europa.eu/public_opinion/flash/fl_313_en.pdf (accessed 15 November 2013).

European Commission. 2012. *Special Eurobarometer 386. Europeans and their languages*. Brussels. http://ec.europa.eu/public_opinion/archives/ebs/ebs_386_en.pdf (accessed 15 November 2013).

Eysenbach Gunther & James E. Till. 2001. Ethical issues in qualitative research on internet communities. *BMJ* 323. 1103-1105.

Ferguson, Gibson. 2006. *Language planning and education*. Edimburgh: Edimburgh University Press.

Ferguson, Gibson. 2012. The practice of ELF. *Journal of English as a Lingua Franca* 1(1). 177-180.
Ferrara Kathleen, Hans Brunner and Greg Whittemore. 1991. Interactive written discourse as an emergent register. *Written Communication* 8(1). 8-34
Ferri, Paolo, Nicola Cavalli, Elisabetta Costa, Andrea Mangiatordi, Stefano Mizzella, Andrea Pozzali & Francesca Scenini – Osservatorio sui Nuovi Media "Numedia Bios" Università degli Studi di Milano-Bicocca. 2010a. *Gli studenti universitari italiani e le nuove tecnologie digitali di comunicazione [Italian university students and new communication digital technologies]. International Journal of Information Sciences for Decision Making* 39: art. 662. http://isdm.univ-tln.fr/articles/num_archives.htm#isdm39 (accessed 15 November 2013).
Ferri, Paolo, Nicola Cavalli, Elisabetta Costa, Andrea Mangiatordi, Stefano Mizzella, Andrea Pozzali & Francesca Scenici. 2010b. Snack culture? La dieta digitale degli studenti universitari [The digital diet of university students]. Presentation given at *Digital Learning: Scuola, Apprendimento e Tecnologie Didattiche* Conference. http://www.numediabios.eu/giovani-e-media-digitali/snack-culture-2010/ (accessed 15 November 2013).
Ferri, Paolo. 2011. *Nativi digitali*. Milano / Torino: Mondadori/Pearson Italia.
Fialkova, Larisa. 2005. Emigrants from the FSU and the Russian-Language Internet. *Toronto Slavic Quarterly* 12. http://www.utoronto.ca/tsq/12/fialkova12.shtml (accessed 15 November 2013).
Firth, Alan. 1996. The discursive accomplishment of normality: on 'lingua franca' English and conversational analysis. *Journal of Pragmatics* 26. 237-259.
Firth, Alan. 2009a. The lingua franca factor. *Intercultural Pragmatics* 6(2). 147-170.
Firth, Alan. 2009b. Doing *not* being a foreign language learner: English as a *lingua franca* in the workplace and (some) implications for SLA. *IRAL* 47. 127-156.
Firth, Alan & Johannes Wagner. 1997. On discourse, communication, and (some) fundamental concepts in SLA research. *The Modern Language Journal* 81. 285-300.
Fono, David & Kate Raynes-Goldie. 2006. Hyperfriends and beyond: friendship and social norms on LiveJournal. In Mia Consalvo & Caroline Haythornthwaite (eds.), *Internet research annual Volume 4: Selected papers from the Association of internet researchers conference*. New York: Peter Lang. http://k4t3.org/publications/hyperfriendship.pdf (accessed 15 November 2013).
Franceschi, Valeria. 2014. *ELF users as creative writers: plurilingual practices in fan fiction*. Verona: University of Verona Unpublished PhD dissertation.
Franceschini, Rita. 2009. The genesis and development of research on multilingualism: Perspectives for future research. In Larissa Aronin & Britta Hufeisen (eds.), *The Exploration of Multilingualism: Development of Research on L3, Multilingualism and Multiple Language Acquisition*, 27-61. Amsterdam & Philadelphia: John Benjamins.
Garafanga, Joseph. 2007. Code-switching as a conversational strategy. In Peter Auer & Li Wei (eds.), *Handbook of multilingualism and multilingual communication*, 279-313. Berlin & New York: Mouton de Gruyter.

Garcia, Angela & Janet Jacobs. 1999. The eyes of the beholder: understanding the turn-taking system in quasi-synchronous Computer Mediated Communication. *Research on Language and Social Interaction* 32(4). 337-367.

Gardner, Colin. 2007. English and new media. In Sharon Goodman, David Graddol & Theresa Lillis (eds.), *Redesigning English*, 205-230. London / Milton Keynes: Routledge/The Open University.

Gardner, Rod & Johannes Wagner (eds.). 2004. *Second language conversations*. London: Continuum.

Georgakopoulou, Alexandra. 1997. Self-presentation and interactional alliances in e-mail discourse: the style- and code-switches of Greek messages. *International Journal of Applied Linguistics* 7(2). 141-164.

Gerritsen, Marinel, Catherine Nickerson, Andreu van Hooft, Frank van Meurs, Ulrike Nederstigt, Marianne Starren & Rogier Crjins. 2007. English in product advertisement in Belgium, France, Germany, the Netherlands and Spain. *World Englishes* 26(3). 291-315.

Giltrow, Janet & Dieter Stein. 2009. Innovation, evolution, and genre theory. In Janet Giltrow & Dieter Stein (eds.), *Genres in the internet*, 1-25. Amsterdam & Philadelphia: John Benjamins.

Gitlin, Todd. 1998. Public sphere or public sphericules? In Tamar Liebes & James Curran (eds.), *Media, ritual and identity*, 168-174. London: Routledge.

Gnutzmann, Carl (ed.). 1999. *Teaching and learning English as a global language*. Tubingen: Stauffenburg Verlag.

Gnutzmann, Carl & Frauke Intemann. 2008 [2005] Introduction: the globalisation of English. Language, politics, and the English language classroom. In Carl Gnutzmann & Frauke Intemann (eds.), *The globalisation of English and the English language classroom*, 9-24. Tübingen: Gunter Narr Verlag.

Goldbarg, Rosalyn Negrón. 2009. Spanish English code switching in Email communication. *Language@internet* 6. http://www.languageatinternet.org/articles/2009/2139 (accessed 15 November 2013).

Görlach, Manfred (ed.). 2002. *English in Europe*. Oxford: Oxford University Press.

Gorny, Eugene. 2004. Russian LiveJournal: national specifics in the development of a virtual community. Russian Cyberspace Project *Russian-cyberspace.org*. http://www.nettime.org/Lists-Archives/nettime-l-0406/msg00029.html (accessed 15 November 2013).

Graddol, David. 1996. Global English, global culture? In Sharon Goodman & David Graddol (eds.), *Redesigning English*, 243-279. London / Milton Keynes: Routledge/The Open University.

Graddol, David. 1997. *The Future of English*. London: The British Council.

Graddol, David. 2006. *English Next*. London: The British Council.

Granieri, Giuseppe. 2007 [2005]. *Blog Generation*. Roma / Bari: Laterza.

Grau, Maike. 2009. Worlds apart? English in German youth cultures and in educational settings. *World Englishes* 28(2). 160-174.

Grazzi, Enrico. 2012. English as a lingua franca and wikis as new affordances for the language classroom. The case of cooperative writing and fanfiction. In Geraldine Ludbrook & David Newbold (eds.), *English lingua franca: Contexts, strategies and international relations. Papers from a conference held at Ca' Foscari Unir versity of Venice October 2011*, 79-89. Venice: Cafoscarina.

Grazzi, Enrico. 2013. Intercultural telecollaboration and ELF: an Italian-American research project. Presentation given at the *ELF6 Conference, Intercultural Communication: new perspectives for ELF*, Rome, 4-7 September 2013.

Greenbaum, Sidney. 1996. *The Oxford English grammar*. Oxford: Oxford University Press.

Grosjean, François. 2010. *Bilingual: life and reality*. Cambridge, MA: Harvard University Press.

Gross, Steven. 2000. Intentionality and the markedness model in literary code-switching. *Journal of Pragmatics* 32(9). 1283-1303.

Gumbrecht, Michelle. 2004. Blogs as "protected space". *Proceedings of the 13th international conference on World Wide Web, WWW 2004*. http://psych.stanford.edu/~mgumbrec/Blogs_as_Protected_Space.pdf (accessed 15 November 2013).

Gumperz, John J. 1982. *Discourse strategies*. Cambridge: Cambridge University Press.

Gunnarsson, Britt-Louise, Lena Bergström, Gerd Eklund, Staffan Fridell, Lise H. Hansen, Angela Karstadt, Bengt Nordberg, Eva Sundgren & Mats Thelander (eds.). 2004. *Language variation in Europe*. Papers from ICLaVE 2, 99-111. Uppsala: Uppsala University Press.

Guth, Sarah & Francesca Helm. 2011. Developing multiliteracies in ELT through telecollaboration. *ELT Journal* 66(1): 42-51.

Hasebrink, Uwe. 2007. English, youth and media environments. In Margie Berns, Kees de Bot & Uwe Hasebrink (eds.), *In the presence of English: media and European youth*, 89-110. New York: Springer.

Hasebrink, Uwe, Margie Berns & Kees de Bot. 2007. In the presence of English: a resume after step one of an international study. In Margie Berns, Kees de Bot & Uwe Hasebrink (eds.), *In the presence of English: media and European youth*, 111-119. New York: Springer.

Hearst, Marti A. & Susan T. Dumais. 2009. Blogging together: an examination of group blogs. *Proceedings of the third international conference on weblogs and social media (ICWSM 2009)*, 226-229. San Jose, CA 2009.. http://people.ischool.berkeley.edu/~hearst/papers/icwsm09_blogs.pdf (accessed 15 November 2013).

Held, David, Anthony McGrew, David Goldblatt & Jonathan Perraton. 1999. *Global transformations: politics, economics and culture*. Cambridge: Polity Press.

Hellekson, Karen & Kristina Busse. 2006. Introduction: work in progress. In Karen Hellekson & Kristina Busse (eds.), *Fan fiction and fan communities in the age of the internet*, 5-32. Jefferson: McFarland & Company.

Heller, Monica. 2007a. Bilingualism as ideology and practice. In Monica Heller (ed.), *Bilingualism: a social approach*, 1-21. Basingtoke & New York: Palgrave-MacMillan.

Heller, Monica (ed.). 2007b. *Bilingualism: a social approach*. Basingtoke & New York: Palgrave-MacMillan.
Herring, Susan C. 1996. Linguistic and critical research on computer-mediated communication: Some ethical and scholarly considerations. *The Information Society*, 12(2). 153-168. http://ella.slis.indiana.edu/~herring/tis.1996.pdf (accessed 15 November 2013).
Herring, Susan C. 1999. Interactional coherence in CMC. *Journal of Computer-Mediated Communication* 4(4). http://jcmc.indiana.edu/vol4/issue4/herring.html (accessed 15 November 2013).
Herring S. C. 2001. Computer-mediated discourse. In Deborah Schiffrin, Deborah Tannen & Heidi E. Hamilton (eds.), *The handbook of discourse analysis*, 612-634. Oxford: Blackwell.
Herring, Susan C. 2002a. Computer-Mediated Communication on the internet. *Annual Review of Information, Science and Technology* 36. 109-168.
Herring, Susan C. 2002b. *The language of the internet: English dominance or heteroglossia?* Keynote presentation, Cultural Attitudes towards Technology and Communication Conference (CATaC), Université de Montréal, July 13 2002. http://ella.slis.indiana.edu/~herring/CATaC.ppt. (accessed 15 November 2013).
Herring, Susan C. 2004. Online communication: through the lens of discourse. In Mia Consalvo, Nancy Baym, Jeremy Hunsinger, Klaus Bruhn Jensen, John Logie, Monica Murero, & Leslie Regan Shade (eds.), *Internet research annual 1*. 65-76. New York: Peter Lang. http://ella.slis.indiana.edu/~herring/ira.2004.pdf (accessed 15 November 2013).
Herring, Susan C. 2007. A faceted classification scheme for Computed-Mediated Discourse. *Language@Internet* 4, Article 1. http://www.languageatinternet.org/articles/2007/761/ (accessed 15 November 2013).
Herring, Susan C. 2008a. Language and the internet. In Wolfgang Donsbach (ed.), *International encyclopedia of communication*, 2640-2645. Oxford: Blackwell Publishers.
Herring S. 2008b. Virtual community. In Lisa M. Given (ed.), *Encyclopedia of qualitative research methods*, 920-921. London & Thousand Oaks: Sage.
Herring, Susan C. 2010a. Computer-Mediated conversation: introduction and overview. *Language@Internet* 7, Article 2. http://www.languageatinternet.org/articles/2010 (accessed 15 November 2013).
Herring, S. C. 2010b. Digital media. In Paul Hogan (ed.), *The Cambridge encyclopedia of the language sciences*. Cambridge: Cambridge University Press.
Herring, Susan C. 2012. Grammar and electronic communication. In Carol A. Chapelle (ed.), *Encyclopedia of applied linguistics*. Hoboken/NJ: Wiley-Blackwell, http://ella.slis.indiana.edu/~herring/e-grammar.2011.pdf (accessed 15 November 2013).
Herring, Susan C. 2013. Discourse in Web 2.0.: Familiar, reconfigured, and emergent. In Deborah Tannen & Anna Marie Tester (eds.), *Georgetown University round table on languages and linguistics 2011: Discourse 2.0: Language and new media*, 1-25. Washington DC: Georgetown University Press.

Herring, Susan C. Inna Kouper, Lois Ann Scheidt & Elijah L. Wright. 2004. Women and children last: the discursive construction of weblogs. *Into the blogosphere: rhetoric, community, and culture of weblogs.* University of Minnesota. http://blog.lib.umn.edu/blogosphere/women_and_children.html (accessed 15 November 2013).

Herring, Susan C., Lois Ann Scheidt, Sabrina Bonus & Elijah L. Wright. 2004. Bridging the gap: a genre analysis of weblogs. *Proceedings of the 37th Hawaii international conference on system sciences*, 101-111. Los Alamitos: IEEE Press.

Herring, Susan C., Lois Ann Scheidt, Elijah L. Wright & Sabrina Bonus. 2005. Weblogs as a bridging genre. *Information, Technology and People* 18(2). 142-171.

Herring, Susan C., Inna Kouper, John C. Paolillo, Lois Ann Scheidt, Michael Tyworth, Peter Welsch, Elijah L. Wright & Ning Yu. 2005. Conversations in the blogosphere. An analysis from the bottom up. *Thirty-Eighth Hawaii international conference on system sciences.* Big Highland-Hi.

Herring, Susan C. & John C. Paolillo. 2006. Gender and genre variation in weblogs. *Journal of Sociolinguistics* 10(4). 439-459.

Herring, Susan C., Lois Ann Scheidt, Inna Kouper & Elijah L. Wright. 2006. A longitudinal content analysis of weblogs 2003-2004. In Mark Tremayne (ed.), *Blogging, citizenship, and the future of media*, 3-20. London: Routledge.

Herring, Susan C. John C. Paolillo, Irene Ramos-Vielba, Inna Kouper, Elijah L. Wright, Sharon Stoerger, Lois Ann Scheidt & Benjiamon Clark. 2007. Language networks on LiveJournal'. *Proceedings of the fortieth Hawai international conference on system sciences* (HICSS-40). Los Alamitos: IEEE Press.

Hickey, Raymond. 2006. Productive lexical processes in present-day English. In Christian Mair, Reinhard Heuberger & Josef Wallmannsberger (eds.), *Corpora and the history of English. A Festschrift for Manfred Markus*, 153-168. Heidelberg: Winter.

Ho, Judy Woon Yee. 2006. Functional complementarity between two languages in ICQ. *International Journal of Bilingualism* 10(4). 429-421.

Hock, E. T. B. 1995. *English in cyberspace*. Singapore: National University of Singapore BA thesis.

Hodkinson, Paul. 2006. Subcultural blogging? Online journals and group involvement among U.K. goths. In Axel Bruns & Joanne Jacobs J. (eds.), *Uses of blogs*, 187-197. New York: Peter Lang.

Hodkinson, Paul. 2007. Interactive online journals and individualization. *New Media & Society* 9(4). 625-650.

Hoffmann, Charlotte. 2000. The spread of English and the growth of multilingualism with English in Europe. In Jasone Cenoz & Ulrike Jessner (eds.), *English in Europe. The acquisition of a third language*, 1-21. Clevedon: Multilingual Matters.

Hollenbaugh, Erin. 2010a. Personal Journal bloggers: profiles of disclosiveness. *Computers in Human Behaviour* 26. 1675-1666.

Hollenbaugh, Erin. 2010b. Motives for maintaining personal journal blogs. *Cyberpsychology* 0(0). 1-8.

Hookway, Nicholas. 2011. 'Entering the blogosphere': some strategies for using blogs in social research. *Qualitative Research* 8(1). 91-113.

Hornby, Albert Sidney (ed.). 2010. *Oxford Advanced Learner's Dictionary OALD* 8th edn. Oxford: Oxford University Press.

Horner, Bruce. 2011. Writing English as a lingua franca. In Alasdair Archibald, Alessia Cogo & Jennifer Jenkins (eds.), *Latest trends in ELF research*, 299-311. Newcastle-upon-Tyne: Cambridge Scholars.

House, Juliane. 2003. English as a Lingua Franca: a threat to multilingualism? *Journal of Sociolinguistics* 7(4). 556-578.

House, Juliane. 2012. English as a lingua franca and linguistic diversity. *Journal of English as a Lingua Franca* 1(1). 173-175.

Huang, D. L. J. 2004. *Code-switching and language use in emails*. Melbourne: The University of Melbourne Unpublished PhD dissertation.

Huffaker, David A. 2006. Teen blogs exposed: the private lives of teens made public. Presented at the *American Association for the Advancement of Science* (*AAAS*), St. Louis, February 16-19. http://www.davehuffaker.com/papers/Huffaker-2006-AAAS-Teen_Blogs.pdf (accessed 15 August 2012).

Huffaker, David A. & Sandra L. Calvert. 2005. Gender, identity, and language use in teenage blogs. *Journal of Computer-Mediated Communication* 10(2). http://onlinelibrary.wiley.com/doi/10.1111/jcmc.2005.10.issue-2/issuetoc (accessed 25 April 2014).

Hülmbauer, Cornelia. 2007. 'You moved, aren't?' – The relationship between lexicogrammatical correctness and communicative effectiveness in English as a lingua Franca. *Vienna English Working PaperS* 16(2). 3-35. http://anglistik.univie.ac.at/fileadmin/user_upload/dep_anglist/weitere_Uploads/Views/Views_0702.pdf (accessed 15 November 2013).

Hülmbauer, Cornelia. 2009. "We don't take the right way. We just take the way we think you will understand" – The shifting relationship of correctness and effectiveness in ELF communication". In Anna Mauranen & Elina Ranta (eds.), *English as a lingua franca: studies and findings*, 323-347. Newcastle-upon-Tyne: Cambridge Scholars.

Hülmbauer, Cornelia. 2010. *English as a lingua franca between correctness and effectiveness. Shifting constellations*. Saarbrüchen: VDM Verlag Dr. Müller.

Hülmbauer, Cornelia. 2011. Old friends? Cognates in ELF communication". In Alasdair Archibald, Alessia Cogo & Jennifer Jenkins (eds.), *Latest trends in ELF research*, 139-161. Newcastle-upon-Tyne: Cambridge Scholars.

Hülmbauer, Cornelia. 2013. From within and without: the virtual and the plurilingual in ELF. *Journal of English as a Lingua Franca* 2(1). 47-73.

Hülmbauer, Cornelia, Heike Böhringer & Barbara Seidlhofer. 2008. Introducing English as a lingua franca (ELF): precursors and partner in intercultural communication. *Synergies Europe* 3. 25-36.

Hymes, Dell. 1972. On communicative competence. In John B. Pride & Janet Holmes (eds.), *Sociolinguistics*, 269-293. Harmondsworth: Penguin.

Hymes, Dell. 1974. *Foundations in sociolinguistics: an ethnographic approach*, Philadelphia: University of Pennsylvania Press.

Hynninen, Niina. 2010. "We try to to to speak all the time in easy sentences" – Student conceptions of ELF interactions. *Helsinki English Studies* 6. 29-43.

Hynninen, Niina. 2013. *Language Regulation in English as a Lingua Franca: Exploring language-regulatory practices in academic spoken discourse*. Helsinki: University of Helsinki Doctoral dissertation. http://urn.fi/URN:ISBN:978-952-10-8639-7 (accessed 15 November 2013).

James, Allan. [2005] 2008. The challenges of the lingua franca: English in the world and types of variety. In Carl Gnutzmann & Frauke Intemann (eds.), *The globalization of English and the English language classroom*, 133-144. Tübingen: Gunter Narr Verlag.

Jang, Chyng.-Yang & Michael A. Stefanone. 2009. I think you know who I am: bloggers' perceived identifiability. *Proceedings of the third international ICWSM conference*: 234-237. https://www.aaai.org/ocs/index.php/ICWSM/09/paper/download/237/513 (accessed 15 November 2013).

Jenkins, Jennifer. 2000. *The phonology of English as an international language*. Oxford: Oxford University Press.

Jenkins, Jennifer. 2002. A sociolinguistically based, empirically researched pronunciation syllabus for English as an international language. *Applied Linguistics* 23(1). 83-103.

Jenkins, Jennifer. 2006a. Points of view and blind spots: ELF and SLA. *International Journal of Applied Linguistics* 16(2). 138-162.

Jenkins, Jennifer. 2006b. Current perspectives on teaching World Englishes and English as a lingua franca. *TESOL Quarterly* 40(1). 157-181.

Jenkins, Jennifer. 2007. *English as a lingua franca: attitude and identity.* Oxford: Oxford University Press.

Jenkins, Jennifer. 2009a [2003]. *World Englishes* 2nd edition. London: Routledge.

Jenkins, Jennifer. 2009b. Exploring attitudes towards English as a lingua franca in the East Asian context. In Kumiko Murata & Jennifer Jenkins (eds.), *Global Englishes in Asian contexts. Current and future debates*, 40-56. Basingtoke: Palgrave.

Jenkins, Jennifer. 2009c. English as a lingua franca: interpretations and attitudes. *World Englishes* 28(2). 200-207.

Jenkins, Jennifer. 2010. ELF still at the gate. In Roberto Cagliero & Jennifer Jenkins (eds.), *Discourses, communities, and global Englishes*, 101-113. Bern: Peter Lang.

Jenkins, Jennifer. 2011a. Accommodating (to) ELF in the international university. *Journal of Pragmatics* 43. 926-936.

Jenkins, Jennifer 2011b. *English as a lingua franca: challenging the 'standard'.* Presentation given at the TESOL Annual Convention, New Orleans, 17 March 2011.

Jenkins, Henry. 1992. *Textual poachers: Television fans and participatory culture*. London: Routledge.

Jenkins, Jennifer. 2014. *English as a lingua franca in the international university. The politics of academic English language policy*. London: Routledge.

Jenkins, Jennifer, Alessia Cogo & Martin Dewey. 2011. Review of developments in research into English as a lingua franca. *Language Teaching* 44. 281-315.

Jessner, Ulrike. 2006. *Linguistic awareness in multilinguals. English as a third language*. Edimburgh: Edimburgh University Press.

Jessner, Ulrike. 2008 [2005]. Expanding scopes and building bridges: learning and teaching English as a third language. In Carl Gnutzmann & Frauke Intemann (eds.), *The globalization of English and the English language classroom*, 231-243. Tübingen: Gunter Narr Verlag.

Jones, Sidney & Susanna. Fox. 2009. *Generations online in 2009*. Pew Internet & American Life Project, Pew Research Center, Washington, D.C. (28 January 2009). http://www.pewinternet.org/files/old-media//Files/Reports/2009/PIP_Generations_2009.pdf (accessed 15 November 2013).

Jørgensen, J. Normann. 2008. Introduction. Polylingual languaging around and among children and adolescents. *International Journal of Multilingualism* 5(3). 161-176.

Kalocsai, Karolina. 2009. Erasmus exchange students: a behind-the-scenes view into an ELF community of practice. *Apples Journal of Applied Language Studies* 3(1). 25-49.

Katsuno, Hirofumi & Christine Yano. 2007. *Kaomoji* and expressivity in a Japanese housewives' chat room. In Brenda Danet & Susan C. Herring (eds.), *The multilingual internet. Language, culture and communication online*, 278-299. Oxford: Oxford University Press.

Kaye, Barbara K. 2005. It's a blog, blog, blog world, *Atlantic Journal of Communication* 13(2). 73-95.

Kecskes, Istvan. 2007. Formulaic language in English lingua franca. In Istvan Kecskes & Laurence R. Horn (eds.), *Explorations in pragmatics. Linguistic, cognitive and intercultural aspects*, 191-219. Berlin & New York: Mouton de Gruyter.

Kecskes, Istvan & Laurence R. Horn (eds.). 2007. *Explorations in pragmatics. Linguistic, cognitive and intercultural aspects*. Berlin & New York: Mouton de Gruyter.

Kelly-Holmes, Helen. 2004. An analysis of the language repertoires of students in higher education and their language choices on the internet (Ukraine, Poland, Macedonia, Italy, France, Tanzania, Oman and Indonesia). *International Journal on Multicultural Societies* 6(1). 52-75.

Kelly-Holmes, Helen. 2005. *Advertising as multilingual communication*. Basingtoke & New York: Palgrave MacMillan.

King, Storm A. 1996. Researching internet communities: proposed ethical guidelines for the reporting of results. *The Information Society* 12(2). 119-127.

Kirkpatrick, Andy. 2011. English as an Asian lingua franca and the multilingual model of ELT. *Language Teaching* 44(2). 212-224.

Klimpfinger, Theresa. 2007. Mind you sometimes you have to mix – the role of code-switching in English as a lingua franca. *Vienna English Working PaperS* 16(2). 36-61. http://anglistik.univie.ac.at/fileadmin/user_upload/dep_anglist/weitere_Uploads/Views/Views_0702.pdf (accessed 15 November 2013).

Klimpfinger, Theresa. 2009. “She’s mixing the two languages together“ – Forms and functions of Code-switching in English as a Lingua Franca. In Anna Mauranen & Elina Ranta (eds.), *English as a lingua franca: studies and findings*, 349-371. Newcastle-upon-Tyne: Cambridge Scholars.

Kohn, Kurt. forthcoming. A pedagogical space for English as a lingua franca in the English classroom. In Yasemin Bayyurt & Sumru Akcan (eds.), *Current perspectives on pedagogy for ELF*, Chapter 4. Berlin & New York: De Gruyter Mouton.

Kontra, Edit H. & Kata Csizér. 2011 “They can achieve their aims without native skills in the field of work or studies”: Hungarian student’s view on English as a lingua franca. *Studies in Second Language Learning and Teaching* 1(1). 135-152.

Kortmann, Bernd & Edgar W. Schneider (eds.). 2004-7. *A handbook of varieties of English: a multimedia reference tool*. Berlin & New York: Mouton de Gruyter. http://www.varieties.mouton-content.com/ (accessed 15 November 2013).

Kortmann, Bernd & Benedikt Szmrecsanyi. 2004. Global synopsis: morphological and syntactic variation in English. In Bernd Kortmann, Edgar W. Schneider, Kate Burridge, Rajend Mesthrie & Clive Upton (eds.), *A Handbook of Varieties of English,* Vol. 2, 1142–1202. Berlin & New York: Mouton de Gruyter.

Kramsch, Claire. 1993. *Context and Culture in language teaching*. Oxford: Oxford University Press.

Kramsch, Claire. 1999. Global and local identities in the contact zone. In Carl Gnutzmann (ed.), *Teaching and learning English as a global language*, 131-143. Tubingen: Stauffenburg Verlag.

Kramsch, Claire. 2002a Introduction. How well can we tell the dancer from the dance?. In Claire Kramsch (ed.), *Language acquisition and language socialization*, 1-30. London: Continuum.

Kramsch, Claire (ed.). 2002b. *Language acquisition and language socialization*. London: Continuum.

Kramsch, Claire. 2009. *The multilingual subject*. Oxford: Oxford University Press.

Kramsch, Claire & Anne Whiteside. 2007. Three fundamental concepts in second language acquisition and their relevance in multilingual contexts. *The Modern Language Journal* 91: 907-922.

Krishnamurthy, Sandeep. 2002. The multidimensionality of blog conversations: the virtual enactment of September 11. Paper given at *Internet Research 3.0: Net / Work / Theory*, Maastricht, October 2002, Association of Internet Researchers.

Kytölä, Samu. 2012. Multilingual web discussion forums. Theoretical, practical and methodological issues. In Mark Sebba, Shahrzad Mahootian & Carla Jonsson (eds.), *Language mixing and code-switching in writing*, 106-127. London: Routledge.

Internet World Stats, 2011. ‘Top ten languages used in the web’. http://www.internetworldstats.com/stats7.htm (accessed 15 Novembre 2013)

Internet World Stats, 2012. ‘Top ten internet countries in Europe’ and ‘Internet penetration in Europe’. http://www.internetworldstats.com/stats4.htm (accessed 15 Novembre 2013)

Ito, Mizuko, Heather Horst, Matteo Bittanti, danah boyd, Becky Herr-Stephenson, Patricia G. Lange, C. J. Pascoe & Laura Robinson. 2009. *Living and learning with new media: summary of findings from the digital youth project.* The John D. and Catherine T. MacArthur Foundation Reports on Digital Media and Learning. Chicago, Illinois: MacArthur Foundation. http://digitalyouth.ischool.berkeley.edu/files/report/digitalyouth-WhitePaper.pdf (accessed 15 November 2013).

Labrie Normand & Carsten Quell. 1997. Your language, my language or English? The potential language choice in communication among nationals of the European Union. *World Englishes* 16(1). 3-26.

Lam, Wan Shun Eva. 2000. L2 literacy and the design of the self: a case study of a teenager writing on the internet. *TESOL Quarterly* 34(3). 457-482.

Lam, Wan Shun Eva 2004. Second language socialization in a bilingual chat room: global and local considerations. *Language Learning and Technology* 8(3). 44-65.

Lamb. Martin. 2004. Integrative motivation in a globalizing world. *System* 23. 3-19.

Lantolf, James P. (ed.). 2000. *Sociocultural theory and second language learning.* Oxford: Oxford University Press.

Lantolf, James P. & Steven L. Thorne. 2006. *Sociocultural theory and the genesis of second language development.* Oxford: Oxford University Press.

Larsen-Freeman, Diane. 2002. Language acquisition and language use from a chaos/complexity theory perspective. In Claire Kramsch (ed.), *Language acquisition and language socialization*, 33-67. London: Continuum.

Lave, Jean & Etienne Wenger. 1991. *Situated learning: legitimate peripheral participation.* Cambridge: Cambridge University Press.

Lee, Carmen & David Barton. 2012. Multilingual texts on web.2: the case of Flick.com. In Mark Sebba, Shahrzad Mahootian & Carla Jonsson (eds.), *Language mixing and code-switching in writing*, 128-145. London: Routledge.

Leech, Geoffrey & Jan Svartvik. 1975. *A communicative grammar of English.* London, Longman.

Lenhart, Amanda & Mary Madden. 2005. *Teen content creators and consumers.* Pew Internet & American Project, Pew Research Center, Washington, D.C., 2. http://www.pewinternet.org/~/media//Files/Reports/2005/PIP_Teens_Content_Creation.pdf.pdf (accessed 15 November 2013).

Lenhart, Amanda & Susannah Fox. 2006. *Bloggers. A portrait of the internet's new storytellers.* Pew Internet & American Project, Pew Research Center, Washington, D.C., 19 July 2006. http://www.pewinternet.org/~/media//Files/Reports/2006/PIP%20Bloggers%20Report%20July%2019%202006.pdf.pdf (accessed 15 November 2013).

Lenhart, Amanda, Mary Madden, Alexandra McGill Rankin & Aaron Smith. 2007. *Teens and social media.* Pew Internet & American Project, Pew Research Center, Washington, D.C., 19 December 2007. http://pewinternet.org/~/media//Files/Reports/2007/PIP_Teens_Social_Media_Final.pdf.pdf (accessed 15 November 2013).

Lenhart, Amanda, Kristen Purcell, Aaron Smith & Kathryn Zickhur. 2010. *Social media & mobile internet use among teens and young adults*. Pew Internet & American Project, Pew Research Center, Washington, D.C., 3 February 2010. http://www.pewinternet.org/~/media//Files/Reports/2010/PIP_Social_Media_and_Young_Adults_Report_Final_with_toplines.pdf (accessed 15 November 2013).

Leppänen, Sirpa. 2007. Youth language in media contexts: insights into the functions of English in Finland. *World Englishes* 26(2). 149-169.

Leppänen S. 2012. Linguistic and generic hybridity in web writing: the case of fan fiction. In Mark Sebba, Shahrzad Mahootian & Carla Jonsson (eds), *Language mixing and code-switching in writing*, 233-254. London: Routledge.

Leppänen, Sirpa, Anne Pitkänen-Huhta, Arja Piirainen-Marsh, Tarija Nikula & Saija Peuronen. 2009. Young People's Translocal New Media Uses: A Multiperspective Analysis of Language Choice and Heteroglossia. *Journal of Computer-Mediated Communication* 14. 1080-1107.

Leppänen, Sirpa & Saija Peuronen. 2012. Multilingualism on the Internet. In Marilyn Martin-Jones, Adrian Blackledge & Angela Creese (eds.), *The Routledge handbook of multilingualism*, 384-402. London: Routledge.

Leung, Constance. 2005. Convivial communication: recontextualizing communicative competence. *International Journal of Applied Linguistics* 15(2). 119-144.

Lewis, Michael. 1993. *The lexical approach*. Hove: Language Teaching Publications.

Lichtkoppler, Julia. 2010. Language use in the European Union. In Dominik Hanf & Elise Muir (eds.), *Langues et construction européenne*, 191-210. Frankfurt/Bern: Peter Lang.

Liebes, Tamar & James Curran. 1998. *Media, ritual and identity*. London: Routledge.

LINEE (Languages in a Network of European Excellence). www.linee.info (accessed 15 November 2013).

Llurda, Enric (ed.). 2005. *Non-native language teachers; perceptions, challenges and contributions to the profession*. New York: Springer.

Llurda, Enric. 2009. Attitudes towards English as an international language: the pervasiveness of native models among L2 users and teachers. In Farzad Sharifian (ed.), *English as an international language. Perspectives and pedagogical issues*, 119-134. Bristol: Multilingual Matters.

Lopriore, Lucilla. 2010. World Englishes and language teacher education. In Cesare Gagliardi & Alan Maley (eds.), *EIL, ELF, global English: teaching and learning issues*, 69-92. Bern: Peter Lang.

Lövheim, Mia. 2011. Personal and popular. The case of young Swedish female top-bloggers. *Nordicom Review* 32(1). 3-16.

Lüdi, Georges. 2005. Code-Switching/Sprachewechsel. In Ulrich Ammon, Norbert Dittmar, Klaus J. Mattheier & Peter Trudgill. *Sociolinguistics – Soziolinguistik. An International Handbook of the Science of Language and Society / Ein internationales Handbuch zur Wissenschaft von Sprache und Gesellschaft*, 2nd completely revised and extended edition, Volume 1, 341-350. Berlin & New York: Mouton de Gruyter.

Lüdi, Georges & Bernard Py. 2009. To be or not to be… a plurilingual speaker. *International Journal of Multilingualism* 6(2). 154-167.

Lyons, John. 1977. *Semantics*. Cambridge: Cambridge University Press.

MacKenzie, Ian. 2011. English as a lingua franca in Europe: bilingualism and multicompetence. *International Journal of Multilingualism* 9(1). 83-100.

Martin, Elisabeth. 2002. Mixing English in French advertising. *World Englishes* 21(3). 375-402.

Martin Elisabeth. 2008. Language-Mixing in French Print Advertising. *Journal of Creative Communications* 3(1). 49-76.

Marwick, Alice. 2008. *LiveJournal users: passionate, prolific and private*. LiveJournal http://www.livejournalinc.com/LJ_Research_Report.pdf (accessed 15 November 2013).

Matsuda, Aya. 2009. Desirable but not necessary? The place of World Englishes and English as an international language in English teacher preparation programs in Japan. In Farzad Sharifian (ed.), *English as an international language: perspectives and pedagogical issues,* 169-189. Clevedon, UK: Multilingual Matters.

Matsuda, Aya. 2012a. Teaching materials in EIL. In In Alsagoff, Lubna, Sandra Lee McKay, Guangwei Lu & Willy A. Renandya (eds.), *Principles and practices for teaching English as an international language*, 168-185. New York / London: Routledge.

Matsuda, Aya (ed.). 2012b. *Principles and practices of teaching English as an international language*. Bristol: Multilingual Matters.

Mauranen, Anna. 2005. English as Lingua Franca: an unknown language?. In Giuseppina Cortese & Anna Duszak (eds.), *Identity, community, discourse*, 269-293. Bern: Peter Lang.

Mauranen, Anna. 2006. Signalling and preventing misunderstanding in English as a lingua franca communication. *International Journal of the Sociology of Language* 177. 123-150.

Mauranen, Anna. 2007. Discourse reflexivity and international speakers – How is it used in English as a lingua franca? *Jezik in Slovstvo* 52(3-4). 1-19.

Mauranen, Anna. 2009. Chunking in ELF: expressions for managing interaction. *Intercultural Pragmatics* 6(2). 217-223.

Mauranen, Anna. 2010a. Features of English as a lingua franca in academia. *Helsinki English Studies* 6. 6-28.

Mauranen, Anna. 2010b. *English as the lingua franca of globalised academia*. Presentation given at Cercles, Helsinki, 2-4 September 2010.

Mauranen, Anna. 2011. Learners and users – Who do we want corpus data from? In Fanny Meunier, Sylvie De Cock, Gaëtanelle Gilquin & Magali Paquot (eds.), *A taste for corpora. A tribute to Professor Sylviane Granger,* 155–171. Amsterdam / Philadelphia: John Benjamins.

Mauranen, Anna. 2012. *Exploring ELF. Academic English shaped by non-native speakers*. Cambridge: Cambridge University Press.

Mauranen, Anna. 2013. Hybridism, edutainment, and doubt: Science blogging finding its feet. *Nordic Journal of English Studies* 13(1). 7-36.
Mauranen, Anna & Maria Metsä-Ketelä. 2006. Introduction. [Special issue]. *Nordic Journal of English Studies*, 5(2). 1-6.
Mayfield, Ross. 2003 *Social networking models*. http://radio.weblogs.com/0114726/2003/03/30.html#a376 (accessed 15 November 2013).
Maynor, Natalie. 1994. The language of electronic mail: written speech? In Michael Montgomery & Greta D. Little (eds.), *Centennial usage studies*, 48-54. Publication of the American Dialect Society Series. Tuscaloosa, Alabama: University of Alabama Press.
McLean, Jennifer 2009. Introduction. Technorati *State of the blogosphere 2009*. http://technorati.com/social-media/article/state-of-the-blogosphere-2009-introduction/ (accessed 15 November 2013).
McKay, Sandra L. 2002. *Teaching English as an international language*. Oxford: Oxford University Press.
McKay, Sandra L. 2006. EIL curriculum development. In Rani Rubdy & Mario Saraceni (eds.), *English in the world. Global rules, global roles*, 114-129. London: Continuum.
McKay, Sandra L. & Wendy D. Bokhorst-Heng. 2008. *International English in its sociolinguistic contexts. Towards a socially sensitive EIL pedagogy*. London: Routledge.
McNeill, Laurie. 2003. Teaching an old genre new tricks: the diary on the internet. *Biography* 26(1). 24-47.
McNeill, Laurie. 2005. Gender Under Construction: The Diary on the internet. *Language@Internet* 2.
McNeill, Laurie. 2009. Brave new genre, or generic colonialism?. In Janet Giltrow & Dieter Stein (eds.), *Genres in the internet*, 143-161. Amsterdam / Philadelphia: John Benjamins.
Meierkord, Christiane. 2002. 'Language stripped bare' or 'linguistic masala". Culture in lingua franca conversation. In Karlfried Knapp & Christiane Meierkord (eds.), *Lingua franca communication*, 109-133. Frankfurt-Main: Peter Lang.
Melchers, Gunnel & Philip Shaw. 2003. *World Englishes*. London: Hodder Arnold.
Metitieri, Fabio. 2009. *Il grande inganno del Web 2.0* [The great fallacy of Web 2.0]. Roma / Bari: Editori Laterza.
Miglietta, Annarita & Alberto. A. Sobrero. 2007. Fra gergo e lingua comune, oltre le regole [Between jargon and everyday language, beyond rules]. In Ugo Cardinale & Dario Corno (eds.), *Giovani oltre* [Young people and beyond], 139-171. Soveria Mannelli: Rubbettino.
Miles, Adrian. 2006. A vision for genuine rich media blogging. In Axel Bruns & Joanne Jacobs (eds.), *Uses of blogs*, 213-222. New York: Peter Lang.
Miller, Carolyn R. & Dawn Shepherd. 2004. Blogging as social action: a genre analysis of the weblog. *Into the blogosphere. Rhethoric, community and culture of weblogs*. http://blog.lib.umn.edu/blogosphere/blogging_as_social_action.html (accessed 15 November 2013).

Miller, Carolyn R. & Dawn Shepherd. 2009. Questions for genre theory from the blogosphere. In Janet Giltrow & Dieter Stein (eds.), *Genres in the internet*, 263-289. Amsterdam & Philadelphia: John Benjamins.

Milroy, Lesley & Pieter Muyksen. 1995. Introduction: code-switching and bilingual research. In Lesley Milroy & Pieter Muyksen (eds.), *One speaker, two languages*, 1-14. Cambridge: Cambridge University Press.

Modiano, Marko. 1999. International English in the global village'. *English Today* 15(2). 14–19.

Modiano, Marko. 2001. Linguistic imperialism, cultural integrity, and EIL. *ELT Journal* 55(4). 339-346.

Modiano, Marko. 2009. EIL, native-speakerism and the failure of European ELT. In Farzad Sharifian (ed.), *English as an international language. Perspectives and pedagogical issues*, 58-77. Bristol: Multilingual Matters.

Mollin, Sandra. 2006. *Euro-English. Assessing variety status*. Tübingen: Gunter Narr Verlag.

Montes-Alcalá, Cecilia. 2007. Blogging in two languages: code-switching in bilingual blogs. In Jonathan Holmquist, Augusto Lorenzino & Lofti Sayahi (eds.). *Selected Proceedings of the third workshop on Spanish sociolinguistics*, 162-170. Somerville, MA: Cascadilla Proceedings Project.

Montgomery, Michael & Greta D. Little (eds.). 1994. *Centennial usage studies*. Publication of the American Dialect Society Series. Tuscaloosa: University of Alabama Press.

Moon, Rosamund. 1998. *Fixed expressions and idioms in English. A corpus-based approach*. Oxford: Clarendon Press.

Moraldo, Sandro M. 2005. Italienische Weblogs. In Peter Schlobinski & Torsten Siever (eds.), *Sprachliche und textuelle Merkmale im Weblogs. Ein internationales Projekt* [Linguistic and textual characteristics in weblogs. An International project]. 131-164. Hannover: Net.Workx.

Mufwene, Salikoko. 2001. *The ecology of language evolution*. Cambridge: Cambridge University Press.

Mufwene, Salikoko. 2008. *Language evolution: Contact, competition and change.* Continuum International Publishing Group.

Myers, Greg. 2010. *Discourse of blogs and wikis*. London: Continuum.

Myers-Scotton, Carol. 1993. *Social motivations for code-switching: evidence from Africa*. Oxford: Oxford University Press.

Myers-Scotton, Carol. 2000. Expanding the role of norms and rationality in code-switching. *Journal of Pragmatics* 32(9). 1259-1271.

Nardi, Bonnie A., Diane J. Schiano, Michelle Gumbrecht & Luke Swartz. 2004a. Why we blog. *Communication of the ACM* 47(12). 41-46.

Nardi, Bonnie A., Diane J. Schiano & Michelle Gumbrecht. 2004b. Blogging as soA cial activity, or, would you let 900 million people read your diary? *Proceedings of the 2004 ACM conference on computer supported cooperative work*, 223-231. Chicago, Illinois: ACM Press.

Negrón Goldbarg, Rosalyn 2009. Spanish-English codeswitching in email communication. *Language@internet* 6, Article 3.

Norton, Bonny. 2001. Non-participation, imagined communities and the language classroom. In Michael P. Breen (ed.). *Learner contributions to language learning: new directions in research*, 159-171. Harlow: Longman.

Nunberg, Geoffrey. 2000. Will the internet always speak English? *The American Prospect* 11(10).

O' Neill, Jacki & David Martin. 2003. Text chat in action. *Proceedings of the 2003 international ACM SIGGROUP conference on supporting group work*, 40-49. New York/ Sanibel Island, Florida: ACM Press.

O'Reilly, Tim. (2005). *What is web 2.0?* http://www.oreillynet.com/pub/a/oreilly/tim/news/2005/09/30/what-is-web-20.html#mememap (accessed 15 November 2013).

Paolillo, John C. 1996. Language choice on soc.culture.punjab. *The Electronic Journal of Communication* 6(3). http://www.cios.org/EJCPUBLIC/006/3/006312.HTML (accessed 15 November 2013).

Paolillo, John C. 2005. Language diversity on the internet. In UNESCO Institute for Statistics (ed.) *Measuring linguistic diversity on the internet*, 43-89. Paris: Unesco.

Paolillo, John C. 2007. How much multilingualism? Language diversity on the internet. In Brenda Danet & Susan C. Herring (eds.), *The multilingual internet. Language, culture and communication online*, 408-428. Oxford: Oxford University Press.

Pavlenko, Aneta. 2002. Poststructuralist approaches to the study of social factors in second language learning and use. In Vivian Cook (ed.), *Portraits of the L2 user*, 275-302. Clevedon: Multilingual Matters.

Pavlenko, Aneta & James P. Lantolf. 2000. Second language learning as participation and the (re)construction of selves. In James P. Lantolf (ed.), *Sociocultural theory and second language learning*, 155-177. Oxford: Oxford University Press.

Pennycook, Alastair. 1994. *The cultural politics of English as an international language*. London: Longman.

Pennycook, Alastair. 1999. Pedagogical implications of different frameworks for understanding the global spread of English. In Carl Gnutzmann (ed.), *Teaching and learning English as a global language*, 147-155. Tübingen: Stauffenburg Verlag.

Pennycook, Alastair. 2007. *Global Englishes and transcultural flows*. London: Routledge.

Pennycook, Alastair. 2010. *Language as local practice*. London: Routledge.

Peterson, Eric E. 2011. How Conversational are weblogs? *Language@Internet* 8, Article 8. http: www.languageatinternet.org/articles/2011/Peterson (accessed 15 November 2013).

Phillipson, Robert. 1992. *Linguistic imperialism*. Oxford: Oxford University Press.

Phillipson, Robert. 2003. *English-only Europe?* London: Routledge.

Piller, Ingrid. 2001. Identity constructions in multilingual advertising. *Language in Society* 30. 153-186.

Piller, Ingrid. 2002. Passing for a native speaker: Identity and success in second language learning. *Journal of Sociolinguistics* 6(2). 179-206.

Piller, Ingrid. 2003. Advertising as a site of language contact. *Annual Review of Applied Linguistics* 23. 170-183.

Pitzl, Marie-Luise. 2009. "We should not wake up any dogs": Idiom and metaphor in ELF. In Anna Mauranen & Elina Ranta (eds.), *English as a lingua franca: studies and findings*, 298-322. Newcastle-upon-Tyne: Cambridge Scholars.

Pitzl, Marie-Luise. 2012a. Creativity meets convention: idiom variation and re-metaphorisation in ELF. *Journal of English as a Lingua Franca* 1(1). 27-55.

Pitzl, Marie-Luise. 2012b. *Preparing teachers for an ELF future: what we CAN tell them*. Presentation given at ELF5, The Fifth International Conference of English as a Lingua Franca, Istanbul, Bogazici University, May 24-26 2102.

Pitzl, Marie-Luise, Angelika Breiteneder & Theresa Klimpfinger. 2008. A world of words: processes of lexical innovation in VOICE. *Vienna English Working PaperS* 17(2). 21-46. http://anglistik.univie.ac.at/fileadmin/user_upload/dep_anglist/weitere_Uploads/Views/views_0802.pdf (accessed 15 November 2013).

Platt, John, Heidi Weber & Mian Lian Ho. 1984. *The New Englishes*. London: Routledge and Kegan Paul.

Pölzl, Ulrike. 2003. Signalling cultural identity: the use of L1/Ln in ELF. *Vienna English Working PaperS* 12(2). 3-24. http://anglistik.univie.ac.at/fileadmin/user_upload/dep_anglist/weitere_Uploads/Views/VIEWS122.PDF (accessed 15 November 2013).

Pölzl, Ulrike & Barbara Seidlhofer. 2006. In and on their own terms: the 'habitat factor' in English as a lingua franca interactions. *International Journal of the Sociology of Language* 177. 151-176.

Posteguillo, Santiago. 2002. Netlinguistics and English for internet purposes. *Ibérica* 4. 21-38.

Preisler, Bent. 1999. Functions and forms of English in a European EFL country. In Tony Bex & Richard J. Watts (eds.), *Standard English: the widening debate*, 239–267. London: Routledge.

Puschmann, Cornelius. 2009. Diary or megaphone? The pragmatic mode of weblogs. Paper presented at *Language in the (new) media: technologies and ideologies*, September 3-6 2009, Seattle, WA, USA. http://ynada.com/pubs/diarymegaphone.pdf (accessed 15 November 2013).

Puschmann, Cornelius. 2010a. *The corporate blog as an emerging genre of Computer-mediated Communication: features, constraints, discourse situations*. Göttingen: Universitätverlag Göttingen.

Puschmann, Cornelius. 2010b. "Thank you for thinking we could" — use and function of interpersonal pronouns in corporate web logs. In Heidrun Dorgeloh & Anja Wanner (eds.), *Approaches to syntactic variation and genre*, 167-194. Berlin & New York: De Gruyter Mouton.

Puschmann, Cornelius. 2013. Blogging. In Susan C. Herring, Dieter Stein & Tuija Virtanen (eds.), *Handbook of the pragmatics of CMC,* 75-100. Berlin & New York: Mouton de Gruyter.

Quirk, Randolph, Sidney Greenbaum, Geoffrey Leech & Jan Svartvik. 1991. *A comprehensive grammar of the English language*. London & New York: Longman.

Rampton, Ben. 1990. Displacing the 'native speaker': expertise, affiliation and inheritance. *ELT Journal* 44(2). 97-101.

Rampton, Ben. 1997. Second language research in late modernity: a response to Firth and Wagner. *The Modern Language Journal* 81(iii). 329-333.

Rainie, Lee. 2005. *The state of blogging*. Pew Internet & American Life Project. Pew Research Center, Washington, D.C., 2 January 2005 http://www.pewinternet.org/files/old-media//Files/Reports/2005/PIP_blogging_data.pdf.pdf (accessed 15 November 2013).

Ranta, Elina. 2006. The 'attractive progressive – why use the –ing form in English as a lingua franca? *Nordic Journal of English Studies* 5(2). 95-116.

Ranta, Elina. 2009. Syntactic features in spoken ELF – Learner language or spoken grammar? In Anna Mauranen & Elina Ranta (eds.), *English as a lingua franca: studies and findings*, 84-105. Newcastle-upon-Tyne: Cambridge Scholars.

Ranta, Elina. 2010. English in the real world vs. English at school: Finnish English teachers' and students' views. *International Journal of Applied Linguistics* 20(2). 156-177.

Raynes-Goldie, Kate. 2004. Pulling sense out of today's informational chaos: LiveJournal as a site for knowledge creation and sharing. *First Monday* 9(12). http://www.firstmonday.org/htbin/cgiwrap/bin/ojs/index.php/fm/issue/view/178 (accessed 15 November 2013).

Rebaza, Claudia. 2008. Online gestures: icon use by fan communities on LiveJournal. *Proceedings of the 41st Hawaii international conference on system sciences*, 150-159. Washington DC, USA: IEEE Computer Society.

Reyes, Pablo & Pierre Tchounikine. 2004. Redefining the turn-taking notion in mediated communication of virtual learning communities. *Intelligent Tutoring Systems. Lecture Notes in Computer Science* 3220. 295-304.

Risager, Karen. 1998. Language teaching and the process of European integration. In Michael Byram & Mike Fleming (eds.), *Language learning in intercultural perspective. Approaches through drama and ethnography*, 242-254. Cambridge: Cambridge University Press.

Risager, Karen. 2007. *Language and culture pedagogy. From a national to a trasnational paradigm*. Clevedon: Multilingual Matters.

Rivoltella, Pier Cesare. 2006. *Screen Generation*. Milano: Vita e Pensiero.

Romaine, Suzanne. 2000. *Language in society. An introduction to sociolinguistics*. Oxford: Oxford University Press.

Romaine, Suzanne. 2001. *Bilingualism*. Oxford: Blackwell.

Rosenberg, Scott. 2009. *Say everything. How blogging began, what it's becoming, and why it matters*. New York: Crown Publishers.

Ross, Nigel J. 1997. Signs of International English. *English Today* 50 13(2). 29-33.
Rubdy, Rani & Mario Saraceni. 2006. An interview with Suresh Canagarajah. In Rani Rubdy & Mario Saraceni. (eds.), *English in the world. Global rules, global roles*, 200-211. London: Continuum.
Russel, Adrienne & Nabil Echchaibi. 2009. *International blogging: identity, politics, and networked publics*. New York: Peter Lang.
Šabec, Nada. n.d. Slovene-English netspeak: linguistic and socio-cultural aspects. http://oddelki.ff.uni-mb.si/filozofija/files/Festschrift/Dunjas_festschrift/sabec.pdf (accessed 15 November 2013).
Sacks, Harvey. 1992. *Lectures on conversation*. Vol. I. Cambridge MA: Blackwell.
Sand, Andrea. 2005. *Angloversals? Shared morphosyntactic features in contact varieties of English*. Freiburg: University of Freiburg Habilitationsschrift.
Saraceni, Mario. 2010. *The relocation of English. Shifting paradigms in the global era*. Basingtoke: Palgrave MacMillan.
Saxena, Mukul & Tope Omoniyi. 2010. Final reflections: globalization and World Englishes. In Mukul Saxena & Tope Omoniyi (eds.), *Contending with globalization in World Englishes*, 211-229. Bristol: Multilingual Matters.
Schendl, Herbert. 2001. *Historical linguistics*. Oxford: Oxford University Press.
Schiano Diane J., Bonnie A. Nardi, Michelle Gumbrecht & Luke Swartz. 2004. Blogging by the rest of us. *Extended abstracts of the 2004 conference on human factors and computing systems*. Chicago, Illinois: ACM Press.
Schlobinski, Peter & Torsten Siever (eds.). 2005. *Sprachliche und Textuelle Merkmale im Weblogs. Ein internationales Projekt*. [Linguistic and textual characteristics in weblogs. An International project]. Hannover: Net.Workx. http://www.mediensprache.net/de/networx/docs/networx-46.aspx (accessed 15 November 2013).
Schmidt, Jan. 2007. Blogging practices: an analytical framework. *Journal of Computer-Mediated Communication* 12(4). 1409-1427. http://onlinelibrary.wiley.com/doi/10.1111/jcmc.2007.12.issue-4/issuetoc (accessed 25 April 2014).
Schneider, Edgar W. 2007. *Postcolonial English. Varieties around the world.* Cambridge: Cambridge University Press.
Schneider, Edgar W. 2011. *English around the world. An introduction*. Cambridge: Cambridge University Press.
Scott, Mike. 1999. *Wordsmith tools software*. Oxford: Oxford University Press.
Seargeant, Philip & Caroline Tagg. 2011. English on the internet and a 'post-varieties' approach to language. *World Englishes* 30(4). 496-514.
Sebba, Mark. 2002. Regulated spaces: Language alternation in writing. *Colloquium on code-switching, class and ideology, 2nd international symposium on bilingualism*, Vigo, October 23-26 2002. http://www.ling.lancs.ac.uk/staff/mark/vigo/regspace (accessed 15 November 2013).
Sebba, Mark 2011. Multilingualism in written discourse. Draft http://www.ling.lancs.ac.uk/staff/mark/MIWD.pdf (accessed 15 November 2013).
Sebba, Mark, Shahrzad Mahootian & Carla Jonsson (eds.). 2012. *Language mixing and code-switching in writing*. London: Routledge.

Seidlhofer, Barbara. 2001. Closing a conceptual gap: the case for a description of English as a lingua franca. *International Journal of Applied Linguistics* 11(2). 133-158.

Seidlhofer, Barbara. 2002. The shape of things to come? Some basic questions about English as lingua franca. In Karlfried Knapp & Christiane Meierkord (eds.), *Lingua franca communication*, 269-302. Frankfurt-Main: Peter Lang.

Seidlhofer, Barbara. 2003. *A concept of international English and related issues: from 'real English' to 'realistic English'?* Strasbourg: Council of Europe Language Policy Division. http://www.coe.int/t/dg4/linguistic/Liste_EN.asp#TopOfPage (accessed 15 November 2013).

Seidlhofer, Barbara. 2004. Research perspectives on teaching English as a lingua franca. *Annual Review of Applied Linguistics* 24. 209-239.

Seidlhofer, Barbara. 2005a. English as a lingua franca. *ELT Journal* 59. 339-341.

Seidlhofer, Barbara. 2005b. English as a lingua franca. In Albert Sidney Hornby (ed.), *Oxford Advanced Learner's Dictionary of Current English*, R 92. Oxford: Oxford University Press.

Seidlhofer, Barbara. 2006. English as a lingua franca in the expanding circle: What it isn't. In Rani Rubdy & Mario Saraceni (eds.), *English in the world: Global rules, global roles*, 40-50. London: Continuum.

Seidlhofer, Barbara. 2007a. Common property: English as a lingua franca in Europe. In Jim Cummins & Chris Davison (eds.), *International handbook of English language teaching*, 137-153. New York: Springer.

Seidlhofer, Barbara. 2007b. English as a lingua franca and communities of practice. In Sabine Volk-Birke & Julia Lippert (eds.), *Anglistentag 2006 Halle Proceedings*, 307-318. Trier: Wissenschaftlicher Verlag Trier.

Seidlhofer, Barbara. 2008. Of norms and mindsets. *Australian Review of Applied Linguistics* 31(3). 1-7.

Seidlhofer, Barbara. 2009a. Accommodation and the idiom principle. *Intercultural Pragmatics* 6(2). 195-215.

Seidlhofer, Barbara. 2009b. ELF findings: form and function. In Anna Mauranen & Elina Ranta, (eds.), *English as a lingua franca: studies and findings*, 37-59. Newcastle-upon-Tyne: Cambridge Scholars.

Seidlhofer, Barbara. 2009c. Common grounds and different realities. World Englishes and English as a lingua franca *World Englishes* 28(2). 236-245.

Seidlhofer, Barbara. 2010a. Giving VOICE to English as a lingua franca. In Roberta Facchinetti, David Crystal & Barbara Seidlhofer (eds.), *From international to local English and back again*, 147-163. Bern: Peter Lang.

Seidlhofer, Barbara. 2010b. Lingua franca English – The European context. In Andy Kirkpatrick (ed.), *The Routledge handbook of World Englishes*, 355-371. London: Routledge.

Seidlhofer, Barbara. 2011. *Understanding English as a Lingua Franca*. Oxford: Oxford University Press.

Seidlhofer, Barbara, Angelika Breiteneder & Marie-Luise Pitzl. 2006. English as a lingua franca in Europe: challenges for applied linguistics. *Annual Review of Applied Linguistics* 26. 3-34.

Seidlhofer, Barbara & Henry G. Widdowson. 2003. House work and student work: a study in cross-cultural understanding. In Nicole Baumgarten, Claudia Böttger, Markus Motz & Julia Probst (eds.), *Übersetzen, interkulturelle Kommunikation, Spracherwerb und Sprachvermittlung – das Leben mit mehreren Sprachen. Festschrift für Juliane House zum 60. Geburtstag* [Translation, intercultural commuu nication, language acquisition and linguistic mediation – life with several languages. Festschrift for Juliane House for her 60th birthday], 114-126. Bochum: AKS-Verlag. http://zif.spz.tu-darmstadt.de/jg-08-2-3/beitrag/Seidlhofer_Widdowson1.htm (accessed 15 November 2013).

Seidlhofer, Barbara & Henry G. Widdowson. 2007. Idiomatic variation and change in English. The idiom principle and its realization. In Ute Smit, Stefan Dollinger, Julia Hüttner, Gunther Kaltemböck & Ursula Lutzky (eds.), *Tracing English through time. Explorations in language variation. Festschrift for Herbert Schendl*. Austrian Studies in English vol. 95, 359-374. Wien: Braumüller.

Seidlhofer, Barbara & Henry G. Widdowson. 2009a. Accommodation and the idiom principle in English as a lingua franca. In Kumiko Murata & Jennifer Jenkins (eds.), *Global Englishes in Asian Contexts. Current and future debates*, 26-39. Basingtoke: Palgrave.

Seidlhofer, Barbara & Henry G. Widdowson. 2009b. Conformity and creativity in ELF and learner English. In Michaela Albl-Mikasa, Sabine Braun & Sylvia Kalina (eds.), *Dimensionen der Zweitsprachneforschung. Dimensions of Second Language Research. Festschrift for Kurt Kohn*, 93-107. Tübingen: Narr Verlag.

Seybert, Heidi & Anna Lööf. 2010. *Internet usage in 2010 – Households and individuals.* Eurostat/European Commission, Data in Focus. http://epp.eurostat.ec.europa.eu/cache/ITY_OFFPUB/KS-QA-10-050/EN/KS-QA-10-050-EN.PDF (accessed 15 November 2013).

Shang, Rong-An, Chen, Yu-Chen & Chen, Cheng-Min. 2007. Why people blog? An empirical investigation of the task technology fit model. *PACIS 2007 Proceedings 11th Pacific-Asia conference on information systems Paper 5*: 212-225. http://aisel.aisnet.org/pacis2007/5 (accessed 15 November 2013).

Sharifian, Farzad. 2010. Glocalization of English in World Englishes: an emerging variety among Persian speakers of English. In Mukul Saxena & Tope Omoniyi (eds.), *Contending with globalization in World Englishes*, 137-158. Bristol: Multilingual Matters.

Sifakis, Nicos C. 2004. Teaching EIL – Teaching international or intercultural English? What teachers should know. *System* 32. 237-250.

Sifakis, Nicos C. 2006. Teaching EIL – Teaching international or intercultural English? In Rani Rubdy & Mario Saraceni (eds.), *English in the World. Global rules, global roles*, 151-168. London: Continuum.

Sifry, David. 2006 *Sifry's Alerts* (blog), http://www.sifry.com/alerts/archives/2006_11.htm (accessed 15 November 2013).

Sifry, David. 2007 *Sifry's Alerts* (blog), http://www.sifry.com/alerts/archives/000493.html (accessed 15 November 2013).

Sinclair, John M. 1991a. Shared knowledge. In Alatis J. (ed). *Linguistics and language pedagogy: the state of the art*, 489-500. Washington DC: Georgetown University Press.

Sinclair, John M. 1991b. *Corpus, concordance, collocation.* Oxford: Oxford University Press.

Smit, Ute, Stefan Dollinger, Julia Hüttner, Gunther Kaltenböck & Ursula Lutzky (eds.). 2007. *Tracing English through time. Explorations in language variation. Festschrift for Herbert Schendl.* Austrian Studies in English vol. 95. Wien: Braumüller.

Smith, Aaron. 2011. *Why Americans use social media.* Pew Internet & American Life Project, Pew Research Center, Washington, D.C. 15 November 2011. http://www.pewinternet.org/files/old-media//Files/Reports/2011/Why%20Americans%20Use%20Social%20Media.pdf (accessed 15 November 2013)

Sobel, Jon. 2010. Introduction, Day 1, Day 2, Day 3. Technorati *State of the blogosphere* 2010. http://technorati.com/social-media/article/state-of-the-blogosphere-2010-introduction/ (accessed 15 November 2013).

Sobrero Alberto A. 2010. Competenze e bisogni linguistici dei giovani, oggi [Young people's competences and linguistic needs]. In Adriana Bonforte, Giovanni Messina & Cettina Rizzo (eds.), *Educazione linguistica e approccio per competenze. Atti del Seminario Nazionale LEND [Language education and a comapetence-based approach. Proceedings of the LEND National Seminar],* 17-28. Catania, 29-31 October 2009. LEND.

Stefanone, Michael A. & Chyng-Yang Jang. 2007. Writing for friends and family: the interpersonal nature of blogs. *Journal of Computer-Mediated Communication* 13(1). Article 7, 123-140.

Studer, Patrick, Felicia Kreiselmaier & Mi-Cha Flubacher. 2010. Language planning in the European Union. *European Journal of Language Policy* 2(2). 251-270.

Su, Norman M., Yang Wang & Gloria Mark. 2005. Politics as usual in the blogorsphere. *Proceedings of the 4th international workshop on social intelligence design,* March 24-26, (SID05), Palo Alto, USA.

Sussman, Matt. 2009. Day 1, Day 2, Day 3, Day 4, Day 5. Technorati *State of the Blogosphere* 2009. http://technorati.com/blogging/feature/state-of-the-blogosphere-2009/ (accessed 15 November 2013)

Swales, John. 1990. *Genre analysis*. Cambridge: Cambridge University Press.

Szymanek, Bogdan. 2005. The latest trends in English word-formation. In Pavel Štekauer & Rochelle Lieber (eds.), *Handbook of word-formation*, 429-448. Dordrecht: Springer.

Tarkowski, Alek. 2005. Peer production of popular culture at the LiveJournal site. Banal blogging, or cultural struggle? Paper presented at the *RE: Activism: Re-Drawing the Boundaries of Activism in New Media environment,* 1-18. Budapest, October 14-15, 2005.

Technorati. 2009. *State of the Blogosphere* 2008. Columnists: White, Dave (Day 1, Day 2, Day 3, Day 4) & Winn, Philip (Introduction), http://technorati.com/blogging/feature/state-of-the-blogosphere-2008/ (accessed 15 November 2013)

Technorati. 2009. *State of the Blogosphere* 2009. Columnists: McLean, Jennifer (Introduction) & Sussman, Matt (Day 1, Day 2, Day 3, Day 4, Day 5), http://technorati.com/blogging/feature/state-of-the-blogosphere-2009/ (accessed 15 November 2013)

Technorati. 2010. *State of the Blogosphere* 2010. Columnist: Sobel, Jon (Introduction, Day 1, Day 2, Day 3), http://technorati.com/blogging/feature/state-of-the-blogosphere-2010/ (accessed 15 November 2013)

Technorati Media. 2011. *State of the Blogosphere* 2011. http://technorati.com/social-media/feature/state-of-the-blogosphere-2011/ (accessed 15 November 2013)

Thelwall, Mike. 2009. MySpace Comments. *Online Information Review* 33(1). 58-76.

Thurlow, Crispin. 2001. The Internet and Language. In Rajend Mesthrie & Asher Ron E. (eds.), *The concise encyclopedia of sociolinguistics*, 287-289. London: Pergamon.

Thurlow, Crispin & Kristine Mroczek (eds.). 2011a. *Digital discourse: language in the new media*. Oxford / New York: Oxford University Press.

Thurlow, Crispin & Mroczek Kristine 2011b. Fresh perspectives on new media sociolinguistics. In Crispin Thurlow & Kristine Mroczek (eds.), *Digital discourse: language in the new media*, 220-250. Oxford / New York: Oxford University Press.

Thurlow, Crispin. 2012. Determined creativity: language play, vernacular practice and new media discourse. In Rodney H. Jones (ed.), *Discourse and creativity*, 169-190. Harlow: Pearson Education.

Todd, Loreto. 1990. *Pidgins and creoles*. London: Routledge.

Tomlinson, Brian. 2006. A multi-dimensional approach to teaching English for the world. In Rani Rubdy & Mario Saraceni (eds.), *English in the world. Global rules, global roles*, 130-150. London: Continuum.

Tosi, Arturo. 2001. *Language and society in a changing Italy*. Clevedon: Multilingual Matters.

Treem, Jeffrey William & Kristin Yates Thomas. 2010. What makes a blog a blog? Exploring user conceptualizations of an old "new" online medium. *Proceedings of the fourth international AAAI conference on weblogs and social media*, 347-350. Washington, D.C., May 23-26.

Trudgill, Peter. 1999. *The dialects of England* 2nd edition. Oxford: Blackwell.

Trudgill, Peter. 2002. *Sociolinguistic variation and change*. Edimburgh: Edimburgh University Press.

Trudgill, Peter & Jean Hannah. 1985. *International English: A guide to varieties of Standard English*. London: Arnold.

Trudgill, Peter & Jean Hannah. 2008. *International English. A guide to the varieties of Standard English*. 5th edition. London: Hodder Education.

Tsiplakou, *Stavroula*. 2009. Doing (bi)lingualism: language alternation as performative construction of online identities. *Pragmatics* 19(3). 361-391.

Turnbull. Giles. 2002. The state of the blog – Part 2: blogger present. In John Rodzvilla (ed.), *We've got blog: how weblogs are changing our culture*, 81-85. Cambridge, MA: Perseus Publishing.

Ungerleider, Neal. 2012. *The return of LiveJournal*. http://www.fastcompany.com/1809674/the-return-of-livejournal (accessed 15 November 2013).

van Dijck, José. 2004. Composing the self: of diaries and lifelogs. *The Fibreculture Journal* 3. http://three.fibreculturejournal.org/fcj-012-composing-the-self-of-diaries-and-lifelogs/ (accessed 15 November 2013).

van Els, Theo. 2005. Multilingualism in the European Union. *International Journal of Applied Linguistics* 15(3). 263-281.

van Lier, Leo. 2002. An ecological-semiotic perspective on language and linguistics. In Claire Kramsch (ed.), *Language acquisition and language socialization*, 140-164. London: Continuum.

Verschik, Anna. 2010. Russian-Estonian code-copying in Live-Journal blogs: a preliminary overview. In Arto Mustajoki, Ekaterina Protassova & Nikolai Vakhtin (eds.), *Sociolinguistic approaches to non-Standard Russian, Slavica Helsingiensia* 40. 355-365.

Vertovec, Steven. 2007. Super-diversity and its implications. *Ethnic and Racial Studies* 30(6). 1024-1054.

Vettorel, Paola. 2010a. EIL/ELF and representation of culture in textbooks: Only food, fairs, folklore and facts?. In Cesare Gagliardi & Alan Maley (eds.), *EIL, ELF, global English: teaching and learning issues*, 153-185. Bern: Peter Lang.

Vettorel, Paola. 2010b. Teaching (and learning) Englishes. *SELM Scuola e Lingue Moderne.* Anno XLVIII 8-9. 18-23.

Vettorel, Paola. 2012. Blogging ELFers. In Geraldine Ludbrook & David Newbold (eds.), *English lingua franca: Contexts, strategies and international relations. Papers from a conference held at Ca'Foscari University of Venice October 2011*, 67-78. Venice: Cafoscarina.

Vettorel P. 2013a. ELF in international school exchanges: stepping into the role of ELF users. *Journal of English as a Lingua Franca* 2(1). 147-173.

Vettorel, Paola. 2013b. English in Italian advertising. *World Englishes* 32(2). 261–279.

Vettorel, Paola. 2013c. Primary school teachers' perceptions: English*es*, ELF, classroom practices and international partnerships, presentation given at the Symposium *New Frontiers in Teaching and Learning English*, University of Verona, 15 February 2013, http://prin-confs-2013.dlls.univr.it/prin/newFrontiers.html (accessed 15 November 2013).)

Vettorel, Paola. in preparation. English, Englishes, ELF: a project with primary school pupils. In Bayyurt, Yasemin & Nicos C. Sifakis (eds.), *English language education policies and practices: A mediterranean perspective.* London: Pearson.

Vettorel, Paola & Sara Corrizzato. 2012. World Englishes and ELF in ELT textbooks: how is plurality represented? In Roberta Facchinetti (ed.), *A cultural journey through the English lexicon*, 201-234. Newcastle-upon-Tyne: Cambridge Scholars.

Vettorel, Paola & Valeria Franceschi. 2013. English and lexical inventiveness in the Italian linguistic landscape. *English Text Construction* 6(2). 238-270.

Vettorel, Paola & Lucilla Lopriore. 2013. Is there ELF in ELT course-books? *Studies in Second Language Learning and Teaching* 4(3). 483-504.

Viégas, Fernanda B. 2005. Bloggers' expectations of privacy and accountability. An initial survey. *Journal of Computer-mediated Communication* 10(3). http://onlinelibrary.wiley.com/doi/10.1111/jcmc.2005.10.issue-3/issuetoc (accessed 25 April 2014).

Vigo, Francesca. 2012. Unexpected lexical creativity: the rise of context-dependent cultures? In Roberta Facchinetti (ed.), *A cultural journey through the English lexicon*, 183-200. Newcastle-upon-Tyne: Cambridge Scholars.

VOICE. 2011. *The Vienna-Oxford International Corpus of English* (version 1.1 online). Director: Barbara Seidlhofer; Researchers: Angelika Breiteneder, Theresa Klimpfinger, Stefan Majewski, Ruth Osimk, Marie-Luise Pitzl. http://voice.univie.ac.at (accessed 15 November 2013).

Walker Rettberg, Jill. 2008a. *Blogging*. Cambridge: Polity.

Walker Rettberg, Jill W. 2008b. Blogs, literacies and the collapse of private and public. *Leonardo Electronic Almanac* 16(2-3) (September 2008). http://jilltxt.net/txt/Blogs--Literacy%20-and-the-Collapse-of-Private-and-Public.pdf (accessed 15 November 2013).

Walther, Joseph B. 2002. Research ethics in Internet-enabled research: Human subject issues and methodological myopia. *Ethics and Information Technology* 4(2). 205-216.

Warschauer, Mark. 2002. Languages.com: the Internet and linguistic pluralism. In Ilana Snyder (ed.), *Silicon literacies: communication, innovation and education in the electronic age*, 62-74. London: Routledge.

Warschauer, Mark & Inez De Florio-Hansen. 2003. Multilingualism, identity, and the internet. In Adelheid Hu & Inez De Florio-Hansen (eds.), *Multiple identity and multilingualism*, 155-179. Tübingen: Stauffenburg.

Warschauer, Mark, & Douglas Grimes. 2007. Audience, authorship, and artifacts. The emergent semiotics of Web 2.0. *Annual Review of Applied Linguistics* 27. 1-23.

Warschauer, Mark, Ghada R. El Said & Ayman G. Zohry. 2002. Language choice online. In Brenda Danet & Susan C. Herring (eds.), *The multilingual internet. Language, culture and communication online,* 303-318. Oxford: Oxford University Press.

Warschauer, Mark, Rebecca Black & Yen-Lin Chou. 2010. Online Englishes. In Andy Kirkpatrick (ed.), *The Routledge handbook of World Englishes*, 490-505. London: Routledge.

Waskul, Dennis & Mark Douglas. 1996. Considering the electronic participant: some polemical observations on the ethics of on-line research. *The Information Society* 12(2). 129-139.

Wei, Li. 1998. The 'why' and 'how' questions in the analysis of conversational code-switching. In Peter Auer (ed.), 1998. *Code-switching in conversation*, 156-176. London: Routledge.

Wellman, Barry & Gulia, Milena. 1999. Net Surfers Don't Ride Alone: Virtual Communities as Communities. In Barry Wellman (ed.), *Networks in the global village*, 331-367. Boulder, CO: Westview Press.

Wenger, Etienne. 1998. *Communities of practice. Learning, meaning and identity*. Cambridge: Cambridge University Press.

Wenger, Etienne, Richard McDermott & William M. Snyder. 2002. *Cultivating communities of practice*. Cambridge M.A.: Harvard Business School Press.

Wenger, Etienne & Trayner Beverly. 2011. Blogs and communities? (Blog post) http://wenger-trayner.com/resources/how-do-communities-use-blogs/ (accessed 15 November 2013).

Werry, Christopher C. 1996. Linguistic and interactional features of internet relay chat. In Susan C. Herring (ed.), *Computer-mediated Communication. Linguistic, social and cross-cultural perspectives*, 47-61. Amsterdam / Philadelphia: John Benjamins.

Wesch, Michael. 2007. *The machine is us/ing us*. http://www.youtube.com/watch?v=NLlGopyXT_g (accessed 15 November 2013).

White, Dave. 2009. Day 1, Day 2, Day 3, Day 4. Technorati *State of the blogosphere* 2008. http://technorati.com/blogging/feature/state-of-the-blogosphere-2008/ (accessed 15 November 2013).

Widdowson, Henry G. 1994. The ownership of English. *TESOL Quarterly* 28. 377-389.

Widdowson H. G. 1997. EIL, ESL, EFL: global issues and local interests. *World Englishes* 16(1). 135-146.

Widdowson, Henry G. 2003. *Defining issues in English language teaching*. Oxford: Oxford University Press.

Widdowson, Henry G. 2009. The linguistic perspective. In Karlfried Knapp & Barbara Seidlhofer (eds.) (in cooperation with Henry G. Widdowson), *Handbook of foreign language communication and learning*, 193-218. Berlin & New York: Mouton de Gruyter.

Widdowson, Henry G. 2012. ELF and the inconvenience of established concepts. *Journal of English as a Lingua Franca* 1(1). 5-26.

Willis, Paul. 1998. Notes on common culture: towards a grounded aesthetics. *European Journal of Cultural Studies* 1(2). 163–176.

Willis, Dave & Jane Willis. 2007. *Doing task-based teaching*. Oxford: Oxford University Press.

Winer, Dave. 2001. The history of weblogs. *UserLand Software*. http://www.userland.com/theHistoryOfWeblogs (accessed 15 November 2013).

Winn, Philip. 2009. Introduction. Technorati *State of the blogosphere* 2008. http://technorati.com/social-media/article/state-of-the-blogosphere-introduction/ (accessed 15 November 2013)

Wodak, Ruth & Scott Wright. 2007. The European Union in cyberspace. In Brenda Danet and Susan C. Herring (eds.), *The multilingual internet. Language, culture and communication online*, 385-407. Oxford: Oxford University Press.

Wright, Sue. 2004. *Language policy and language planning*. Basingtoke: Palgrave MacMillan.
Yates, Simeon. 1996. English in cyberspace. In Sharon Goodman & David Graddol (eds.), *Redesigning English. New texts, new identities*, 106-140. London / Milton Keynes: Routledge/The Open University.
Zimmer, Karl. 1964. *Affixal negation in English and other languages: an investigation of restricted productivity* (Supplement to *Word 2.0*). London: Clowes.

Index

Bei Fragen zur Produktsicherheit wenden Sie sich bitte an:
If you have any questions regarding product safety,
please contact:

Walter de Gruyter GmbH
Genthiner Straße 13
10785 Berlin
productsafety@degruyterbrill.com